WHEN
DOWN
SYNDROME
AND
AUTISM
INTERSECT

WHEN
DOWN SYNDROME
AND AUTISM INTERSECT

A Guide to DS-ASD for Parents and Professionals

SECOND EDITION

MARGARET FROEHLKE, RN, BSN
& ROBIN SATTEL, MS

Passion Flower Press

DENVER COLORADO

WHEN DOWN SYNDROME AND AUTISM INTERSECT
A Guide to DS-ASD for Parents and Professionals
Second Edition

Margaret Froehlke, RN, BSN & Robin Sattel, MS

Published by Passion Flower Press
Denver, Colorado

First Edition published by Woodbine House 2013

Copyeditor: Russell Santana, www.e4editorial.com Index: Russell Santana, www.e4editorial.com
Cover and Interior Design and Layout: Yvonne Parks, www.pearcreative.ca
Library of Congress Control Number: 2023921978

ISBN: 978-1-962968-04-1 (paperback)
978-1-962968-05-8 (Kindle)
978-1-962968-06-5 (ePub)

Quantity discounts are available on bulk purchases of this book for educational, gift purposes, or as premiums for increasing magazine subscriptions or renewals. Special books or book excerpts can also be created to fit specific needs. For information, please contact requests@passionflowerpress.pub.

Names:	Froehlke, Margaret, author, editor. | Sattel, Robin, author, editor.
Title:	When Down syndrome and autism intersect : a guide to DS-ASD for parents and professionals / [edited by] Margaret Froehlke, RN, BSN & Robin Sattel, MS.
Description:	Second edition. | Denver, Colorado : Passion Flower Press, [2024] | Includes bibliographical references and index.
Identifiers:	ISBN: 978-1-962968-04-1 (paperback) | 978-1-962968-05-8 (Kindle) | 978-1-962968-06-5 (ePub) | LCCN: 2023921978
Subjects:	LCSH: Developmentally disabled children--Care. | Children with mental disabilities--Care. | Autism in children. | Down syndrome.

Classification: LCC: RJ506.D47 W44 2024 | DDC: 362.4--dc23

DEDICATIONS

MARGARET:

To Brennan for being a light of Christ's love and an inspiration to our family, friends, community, and countless people throughout his life.

ROBIN:

To Janet Kay, who took me gently by the hand and led the way on our uncharted DS-ASD expedition together. The tiny baby, who wasn't expected to survive infancy, changed more lives than I can count during her 15 years on this earth. Her legacy, in part, is this book, as well as a national support group (The Down Syndrome-Autism Connection) dedicated to DS-ASD awareness, information, and support. I thank God every single day that we found each other through the miracle of adoption.

To my children Joe, Tommy, and Caroline, for walking this DS-ASD journey with me, and for loving your sister with all your hearts. You filled her life with a radiant and boundless love.

CONTENTS

FOREWORD

Noemi Alice Spinazzi, MD, FAAP

Medical Director of Charlie's Clinic (Down syndrome clinic, UCSF Benioff Children's Hospital) Primary Care, UCSF Benioff Children's Hospital Oakland
Associate Clinical Professor, UCSF School of Medicine
Director of the Developmental and Behavioral Pediatrics Resident Rotation

A lot has changed for individuals with Down syndrome over the past several decades, including a significant increase in life expectancy thanks to protections against discrimination in treatment provision for health conditions such as leukemia and congenital heart disease. As society has moved away from institutionalization and has instead promoted community-based living and learning, medical and education specialists have been able to learn more about individuals with Down syndrome, including their learning styles, developmental profiles, and the impact of various medical conditions on their health and wellness. Thanks to greater investment in research, the body of literature on Down syndrome has grown immensely over the past several decades, allowing for the development and refining of guidelines for health care maintenance and developmental support and monitoring.

One of the lessons learned in the past several years is that autism is actually very common in individuals with Down syndrome, though unfortunately underdiagnosed and undersupported. Nonprofit organizations, like the Down Syndrome Medical Interest Group (DSMIG), have advocated for increased awareness about the dual diagnosis and have been working tirelessly to catalyze research in the field. Support organizations, like the Down Syndrome-Autism Connection, have grown in membership and have created a safe space for the DS-ASD community to gather and share knowledge and experiences.

If you have picked up this book, you may be a parent or caregiver wondering if your loved one may have a dual diagnosis of Down syndrome and autism. Perhaps your loved one just received a diagnosis. Or you may be an educator or health care provider eager to learn more about DS-ASD. Regardless of who you are, please remember that receiving a diagnosis of autism does not fundamentally change who your loved one is; rather, it can help explain why they may be struggling in some areas and elucidate how best to support their learning and development. A diagnosis can inform how health care services are delivered and can open the doors to additional services and supports that previously may have been denied by school districts or insurance companies. This is why I recommend that caregivers pursue an evaluation when suspicion for a dual diagnosis arises, and why I never hesitate to share my observations with families, educators, and other professionals. Recognizing the presence of autism and supporting the individual with evidence-based tools and services can make a huge difference in the whole family's life.

As a community, we have a lot of work left to do. Individuals are receiving their autism diagnosis way too late, in part due to encountering many barriers in their journey to an evaluation. Services are difficult to access, even when approved, and families have to continually advocate for their child to receive the support that they deserve. There is still little evidence on best practices for evaluation, diagnosis, education, and treatment for children with DS-ASD. And individuals with DS-ASD do not get much visibility in Down syndrome spaces. Yet, I am hopeful, because I have seen the tremendous progress that has been made, and I work alongside a vibrant group of physicians, psychologists, therapists, and advocates who continue to move the needle forward to improve the care for those with DS-ASD.

In this book, you will find up-to-date, evidence-based information and many helpful resources. Some may be most relevant to your day-to-day life, while others may be good resources to share with professionals that you interact with. You can read it from cover to cover or choose to start with chapters that feel most relevant to you. I encourage you to use this book as a resource over the years, and to share its lessons with your loved one's educators, service providers, medical professionals, and family. And as always, I encourage you to speak up about your observations, as you know your loved one best, and they deserve your fierce advocacy.

INTRODUCTION

Margaret Froehlke, RN, BSN
Robin Sattel, MS

The opportunity to contribute content, prepare, edit, and present the second edition of this resource book was a dream and an honor for us. Ten years ago, as parents of teenagers with co-occurring Down syndrome and autism spectrum disorder (DS-ASD), we conceived this book because there was little available to guide us during the time our children were first exhibiting autism behaviors, during the diagnosis phase, and beyond. We remember the disappointment and isolation of not quite fitting in with the greater Down syndrome community. We remember wondering why our children were not developing like their peers with Down syndrome, even though we felt like we were working twice as hard as other parents with fewer results. We dreamed of a resource guide to help families and professionals alike, so that their journeys would not be as frightening, frustrating, and difficult as ours were.

The second edition of *When Down Syndrome and Autism Intersect: A Guide to DS-ASD for Parents and Professionals* was written collaboratively by a team of professional experts and experienced parents who care for and work with individuals of all ages with DS-ASD. The topics discussed cover the lifespan and provide updated information, data, and insights that establish best practices aimed at improving the lives of people with DS-ASD. The topics covered herein are also intended to provide support to those who care for people with DS-ASD.

For many of you, this topic may be a brand-new concept. Parents who are reading this book may have just received the diagnosis of autism for their child who has Down syndrome, and they want to learn as much as possible about how autism may affect their young child or adult child. Many parents report that even though they have suspected autism for a while, upon diagnosis they feel as if their world has been turned upside down *again*, and they may experience a new and different type of grieving and adaptation process. Others may be in disbelief that their child could possibly receive a second major diagnosis and wonder about the odds of this happening to them. And still other parents, dealing with multiple medical and/or psychiatric conditions on top of Down syndrome and autism, may feel like, "Why not? She has everything else!"

Health care providers, school personnel, and others who may be new to the dual diagnosis of DS-ASD might be at a loss about how to help the individuals with DS-ASD and families in their care. We sincerely hope that this book will be a valuable resource to you in your workplace.

We believe that it is imperative to spread awareness of DS-ASD. We also believe that it is vital to increase compassion and understanding for individuals with DS-ASD, their families, and the professionals who serve them, with the goal of enabling people with DS-ASD to live healthy, safe, and joyful lives. It is our desire that every single family member and professional caring for a child or adult with DS-ASD will get the support they need and come to the clear realization that they are not alone.

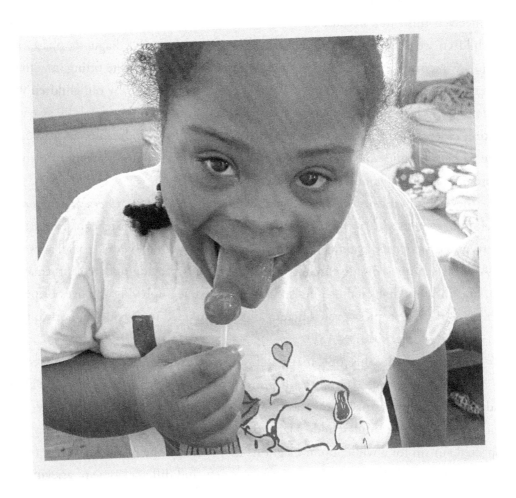

LANGUAGE GUIDELINES

Language guidelines in the world of intellectual and developmental disabilities (IDD) continually evolve. Many individuals who have autism, for example, prefer to be called autistic rather than "having autism"; this is an example of identity-first language (Loftus, 2021). Parents who have children with IDD, however, tend to prefer person-first language when discussing their children with IDD, for example, "This student has Down syndrome," or "She is a student with Down syndrome." Additionally, person-first language is the current preference for academic and professional writing; therefore, in this book, you will see person-first language being used often, although identity-first language may be used, as applicable. Our desire is to feature language that conveys utmost respect to individuals with DS-ASD and their families, and we hope if language preferences change over time that our readers will focus on the spirit of dignity and love in which we present this valuable information.

TERMS AND ACRONYMS YOU WILL SEE IN THIS BOOK

- Down syndrome, DS
- Trisomy 21 (medical term for Down syndrome)
- Autism, autism spectrum disorder, ASD
- DS-ASD (dual diagnosis of Down syndrome and autism)
- IDD (Intellectual and Developmental Disabilities)
- ID (Intellectual Disability)

REFERENCES

Loftus, Y. (2021, June 22). *Autism language: Person-first or identity-first? Autism Parenting Magazine.* https://www.autismparentingmagazine.com/autism-language-person-first/

CHAPTER ONE

THE FROEHLKE FAMILY'S JOURNEY: AN INTRODUCTION TO DS-ASD

Margaret Froehlke, RN, BSN
Robert Froehlke, MD

The dual diagnosis of Down syndrome with autism was not widely recognized until recently. Historically, it was thought that people with Down syndrome only rarely, if ever, also had autism. In fact, some suggested that individuals with Down syndrome were somehow "protected" from developing autism (Turk, 1992) and they attributed autistic characteristics and behaviors to the individual's intellectual developmental disability.

Brennan was born in 1993 and is the third of our four children—Elizabeth, Alex, and a younger sister, Sarah. Brennan was diagnosed with Down syndrome at birth and was the first member of any of our immediate or extended families to have Down syndrome. Even though we are both health care providers, prior to Brennan's birth our experience with persons with Down syndrome was minimal. We immediately began to research and learn everything we could to better understand Down syndrome. We devoured books and articles, joined local support groups, and sought any educational materials that supported persons with Down syndrome.

Becoming well-informed proved to be the best way to advocate for Brennan, even among our own families and friends. However, it was emotionally and physically exhausting to both care for Brennan and our other children, and to be the "experts" on Down syndrome.

Thankfully, Brennan did not have immediate serious health concerns at birth. He did struggle to suckle and nurse, which impeded his growth and weight gain for the first few months. Working to teach him to nurse while providing pumped breast milk and using special oral nursing aids eventually paid off. Over time, Brennan grew stronger and was able to nurse normally. That solved, our attention turned to helping him reach developmental milestones.

The "Early On" program in Michigan (see chapter sixteen for more information) began for Brennan around two months. His Early On team included regular in-home visits with physical, occupational, and speech and language therapists plus a program coordinator. They rotated their services visiting our home two days a week, plus we attended a monthly therapist-facilitated playgroup session with other local Early On families and their children. These meetings were a helpful way to meet other families with children with developmental disabilities and gave us an opportunity to observe how other children with Down syndrome were progressing. Brennan's therapy team remarked on how well he responded to praise as motivation, whereas many of their other young clients were harder to motivate.

We could tell Brennan was a hard worker and we loved watching his face light up with our applause for his accomplishments. By five months, Brennan was able to hold his head up, roll over, and was cooing and vocalizing all the time. He was showing great progress in his attempts at sitting up. His overall development was still within the range of a five-month-old neurotypical child's milestones. Later that same month, things drastically changed.

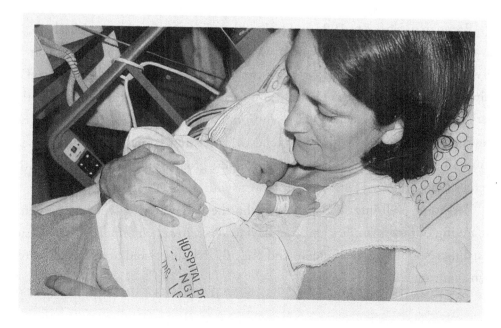

UNEXPECTED CONCERNS

It was just after Thanksgiving when we noticed Brennan was showing signs of a seizure disorder called "infantile spasms." This is a particularly severe seizure disorder. It is typically extremely difficult to control and usually causes the child to have long-lasting devastating neurologic and developmental outcomes—sometimes even death.

We went through a traumatic few weeks full of neurologists' visits, CT and PET Scans, EEGs, and administering injections of a medication called ACTH into our little baby Brennan. It seemed as if the treatment and the seizures would kill him. Neither of the neurologists who treated Brennan were very encouraging about his prognosis. Fortunately, after much concentrated prayer, faith, and hope, Brennan's health improved and his seizures miraculously, abruptly stopped.

Sadly, following the seizures, Brennan lost almost all his prior developmental gains. We started over with all his therapy goals and painstakingly watched him slowly make progress. Brennan no longer made cooing and vocalizing sounds. Instead, he was eerily silent. His development also began to include new behaviors that were different from the typical behavior of his same-aged peers with Down syndrome. Our therapy team also observed Brennan's unusual behavior and agreed that it was unlike behaviors compared to other children with Down syndrome. These behaviors were peculiar and included his inattentiveness to our voices, resistance to making eye contact, his complete fixation on making shadows with his hands using the light in the room and being captivated by ceiling fans.

During this time, breaking Brennan's attention from these activities was challenging, but we learned to work around them. For example, we would settle him down by quietly singing familiar calming songs to him such as "Home on the Range."

Although we made some progress working around these behaviors, the regression in his development and these odd new behaviors did not go away. We eventually learned that these signs were harbingers of autism. Studies show that infantile spasms in persons with Down syndrome are a significant risk factor for a diagnosis of autism (Lott & Dierssen, 2010; Molloy et al., 2009).

By age 1, certain types of voices and sounds really upset Brennan. His father's voice and laughter were among the most stressful. When his father (Bob) would laugh, or even speak, Brennan would often go into a meltdown of screaming. Nothing would calm him down except Bob's silence. These unsettling behaviors continued and were very disruptive for all of us. No one in our network of Down syndrome parents, Early On therapists, or our pediatrician had any helpful answers. We were told these behaviors were related to a lower cognitive function related to his Down syndrome diagnosis; however, this answer did not accurately portray all that was going on. We asked our pediatrician for his help with strategies to stop the screaming. He suggested we record Brennan's screaming and play it back to him. He also recommended that we use a blow-horn whenever Brennan screamed. This was disheartening.

Watching Brennan regain skills was like watching a movie in slow motion. With each phase of physical development, he would first achieve a series of complex smaller steps which set the foundation for the larger skill (such as rolling over, sitting up, crawling, and walking). This slower process did not seem to discourage Brennan and witnessing all his hard work made us even more excited when he finally achieved a new goal. Amazingly, he did not grow weary of the energy and time needed to recapture lost skills. His response to applause and cheers of excitement continued to motivate him and fill him with joy.

Brennan walked independently at 33 months. Once he was mobile, he was not going in slow motion anymore! He quickly used this new skill to run away from us at will. Because he was so quiet, we would not immediately realize he was gone until it was too late. There were several frightening experiences even at this early age. Once, early on a Saturday morning, unbeknownst to us, he left our house—we were in a panic! Thankfully, we quickly found him around the block from our house, sitting on a neighbor's front porch quietly dangling his Sesame Street Ernie doll. Another time, while there was street construction going on outside our house, we found him walking along an adjacent street heading out of the neighborhood toward a busy road. We noticed that he tended to escape from settings more frequently wherein adults were engaged in conversation, or where stress or emotions were running high. For example, if a baby were crying at church, or there were raised voices in a room, he would react immediately and either start screaming, bolt, or both. To this day, unplanned or long conversations between adults, including phone calls, and crying babies are still hard for him and can be a trigger for him to get upset.

When Brennan started preschool, he began using aggressive behaviors to communicate, including biting, kicking, and hitting his classmates. During an IEP (Individualized Educational Plan) meeting discussing how to solve these challenging behaviors, the school principal recommended we get some "cat toys" for him and that we put him in a pen with a muzzle. We were shocked by this response and began to investigate other educational settings that would be a better fit for Brennan. Well-meaning family and friends also tried to "help" by suggesting better parenting and discipline of Brennan.

We began to feel increasingly confused and isolated, not only in knowing how to care for and help Brennan, but also from friends, family, and professional "support" communities.

GETTING THE AUTISM DIAGNOSIS

It was increasingly clear that Brennan had more than just Down syndrome. An article by Joan Medlen (1999), in which she shared the story of her teenage son who had Down syndrome and autism spectrum disorder (DS-ASD), was the first article we discovered that rang true about Brennan. It provided some welcome direction and was a ray of hope for us. We then had Brennan formally evaluated for autism; he was diagnosed at age 6 with PDD NOS (Pervasive Developmental Disorder-Not Otherwise Specified), now known as autism spectrum disorder.

Armed with the DS-ASD diagnosis, we added his ASD diagnosis to his IEP at school and shared the article with Brennan's IEP team and pediatrician. Our search for additional literature, studies, and resources to help us learn more about DS-ASD was essentially fruitless, as at that time there was little to no research on the subject. However, we were greatly helped by a psychologist familiar with autism who developed a behavior plan for Brennan, which was based on ABA (Applied Behavioral Analysis) approaches used to address maladaptive behaviors in children with autism. We began incorporating the behavior plan into that year's IEP, as well as into all subsequent IEPs.

Just knowing that Brennan had something other than Down syndrome gave us solace that we were not doing something wrong and eventually provided us with information that we could share with family and friends to help explain his behavioral challenges.

We transferred Brennan to a kindergarten through grade 2 developmental program in a neighboring school district that provided more support and progressive learning methods. Nevertheless, as Brennan was the program's first student with DS-ASD, they did not have a playbook for how to best work with him. We used his behavior plan and worked together as a team through many trials and errors to figure out the best strategies to help support him. We used visual schedules to improve communication, built-in time, and cues for transitions, minimized sensory overload, and included activities that supported social engagement. Additionally, we learned that anything that was new and unpredictable was a challenge for Brennan. We found planning pre-visits to settings that were not in Brennan's normal routine (haircuts, doctor visits, blood draws, school photography days, dental visits, etc.) and the use of desensitization techniques helped to reduce his anxiety and helped him manage the situations more successfully (see chapter nine for more information). These pre-visits gave Brennan time to explore the settings and meet the staff. We kept a close eye on his reactions and would quietly praise him and gently guide him back to the car as soon as we saw any indication that he was getting anxious. With a few successes under his belt, we added more challenging settings such as his siblings' sporting events, school plays, and plane travels. And, our biggest success, Brennan even went to an American Idol concert, and he loved it!

Our ability to read all the triggers that upset Brennan continued to be challenging and the pre-visit method was not an option for everything. Holidays, family gatherings, and get-togethers with friends were sources of stress, worry, anxiety, and exhaustion for him and us. Our family learned that when we were outside of the "safety of our home," we needed to be vigilant and watchful of what was happening all around us. We became like a secret service team of bodyguards to ensure he did not run away into parking lots, traffic, swimming pools, etc. We were on high alert and prepared to make a quick getaway from activities should he "blow." It was clear that his behavior was negatively impacting his reputation within our extended family and community, and we started to decline invitations.

Sleep and rest escaped him (and us!). Regardless of routine nap times, strict bedtime practices, and blackout shades in his bedroom, by age 6, Brennan was still not sleeping through the night. Each night around midnight, he would start to run in circles in his room and our attempts to get him back to bed proved futile. We were saved finally when a parent of an older child with autism told us to try melatonin and eureka! It worked.

STRATEGIES FOR SUCCESS

Beginning in third grade, an experienced autism consultant was added to Brennan's IEP team. She provided the latest ideas and strategies such as the ABC (Antecedent, Behavior, Consequence) method which helped us to better identify triggers. This approach, along with the behavior plan was refined and agreed upon by us and his IEP team and was put in place to provide consistent responses to managing behavioral issues both at school and at home. With time, we all got better at reading his cues, avoiding triggers, and supporting him in navigating social situations (see chapter ten for more information).

Throughout the elementary years, Brennan's inclusion with neurotypical peers provided learning opportunities that helped him gain social skills. His general education classroom teachers were completely on board and integrated friendship skills and acceptance into their lessons. The benefit of this nurturing culture led to genuine interest and friendship between Brennan and his classmates.

Outside of school, our family was actively involved in our faith life. We are Roman Catholic, and when Brennan was 11 years old, his younger sister, Sarah, who was 7 years old, was preparing for her First Communion. For many years, attending church had been one of the most difficult settings for Brennan. We had already lived through lots of outbursts and worse. Thus, we had not really thought about Brennan receiving his First Communion or other Sacraments. One Sunday after Mass, we found Brennan alone in his room kneeling and praying in front of his dresser where there was a small statue of Our Lady of Guadalupe—something he had never done before. We took it as a sign that he might be ready to receive Communion. Brennan was able to join Sarah and her second-grade class as they prepared and practiced how to line up and approach the altar for the big day.

On the First Communion Day, the church was packed with over 100 First Communicants, their families, and visitors—a setting that might turn into the perfect storm. As Brennan lined up beside Sarah as his partner, the last twosome in the line, we held our breath. They made their way slowly, up the center aisle, reached the priest, and Brennan successfully received his First Communion! We felt such joy and were so proud of him. We were also proud of Sarah who, a few years later, partnered again with Brennan as he learned to become an altar server and then, a few years after that, to receive the Sacrament of Confirmation. Having Sarah as a companion and supportive "peer" was a major help to Brennan and his progress throughout not just his Faith life, but many other childhood experiences.

Peer-modeling strategies continued to be successful for Brennan in participating in school sports with typical peers. In sixth grade, the cross-country team coach welcomed Brennan's participation, and the high school provided a volunteer to support Brennan. He practiced weekly with his team who encouraged him by taking time to say hello and giving him high fives to keep him moving.

When the time came for his first cross-country meet, we were all very anxious. In addition to his familiar classmates, there were over 100 other noisy participants and their fans gathered for the event. Normally, this would have been a situation that Brennan would have run away *from*, rather than run *with*. However, with the gentle support of his high school volunteer, and the encouragement of his teammates, Brennan willingly lined up with all the other runners at the starting line. The gun went off, and so did the 100-plus runners, with Brennan among them!

We followed the spectators and families to the bleachers set up near the finish line and anxiously awaited Brennan's return. Soon the fastest runners appeared, running out from the wooded trail; then more runners crossed the finish line—Brennan nowhere in sight. Finally, Bob discreetly walked up the final stretch of the course looking for Brennan and found him sitting on the trail with his volunteer about 400 yards short of the finish line. Just as Bob was about to intercede, he heard a lot of voices approaching from the finish line end of the trail. It was a group of Brennan's teammates who called to him and encouraged him to join them. One teammate took his hand to lead him. Suddenly, Brennan was in the center of about a dozen classmates, running with them toward the finish line. He may have been the last runner to cross the tape that day, but the audience's cheers for him were the loudest. The fans in the stands, regardless of which school they represented, were cheering him on! Tears were streaming down the faces of people who did not even know who he was. It was a Hallmark Movie moment and Brennan was beaming!

In addition to Brennan successfully responding to autism strategies, peer-modeling, and lots of cheerleading, he was also developmentally maturing. At age 13, he finally was fully toilet trained. That was a game changer that we never thought would happen.

While the desensitization and peer-modeling methods worked well in his earlier years, it was not as easy to orchestrate during middle and high school years. Much of the change was because we moved to Colorado as Brennan was entering eighth grade and into a larger school district where he was placed in a self-contained resource room. We continued to use our toolbox of working strategies and he successfully participated on the middle school and high school track teams, enjoyed his new resource room classmates, and loved playing basketball with high school volunteers on the Special Olympic Basketball Team.

Outside of school, a neighborhood high schooler volunteered and supported Brennan as a swimmer on our neighborhood swim team. He loved being a part of the team and during the local meets, both the neighborhood families and opposing team families crowded around the pool's edges to watch him swim and cheered him on enthusiastically. He would swim the backstroke with his head propped out of the water while waving one hand with each stroke to the delight of his audience. He also learned to downhill ski with an adaptive ski program in Breckenridge, enjoyed going to a few high school dances, and altar-serving with a peer helper at our church.

MOVING INTO ADULTHOOD

After he graduated from high school, Brennan spent two years in our school district's transitional vocational training program. Verbal communication had never been Brennan's strong suit. Historically, he used signs sparingly and was disinterested in his Augmentative and Alternative Communication (AAC) device. To our surprise, in the new program Brennan became more verbal, which we credited to the slower pace and more one-on-one, hands-on support and creative curriculum. He grew in his sense of confidence and pride in his achievements. During these years, he put two and three words together more frequently, improving his ability to communicate with staff and peers. Brennan enjoyed the vocational opportunities and even won an award for folding the most pizza boxes in one sitting! Yet, when Brennan reached the maximum age for services in the Colorado public education system, he still required one-on-one support for safety and other reasons and was therefore not a candidate to go forward and pursue a job. Instead, we focused on finding a good day program.

Leaving the support of the educational system behind was scary. We felt we were crossing a threshold into unfamiliar territory, and we did not know if it would provide the safety or the support Brennan needed. We visited several local day programs and were not impressed. They not only lacked the support Brennan needed but did not share a cultural belief that promoted dignity and respect for the participants. Thankfully, our prayers were answered when we found an incredible day program called Wellspring Community. Their mission was Christ-centered and committed to the well-being and dignity of each participant as the core of all their programming. They welcomed Brennan. He was their first participant with Down syndrome and autism and the leadership and staff were open to learning how to best support him. They readily adapted activities and provided learning opportunities to meet Brennan's needs. Today, in addition to participating in Wellspring's day program activities, Brennan also works as a paid Barista at the Wellspring/Castle Rock Collective Café for a half day each week. He loves it! He has made many friends at Wellspring, and it has become a beloved second family for our whole family.

Brennan's adult years have involved managing health issues that included foot surgeries, dental implants, and several endoscopies. Each circumstance required adapting the collection of known and familiar strategies to successfully prepare him for each situation and setting. Today his day-to-day life is consistent and structured with predictable schedules and routines and supports that allow him to confidently navigate his world. He even looks forward to family trips and vacations when he has proper forewarning. However, when we forget to set something up properly, his stress level and anxiety kicks in and reminds us how fragile his coping skills really are.

Although we do not want to think about a time in the future where we will not be Brennan's main support team, we know it is a reality. Our life's focus is to ensure Brennan continues to receive high-quality, loving, and supportive care centered on respect and dignity. We are confident that with the appropriate level of support and the right environment, Brennan can live a joyful life and successfully engage in his world.

It took us many years to understand Brennan and to apply strategies that worked for him to succeed. At times we stumbled along with only our unfailing love and faith keeping us strong. There were times in the early days when we felt alone and isolated. Having a child with DS-ASD is difficult and challenging, but we have experienced many more joys than sorrows and are ever grateful for the gift of Brennan's life. People who meet Brennan comment on the love they feel from him and how he has a beautiful way of making others feel good. Through his gentle and joyful ways, he has touched hundreds of lives and changed the world for the better, one person at a time.

In closing, Brennan's favorite song, "The Little Drummer Boy," reminds us that earthly wealth, position, and power do not determine the value of an individual, but rather that each person inherently has value, no matter how humble their gifts may seem.

REFERENCES

Lott, I. T., & Dierssen, M. (2010). Cognitive deficits and associated neurological complications in individuals with Down's syndrome. *The Lancet Neurology, 9*(6), 623–633. https://doi.org/10.1016/S1474-4422(10)70112-5

Medlen, J. E. G. (1999). More than Down syndrome: A parent's view. *Disability Solutions, 3*(5–6), 1-7.

Molloy, C. A., Murray, D. S., Kinsman, A., Castillo, H., Mitchell, T., Hickey, F. J., & Patterson, B. (2009). Differences in the clinical presentation of Trisomy 21 with and without autism. *Journal of Intellectual Disability Research, 53*(2), 143–51. https://doi.org/10.1111/j.1365-2788.2008.01138.x

Turk, J. (1992). The fragile X syndrome: On the way to a behavioural phenotype. *British Journal of Psychiatry, 160*. 24–35. https://doi.org/10.1192/bjp.160.1.24

CHAPTER TWO

THE AUTISM PHENOTYPE

Darren Olsen, PhD

When discussing people with both Down syndrome and autism it is important to understand autism as a standalone diagnosis. Autism is very prevalent in the media, with the rates of autism seemingly ever increasing and new research coming out all the time. There are also many controversies associated with autism that can be hard to sift through, such as vaccines, treatments, and others.

During my clinical work with teenagers and adults with autism, I've heard autism described in many ways. Some describe it like tools in a toolbox. Everyone has a set of tools in their toolbox that they use to go about their lives. However, the person with autism has a different set of tools in their toolbox than do most other people. There's nothing good or bad or right or wrong about their tools, they are just different from most other people's tools. But, the person with autism discovers that the world they live in has been built with other tools, not theirs. So, they spend their life trying to figure out how to use or modify the tools they have to get by in a world designed by people who are not quite like them.

WHAT IS AUTISM?
History

Although autism may seem like a relatively new phenomenon, the term itself has been around for a while. The word "autism" was first used to describe schizophrenic patients all the way back in the early 1900s. In the 1940s, psychiatrist Leo Kanner studied a group of individuals who demonstrated social deficits, repetitive behaviors, sensory sensitivities, and the tendency to repeat noises or words. He used the term "autism" in describing these individuals. Around the same time Hans Asperger was studying children who seemed to talk like adults, with their word knowledge being above what you'd expect for their age. However, at that time many people who would be diagnosed with autism today were being diagnosed with disorders such as childhood bipolar disorder or childhood schizophrenia, while many others were not identified at all. Through the 1960s and beyond, there was a theory that the mothers of children with autism-like symptoms were causing their child's autism by not loving the child enough. The term "refrigerator mothers" and the effects of such a damaging theory lasted for decades. In 1980, autism appeared for the first time as a separate and distinct diagnosis in the third edition of the *Diagnostic and Statistical Manual of Mental Disorders* (American Psychiatric Association, 1980), the official source for health care professionals to make mental health diagnoses in the United States.

In the 1990s, public awareness of autism grew as adults with autism such as Temple Grandin wrote about their experiences (Grandin, 1995). The idea that autism might be more subtle or less obvious in some people also started to take hold. In the late 1990s and early 2000s, the idea of vaccinations causing autism ensnared the diagnosis in controversy. The idea spurring the controversy was thoroughly discredited with research consistently showing no link between vaccines and autism, yet it still helped cultivate an anti-vaccination movement. The fourth edition of the DSM in 1994 (American Psychiatric Association, 1994) listed autistic disorder and Asperger's syndrome as separate diagnoses. In 2013, the fifth edition of the DSM (American Psychiatric Association, 2013) was updated to include autism spectrum disorder (ASD). This "spectrum" of a disorder was created by combining multiple diagnoses including autistic disorder, Asperger's disorder, Pervasive Developmental Disorder-Not Otherwise Specified (PDD-NOS), and Rett's syndrome. Moving forward, properly classifying subgroups within the spectrum remains an area of significant scientific and public interest.

Criteria/Symptoms

So, how is the medical diagnosis of autism spectrum disorder defined? Formal testing done by a professional in the field of autism assessment is an important step. The professional looks for several key indicators and symptoms. According to the DSM-5, which is used in the United States, there are a number of symptom clusters that are consistent with autism. However, it must be remembered that every person with autism is different and each has their own strengths and weaknesses. None of the following examples are universally seen in individuals with autism.

Social Communication

Differences in social communication can manifest themselves in many ways. One way is in difficulty with the "back and forth" of conversation, play, and other social exchanges. Interaction may feel more one-sided or side-by-side rather than back-and-forth; the person may need lots of reminders to include others in what they are doing; or, they approach others in an unusual way, or walk away during the middle of an interaction. It may look like difficulties in sharing or understanding emotions. It could also be that the person seems to ignore other people some or all the time.

Social differences must also be present in nonverbal communication. People with autism may have difficulty *integrating* eye contact, body language, facial expression, or gestures in combination with each other and words. Integration of these nonverbal behaviors is the key. People with autism probably do point, look you in the eye, and show various expressions on their faces sometimes. How often they use them and how well those behaviors link up (or integrate) to each other and to vocalizations is important.

Creating and maintaining deeper relationships is another important form of social communication. People with autism may have differences in the way they form and maintain bonds with others. They may have a hard time adjusting their actions to fit the situation they are in. They may not show the expected interest in making friends or in even being around people at all. There are many other ways that these social differences can manifest, and this list is not exhaustive.

It must be pointed out that the idea of people with autism not liking people or being unable to feel or express love and other emotions is completely false. People with autism absolutely do like and love others, desire connection, and feel a whole array of emotions. The way it looks on the outside may be different from what people are used to.

Stereotyped or Repetitive Motor Movements/Use of Objects or Speech

Many people with autism repetitively engage in unusual or very specific ("stereotyped") behaviors. These behaviors may have no apparent goal or external function, instead satisfying an internal drive that others may not fully understand. These repeated behaviors can be vocal, such as humming, babbling, blowing raspberries, yelling, screaming, squealing, or saying words that are out of context. This can also include echolalia when a person repeats what they hear others saying. Verbal/vocal stereotypy can also be repetition of many other sounds, words, or phrases not listed here. Repetitive behaviors can be physical, such as rocking back and forth, swaying, dipping down, flapping hands, twisting fingers, shaking the head or other body parts, stiffening body parts, jerking motions, jumping, facial grimacing, picking at self or objects, clenching teeth, waving, pacing, spinning, and many others. Sometimes these behaviors are relatively easy to see, while others are much more subtle. Sometimes these behaviors happen more when the person is feeling a strong emotion such as happiness or distress, and individuals often report the behaviors support their self-calming. Another way that these can be manifested is in the repetitive use of objects such as lining up objects, setting objects up in specific sets or scenes, shaking/tapping/hitting objects over and over, dangling, categorizing, flipping, or using toys in repetitive ways outside of what they are intended for.

Insistence on Sameness/Inflexible Adherence to Routines/ Ritualized Patterns of Verbal or Nonverbal Behavior

This section broadly refers to what is commonly referred to as "rigidity." One way that rigidity can manifest is in the need to have things be consistent or predictable. When things are not consistent or predictable, the person may become upset, distressed, or anxious. The person may not want things to change around them (objects in their bedroom, house, or school). They may become very upset when objects are moved from where they left them. Other rigidity could be wanting to wear the same clothes or eat the same foods or being highly adherent to time. The person may have a strong desire to stick to a routine or do activities in the same order each time. Routines or rituals can show up in getting ready for bed the same way each night, being very distressed when the school day does not go as usual (e.g., assembly, substitute teacher), or being upset when going to an appointment after school rather than going directly home. The person may need to touch objects in a certain order or must take a bath before getting ready for bed or say phrases in a certain way to move on with their day. Sometimes when the rituals are not completed the person becomes very distressed or upset.

Highly Restricted/Fixated Interests That Are Abnormal in Intensity or Focus

Another major area in autism is restricted or fixated interests. These are very strong interests with a relatively narrow focus. This can look like being interested in objects that most others are not particularly interested in, such as strings, bottle caps, dangling objects, rocks, bags, and other objects. It can be a high interest in matching, small, or unique objects. It can also be very a strong interest in more common objects, such as screens, balls, or toys. In discussing interests, which all people have, it is important to think about how easily the person comes away from their preferred object or activity. Fixated or intense interests are such that a person would likely drop everything else to get to the object or activity and may become very upset when it is taken away. Interests that are narrow in focus may look like being very focused on a part of an object such as the wheels or doors of a toy car rather than the whole car or the eyes of a baby doll, rather than the doll as a whole.

Hypo- or Hyperreactivity to Sensory Input or Unusual Interest in Sensory Aspects of the Environment

The final area to discuss is sensory differences. It is very important to note that sensory differences can show up as either the person wanting to get high levels of sensory input from the environment and/or wanting to get away from or avoid sensory input. A vast majority of people with autism display both sensory seeking and sensory avoidance behaviors. For example, a person may chew on objects constantly (seeking oral feedback) while simultaneously avoiding and being highly sensitive to loud noises. Each of the five senses can have sensory differences. Sight sensitivity could be aversion to bright lights or commotion. Sight seeking could be a strong attraction to flashing lights or spinning parts. It could also be that the person brings objects up close to their eyes or peers at them out of the side of their eyes. Hearing sensitivity to talking, laughing, buzzing, clicking, breathing, or toilet flushing are common, sometimes resulting in covering ears. Seeking auditory input may involve holding noisemaking objects to their ears or yelling for no apparent reason. Taste/oral aversion may manifest in significant pickiness, restricted eating, or gagging/vomiting with certain food textures. Taste/oral seeking could involve thoroughly enjoying food to the point of overeating, putting objects in their mouth, or eating nonfood items. Smelling or olfactory sensitivity may show as aversion to smells, good or bad. Olfactory seeking may present as frequently smelling objects or bringing objects close to the person's nose. For touch, the person may avoid or strongly dislike tight clothes, physical touch initiated by others, restriction, wetness, feeling dirty, or stickiness. Touch seeking may be a desire to rub or feel soft textures, be bundled up in blankets, or have deep pressure touch. It could also be in the form of self-stimulatory behaviors such as banging their head or other body parts. Pain tolerance also falls under this category as people with autism may have very high or low tolerance.

Throughout all discussion of autism spectrum disorder, it is very important to remember that ASD defies generalization. For example, statements such as "people with autism aren't social" is false because there is a continuum of differences of socialization. Other examples include, "people with autism don't like to be touched," or "don't give hugs," or "don't look you in the eye" are incorrect generalizations. Some with autism prefer to be left alone at times (though that does not mean they are not social) while others with autism can be highly social, to the point of being referred to as "intrusive," or so social that they lack appropriate boundaries or treat nearly anyone as family and could happily walk off with a stranger if given the opportunity. All are *differences*, and all are found on the autism spectrum. Given the nuances and variability in presentation and needs across the spectrum (as well as cultural and regional variations in social and communication practices), formal evaluation by a professional is needed to confirm a medical diagnosis of autism. This is especially true for people with Down syndrome (DS) whose developmental and behavioral differences may intersect with the autism spectrum.

Course

Autism is a neurodevelopmental disorder, which is to say that during the developmental period (starting before birth), differences in brain functioning developed. Said more plainly, people with autism have autism before they are born even though some or many of the symptoms may not be completely obvious until they are older. As the person grows up, the differences in socialization, the repetitive behaviors, sensory sensitives, and/or other behaviors that were discussed earlier in the chapter will become increasingly apparent. The age at which those differences can be identified as autism varies. For some people, the differences will be pronounced while they are toddlers and, in some cases, even younger. Some signs of autism that may begin to be noticed in these young ages is the use of gaze as a form or communication. Small social behaviors may be lacking, sensory sensitivities may emerge as fussiness, and sometimes repetitive use of toys becomes apparent. For others, the differences may not be recognizable until they are in school. School is a time when children are separated from their caregivers for long stretches, there is often more structure, more demands, more transitions, new sensory input, and of course, more kids, all of which can bring out indicators of autism. The start of school may be the first time parents get feedback from other adults such as the school staff as well. For others, a diagnosis of autism may not come until they are teenagers. Adolescence is a time when friends and "fitting in" are increasingly important. The person's social differences may make socialization more difficult and more apparent as the social gap between themselves and their peers widens. People at this and other ages may attempt to "camouflage" or actively work to minimize their autism symptoms, especially in social situations (Hull et al., 2017). For others still, they may not be identified as having ASD until they have reached adulthood. Getting a first diagnosis at this time of life may be a product of increased awareness and the individual's recognizing symptoms and differences in themselves. They may struggle at work and/or with relationships, have set routines, and sensory profiles that they have had to adapt to. Of course, there are some who will never be diagnosed with autism despite living with the symptoms all their lives.

Current Statistics

As of 2023, 1 in 36 children in the US were estimated to have been diagnosed with autism spectrum disorder. Research has found that autism is nearly four times more common in boys as in girls, and it occurs across all racial, ethnic, and socioeconomic groups (Maenner et al., 2023). The number of people actually being identified as having autism varies widely across the world, which likely has a lot to do with the amount of resources governments dedicate to identification (Zeidan et al., 2022).

Most of the people received their autism diagnosis after the age of 4 years old. Globally, the most recent data shows that around 1 in 100 children are diagnosed with ASD, varying significantly by location, ethnicity, and sex, though it is seen across all demographics (Zeidan et al., 2022).

Where Does It Come From?

The question of what causes autism has been at the heart of decades of research, theory, and conjecture. Research has not identified a single cause for autism, nor do we expect that a single cause will be found. Autism appears to have many different possible contributing genes, and research is ongoing. The lack of knowledge in this area makes understanding to what extent or through what pathways Trisomy 21 itself directly or indirectly contributes to autism risk that much more difficult. However, the following research has shown promise in identifying some of the potential pathways to developing autism.

Large studies that cover multiple countries have found that heritability (passing on characteristics to children through genes) was very high in autism. These studies have shown little "shared environment" effect. This term means that the parents' actions or the child's experiences have very little, if anything at all, in determining if the person develops autism (Bai et al., 2019; Tick et al., 2016). Research has shown that a decent amount of what accounts for a person's development of autism is tied directly back to their own genetic code, with some considering autism one of the most heritable disorders in the mental and behavioral health field (Thapar & Rutter, 2015). Overall, most studies show autism being caused by two or more genes interacting in a complex way that could lead a person to be far more likely to have autism (Risch et al., 1999), although an exact combination of genes has not been determined.

However, there is research showing that genes and the environment can work together to cause autism symptoms to show up more readily. At present, many researchers believe that autism shows up when there is an interaction between our genes (what we have at and before birth) and what we are exposed to and do after birth, which is called epigenetics. Other theories include genomic imprinting, which is genes being expressed or not depending on if they come from the mother or father, and epimutations which is inherited change that does not impact DNA sequences though changes gene expression playing major roles in if a person has autism (Jiang et al., 2004; Samaco et al., 2005).

Despite the advances in knowledge, there is still much that is not known about where autism comes from. When so much is unknown about a topic it creates a knowledge gap. That gap will sometimes be filled by theories and ideas with little to no evidence to support them. Take, for example, the "refrigerator mothers" theory that was discussed at the beginning of this chapter. Without knowledge of what was causing autism (knowledge gap), a theory or idea was created to fill the gap. Because it could not be disproved quickly, the idea spread and was accepted as truth. With that, many of the most vulnerable and loving mothers were being told their child's diagnosis was a direct result of them being cold toward their children. Similar theories have attempted to fill the knowledge gap. Recently, vaccinations were a strong candidate in attempting to fill that gap. Though the peak of this idea appears to have passed, or at least lessened, the lingering confusion about the link between vaccinations and autism continues despite clear empirical evidence that vaccinations do not increase a person's risk of autism (Hurley et al., 2010; Price et al., 2010).

COMMON CO-OCCURRING CONDITIONS

There are many other conditions that have been associated with autism. In fact, as many as 95% of children with autism may have at least one co-occurring condition or set of symptoms (Soke et al., 2018). The following is a non-exhaustive list of various disorders and conditions that have been found to be associated with autism.

ASSOCIATED GENETIC CONDITIONS

(Note: Some information in this section has been carried over from the first edition of this book written by Ellen Roy Elias, MD, FAAP, FACMG.)

Chromosomal Abnormalities

Chromosomal abnormalities associated with intellectual disability can also be present with features seen in autism (Marshall et al., 2008). Many abnormalities associated with autism are seen on genes 1p, 2q, 7q, 13q, 16p, and 19q. High rates of autistic features are found in Trisomy 13 and chromosome 15 as well as Trisomy 21.

Fragile X Syndrome

Fragile X Syndrome is a common genetic disorder caused by a mutation in the FMR1 gene, which is located on the A chromosome (Hatton et al., 2006). Many features of fragile X are similar to autism. In fact, 46% of men and 16% of women with fragile X have autism according to the CDC. Some studies suggest that the prevalence of autistic traits in fragile X is significantly higher (Hernandez et al., 2009).

Rett Syndrome

Rett syndrome is a rare genetic disorder seen almost exclusively in females. The mutation on the MECP2 gene is generally lethal to male fetuses. Generally, after a period of typical development there is a regression in skills and seizures begin along with features of autism. Rett syndrome, previously categorized under the umbrella of autism, is now considered a separate and distinct disorder.

Angelman Syndrome

Angelman syndrome affects the UBE3A gene, causing autism and/or many traits of autism, intellectual disability, seizures, increased muscle tone, and characteristic facial features (Clayton-Smith & Laan, 2003).

Trisomy 21

As will be discussed at length in this book, Trisomy 21, or Down syndrome, is the most common chromosomal abnormality in humans. There can be significant overlap in the symptoms of autism and Down syndrome including intellectual disability and repetitive behaviors among others. The prevalence of autism in Down syndrome is roughly 16%–18% which is higher than autism in the general population making it one of the conditions more strongly associated to autism (Richards et al., 2015).

MENTAL/BEHAVIORAL HEALTH CONDITIONS

It is important to remember that being diagnosed with autism does not prevent the person from also having other mental or behavioral health conditions, and in some cases increases the likelihood of having at least one other psychiatric disorder (Rosen et al., 2018). Further, roughly half of children and adolescents with autism meet criteria for two or more co-occurring disorders (Simonoff et al., 2008), making co-occurring mental health conditions closer to the rule than the exception.

Anxiety disorders are intense and persistent worries and fears about specific or general situations or objects. Examples of anxiety disorders include specific phobias to a vast number of things, such as snakes, elevators, vomit, dogs, airplanes, and others. Social anxiety is a disorder in which fear is brought on by being around or in front of other people, with a strong fear of being judged or evaluated. Generalized anxiety is what it sounds like, anxiety that is general or wide-ranging. Anxiety in people with autism can be manifested as withdrawing from situations, crying, irritability, shaking, increase in repetitive motor movements, increase in scripted speech, sleep difficulties, repetitive questions about the future, refusal to leave the house, and other behaviors.

Depressive disorders, such as major depressive disorder, persistent depressive disorder, premenstrual dysphoric disorder, seasonal affective disorder, and others are states in which a person's mood is down, depressed, blue, slowed down, or irritable most of the day for most days. These may follow patterns, such menstruation, the seasons, or the school year. It may be chronic in which a person has very little break in their symptoms, seemingly becoming a part of them. Depression may be manifested in people with autism in ways such as increased crying, less interest in things that generally make them happy, refusal to leave the house, increasingly morbid written or drawn communications (e.g., tombstones, death, blood), regression in self-care abilities, more social withdrawal, more irritability, and more oppositional behavior. These symptoms should be viewed as differences from the person's baseline.

Attention Deficit Hyperactivity Disorder (ADHD) is a neurodevelopmental disorder (like autism) in which the person has significant inattentive (e.g., off-task, difficulty sustaining focus, disorganization, etc.) and/or hyperactive-impulsive symptoms (e.g., constantly moving, excessive fidgeting, interrupting others, etc.). These symptoms appear before the person is 12 years old. ADHD manifests itself in the same way it does in those without autism.

OTHER CONDITIONS OR SETS OF SYMPTOMS COMMON IN AUTISM THAT ARE NOT NECESSARILY DIAGNOSED BUT CAN BE IMPAIRING AND WARRANT INTERVENTION

Eating

Difficulties with eating in people with autism are common and well documented. Difficulties with eating include picky eating, being very selective with textures, and selectivity with the way food looks or smells. They may not want foods to touch and may not be open to trying new things. They may also experience food jags, which is when a person will only eat one or a few different foods prepared the same way. After a period of time, the person stops eating the food altogether, further reducing their list of preferred foods.

Toileting

Difficulties with toileting is another very common condition in people with autism. Common presentations of these difficulties include difficulties toilet training, knowing and communicating that they need to use the bathroom, sensory difficulties/sensitivities to bathrooms and/or the sensation of bodily functions, cleaning/wiping themselves, fecal smearing/playing with feces, wetting the bed, and constipation.

With both eating and toileting, it is important to remember that some of these challenges may be traced back to something medical, as gastrointestinal problems are very common in people with autism. For example, if a person with autism is highly selective with food there is a chance they are not feeling well due to constipation, acid reflux, or irritable bowel syndrome.

Sleep

Challenges with sleep are very common in people with ASD, as well. Difficulties can be any combination of the ability to fall asleep, stay asleep, and/or wake at an appropriate time in the morning. Circadian rhythms may be different. (Please see chapter eight for more information.)

Fine/Gross Motor Delays

Fine motor difficulties may include delayed ability or inability to use pincer grip, scissors, pencils, or utensils. Gross motor difficulties may include clumsiness, awkward gait, difficulties riding a bike, or delayed onset of walking, crawling, or crossing the midline.

CONCLUSION

In all, it is important to remember that a lot more goes into autism than the "classic symptoms" people generally think of first. Understanding autism as a standalone diagnosis with all its complexities is an important step in understanding how an individual with Down syndrome can also have autism.

REFERENCES

American Psychiatric Association. (1980). *Diagnostic and statistical manual of mental disorders* (3rd ed.).

American Psychiatric Association. (1994). *Diagnostic and statistical manual of mental disorders* (4th ed.).

American Psychiatric Association. (2013). *Diagnostic and statistical manual of mental disorders* (5th ed.). https://doi.org/10.1176/appi.books.9780890425596

Bai, D., Yip, B. H. K., Windham, G. C., Sourander, A., Francis, R., Yoffe, R., Glasson, E., Mahjani, B., Suominen, A., Leonard, H., Gissler, M., Buxbaum, J. D., Wong, K., Schendel, D., Kodesh, A., Breshnahan, M., Levine, S., Partner, E., Hansen, S., … Sandin, S. (2019). Association of genetic and environmental factors with autism in a 5-country cohort. *JAMA Psychiatry, 76*(10), 1035–1043. https://doi.org/10.1001/jamapsychiatry.2019.1411

Clayton-Smith, J., & Laan, L. (2003). Angelman syndrome: a review of the clinical and genetic aspects. *Journal of Medical Genetics, 40*(2), 87–95. https://doi.org/10.1136/jmg.40.2.87

Grandin, T. (1995). *Thinking in pictures: and other reports from my life with autism.* Doubleday.

Hatton, D. D., Sideris, J., Skinner, M., Mankowski, J., Bailey, D. B., Jr., Roberts, J., & Mirrett, P. (2006). Autistic behavior in children with fragile X syndrome: Prevalence, stability, and the impact of FMRP. *American Journal of Medical Genetics Part A, 140*(17), 1804–1813. https://doi.org/10.1002/ajmg.a.31286

Hernandez, R. N., Feinberg, R. L., Vaurio, R., Passanante, N. M., Thompson, R. E., & Kaufmann, W. E. (2009). Autism spectrum disorder in fragile X syndrome: a longitudinal evaluation. *American Journal of Medical Genetics Part A, 149*(6), 1125–1137. https://doi.org/10.1002/ajmg.a.32848

Hull, L., Petrides, K. V., Allison, C., Smith, P., Baron-Cohen, S., Lai, M., & William, M. (2017). "Putting on my best normal": Social camouflaging in adults with autism spectrum conditions. *Journal of Autism and Developmental Disorders, 47*(8) 2519–2534. https://doi.org/10.1007/s10803-017-3166-5

Hurley, A. M., Tadrous, M., & Miller, E. S. (2010). Thimerosal-containing vaccines and autism: A review of recent epidemiologic studies. *The Journal of Pediatric Pharmacology and Therapeutics, 15*(3), 173–181. https://doi.org/10.5863/1551-6776-15.3.173

Jiang, Y. H., Sahoo, T., Michaelis, R. C., Bercovich, D., Bressler, J., Kashork, C. D., Liu, Q., Shaffer, L. G., Schroer, R. J., Stockton, D. W., Spielman, R. S., Stevenson, R. E., & Beaudet, A. L. (2004). A mixed epigenetic/genetic model for oligogenic inheritance of autism with a limited role for *UBE3A. American Journal of Medical Genetics Part A, 131*(1), 1–10. https://doi.org/10.1002/ajmg.a.30297

Maenner, M. J., Warren, Z., Williams, A. R., Amoakohene, E., Bakian, A. V., Bilder, D. A., Durkin, M. S., Fitzgerald, R. T., Furnier, S. M., Hughes, M. M., Ladd-Acosta, C. M., McArthur, D., Pas, E., Salinas, A., Vehorn, A., Williams, S., Esler, A., Grzybowski, A., Hall-Lande, J., … Shaw, K. A. (2023). Prevalence and characteristics of Autism Spectrum Disorder among children aged 8 Years — Autism and Developmental Disabilities Monitoring Network, 11 sites, United States, 2020. *Morbidity and Mortality Weekly Report Surveillance Summaries, 72*(2), 1–14. https://doi.org/10.15585/mmwr.ss7202a1

Marshall, C. R., Noor, A., Vincent, J. B., Lionel, A. C., Feuk, L., Skaug, J., Shago, M., Moessner, R., Pinto, D., Ren, Y., Thiruvahindrapduram, B., Fiebig, A., Schreiber, S., Friedman, J., Ketelaars, C. E. J., Vos, Y. J., Ficicioglu, C., Kirkpatrick, S., Nicolson, R., … Scherer, S. W. (2008). Structural variation of chromosomes in autism spectrum disorder. *The American Journal of Human Genetics, 82*(2), 477–488. https://doi.org/10.1016/j.ajhg.2007.12.009

Price, C. S., Thompson, W. W., Goodson, B., Weintraub, E. S., Croen, L. A., Hinrichsen, V. L., Marcy, M., Robertson, A., Eriksen, E., Lewis, E., Bernal, P., Shay, D., Davis, R. L., & DeStefano, F. (2010). Prenatal and infant exposure to thimerosal from vaccines and immunoglobulins and risk of autism. *Pediatrics, 126*(4), 656–664. https://doi.org/10.1542/peds.2010-0309

Richards, C., Jones, C., Groves, L., Moss, J., & Oliver, C. (2015). Prevalence of autism spectrum disorder phenomenology in genetic disorders: a systematic review and meta-analysis. *The Lancet Psychiatry, 2*(10), 909–916. https://doi.org/10.1016/S2215-0366(15)00376-4

Risch, N., Spiker, D., Lotspeich, L., Nouri, N., Hinds, D., Hallmayer, J., Kalaydjieva, L., McCague, P., Dimiceli, S., Pitts, T., Nguyen, L., Yang, J., Harper, C., Thorpe, D., Vermeer, S., Young, H., Hebert, J., Lin, A., Ferguson, J., … Myers, R. M. (1999). A genomic screen of autism: evidence for a multilocus etiology. *The American Journal of Human Genetics, 65*(2), 493–507. https://doi.org/10.1086/302497

Rosen, T. E., Mazefsky, C. A., Vasa, R. A., & Lerner, M. D. (2018). Co-occurring psychiatric conditions in autism spectrum disorder. *International Review of Psychiatry, 30*(1), 40–61. https://doi.org/10.1080/09540261.2018.1450229

Samaco, R. C., Hogart, A., & LaSalle, J. M. (2005). Epigenetic overlap in autism-spectrum neurodevelopmental disorders: *MECP2* deficiency causes reduced expression of *UBE3A* and *GABRB3*. *Human Molecular Genetics, 14*(4), 483–492. https://doi.org/10.1093/hmg/ddi045

Simonoff, E., Pickles, A., Charman, T., Chandler, S., Loucas, T., & Baird, G. (2008). Psychiatric disorders in children with autism spectrum disorders: Prevalence, comorbidity, and associated factors in a population-derived sample. *Journal of the American Academy of Child & Adolescent Psychiatry, 47*(8), 921–929. https://doi.org/10.1097/CHI.0b013e318179964f

Soke, G. N., Maenner, M. J., Christensen, D., Kurzius-Spencer, M., & Schieve, L. (2018). Prevalence of co-occurring medical and behavioral conditions/symptoms among 4-and 8-year-old children with autism spectrum disorder in selected areas of the United States in 2010. *Journal of Autism and Developmental Disorders, 48*(8), 2663–2676. https://doi.org/10.1007/s10803-018-3521-1

Thapar, A., & Rutter, M. (2015). Neurodevelopmental disorders. In A. Thapar, D. S. Pine, J. F. Leckman, S. Scott, M. J. Snowling, & E. Taylor (Eds.), *Rutter's child and adolescent psychiatry* (6th ed., pp., 31–40). Wiley-Blackwell.

Tick, B., Bolton, P., Happé, F., Rutter, M., & Rijsdijk, F. (2016). Heritability of autism spectrum disorders: a meta-analysis of twin studies. *Journal of Child Psychology and Psychiatry, 57*(5), 585–595. https://doi.org/10.1111/jcpp.12499

Zeidan, J., Fombonne, E., Scorah, J., Ibrahim, A., Durkin, M. S., Saxena, S., Yusuf, A., Shih, A., & Elsabbagh, M. (2022). Global prevalence of autism: a systematic review update. *Autism Research, 15*(5), 778–790. https://doi.org/10.1002/aur.2696

CHAPTER THREE

WHAT AUTISM LOOKS LIKE IN A PERSON WITH DOWN SYNDROME: THE BEHAVIORAL PHENOTYPE

Deborah Fidler, PhD

Susan Hepburn, PhD

Dennis McGuire, LCSW, PhD

Brian Chicoine, MD

INTRODUCTION

For years, most professionals and parents regarded the co-occurrence of autism and Down syndrome to be very rare. In fact, given the social strengths that were often reported in people with Down syndrome, it seemed particularly improbable that a condition that impacts social communication would be evident in a person with Down syndrome.

However, as more and more parents expressed concerns about the different developmental path their sons or daughters with Down syndrome seemed to be taking, clinical researchers began to take note of the possibility that some children with Down syndrome could also be challenged by an additional behavioral diagnosis—an autism spectrum disorder (ASD). Because of the work of pioneering clinicians and researchers in the field, there is much better awareness among professionals and caregivers that ASD can coexist with Down syndrome (DS) (Capone, 1999; Reilly, 2009). Over the past ten years or more, there have been presentations on this topic at national conferences, and children with DS-ASD are now far more likely to be diagnosed with this condition than in the past. Still, there is a great deal of overlap in the descriptions and behaviors of both DS and autism and it is not always clear to parents or professionals how the two syndromes differ.

This chapter is organized into three parts. In Part I, we begin by briefly covering important foundational topics, including basic facts about DS, basic facts about ASD and how ASD is identified. More information on ASD is presented in chapter two and more information on the diagnostic process is presented in chapters four and five. Our goal here is to set the stage for the rest of our chapter on the behavioral presentation of individuals with both conditions across the lifespan. Part II of the chapter focuses on what autism symptoms look like in children of different ages and developmental levels. We use a case vignette approach to describe how children with DS with and without ASD symptoms may present. Part III discusses how autism symptoms present in teenagers and adults with Down syndrome.

PART I:

BASICS ABOUT DS, ASD, AND THE DIAGNOSTIC PROCESS

Susan Hepburn, PhD & Deborah Fidler, PhD

BASIC FACTS ABOUT DOWN SYNDROME

Before we can talk about what autism looks like in a person with Down syndrome, we first consider a few points about general development in Down syndrome, when an ASD is not thought to be part of a child's clinical presentation.

- The incidence rate of Down syndrome is approximately 1 in 772 when averaged across all maternal ages (de Graaf et al., 2022). The likelihood of having a child with Down syndrome increases with maternal age, and by age 40, the likelihood of having a child with Down syndrome is approximately 1 in 25.
- The majority of cases of Down syndrome are caused by "non-disjunction," an event that occurs during cell division when gametes are formed (ovum for women, sperm for men). As a result of this event, when fertilization takes place, three copies of chromosome 21 are found in the fertilized egg instead of two. In other, less frequent cases, cell division events happen after fertilization, which can lead to "mosaicism." Another rare cause of Down syndrome occurs when a parent passes along a chromosome that has additional information from chromosome 21 attached to it, which is called a "translocation."
- Trisomy 21 affects the activity of over 300 genes and their associated proteins and enzymes, and therefore affects multiple systems (Gardiner & Costa, 2006).
- Down syndrome is often associated with specific physical features, which may include a distinctive craniofacial structure, brachycephaly (abnormally wide head shape), short neck, congenital heart defects, muscular hypotonia, and musculoskeletal hyperflexibility. A unique craniofacial appearance

is also found in Down syndrome, which often includes some or all the following features: upslanting palpebral fissures, epicanthal folds, Brushfield spots, flat nasal bridge, dysplastic ear, and a high arched palate.

· In addition to specific physical features, Down syndrome predisposes an individual to specific behavioral outcomes. Recent work in this area suggests that many individuals with Down syndrome show patterns of relative strength in some aspects of visual processing, language understanding, and some aspects of social relatedness. Challenges have been reported in the areas of expressive language, working memory, and some aspects of movement development. It is important to note that not every individual with Down syndrome will show all aspects of the behavioral profile. Rather, the likelihood that individuals with Down syndrome will show this pattern of outcomes is higher than in other children with developmental disabilities who do not have Down syndrome.

· The majority of children with Down syndrome score in the mild (55–70) to moderate (40–55) range of intellectual disability, though the range of outcomes includes mild to profound levels. Over the first few years of life, most children with Down syndrome make steady progress in development, but they do not make these gains at the same rate as other children without disabilities. Thus, their IQ scores tend to become gradually lower throughout childhood.

· Speech and expressive language skills tend to be delayed in Down syndrome relative to nonverbal abilities. However, receptive language (language understanding) seems to develop with relative competence in Down syndrome, with the majority of children aged birth to five showing mental-age-appropriate receptive language skills. While the majority (though not all) children with Down syndrome show a profile of relative strengths in receptive over expressive language, there may be different pathways leading to this outcome.

· Many children with Down syndrome generally show delays in the transition from prelinguistic communication to meaningful speech. Young children with Down syndrome may show an average productive (signed or spoken) vocabulary of 28 words at 24 months, 116 words at 36 months, 248 words at 48 months, and 330 words at 72 months. When considering only spoken (not signed) vocabulary words, only 12 percent of 1-year-olds with Down syndrome have produced their first words, and only 53 percent of 4-year-old children have vocabularies larger than 50 words, a level that would be on par with a typically developing 16-month-old child.

- The use of gestures seems to be an area of strength in many children with Down syndrome, and some studies report that individuals with Down syndrome use more advanced gestures than expected based on their general language development levels, and a wider repertoire of functional, symbolic, and pretending gestures than typically developing children at the same language level.

- Young children with Down syndrome tend to show mental age-appropriate levels of nonverbal joint attention, or the use of eye contact, gesture, and vocalization for the purposes of social sharing, according to most studies. But difficulties are observed in nonverbal requesting behaviors, or the use of eye contact, gesture, or vocalization for the purposes of obtaining a certain outcome (a desired toy, food item, etc.).

- Motor development is an area of delay in many children with Down syndrome. Atypical development of reflexes, low muscle tone, and hyperflexibility are often observed.

- During early development, many children with Down syndrome reach social relatedness milestones with competence. Infants with Down syndrome show longer looking times at people versus objects, and show increased melodic sounds, vocalic sounds, and emotional sounds when interacting with people rather than objects (Legerstee et al., 1992). Toddlers with Down syndrome also achieve competence in the areas of joint attention, sharing objects with others, and other social initiations. Socialization skills in the school years have often been cited as an area of strength within the larger area of adaptation.

- Many individuals with Down syndrome show difficulty with aspects of problem-solving and goal-directed behavior. Some individuals may develop a style in which they abandon difficult tasks more quickly than other children.

- Individuals with Down syndrome may have some difficulty with perspective-taking and understanding other people's motives, desires, and feelings.

- Down syndrome may predispose some children to specific behavior problems, including oppositionality, inattentiveness, and hyperactivity. Other conditions, such as anxiety and depression, are reported to occur less frequently in children with Down syndrome than in other children with developmental disabilities, but their rates are higher than in typically developing children. Issues related to mood may become more common during transitions to adolescence and as individuals reach adulthood.

BASIC FACTS ABOUT AUTISM SPECTRUM DISORDERS

There are a few other things to know about autism spectrum disorders before we discuss what an ASD can look like in a child with Down syndrome.

1. ASD is a developmental disability that can be identified only through a developmental/behavioral evaluation process. There is no medical test for autism, so the skill and experience of the people evaluating a child with another known developmental disability is especially important in determining if this second condition is in the picture.

2. ASD is a biologically based condition that involves disorders of development of the nervous system, including the brain.

3. Many different biological systems may or may not be involved in a particular child's ASD; such as the motor system, speech-language system, immune system, sleep/regulatory systems, gastrointestinal system, sensory processing systems (including vision, hearing, tactile sensitivity, taste/smell, vestibular, and pain sensitivity). Researchers are studying the "multisystem" nature of ASD very actively. For updated information on the medical aspects of ASD, check the websites for the American Academy of Pediatrics (www.aap.org/healthtopics/autism.cfm) or the Centers for Disease Control and Prevention (www.cdc.gov/ncbddd/autism).

4. ASD is not caused by poor parenting. Although we do not know the specific causes of ASD, scientists think that the condition is strongly genetic, but in a very complex way, such that several different genetic differences need to happen at the same time for the "scene to be set" for an ASD to develop. Then, most scientists think, this "genetic vulnerability" to an ASD needs to be "turned on" by some kind of environmental or experiential factor. This would explain how studies of identical twins (children who share the exact same genetic makeup) report that it is possible for one twin to have an ASD and the other to be developing typically. Or, as happens more often, how one twin can be more severely affected by ASD symptoms than his or her co-twin. Scientists are actively studying the genetics of ASD, and the observation that children with Down syndrome are at particular risk for an ASD is leading some to examine chromosome 21 as a potential site for genes that are relevant to ASD as well.

5. The biological underpinnings of ASD have not been found to exist in any one part of the brain. Rather, they are more likely to involve problems in the brain's connectivity, or the efficiency with which the brain can send messages across neural structures and integrate information from different brain regions.

6. Recent research suggests that there is an increase in children with ASD throughout the developing world that cannot be accounted for by better diagnostic methods or changes in clinical practice. Current studies suggest that 1 in 44 children presents with features of ASD (as detected in surveillance studies, which are based on record reviews; Maenner et al., 2023), which is significantly higher than estimates generated 20 years ago of 1 in 2500 children (American Psychiatric Association, 2000). This dramatic increase is being actively studied by epidemiologists, who are examining several environmental and biological factors that may be involved in the increased numbers of children affected worldwide.

7. ASD is reported to occur in children of all different racial, ethnic, and socioeconomic groups. However, there is some evidence for disparities in the age of diagnosis, such that children with higher socioeconomic status, those living near medical centers, and possibly those of Caucasian ethnicity tend to receive the diagnosis earlier.

8. ASD is found to occur more often in males; approximately 4 to 5 boys are identified for every girl. The reasons for this are unknown, leading researchers to examine x-linked genetic conditions, hormonal influences, and the evolutionary biology of brain development. (For example: Are there differences in the male and female brains? If so, do these differences yield clues to the possible brain regions involved in ASD?)

9. There are a lot of ways that children with a diagnosis of an ASD differ from each other. Clinicians and researchers would say that the disorder is "heterogeneous" or "has a lot of variability." Possible sources of these individual differences in how an ASD presents in each individual child are listed in table 3.1.

Table 3.1: Possible Sources of Individual Differences in Symptom Presentation in ASD

	How Differences Impact Symptom Presentation
Chronological Age	Younger children show different forms of social, communicative, and behavioral differences than older children. For example, children with ASD under the age of 3 years rarely understand what simple gestures such as pointing mean, and they are not likely to follow an adult's pointed finger with their eye gaze to see what is of interest. However, most children with ASD learn to follow another person's point by the time they enter kindergarten. Therefore, failure to follow a point is an important symptom to look for in toddlers and preschoolers but does not differentiate children with ASD from others in the school years.
Overall Developmental Level	A child's overall developmental level is important to consider when setting expectations for social and communicative skills.
Patterns of Cognitive Strengths and Weaknesses	Some children with ASD are better at solving problems without language, others are better at verbal reasoning. Some children with ASD learn best with lots of visual supports, while others tend to learn better through auditory (e.g., listening) or kinesthetic means (e.g., moving/doing).
Temperament	Behavioral style, one's individual manner of operating in the world, a constitutional tendency to respond to certain situations in predictable ways.
Activity Level	Some children with ASD are highly active and in constant motion. Others are more lethargic, slow to respond, and seem to have difficulty getting started.

Emotional Intensity	Some children are very emotionally reactive and show strong feelings regularly. Others may seem unusually nonreactive to emotional or charged situations and experiences.
Adaptability or "Behavioral Flexibility"	Some children can "go with the flow" better than others and tend to be able to adjust to changes in situations or expectations. Others have intense difficulty being flexible, managing transitions, and integrating new experiences.
Persistence or "Mastery Motivation"	Some children show a drive to complete a task or achieve a goal of some kind that is remarkably focused. Others give up much more easily or avoid trying new challenges completely. Many parents report that their children with ASD show different levels of persistence in different tasks/activities (e.g., persistent with a special interest—such as lining up toy cars—but not persistent in learning to write letters).
Distractibility	Some children are difficult to distract from what they are doing ("overly focused"), and others seem distracted ("unfocused") much of the time. And some children show both attentional styles at different times.

A diagnosis of ASD is only relevant if a person's difficulties in social functioning and nonverbal communication abilities are more severe than would be expected for the person's developmental level, not his chronological age. For example, let's say that an 8-year-old boy with Down syndrome is functioning more like a 4-year-old. (Note: This kind of developmental estimate can be obtained through standardized testing, accompanied by some assessment of the child's skills and abilities in real life, known as "adaptive functioning," which is usually assessed by interviewing parents and caregivers who know the child well, using a standardized tool such as the Vineland Scales of Adaptive Behavior; Sparrow et al., 2005). In this case, the child's chronological age is 8 years, and his developmental age is 4 years. If, during a specific evaluation of social reciprocity and nonverbal communication (which are the hallmarks of ASD), the child demonstrates social and nonverbal communicative behaviors that are similar to those seen in a 4-year-old with Down syndrome, then their challenges are interpreted to be part of their developmental delay, but not indicative of a co-occurring ASD. If, however, the child lacks the social and nonverbal communication behaviors seen in most 4-year-olds, then an ASD may be relevant for this child. See table 3.2 for an overview of the developmental ages associated with several important social communication behaviors.

Table 3.2: Developmental Ages Associated with Specific Social-Communicative Behaviors

Social/Communicative Behaviors	Expected age of accomplishment
Expresses a variety of emotions (including happiness, sadness, interest, surprise, anger, fear, disgust)	By the age of 6 months
Demonstrates a predictable social smile (i.e., a smile that is clearly directed at or shared with another person)	By the age of 6 months
Matches the emotions expressed by an adult in face-to-face interactions	By the age of 6 months
Shows nervousness with strangers (and therefore is differentiating familiar and unfamiliar people)	Between 7 and 12 months
Relies on caregiver to be a secure base while exploring environment	Between 7 and 12 months
Uses social referencing (looking back at caregiver) to pick up cues about how to react in new situations	Between 7 and 12 months
Readily joins in play with familiar children, such as siblings, cousins, etc.	Between 13 and 18 months
Recognizes image of self in mirrors and pictures	Between 13 and 18 months
Begins to show empathy for others (by trying to comfort others or directing sympathetic facial expressions to others who are hurt or unhappy)	Between 13 and 18 months

Able to follow simple directions given by familiar caregiver	Between 13 and 18 months
Expresses more subtle, more complex emotions, such as shame and embarrassment (these emotions are indicative of developmental growth in social cognition)	Between 19 and 24 months
Verbally expresses a variety of emotion words	Between 19 and 24 months
Begins to use communication as a tool for self-regulation (uses verbal and nonverbal communication to express feelings, make requests)	Between 19 and 24 months
Uses own name and personal pronouns	Between 19 and 24 months
Understands basic categories that are associated with people, such as age and sex	Between 19 and 24 months
Distinguishes between intentional and unintentional acts by self and others	Between 2 and 3 years (25–36 months)
Shows ability to be cooperative with caregivers	Between 2 and 3 years (25–36 months)
Shows emerging understanding of how actions cause feelings and vice versa	Between 2 and 3 years (25–36 months)
Demonstrates greater capacity for empathy, characterized by sharing and increased acts of generosity to comfort others	Between 2 and 3 years (25–36 months)

Expression of complex emotions (such as shame, embarrassment, guilt, pride) increases	Between 2 and 5 years (25-60 months)
Engages in first friendships	Between 2 and 5 years (25-60 months)

Note: Adapted from *Infants, Children, and Adolescents* (3rd ed.), by L. E. Berk, 2009, Allyn & Bacon.

BRIEF DESCRIPTION OF THE DIAGNOSIS PROCESS IN AN ASD EVALUATION

The diagnosis of autism is a deductive process conducted by a group of specialists who are trained in ASD evaluations. After completing a thorough evaluation, the specialists compare the results with the characteristics described in the current edition of the Diagnostic and Statistical Manual (DSM) of the American Psychiatric Association or in the International Classification of Diseases (ICD) of the World Health Organization (Geneva, Switzerland), both international systems used in the classification of mental disorders. The purpose of the evaluation is to obtain a profile of functioning that will be used for developing appropriate interventions. Early diagnosis of autism is important, as the sooner treatment starts, the better the prognosis, both for the individual and for the family. Parents who are trained to help their young children with ASD improve their response to the environment report less family stress.

The diagnosis of autism in the general population relies on the use of instruments that assess the presence of behaviors typically associated with ASD (see chapter five for more details). The gold standard of autism assessment is based on an interdisciplinary assessment that includes:

a. A complete *medical history,* which should include prenatal and neonatal information, developmental history, family history, medical and educational history, and any prior interventions. A detailed history of sensory issues is also included.

b. A complete *medical evaluation* to determine whether there are any physical problems that may account for the behavioral difficulties and to rule out other genetic disorders that could account for the behaviors (e.g., Fragile X syndrome, tuberous sclerosis, etc.). It is also important to rule out a significant hearing impairment.

c. A *psychological evaluation* to assess cognitive functioning, adaptive behaviors, and the presence of autism.

d. A *speech and language evaluation* to assess communicative intent and ability.

e. An *occupational therapy evaluation* to assess sensory and motor problems typically associated with autism.

f. A *psychosocial evaluation* to assess the individual's home and school environment.

The content and diagnostic process will vary depending on the individual's age and history, whether prior evaluations were conducted, and the individual's general level of functioning. Usually, the evaluation starts with the family's suspicion that there is something different or problematic with their child's functioning.

To receive a diagnosis of an ASD, a person must show significant difficulties in three areas of development: 1) social functioning, 2) nonverbal and verbal communication, and 3) restricted interests and repetitive activities. Within each of these areas, there are several behavioral indicators, or symptoms, that characterize the type of impairment that is relevant to an ASD. In the rest of this chapter, we will describe how these signs and symptoms may present in people with Down syndrome of different ages and functioning levels.

PART II:

WHAT AUTISM WITH DOWN SYNDROME LOOKS LIKE IN CHILDREN

Susan Hepburn, PhD & Deborah Fidler, PhD

As noted in table 3.2, one of the important sources of individual differences in how an ASD presents is whether the child has another diagnosis that affects behavior or development. This brings us to the mission of this chapter, which is to describe how an ASD is likely to present in a person with Down syndrome—which, we believe (as do others in the field) has a characteristic "feel" or clinical picture. That is, while children with both Down syndrome and ASD have many things in common, the presence of both conditions in a child influences development in unique ways. In our clinical experience, the presentation differs from what we see in children with Down syndrome alone or ASD alone.

In other words, having both conditions (Down syndrome plus ASD) may be a qualitatively different experience from having either one alone—both for the child and for the family. In the sections that follow, we will try to share our clinical observations about how the co-occurrence impacts the child. Family issues will be discussed elsewhere in this volume.

We thought we'd try to use a case study approach to illustrate how having an ASD might impact the behavior of a person with Down syndrome. For this approach to make sense, we need to think developmentally. Therefore, we will describe four children with Down syndrome and ASD, of differing developmental levels and ages, whom we have had the chance to get to know very well through various research studies. We will also describe four of their peers with Down syndrome alone, who are similar in both chronological and mental age as the child with both Down syndrome and ASD. As with any case study approach, we want to emphasize that these examples do not provide a comprehensive view of how the two disorders can co-occur. As discussed previously, there is a multitude of ways that an ASD can present in any person, but hopefully these case examples will show some of the more common patterns we tend to observe. To protect confidentiality, we are changing names and other details not germane to the contrast we are trying to illustrate.

PRESCHOOL-AGED CHILDREN

PRESCHOOL-AGED CHILDREN WHO CURRENTLY FUNCTION MORE LIKE 12- TO 18-MONTH-OLDS

Chronological Age: 3½ years (42 months)
Developmental Age: 12–16 months

Wade: Child with Down syndrome without ASD.

Wade is a quiet young boy with very low muscle tone and difficulty coordinating his body. He scoots his body on the floor in a sort of "commando crawl" and is working on walking. He laughs and smiles when his parents or therapists talk to him and praise his efforts at using his body. He loves music and watches his mother's face intently when she sings to him. If she pauses in the middle of a line in a song that he knows well, he moves his hand excitedly, makes a sound, and looks at his mom with a smile. When she continues the song, he giggles and pats her face. When his mom claps at the end of a song, he tries to do the same, but his hand control makes it hard to clap effectively. This doesn't appear to frustrate him, and he smiles gleefully. Wade likes to play pat-a-cake and tries to do the movements his mom shows him. When she hugs him, he cuddles his body into her. When she calls his name, it takes him a few seconds to turn his head, but he usually turns toward the sound of her voice. Wade vocalizes often while looking at another person but is not yet using words. His favorite activities are cause-and-effect musical toys, singing songs with his mom, and playing in water or sand. He loves the family dog and playing near his big sister.

Ryan: Child with Down syndrome and ASD.

Ryan is a quiet, endearing little boy who looks sort of serious much of the time. He has low muscle tone and learned to walk when he was about 2 years old. Ryan doesn't seem to like being praised by his parents or therapists and sometimes he covers his ears when they clap for him. He likes music, especially when it is sung softly. Ryan will back his body into his mother's and pull her hands around him, moving her body almost as if he is adjusting a piece of furniture to sit on. His mom is very good at knowing what he wants, and she sings one of his two favorite songs when he does this. During the singing, he rocks in her lap, looking forward. When she pauses the song, he becomes distressed and cries, pulls at her body without looking at her, and then gets up and walks away. He doesn't seem to know how to let her know that he would like to hear more. Ryan's mom tries to engage him in pat-a-cake and peek-a-boo, but he walks away. When Ryan is really happy, he laughs and jumps up and down and vocalizes gleefully, but he doesn't look at others or do things to share his emotions. When his mother calls his name, he rarely looks up or pays attention—in fact, his parents wondered if he was deaf and sought hearing tests to rule out a hearing impairment. He isn't yet imitating sounds or gestures, like waving goodbye. His favorite activities are playing with string, swinging, and water play. When his older sister tries to get him to play, he seems to ignore her or walks away.

What to Notice

In these two examples, we have a preschool-aged child who is functioning more like a 12- to 16-month-old, so we want to think about the social and communication skills we would hope to see in a typically developing child at that age. If the child has most of these skills, then an ASD is probably not present. In the example above, Wade has many of the social communication skills we would expect in a 12- to 16-month-old. These are discussed below.

Sharing Affect: Young children direct their facial expressions toward others to share their feelings.

> WHAT DOES WADE DO? When happy, Wade smiles and directs this smile to his mom to share the experience. When sad or frustrated, we expect that Wade probably directs his face toward his caregiver to share that feeling as well.

> WHAT DOES RYAN DO? When happy, Ryan doesn't tend to look at others and share a smile, nor does he direct his distress or frustration toward others. He experiences emotions, sometimes quite strongly, but he doesn't recruit others into his experience or seem to try to share how he is feeling.

Shows a Range of Affect: Young children's feelings change frequently and fluidly, depending on what is happening around or within them. Caregivers can usually tell how they are feeling from their affect—their facial expressions, bodily postures, and the quality of their vocalizations.

> WHAT DOES WADE DO? Even with his motor challenges, Wade uses his face, eyes, and body to send messages about how he is feeling that his mom can understand most of the time. His emotions seem to make sense, given what is happening around him.
>
> WHAT DOES RYAN DO? Ryan has a somewhat flat, or less variable, facial expression much of the time. It can be hard to know how he is feeling. His emotions seem hard to predict and he can become intensely upset, even though it doesn't seem like anything is happening to cause the distress. Sometimes he laughs when others cry.

Sharing Attention with Another Person: Young children learn about the world by focusing on the same activity as another person and thus building skills, such as word learning, by being "on the same page" as a caregiver.

> WHAT DOES WADE DO? During the song games with his mom, Wade participates with her, clearly sharing attention to the song. If his mom showed him a book, Wade would look at the pictures she was showing him.
>
> WHAT DOES RYAN DO? During the song game with his mom, Ryan doesn't participate actively and abandons the shared activity early. If his mom showed him a book, it is likely that Ryan would not look at the book with her, even briefly.

Responding to His Name: Young children with good hearing and motor control will turn their heads toward their caregiver's voice when their name is called. This is an early emerging form of social orienting.

> WHAT DOES WADE DO? Even with his motor challenges, Wade attempts to turn his head toward the sound of his mother's voice and he knows she wants his attention.

WHAT DOES RYAN DO? Ryan rarely shifts his attention from what he is doing to look up when his mom calls his name. It seems as if he is more interested in objects than in people, and if he is looking at an interesting object, the social bid of a person doesn't capture his attention.

Attempting to Make Needs/Wants Known: Even before they develop words, young children have many different nonverbal strategies for getting their needs met. These include directing their eye gaze to a caregiver and then to something they want, making sounds and looking at what they want, and reaching or using gestures to indicate they want something.

WHAT DOES WADE DO? Wade has an instinct for how to use his body, his face, and his voice to send messages to his caregiver. He may not integrate all these methods of communicating very well, due to his motor difficulties, but he clearly is attempting to communicate and will try a different strategy if the first one doesn't work.

WHAT DOES RYAN DO? Ryan seems not to understand what communication is and he rarely attempts to use his voice, eyes, face, or body to send clear messages to others. If he wants something, he usually tries to get it himself, or he may take another person's hand and use it like a tool to meet his needs—for example, backing into his mom and wrapping her arms around him is a less-social way of requesting being held.

Attempting to Imitate: By around 12–14 months, most children will attempt to imitate simple motor movements and will play imitative games, such as pat-a-cake. They also imitate simple gestures, such as clapping and waving goodbye.

WHAT DOES WADE DO? Wade is socially tuned-in and tries to match the behaviors of others. Even if his motor challenges compromise the precision of his hand movements, he tries to copy simple movements.

WHAT DOES RYAN DO? Ryan does not attempt to copy or match the behaviors of others. He resists attempts to participate in social games that involve simple imitative play.

Activities/Interests: 1-year-olds play with cause-and-effect toys and enjoy sensory-motor play. They also play near other children and are usually receptive to the social approach of a familiar person, such as a brother or a sister.

WHAT DOES WADE DO? Wade is playing as one might expect in a 1-year-old (simple cause-and-effect and other forms of sensory-motor play). He seems to be interested in and responsive to his sister.

WHAT DOES RYAN DO? Ryan is also playing in a sensory-motor way, but he may be less open to new activities than Wade. He tends to play on his own and is not very responsive to his sister when she tries to get him to play.

PRESCHOOL-AGED CHILDREN WHO CURRENTLY FUNCTION MORE LIKE 2½- TO 3-YEAR-OLDS

Chronological Age: 4½ years
Developmental Age: 32–36 months

Jacqueline: Child with Down syndrome without ASD.

Jacqueline is an energetic young girl who usually carries one of her dolls with her almost everywhere she goes. She speaks in 2- to 4-word phrases and sentences most of the time and consistently looks right at the person she is speaking to. It can be hard to understand her words, due to some articulation difficulties, but Jacqueline is quick to add gestures and miming motions to clarify her message. For example, she frequently uses a "come here" gesture of her right arm to recruit another child or adult to see her doll. She also shakes her finger at others, says "no, no, no," and frowns intently if she wants others to stop doing something. She loves books and story time and frequently stands up in circle time and directs a "shh" gesture to all her children in the circle. She has an imaginary friend, who she talks to and directs others to greet. Jacqueline tends to hug other children somewhat indiscriminately and can be unintentionally rough physically when intent on hugging a friend. If another child is sad or hurt, Jacqueline tries to comfort her by patting her back and saying "there . . . there . . . there. You sad." Jacqueline likes to play in the kitchen area during free play best of all, but she will also follow a friend to another play center. She seems to enjoy new experiences and expresses her enthusiasm by smiling and saying "cool" with an excited lilt to her voice.

Nora: Child with Down syndrome and ASD.

Nora is an independent, curious little girl who loves Buzz Lightyear and frequently says "tofinobeyo!" (which means "to infinity and beyond," a line from the *Toy Story* movies). Her words are directed to no one as she runs and jumps and sometimes throws a toy. She doesn't seem to be aware that she could bump into someone else or accidentally hit them with her toy. Nora can talk in 3- to 4-word sentences, but most of her sentences were learned in chunks and come from scripts of her favorite movies or cartoons. She refers to herself as "Nora" and doesn't use pronouns such as "I" and "you" correctly. When she wants something, she says "Nora's turn."

It is often difficult to understand what Nora is saying and it is not always clear to whom she is speaking. When someone tries to understand and asks her to clarify, she usually walks away and doesn't add gestures or show others what she is talking about. She rarely tries to get another child to play with her and she rarely responds to another child's invitation to play, unless the game is tag, which she usually plays through one turn before wandering away from the game. She does not greet others. Nora loves to swing and will try to physically move other children from the swings to get a turn. Circle time seems to be her least favorite part of the preschool day and she frequently leaves the area or pushes other children who get too close.

What to Notice

In these two examples, we have a 4½-year-old child who is functioning more like a 3-year-old, so we want to think about the social and communication skills we would hope to see in a 3-year-old. In the example above, Jacqueline has many of the social communication skills we would expect in a 32-to-36-month-old. These are described below.

Coordinating Eye Contact with Her Words: As spoken language develops, young children coordinate their eye gaze with increasing effectiveness and can use nonverbal cues to clarify their messages.

WHAT DOES JACQUELINE DO? Jacqueline consistently initiates and sustains a coordinated eye gaze with her listener when she is talking. Because she has difficulty with articulation, her listener may need additional nonverbal cues to understand her message and Jacqueline uses her eyes in a communicative way.

WHAT DOES NORA DO? Nora rarely looks directly toward the person to whom she is speaking. If her listener doesn't seem to understand the message, Nora doesn't use her eyes in a communicative way (such as looking at the person, looking at a desired toy, then looking at the person again).

Using Gestures, Voice Quality, and Facial Expressions to Support Verbal Communications: Children who are emerging talkers (i.e., using phrases and some full sentences comprised primarily of verbs and nouns, such as "I go swing"; "You eat pizza. Good?") frequently add gestures, alter their intonation patterns, and/or or change their facial expression to punctuate their message, clarify their intention, and/or add emphasis or emotion.

WHAT DOES JACQUELINE DO? Jacqueline frequently adds descriptive or instructive hand movements to her words. Her gestures, though imprecise, carry emotion and she can convey the strength of her feeling by altering the speed or forcefulness of the movements. She changes the rate and rhythm of her speech, as well as her intonation patterns, when she is communicating for different reasons. For example, she raises her intonation and tips her head when asking if the food is good to the adult, indicating she is asking a question with clear, culturally learned gestures, vocal quality, and postures. She uses a clearly differentiated directive tone when insisting that her peers be quiet.

WHAT DOES NORA DO? Nora does not gesture spontaneously very often, either to clarify a message or to add emotion to it. Her voice tone doesn't vary, and she doesn't provide additional information in her facial expressions or changes in posture.

Showing Empathy for Others: Preschool-aged children begin to understand that other people have feelings and sometimes need help to feel better. Typically developing 3-year-olds usually notice when another child is sad or hurt and often make some attempt to comfort the person, particularly if he or she is a familiar person.

WHAT DOES JACQUELINE DO? Jacqueline appears to be very aware of other people's emotions, even labeling them spontaneously and trying to offer comfort when another child is hurt.

WHAT DOES NORA DO? Nora does not show awareness of other people's feelings. This lack of regard for others can look intentional, but usually reflects a basic lack of understanding that other people experience the world differently than you.

Spontaneity and Flexibility of Spoken Language: Preschool-aged children learn to use their words for a variety of purposes—to request something, to comment on it, to ask questions, to share information, to demand something, etc. They also generate new combinations of words, make predictable errors in grammar and syntax, and improve the complexity of their speech as they practice.

WHAT DOES JACQUELINE DO? Jacqueline communicates for lots of different reasons and puts together original phrases and verbal combinations.

WHAT DOES NORA DO? Nora tends to communicate for fewer reasons (usually to get a need met). She also seems to use phrases in chunks and many of her verbalizations are not spontaneous constructions she has created, but rather come from scripts in familiar books or movies. Nora also demonstrates some of the unusual language features that are associated with ASD, including: reversing the pronouns "I" and "you," calling herself by her own name, and reusing the same phrases over and over without clear regard for the context.

Social Quality of Initiations and Responses to Other Children: Children in the preschool years are developing appropriate social behaviors and learning how to behave in a variety of play scenarios. Children of this age learn to join others in play and invite others to play with them. They also begin to understand that sometimes you play a game longer than you might want to, and then you can switch the game to what you like best.

WHAT DOES JACQUELINE DO? Jacqueline frequently initiates toward other children and tries to recruit them to join her in her play interests. She also tries to participate in group games and responds to the social bids of her peers. She is an active participant in group instruction (circle time).

WHAT DOES NORA DO? Nora rarely initiates interactions with her peers and may respond to a play invitation, but only in a limited way (such as in certain games or only for a turn or two). She doesn't tend to persist in a game for the pure social enjoyment of playing but abandons activities without communicating with her friends. Group instruction (circle time) is not an enjoyable learning venue for her, and she does not seem comfortable when physically close to other children.

ELEMENTARY-AGED CHILDREN (KINDERGARTEN–FIFTH GRADE)

ELEMENTARY SCHOOL-AGED CHILD WHO CURRENTLY FUNCTIONS LIKE A 2-YEAR-OLD

Chronological Age: 10 years
Developmental Age: 18–30 months

Alicia: Child with Down syndrome without ASD.

Alicia is a quiet, shy, sweet-tempered fourth-grade student. She is accompanied by a teaching assistant to music, gym, recess, and lunch. She is also in remission after treatment for leukemia. She has bravely endured a lot of medical procedures in her young life, and her health is improving. Alicia learned to walk when she was 4½ years old and continues to develop slowly, particularly in motor skills. She has low muscle tone, and it takes her a little while to organize and initiate movement.

Alicia seems happiest when she is listening to music, sitting in the sun at the park, and being near animals. She has a therapy dog, Rocco, that comes with her to school, which has seemed to help her to adjust to being back at school after being in the hospital. The other children are interested in her dog and frequently approach Alicia to ask if they can pet him. Alicia smiles broadly when her peers approach her, and she nods her head vigorously at their request. She communicates primarily through simple gestures and signs and can request 'food, Rocco, music, hugs, and outside.' She is very affectionate, particularly with adults, and seeks being near an adult in most situations. She watches other children play, but rarely joins them on her own initiative. If an adult or another child who is familiar to her actively recruits her to join a game, she usually does so timidly, often showing more and more pleasure in the activity as it continues. When she listens to music, Alicia often rocks back and forth and smiles to those around her, giggling when her favorite parts are played. She is not interested in television, movies, or the computer, but can be very content sitting with a familiar adult and looking at picture books, particularly of animals.

Rose: Child with Down syndrome with ASD.

Rose is also a fourth-grade student who participates in school activities along with her peers. Attempts to include her with peers in activities such as music and gym have not been very successful, and Rose seems agitated when escorted to these classrooms. When her peers try to approach her or give her something (like a tambourine in music class), she turns away or walks away without really regarding them. Rose rarely smiles and often looks serious. Sometimes she laughs at unusual times, such as when someone is crying or gets hurt. She is very quiet and rarely vocalizes unless she is very happy or very upset. Rose is physically very active and is rarely ill. She loves swinging, spinning in circles, and jumping.

Rose's educational team has been working hard to help her learn how to communicate basic requests, but Rose's responses are inconsistent. Sometimes she uses a sign to indicate "more"; however, most of the time she does not try to communicate. Rose likes to always carry an object in each hand and becomes distressed when her teachers try to get her to put the objects down to do an activity. Transitions between activities can be very challenging. During free play, Rose sits on the floor with her legs outstretched and rocks back and forth vigorously while moving her hands rapidly in front of her face. Sometimes a teacher can get her interested in a three-piece puzzle or a cause-and-effect music toy, but usually Rose has difficulty initiating play with toys on her own.

What to Notice

Importance of Medical History: Some children with Down syndrome have a complicated medical history and have received extensive medical interventions. Sometimes, development is slower in children with health problems, either because of the illness itself or because of the learning opportunities the children miss during medical treatment. It is very important to consider a child's medical history when considering an additional diagnosis of ASD, as part of the criteria for autism involves ruling out any other possible explanations for the child's social, communication, and play behaviors.

WHAT DOES ALICIA DO? Alicia presents as a shy child with significant developmental delays, and her long-standing experience with medical treatment for leukemia poses challenges to her overall development. The chemotherapy she received has been associated with memory problems and she is often fatigued and not able to attend school. Understanding her history helps to clarify that there could be another explanation for her slow developmental progress.

WHAT DOES ROSE DO? Conversely, Rose does not have co-occurring medical conditions and her slow developmental progress cannot be attributed to illness.

Social Orientation. At a developmental age of two years, toddlers show awareness of others by watching them, smiling upon their approach, and seeking to be near them. These behaviors demonstrate that the child is engaged socially and is participating with others in a manner that is appropriate for his or her developmental level.

WHAT DOES ALICIA DO? Alicia shows interest in other children and responds positively when they come to her to ask about her dog. She seeks out being close to familiar people. Subjectively, she feels "connected" to adults and other children, even when she is not at the same skill level as the peers around her.

WHAT DOES ROSE DO? Rose does not appear to be interested in other children and tends to wander away when they try to interact with her. Being with her peers in a large group seems more distressing than pleasurable to her. She seems to act as if no one else is around and her attention is focused inwardly, as opposed to outwardly.

Attempts to Communicate. Developmentally, toddlers (1- to 2-year-olds) are developing ways to communicate what they want, either through words, gestures, making sounds, or using their eyes. Even if their communicative efforts are hard to understand, young children who try to send messages to others understand the basics of social communication.

> WHAT DOES ALICIA DO? Like other children of a similar developmental age (i.e., about 2 years), Alicia has learned how to indicate basic requests using nonverbal means (e.g., gestures or signs). Her vocabulary is small, but very useful to her and she sends simple messages to others frequently throughout the day.
>
> WHAT DOES ROSE DO? Like other young children with ASD, Rose does not seem to understand the process of communication, and she rarely tries to send messages to others, either through verbal or nonverbal means.

Play Behaviors. Developmentally young children usually have relatively limited play skills and tend to seek out sensorimotor play (exploring the sensory features of objects and not yet developing play schemes). In fact, the sophistication of a child's play is thought to reflect his or her language ability.

> WHAT DOES ALICIA DO? Alicia's interests are consistent with sensorimotor play; she tends to enjoy passive listening or sensory exploration and is not yet engaging in multistep play schemes. Her play skills reflect her overall receptive language ability.
>
> WHAT DOES ROSE DO? Rose also tends to engage in sensorimotor play, although her preference is for high-intensity motor activities, such as swinging, spinning, and jumping. During toy time, she rarely shows interest in playing with objects, but rather engages in repetitive body movements.

Self-Soothing Strategies. One of the developmental tasks of early childhood is to develop strategies for coping with distress. Most young children seek comfort from others and find it calming to be near familiar people.

> WHAT DOES ALICIA DO? Alicia seeks being close to familiar people, particularly when she is feeling shy or if she is in a new situation. She has the social instinct to trust others to care for her.

WHAT DOES ROSE DO? Rose does not rely on others for comfort; rather, she seems calmed by carrying objects or getting a lot of movement and stimulation. She does not seem to have the same sort of social affiliation or sense of trust and connectedness that Alicia demonstrates.

ELEMENTARY SCHOOL-AGED CHILD WHO CURRENTLY FUNCTIONS LIKE A 5- TO 7-YEAR-OLD

Chronological Age: 10 years
Developmental Age: 5 to 7 years

Porter: Child with Down syndrome without ASD.

Porter is a fourth-grade student who likes being in his homeroom and always checks the job chart with enthusiasm each morning. He particularly likes the job of feeding the classroom's fish and sometimes he will feed them, even if it isn't his job. When Porter has decided he is going to add an extra feeding (which he knows is against the rules), he first looks around to see where his teachers are and tries to lift the top of the tank quietly. If his teacher sees him, Porter cries and covers his face with his arm and says, "I sorry."

Porter likes the classroom routine but can also be fairly flexible when changes in his schedule occur. He tends to "go with the flow." Porter's expressive and receptive language skills are lower than his classmates', and this sometimes frustrates him. However, he has learned that if he does not understand an adult's direction, he can watch what other kids do and follow their lead.

Porter plays a variety of games with other children during recess and play time. He likes to serve snacks to stuffed animals and will try to get others to join him in this game. Whenever he gives a stuffed animal a snack, he asks if it's good by looking right at the animal's face, holding both palms open in front of him in a questioning gesture, tilting his head and raising his tone of voice at the end of the word in an inquiring manner. Then he appears to wait for a response from the stuffed animal, says "Yeah, yeah, yeah," and nods his head vigorously, sometimes rubbing his belly. Porter plays this way frequently and may repeat the same play scheme over and over and over, enjoying it each time.

Nathan: Child with Down syndrome and ASD.

Nathan is also a fourth-grader. He learns best when there are fewer people around and he appears to be "in his own world" when in the general education classes with his peers. He is learning to greet people and responds to a visual reminder from his teacher to say "hi." He understands many of the classroom rules and likes predictable routines. He gets upset if he is not the Line Leader and will not readily participate in any other classroom job. When another child is Line Leader, he will physically put himself in that position and it can be difficult to redirect him to another place in line. Teachers have tried to prompt him to apologize after hitting another child, but he doesn't seem to understand what they want him to do, which confuses and upsets him.

Nathan's favorite activity is working on the computer, and he has figured out how to get online and search the internet for his favorite websites. He also operates electronics and effortlessly finds his favorite section of a movie and replays it over and over. He likes to watch the credits of movies several times and becomes very distressed if interrupted before they are finished. Nathan is already showing some good reading skills and seems to have improved his talking as he became a better and better reader. Even though he has some very nice problem-solving and academic skills, he is not yet toilet trained during the day. He prefers yellow and gets upset if someone else gets an item of this color instead of him. When distressed, he is very difficult to console. Nathan doesn't sleep well, and he only eats a few foods, including macaroni and cheese, chicken nuggets, and pizza crust.

WHAT TO NOTICE

Social Orientation: Thinking about Other People: During the middle childhood years, children become increasingly aware of other people's thoughts, feelings, and intentions. Children five years and older become more likely to change their behavior based on what they think other people will think about it.

> WHAT DOES PORTER DO? Porter is aware that his additional fish-feedings are against classroom rules, and he has the social understanding to look around and make sure his teacher isn't watching when he tries to sneak the fish a snack.

WHAT DOES NATHAN DO? Nathan seems unaware of the thoughts and feelings of others in his classroom and doesn't often change his behavior spontaneously because of what others might be thinking. For example, his insistence on being Line Leader precludes him from considering how the "real" Line Leader might feel about his intrusion.

Social Conventions: Seeking reassurance and engaging in social conventions, such as greeting others and apologizing to someone you have annoyed, develops in early to middle childhood. Demonstrating knowledge of social conventions and attempting to repair an interaction are developmentally appropriate social behaviors for elementary-aged kids.

WHAT DOES PORTER DO? Porter spontaneously greets others and initiates a routine for apologizing and demonstrates knowledge of the social convention for apologizing and he attempts to repair the interaction. Even though feeding the fish is intensely fun, he also doesn't want his teacher to be mad at him.

WHAT DOES NATHAN DO? Nathan doesn't understand or enact basic social conventions, such as greeting others, saying "excuse me" when he bumps into someone, or apologizing if he hurts someone. This "unwritten" social code is not meaningful to him. His lack of social niceties is sometimes misunderstood by others as meanness, but he is completely unaware of many seemingly basic social conventions, such as greetings.

Developing Strategies to Help Cope with Language Problems: Children with communication difficulties, such as problems understanding complex language or challenges in pronouncing words clearly and consistently, often develop strategies to help them to function when their language challenges get in the way. If the child also has an ASD, the child is much less likely to develop and initiate some of the social learning strategies that can help—such as watching what other kids do and then doing what they are doing.

> WHAT DOES PORTER DO? Porter has learned that when he doesn't understand what someone has said, he can look to see what other kids are doing and imitate their actions. This strategy has served him well in many new situations.
>
> WHAT DOES NATHAN DO? Nathan does not seem to attend to the actions of other children, and he is rarely seen spontaneously copying what they do—either in play or during schoolwork. Instead of relying on imitation or looking to others to solve problems, Nathan usually tries to solve a problem by himself and either succeeds or abandons it.

Variety in Play: As children are learning a new skill, they will repeat it and repeat it until it is mastered. Some repetition, therefore, is adaptive and part of typical development. Children with a developmental delay of any kind are more repetitive in their play than children without a developmental disability. Therefore, some repetitive play is to be expected in children with Down syndrome, whether or not they also have an ASD.

> WHAT DOES PORTER DO? Porter likes familiarity and routine and repeats the "feeding the animals" play scheme quite often. However, he is also open to participating in other activities and doesn't solely play in the same way each time.
>
> WHAT DOES NATHAN DO? Nathan has limited play skills and repeats the same activities on the computer over and over and watches the same sections of movies several times. It is difficult to interest him in novel activities.

Behavioral Flexibility: As children get older, they are challenged more and more to be flexible and to "go with the flow." Being adaptable to changes and managing transitions between activities becomes an age-appropriate skill that is necessary to accomplish before kindergarten.

WHAT DOES PORTER DO? Porter follows the classroom routine and moves between activities without additional interventions. He prefers certain toys but can usually accept a replacement. He may balk at some transitions, but overall is able to "go with the flow."

WHAT DOES NATHAN DO? Nathan becomes overly focused on certain events or activities (like being the Line Leader), has difficulty with transitions and unexpected events, and needs additional help leaving preferred activities, such as recess. He gets fixated on yellow and has a hard time being flexible and allowing another child to have something yellow.

The final section of this chapter will discuss how autism symptoms present in teenagers and adults with Down syndrome.

WHEN AUTISM IS SUSPECTED FOR TEENS AND ADULTS WITH DOWN SYNDROME

Dennis McGuire, LCSW, PhD & Brian Chicoine, MD

One common concern voiced by families and caregivers of adults with DS is whether the behavior or characteristics of their family member with DS is an indication of an autism spectrum disorder (ASD). These issues are particularly confusing to parents of people with DS who are in their late teens and adult years. For many of these families, there was little information and awareness of ASD associated with DS while their children were growing up. In fact, many parents who had concerns have reported that they could not find professionals who could help them, or they were told that ASD did not occur in people with DS.

This part of the chapter will look at the behavior and characteristics of ASD and DS in teens and adults to help caregivers and professionals better differentiate whether autism is a true concern. We will also discuss strategies to use when ASD is diagnosed. We will draw on our experience to discuss these issues, but we were also able to elicit the assistance of our colleague Dr. Elina Manghi to help us write this chapter. The late Dr. Manghi was a psychologist by training and an expert on ASD, and she had extensive experience with ASD and DS. She also added a key component to this chapter with her discussion of the complex art and science of the diagnosis of ASD.

FINDINGS IN ADULTS WITH DOWN SYNDROME

Like the section on children with DS, adults without ASD will be compared to adults with DS-ASD. The focus in this section will be on individuals who are younger than 30 because the idea that ASD could coexist in DS has only been more widely accepted in the past 15 to 20 years. The description of adults having ASD will include those diagnosed in childhood and those who we believe have ASD because of symptoms and behaviors. It is not uncommon for an adult with DS who also has features of ASD to have not been diagnosed in childhood. The lack of acknowledgment in the past that ASD could coexist likely contributes to that finding as does the lack of understanding of the differences between people with DS with and without ASD. We will also discuss how to differentiate those with DS alone with those who also have ASD, how to diagnose ASD in this population, and what treatment strategies are effective when ASD is found.

PARENT RECOLLECTION OF CHILDHOOD HISTORY

We will briefly discuss a general childhood history of individuals based on parental interviews and available records. There are some obvious inaccuracies and omissions in the parental interviews because they are based on a recollection of events and observations that occurred years in the past when their now adult son or daughter was a child. Still, parental reports can be quite consistent. It is interesting to note, too, that many families recall painful experiences in the past. Most commonly, these painful experiences were due to critical or negative comments from family or friends as well as from teachers, staff, neighbors, and even strangers.

Parents clearly interpreted these criticisms to imply that if they were better parents, their child's problems would go away. Many parents also reported at least one incident in public settings where strangers accused them of being bad or abusive parents when their child displayed a tantrum or problem behavior. On the other hand, many of these same parents remembered other family, friends, teachers, staff, and professionals who took the time to understand and support them and their child despite whatever behavior the child displayed. These individuals made life far more tolerable for them.

Two Categories

Most families' descriptions of their child's history fit into one of two categories, which are like categories reported by Dr. George Capone (1999). In the first category, the child displayed autistic symptoms and behaviors from very early in childhood and the families do not recall this as a regression. In the second category, the child was reported to have had a major regression of previously mastered skills. Parents reported that the age of regression tended to be older, from 3 to 8 years, compared to the age of 2 to 3 years reported in the general population (who developed ASD). The later date of regression may be due to a delay in development for children with DS compared to the general population.

In families reporting a regression, some reported the type of severe and dramatic regression similar to what Joan Medlen (1999) described so eloquently in her article "More than Down Syndrome: A Parent's View." For example, many children had verbal language, were social with caregivers and peers, and had creative play and other skills, before seemingly losing all these skills in a regression. Other parents, however, described a major regression, but also observed some differences in their sons and daughters even before the regression. Many noted there were differences in their child's response to them or to other children compared to other children with DS. They also frequently noted more fussiness and irritability, the presence of stereotypic behaviors (such as rocking and hand flapping), and a greater sensitivity to sensory stimuli (such as to touch, light, or sounds), as well as eating and sleeping difficulties. Thus, for some individuals, the distinction between the first and second categories appears to be less clear or obvious.

Symptoms and Behaviors of ASD

Regardless of parents' reporting their child's history of exhibiting signs and symptoms of ASD at an early age or that they experienced regression of previously acquired skills later in childhood, both categories reported similar autism characteristics, as described below.

Difficulties with Social Skills. Most notably, parents observed a significant lack of social response or relatedness with family or friends. Parents also noted a definite lack of interest or ability in developing relationships with peers. Many children were antisocial, anxious, or fearful in the presence of people they did not know, even when they encountered visitors in their own home. In the literature (Capone, 1999), individuals with DS-ASD have been reported to be a little more social than those with ASD without DS, and this was also reported by parents in our experience. Despite this, we have found that there is still a significant difference in social relatedness between individuals with DS who have ASD and those with "just" Down syndrome, as we will discuss at some length later in this chapter.

Difficulties in Communication. Most families in the second category who noted regression reported a total loss of verbal communication, but many children in the first category, who did not have a major regression, also had significant expressive language limitations, and quite a few were nonverbal.

Repetitive Behaviors. In both groups, most individuals developed or intensified stereotypic and repetitive motor behaviors such as hand flapping, spinning, or rocking. Many also developed an obsession or fascination with inanimate objects such as strings, lights, fans, mirrors, hands, fingers, and water. Many also lost the ability or interest in creative play, preferring instead to manipulate objects (often repetitiously) in rigid ways, such as lining up toys or other objects in fixed positions.

Sensory Issues. Many children also developed or intensified sensitivity to certain sensory inputs, such as hearing, touch, taste, smell, sight, and less-known body senses.

Behavioral Challenges. Findings included behavioral challenges, including frequent tantrums and outbursts, as well as verbal and physical aggression. Many parents noted great difficulty in adjusting to transitions and that a common strategy when refusing to respond to a change was to drop to the ground and refuse to move. This is a particularly difficult strategy to counter because the person's body becomes dead weight. Families universally dread this behavior. Many had a name for it such as a "meltdown" or a "drop-and-flop."

Typical Signs of ASD in Teens and Adults with Down Syndrome

- Significant lack of social response or relatedness with family or friends
- Lack of interest in or ability to develop relationships with peers
- Antisocial, anxious, or fearful in the presence of people they do not know
- For some, a history of regression, with loss of verbal communication
- If no regression, significant expressive language limitations or being nonverbal
- Intensified stereotypic and repetitive motor behaviors (e.g., hand flapping, spinning, or rocking)
- Obsession or fascination with inanimate objects such as strings, lights, fans, mirrors, hands, fingers, and water
- Lack of ability or interest in creative play
- Manipulation of objects in rigid ways, such as lining up toys or other objects in fixed positions
- Intensified sensitivity to certain types of sensory input (hearing, touch, taste, smell, sight)
- Frequent tantrums and outbursts, as well as verbal and physical aggression
- Great difficulty in adjusting to transitions
- Dropping to the ground and refusing to move—a common strategy when refusing to respond to a change
- A little more social than those with ASD without DS

HISTORY OF ADULTS WITH DS AND ASD

ASD is a spectrum disorder and there are some differences in the intensity or severity of symptoms for adults with DS. All have some features of ASD. However, there can be important distinctions depending on how or when they were diagnosed or identified as having an ASD.

The first group was diagnosed with ASD in childhood, by a reputable diagnostician. Still, many of the parents in this group reported that they had problems locating a professional to diagnose their child.

The second group was not formally diagnosed by a trained psychologist or diagnostician, but they were told by someone who worked in some professional capacity that their child probably had an ASD, and this person had extensive contact with their son or daughter. Many times, parents respected the opinion of this person or professional. Many of these parents followed up with their own review of the literature (on ASD and DS-ASD) and were knowledgeable about the issues. Families in this group gave several reasons why they did not seek a formal diagnosis. Some reported that they simply could not find a practitioner or a center that diagnosed ASD in people with DS, some could not afford an evaluation, others report that they felt no need because they already knew, and still others reported they simply did not find the time because of the demands of raising their child with DS-ASD.

The third group of individuals was also not diagnosed with ASD in childhood. Families in this group clearly had grave concerns that something was wrong, and some even suspected ASD (given what they heard of the disorder), but they were not able to find a practitioner or any reputable source to help them give a name to their concerns.

MENTAL HEALTH DIAGNOSES AND TREATMENTS

Despite the differences in when or how individuals were diagnosed, there was one major similarity for all groups. Most were diagnosed and treated by a variety of other mental health practitioners and were given a variety of other mental health diagnoses. Even families in the first group were quite often given other diagnoses and a host of treatments before finding the "right" diagnostician to identify the ASD.

Common diagnoses given included attention deficit disorder, oppositional defiant disorder, obsessive-compulsive disorder, bipolar disorder, impulse control disorder, and atypical psychosis. The psychotropic medications prescribed included those that were the norm for treatment of these disorders, including the atypical antipsychotics, antidepressants, and mood stabilizers. Some families reported that some of these treatments helped, while others reported that they did not. Quite a few of the families reported at least some problems with side effects associated with these medications, including weight gain followed by agitation and sedation.

It is interesting to note that many parents, across all the groups, were told by medical and mental health practitioners that people with DS could not have ASD.

SYMPTOMS AND FINDINGS IN ADULTHOOD

Regardless of which of the above three categories families were in, many reported that whatever positive strategies they learned to help support their child's development and behavior in childhood were often undermined by the developmental, physical, and environmental changes and challenges in the teen and adult years. These changes and challenges tended to create more extreme and unmanageable levels of stress. We found that most individuals with DS and ASD simply had too many stressors and vulnerabilities to come through the teen and adult years without experiencing significant challenges.

Stressors and Vulnerabilities

Like all individuals with DS, those with ASD are at greater risk for a variety of health issues (when compared to those without DS), such as thyroid disorders, sleep apnea, and gastrointestinal conditions including celiac disease (inability to process gluten)— all of which may have a profound effect on the person's physical and mental well-being (Chicoine & McGuire, 2010). Additionally, sleeping and eating difficulties, as well as bowel and bladder issues, continued well beyond childhood for many people in the sample, creating enormous stress for parents, as well as for their son or daughter. For example, in addition to sleep apnea many individuals have other problems with sleep. Agitation because of stress in their lives likely contributes to some of the sleep disturbance. This agitation can continue well into the nighttime hours, affecting their own and their parents' sleep. Over time, the detrimental effect on the family and person with DS increases as the sleep problems and sleep deprivation continue.

Hormonal changes also are a potential cause of stress for teens. The hormonal changes for people with DS (with and without ASD) tend to occur close to the age that people in the general population experience them (McGuire & Chicoine, 2021). Adolescence brings on major physical changes in the body, such as the growth of body hair, the need for deodorant, the maturation of genitalia, and the onset of menses in women and nocturnal emissions in men. The latter two changes were understandably most disturbing to teens with DS-ASD.

Accompanying these hormonal changes are the notorious *fluctuations in mood* that are the hallmark of adolescence. This is a difficult and tumultuous period for people without intellectual disabilities. We found similarities in mood and behavior for adolescents with DS and those in the general population, but for teens with DS-ASD the effect was even more intense and disruptive. No doubt the effect of hormonal changes is increased by communication difficulties that make it far more difficult for parents, teachers, or professionals to explain to these individuals what is happening to their bodies. Even parents who had other teenagers and who were prepared for a rocky road were surprised by the intensity and severity of mood and behavior fluctuations. Families reported a marked increase in anxiety and agitation, temper tantrums, oppositional behavior, rigid compulsions, and refusals to do just about anything.

For many individuals, there are other *problems in public settings.* For example, some refuse to use public toilets, which greatly limits activities in the community. For others, using a public toilet can too easily create trauma, which affects all elimination behavior.

Eating problems also continue to be a concern in the teen and adult years. Many individuals are fussy eaters or have peculiar tastes, habits, or rituals when eating. Often, odd eating habits are precipitated by sensory issues, such as having an aversion to certain textures, smells, or sensations when eating. Whatever the cause of the eating habits or issues, the effect for many families is to create stress and a battleground at meals, particularly if the person's food choices are unreasonable or unhealthy.

We found that many teens and adults with DS are susceptible to *sensory perception differences,* including vision, hearing and touch. These issues appear to be far more common and intense for those who also have ASD and interfere with their ability to go freely into the community. These individuals often find sensory stimuli such as lights, noises, large spaces, or crowds quite aversive.

Social Relatedness Issues

Perhaps the most important area of stress and vulnerability is related to social skills and social relatedness. This is also the one key area different for persons with DS-ASD versus individuals with DS-only (as we will discuss later). We live in a social world; thus, our ability to deal with others may have a profound effect on all areas of our life.

Most people with DS have the ability to engage others because of good social skills. This ability to interact may go a long way toward instilling goodwill and assistance from others, especially when experiencing problems or in times of need. In contrast, those with ASD do not have this social ability. As a result, the lack of a smile or attempt to reach out to others may too easily result in a lack of understanding, patience, and sensitivity from others—in schools, recreation centers, extended family, and community settings. The families find that their sons' or daughters' problems with social skills often make it more difficult to get help and support when needed or to resolve issues when they occur.

Environmental Changes/Challenges

As people with DS grow out of the childhood years, changes in the school system, especially when coupled with other stressors, may create enormous strain for them. This strain is often magnified tenfold for teens and young adults who also have ASD. The small school and single class of the elementary years gives way to bigger middle schools and high schools and the need to adapt to far larger and more complex settings. These settings have more students and staff and the potential to cause intolerable sensory overstimulation for those with DS-ASD.

Finally, the ability to communicate the cause, source, or presence of a problem is often difficult for teens and adults with DS, but even more difficult for those with ASD. Many times, it seems that the only recourse those with DS-ASD have to let others know they are stressed is to shut down or to become agitated or aggressive, especially as the stress becomes increasingly intolerable to them.

Areas of Stress That May Arise

There are many possible points of stress or areas of vulnerability that may arise for those with DS-ASD, which may include impaired sleep, mystifying hormonal changes, eating problems, bowel and urinary function or dysfunction, significant communication limitations, a limited number of persons in one's support system (due in part to lack of social skills and relatedness), a tendency toward rigidity in one's daily routine (obsessive-compulsive behaviors), and a much higher sensitivity or reaction to sensory stimuli (sensory integration impairment). There can be a higher incidence of health issues affecting people with DS and major environmental changes as the child progresses into middle school and high school.

Each one of these areas of vulnerability can create added stressors and can have a negative effect on other areas of life, as well. In other words, one major change or series of changes can result in what families often called a "breakdown" or a "shut down." In these instances, the person with DS-ASD may benefit by the care providers building in additional time for transitions and new routines to help with the adjustments to new situations and mitigate escalating behaviors.

GAINING AN UNDERSTANDING OF DS-ASD

At least partly due to not receiving a diagnosis in childhood, families have various levels of understanding regarding ASD. Some are quite informed, others less so, and still others believing what they were told about ASD not being possible in people with DS. Generally, we find that all are open to, and interested in, identifying and resolving problems arising from areas of vulnerability and stress. Despite the severity of symptoms and behaviors, and the fact that many families present in crisis, we find many have a number of strengths and resources in the family. Many families are also able to find help from professionals and from others in the community, which allows creative and fruitful ways to get people back on track. This is especially true when they now have a better understanding of the diagnosis and the differences in someone with "just" Down syndrome and someone with DS-ASD.

Strengths of the Families

We have found over the years that most families exhibited great resilience when facing challenges. They have learned from their experiences and know their child well and are determined to handle each new challenge. We found that there are many good reasons why they were able to do this. First, most parents and their children with DS-ASD have learned to better communicate, respect, and respond to each other. Parents are quite often particularly good observers and interpreters to begin with, but most of these parents fine-tune this skill to understand even subtle cues from their son's or daughter's behavior. This, in turn, had a positive effect on the child-parent relationship. We also found that these families were far more patient and more accepting of their sons' and daughters' idiosyncrasies.

SOME ADDITIONAL THINGS TO KNOW ABOUT DIAGNOSING ASD IN ADULTS WITH DOWN SYNDROME

The diagnosis of ASD in adults with DS is complicated because of several factors, which include:

a. The lack of appropriate diagnostic tools.
b. The reliance on caregivers' memory to recall behaviors that existed in early childhood.
c. The lack of professional knowledge that both diagnoses may coexist.

    d.   The scarcity of professionals trained to appropriately diagnose autism in adults with DS.

Despite the above difficulties, the diagnosis of ASD in adults with DS is possible and should be conducted by professionals experienced in recognizing ASD in individuals with intellectual disabilities. To appropriately diagnose ASD in adults with DS, caregivers need to understand that the diagnosis is a process that cannot be accomplished in one office visit. Unfortunately, there is no blood test or imaging (such as X-rays or magnetic resonance imaging/MRI) that allows us to determine whether an individual has ASD. (See chapter five for more details on the diagnostic evaluation process.)

PREPARING FOR AN ASD EVALUATION OF AN ADULT WITH DOWN SYNDROME

The first step in the diagnostic process is to gather a detailed medical history. It is important that caregivers provide the diagnostic team with complete medical records, if possible, prior to the first appointment. This gives the team an opportunity to review the records and prepare pertinent questions. We also recommend that the caregivers review both childhood and current pictures and videos to aid in the recollection of early history.

The gold standard for the ASD evaluation of teens and adults with DS is a clinical diagnosis by the multidisciplinary clinical team. Therefore, the teen or adult suspected of having ASD must be prepared to meet several professionals over a period of a few clinic visits. Professionals also must be sensitive to the difficulties that the person with suspected ASD might have in working with many unknown people. Efforts should be made to schedule shorter sessions, be sensitive to sensory issues, and provide many breaks to facilitate the evaluation.

DIAGNOSING ASD IN TEENS AND ADULTS WITH DOWN SYNDROME

The most difficult aspect of the diagnosis of ASD in adults with DS is identifying appropriate instruments, which would allow the interdisciplinary team to determine the appropriate clinical diagnosis. Expert clinicians are using several tools that aid in the diagnosis of ASD in this population. For example, the two gold standard tools for the assessment of ASD are the Autism Diagnostic Interview-Revised (ADI-R) and the Autism Diagnostic Observation Schedule (ADOS).

The ADI-R is a very detailed interview conducted with the parents or caregivers. It assesses early and current history of ASD behaviors. The ADOS is an observational tool used for the diagnosis of ASD from toddlers to adults. The ADOS does not provide materials or diagnostic algorithms for nonverbal adolescents and adults with ASD. Thus, when testing a nonverbal adult or teen with DS and possible ASD, it is important to combine information from all sources, including medical history, history of restricted and repetitive behaviors, creative play, obsessions, stereotyped behaviors, etc.

Activities from the ADOS allow the assessment of current communication and social relationship issues, as well as the observation of behaviors that are typically seen in individuals with ASD (e.g., lack of eye contact, difficulties with reciprocity, etc.). It is important for caregivers to understand that the examiner is observing how the individual behaves with someone he does not know and how he regulates social interaction.

The ADI-R is a detailed interview with the parents or other caregivers that is used to assess the history and current presence of behaviors also related to ASD. The ADI-R can be used with teens and adults suspected of having ASD, if their mental age is above 2 years, 0 months. The interview evaluates three functional domains: 1) language/communication; 2) reciprocal social interaction; 3) restricted, repetitive, and stereotyped behaviors and interests.

The Aberrant Behavior Checklist (ABC; Aman & Singh, 2017; Aman et al., 1985) is also used for assessing problem behaviors in children and adults with intellectual disabilities. The scale provides information in five areas: 1) irritability and agitation; 2) lethargy and social withdrawal; 3) stereotypic behavior; 4) hyperactivity and noncompliance; 5) and inappropriate speech.

Assessing cognitive functioning is important to develop the best interventions consistent with the individual's functioning. However, cognitive assessment is complicated by the lack of appropriate norms. That is, none of the tests used to assess IQ have been normed or tested on a large number of people with DS to determine what the average, below average, and above average range of scores is for each subtest of individuals. Nor have any of the tests been normed on people with ASD and DS. The Leiter-R is a nonverbal cognitive test that is better suited to use with individuals with intellectual disabilities than are the more commonly used tests such as the Wechsler or Stanford-Binet. However, the test requires the understanding and use of gestures, which is difficult for individuals with ASD. One group of researchers suggests the use of a developmental quotient score to calculate how much an individual's skill level deviates from his or her chronological age (di Pellegrino et al., 1992). This method may be used when selecting an assessment tool developed for individuals in an age range different from the individual being tested (e.g., the Wechsler scales).

The assessment of adaptive behaviors is another helpful area when selecting appropriate testing instruments and creating developmentally appropriate interventions. Understanding what the individual can do is the foundation for successful strategies to improve lacking skills.

A current speech and language evaluation is helpful to determine the extent of the person's communicative intent, speech, and language ability. If possible, this evaluation should be conducted prior to the psychological evaluation. Understanding the person's speech abilities will aid in the selection of the most appropriate cognitive assessment tool, and the appropriate ADOS module.

Individuals with DS and ASD have sensory and motor problems that may impede normal functioning. An occupational and physical therapy evaluation may therefore aid in determining the most appropriate interventions and/or environmental changes needed.

Finally, an understanding of the individual's current home and school environment is important to facilitate the development of treatment strategies. In addition, a psychosocial assessment by a psychologist, social worker, or a related professional, on the issues discussed at some length in the section "Symptoms and Findings in Adulthood" (above) provide clear guidelines as to what services are needed to improve the individual's community functioning.

When conducting an ASD assessment for individuals with DS, it is important to remember that there are some behaviors that are present in people with DS with or without ASD but that look different when the individual has DS-ASD. For example, obsessional behaviors are present in both, but there are qualitative differences. For example, the compulsions of someone with DS-ASD are more likely to be less functional or out of sync with normal activities or patterns of behavior (e.g., arranging toys in a rigid manner). In contrast, for a person with just DS, obsessional behavior is more likely to involve the repetition of a more functional behavior (e.g., rigidly adhering to a schedule or routine).

Also, keep in mind that difficulties in social relatedness may be due to a hearing impairment or may be part of ASD. Distinguishing ASD behaviors from behaviors associated with the level of cognitive impairment is also a diagnostic challenge. For example, adults with significant levels of intellectual disability may engage in repetitive, stereotyped movements regardless of if they have ASD.

Every effort should be made to include a variety of instruments and interviews to aid in the refinement of the ASD diagnosis. The best approach is to consult an interdisciplinary team with experience in diagnosing ASD in adults with DS.

DIFFERENTIAL DIAGNOSIS

When a teen experiences a loss of skill or function, it is important to rule out any other possible causes or explanations other than autism. Ideally, the person can be evaluated at a multidisciplinary clinic staffed by health and mental health professionals with staff who can look at a wide variety of health, sensory (vision and hearing), and environmental stressors that may be associated with a loss of function. When there are symptoms or behaviors of concern, we recommend considering the following.

Communication

People with DS have expressive language limitations, and they cannot always communicate the cause or source of problems, even when they have a considerable degree of emotional or physical discomfort or pain. Many times, parents and other caregivers are extremely good observers and interpreters of the people with DS in their care. We recommend including parents/caregivers in any evaluations to help better communicate possible issues and concerns for the person with DS.

Lower Functioning Individuals

Many people who have significant expressive and adaptive skill limitations may appear to have ASD because of more extreme communication limitations and stereotypic behaviors. It is important to gather information from knowledgeable informants in the person's residence, work, and recreation settings. The presence or absence of social skills and relatedness is often very easy to discern by credible and caring caregivers who are often excellent interpreters and observers of the individual's subtle and not-so-subtle nonverbal communication.

Social Deprivation

Some home and community environments may deprive people of the opportunity to learn social skills and social relatedness. It is not that these individuals cannot learn, just that they have not had adequate training or experience. In most cases, it is possible to tell whether the person has social skills and the ability to learn them by observing how the person acts with other people.

Sensory Issues

People with DS have a high incidence of vision and hearing difficulties, which may make them appear unresponsive and unaware of their social and natural environments. Hearing and vision testing is highly recommended. Also, as mentioned previously, many people with DS have sensory processing or sensory integration disorders. A sensory evaluation by an experienced occupational therapist trained to evaluate these problems is highly recommended.

Health Issues

People with DS are at greater risk for several health issues that may create a significant change in mood or behavior. The most common of these issues include hypothyroidism or hyperthyroidism, sleep apnea, and celiac disease (but there are many others). A complete physical exam by a knowledgeable physician or medical professional is highly recommended to diagnose and treat any health conditions.

Additionally, pain and medical illness may have a significant effect on the person's mood and behavior. It is important to note that many people with DS appear to have a higher threshold of pain (although this may be based on limited ability to report or localize pain or delayed response to pain). When coupled with communication problems (above), this may delay diagnosis and treatment.

MENTAL HEALTH AND BEHAVIORAL PROBLEMS

Many individuals with DS have mental health and behavioral disorders that may generate concern about the possibility of ASD. The disorders of greatest concern include depression, trauma, obsessive-compulsive disorder (OCD), obsessional slowness, and attention deficit disorder. These disorders will be discussed in more detail later.

Down Syndrome Regression Disorder

A condition that appears to have neurological and psychological features has been unofficially called Down syndrome regression disorder. Another of the names it has been called is Down Syndrome Disintegrative Disorder, which highlights that some of the features look like ASD. However, this condition, which includes loss of skills and behavioral changes, typically has onset in the teenage or early adult years rather than childhood for ASD. There are other features that are different as well.

First, it is important to discuss the interaction of mental, physical, sensory, and environmental causes. In our experience, too often people are referred for psychiatric treatment without looking for and treating underlying causes and precipitants, and, as a result, these conditions may continue or worsen. This is particularly the case for a person with DS who cannot easily verbalize or articulate the cause or source of problems. We cannot stress enough the need to look for and treat all health and sensory problems and to identify and reduce environmental stressors associated with a mental health behavioral problem. We have written extensively about these issues in previous works (Chicoine & McGuire, 2010; McGuire & Chicoine, 2021).

Depression

Depression is one of the most common mental health problems reported for persons with DS (Chicoine & McGuire, 2010; McGuire & Chicoine, 2021). There are several reasons for this. First, people with DS are more susceptible to health problems that are a known cause of depression, such as hypothyroidism (affecting approximately 40 percent of this population), as well as sleep apnea and celiac disease (Chicoine & McGuire, 2010). Second, sensory and sensory processing difficulties are more common, and these also create stress and tend to isolate the individual, placing them more at risk for depression. Many people with DS may also be more susceptible to depression because of expressive language limitations, which may make it more difficult to identify and resolve situations that are stressful to them.

Some individuals with DS develop more severe forms of depression that sometimes caregivers interpret as symptoms of ASD. Severe depression often results in a more extreme form of withdrawal. Many people with severe depression refuse to leave the house to go to work or to social events and may stop socializing with their family. Many develop odd or unproductive compulsive behaviors, and those who are verbal quite often have agitated self-talk. Perhaps most disturbing to families is the development of a self-absorbed state that takes more and more of the person's attention and focus. Typically, this includes self-talk; even if the person does not talk out loud to himself, they may appear to be communicating with some invisible person or entity. In this state, people appear to be out of touch with the world and reality. Many times, parents and other caregivers report that it is often very difficult to pull people back from this self-absorbed state. This is what caregivers can mistake for ASD.

With more severe forms of depression, the difference between ASD and depression may be difficult to sort out. What we have found is that individuals with more severe depression may stay in a self-absorbed state (described by family members as being "out of it" or "in another world"). This may last for months or years, but still there will be some improvement in time. At first, the individual may show a small but gradually increasing interest in things that he enjoyed previously, such as music, movies, sports, etc. After this, most people gradually return to recreational activities, and then finally they will return to work. Most importantly, with time, people regain enough of their social awareness and responsiveness to function adequately in social, recreational, and vocational settings. Some may not return to the level of function they had prior to the onset of their depressed symptoms, but still regain enough skills to relate to others in the different environments they inhabit.

In comparison, a person with DS who has ASD who has regressed in social skills and relatedness may be able to go through the motions of relating to others with behavioral training. However, even years later the quality of the social relatedness remains quite deficient.

Trauma

Some individuals with DS are known or suspected to have been severely traumatized by physical or sexual abuse or some other traumatic experience. In response to the trauma, many develop symptoms that are very similar to those described above for individuals with more severe forms of depression. Typically, however, the trauma sufferers also have a considerable amount of anxiety.

Many caregivers suspect trauma when the person with DS avoids activities and places that had been a normal and often an enjoyable part of their daily routine. For example, one woman who was sexually abused at her worksite adamantly refused to go to her job, which was the site of the sexual violence. Many others also have general anxiety and fearfulness, and many are fearful of leaving their home or of going to public places, especially places where there are strangers. Additionally, many people regress and become more dependent on others. They may also become clingier and more afraid to be alone or apart from significant others. Again, what is most disturbing to families is the development of a state of self-absorption very similar to that of individuals who are experiencing more severe forms of depression. The self-absorption often takes more and more of the person's attention and focus. In this state, individuals will appear to be out of touch with the world and reality, and, again, this may look very much like autism.

As with the severely depressed, people with DS who are exposed to a severe trauma may take years to recover, but over time there are significant improvements in social relatedness—which will generally not occur to the same degree for people with ASD.

Obsessive-Compulsive Disorder

As discussed previously, we have found that most people with DS have obsessive-compulsive tendencies that we have called "grooves," because people tend to have set patterns and routines in their lives (McGuire & Chicoine, 2021). Under stress, a normally productive groove can become an unproductive obsession or compulsion for many people with DS. We have found that the development of a more rigid or less functional groove is a very common way for people with DS to express stress. If the stress continues, the groove may become an obsession or compulsion that may then begin to interfere in some essential area of life. For example, people may choose to arrange and rearrange personal items or objects in their room rather than to attend a beneficial social or recreational activity that they would normally enjoy.

Obsessions and compulsions may be more odd, extreme, or dysfunctional for teens and adults with DS-ASD compared to those with "just" DS. Still, we have found that many people with DS also have very odd, unusual, and debilitating types of obsessive-compulsive disorder (OCD), particularly in response to more extreme stressors in their lives. Therefore, we recommend being very careful in assuming that someone has ASD based on obsessions or compulsive behaviors.

Obsessional Slowness

One of the most unusual and frustrating patterns of behavior diagnosed in teens and adults with DS is a condition called obsessional slowness. This condition occurs in a relatively small number of individuals, but for these individuals, the disorder is quite debilitating, and it is maddening to caregivers. While the diagnosis has been questioned in those without DS, there is no question that a small subset of people with DS develop this intense slowing. Sometimes the slowness gradually develops over a period, such as months or even years, but other times it may come on suddenly after the person with DS has had a relatively "normal" pattern of behavior for their life.

These individuals move at a pace that is so slow that they cannot go about their daily life and activities without hands-on help and assistance from caregivers. These individuals do not seem to lose the ability to do tasks; rather, their speed prohibits completion in a manner required for life. Additionally, many show very brief bursts of normal speed, but most of the time, movement is painstakingly slow. Adding greatly to the mystery and frustration of this condition is the fact that no effective treatments have been found to date. In most cases, this condition appears to be impervious to psychotropic medications. Some practitioners have found some success with behavioral strategies, but usually even this only provides a small increase in the slow pace.

Because people with obsessional slowness display periods of normal speed, caregivers may wonder if the individual's behavior is purposeful. Caregivers who have observed the slowness over many months and years, however, often come to believe that the individuals who have this condition have little control over their own pace.

Although parents may be concerned that obsessional slowness is a symptom of ASD, most people who have the condition continue to be socially aware and responsive to others. Therefore, caregivers may be dismayed and frustrated by this condition, but the fact that there is a continuation of social relatedness means this is most likely not related to autism.

ADHD

Attention deficit disorder with and without hyperactivity occurs in teens and adults with DS just as it does in the general population. People with DS plus ADHD typically have attention problems, are distractible, and have difficulty controlling their impulses. Individuals with DS and ASD may also be diagnosed with ADHD. The problem for these individuals is not that they are diagnosed with ADHD, but that sometimes they are only given this diagnosis when, in fact, ASD is present.

Therefore, despite the presence of ADHD symptoms or behaviors, we strongly recommend that a more thorough assessment be made, particularly in terms of social skills and relationship issues, if there are suspicions of possible ASD.

ASSESSMENT AND INTERVENTION

Multidisciplinary Approach

A multidisciplinary approach is often beneficial because problems are often the result of a complex interplay of biological, social, and psychological factors. The multidisciplinary team allows the best means for identifying and treating the different factors at play in a problem. This is especially important for teens and adults with DS-ASD because there are so many areas of vulnerability.

For example, the medical staff identify and treat health problems that occur more frequently in individuals with DS (both with and without ASD). This helps to reduce one very important area of vulnerability. For example, people in this group are just as susceptible to such problems as thyroid disorders, celiac disease, GI problems, and sleep apnea as others with DS.

Psychosocial staff and medical staff can work collaboratively to diagnose and treat mental health and behavioral problems. When deemed appropriate by the team, psychotropic medications may be prescribed to help reduce agitation and get the more disruptive or aggressive behavior under better control. Once agitation is reduced, sleep often improves. Medication can also help to reduce depressive withdrawal, as well as compulsive behavior, which allows people to be more flexible in responding to their world.

Visual Cues

Additionally, once the disruptive behavior is better controlled, behavioral strategies are often more effective. Visual cues can be especially effective in helping teens and adults with DS-ASD learn skills, solve problems, communicate, and manage day-to-day functions and frustrations—regardless of what age the cues are introduced. For example, visual cues can help to make the effects of hormonal changes more understandable and manageable. Visual checklists give women a stepwise means to deal with tasks related to menstruation, and calendars help to show when their periods will occur. For both men and women, sex education charts of the human body help to better show how developmental changes occur in adolescents. Even nocturnal emissions are more understandable to men if they can look at charts of the male reproductive system. It is a little more difficult to use visual supports to explain changes in mood and irritability, but at least the cues give individuals some indication as to why they are having problems.

Visual cues are also very helpful in reducing a common area of stress in the family—completing daily living tasks. Visual cues can help people with DS-ASD to do their tasks without interference or supervision, which gives them a needed sense of control and independence.

Visual cues also give parents "the best shot" at managing eating problems. Most parents are willing to try something new after repeated failures with their attempts to enforce "normal" eating habits. Pictures of the food items and a checklist that are appealing to the individual with DS-ASD can be used. This gives a greater sense of independence and control, as well as a much better chance at a more balanced diet and a calmer meal.

In addition, bowel and bladder issues are better managed with visual cues, helping to reduce another very intense and stressful issue for many families. For example, visual cues can be an effective way to teach basic toileting skills to teens or adults who have not yet mastered them.

Many families have been able to use the most up-to-date technology to incorporate visual cues into their adult child's life. For example, they use smart phones with applications that all teens and adults consider helpful and "cool," instead of the old augmentative devices that are often not used because they were too big and clunky and because they can be embarrassing for teen or young adult users. Smart phones are a far more acceptable way to provide visual cues and can give people a means to take part in activities they cannot participate in without a visual "checklist" to follow.

Connecting Families with Needed Resources

It can be quite beneficial to assist families to get in-home behavior management if they do not already have this service. In-home behavior support is a must for families who are otherwise besieged and overwhelmed by the demands of caring for a son or daughter with DS-ASD. This greatly relieves stress and allows most families to return to some semblance of normalcy.

Appropriate resources and funding sources for sensory evaluations, respite services, and other programs and resources for our families can be helpful. However, despite an obvious need, families often learn that services that are available for children are not always available for teens and adults. Sensory integration evaluations are especially difficult to find, and, when they are available, there are often funding issues. This means that many families must pay out of pocket for the service, which can be prohibitively expensive.

Critical Need for the Right School or Vocational Program and Staff

For many of the people in our sample, a key precipitant to an eventual "breakdown" was a school or work environment that was not right for them. For many, one major step to getting things under control is to find a school or work program that is much better suited to their needs. This often includes smaller classes, with teachers who are trained and experienced in working with students with ASD or similar types of challenging conditions. Additionally, many families find beneficial special recreation programs staffed by people who are more sensitive to the needs of their son or daughter. This allows these families peace of mind and a break from the full-time care that had often limited opportunity to leave their homes.

Family Support

Some of the families report that support from extended family and from others in the community becomes more positive as they accept the diagnosis. Still, others report that family and "friends" are not patient or understanding when their son or daughter has an outburst or behaves oddly. They also continue to experience stares and critical looks by others when out of their home and in the community.

On the plus side, many families find there are many more supports available in the community through local support groups for families with a loved one with DS-ASD and other behavioral challenges. This is due to a combination of things—a greater awareness, over the past ten-plus years, that ASD can coexist with DS, and of the greater needs of these individuals and their families. For example, in the Chicago area, the National Association for Down Syndrome (NADS) has for the many years run a "parent getaway weekend" for parents with sons and daughters with significant emotional and behavioral challenges (many of whom are diagnosed with ASD). Many of the families in this group look forward to this weekend all year. Ample care is provided for their children with DS-ASD, as well as respite time for their other children. Additionally, the parents hear advice from experts about a host of important topics (behavioral strategies, medication issues, resources, etc.). Perhaps of greatest importance is the support given by the other families at this getaway weekend.

Considering Residence Outside the Home

The families of many teens and adults with DS consider whether their sons and daughters would benefit from living in a group home. We have discussed these issues at length in the book *The Guide to Good Health for Teens & Adults with Down Syndrome* (Chicoine & McGuire, 2010) and we will not repeat the full discussion here. However, a residential option may be especially important to families of a teen or adults with DS-ASD.

We have found there were at least two reasons why families consider group homes. Some look at group homes when there are no problems occurring at home or in the community. For many, this occurs after a period of crisis and transition into the adult years, but the crisis was dealt with effectively (through in-home and out-of-home behavioral strategies and support, appropriate school, or worksites to meet needs, etc.). For these families, the residential option is viewed as a natural part of development in the teen and adult years, just as for other sons or daughters who left home.

On the other hand, there arc a number of parents whose sons or daughters tended to have more significant challenges and behaviors. These parents consider group homes because they found they could no longer meet their son's or daughter's needs in the teen and adult years. For many, too, the demands of caring for their son or daughter created a major strain on the health and well-being of all family members, including the family member with DS-ASD. Many parents/caregivers find they are restricted in the freedom to leave their homes, not only because of their son's or daughter's behaviors in the community, but also because of the difficulty of finding caregiving help from others.

How do people adapt to the move? Some families are very relieved to find positive changes occurring almost immediately after their son or daughter enters the group home. For others, there is a more tumultuous process of transition. This can be very stressful for these families, but it also gives them a glimpse of how competently staff in these homes can manage behavior in a crisis or transition period. Most of the time, families like what they see. Once past the crisis, most individuals with DS-ASD settle in and do very well. The families in both groups continue to stay very actively involved in their adult children's lives after their moves to group homes.

SUMMARY

People with DS, with and without ASD, share common characteristics that are often associated with autism. These include repetitious behavior, sensory issues, and communication deficits. Relationship issues appear to be the one area where there is a clear and obvious difference between the two groups. That is, in people with DS alone, social skills are often a relative strength, whereas in people with DS and ASD of all ages, social skills are a relative weakness.

It is of great importance that professionals who work with people with DS familiarize themselves with the behavior characteristics of ASD, especially those unique to DS, as well as the medical needs and strategies that are used when ASD is diagnosed in a teen or adult with DS. It is our hope that as the field continues to evolve, ASD will be diagnosed much earlier, since early diagnosis and early intensive interventions allow families to be more successful in managing the ASD characteristics. Autism centers need to be more aware of the coexistence of these two disorders, offer specialized diagnosis, and provide families with the appropriate intervention tools that the field of autism care has. An early, multidisciplinary approach to treatment will no doubt benefit the individual with DS and ASD and his or her family.

ACKNOWLEDGMENTS

Understanding DS-ASD is a community effort. Many thanks to the families who participated in our studies and have been very generous with their time, effort, and wisdom.

With appreciation to our colleagues at JFK Partners, the University Center for Excellence in Developmental Disabilities at the University of Colorado, Anschutz Medical Campus; specifically, Cordelia Robinson, PhD, Carolyn DiGuiseppi, PhD, Nancy Lee, PhD, Amy Philofsky, PhD, and Audrey Blakeley-Smith, PhD. Our collaborations with Dr. Lisa Miller of the Colorado Department of Public Health and the Environment, and Sarah Hartway have been instrumental in shaping our interest in this area.

We also share appreciation to our colleagues, past and present, of the Advocate Medical Group Adult Down Syndrome Center in Illinois.

The founders (specifically Margaret Froehlke, Robin Sattel, and Sarah Hartway) and current leaders of the Down Syndrome-Autism Connection have been instrumental in keeping the work going and in helping us to find relevant ways to share it.

REFERENCES

Aman, M. G., & Singh, N. N. (2017). *Aberrant Behavior Checklist: Manual* (2nd ed.). Slosson Educational Publication, Inc.

Aman, M. G., Singh, N. N., Stewart, A. W., & Field, C. J. (1985). The Aberrant Behavior Checklist: a behavior rating scale for the assessment of treatment effects. *American Journal of Mental Deficiency, 89*(5), 485–491.

American Psychiatric Association. (2000). *Diagnostic and statistical manual of mental disorders* (4th ed., text rev.).

Berk, L. E. (2009). *Infants, children, and adolescents* (3rd ed.). Allyn & Bacon.

Capone, G. T. (1999). Down syndrome and autistic spectrum disorder: A look at what we know. *Disability Solutions, 3*(5/6), 8–15.

Chicoine, B., & McGuire, D. (2010). *The guide to good health for teens & adults with Down Syndrome.* Woodbine House.

de Graaf, G., Skladzien, E., Buckley, F., & Skotko, B. G. (2022). Estimation of the number of people with Down syndrome in Australia and New Zealand. *Genetics in Medicine: Official Journal of the American College of Medical Genetics, 24*(12), 2568–2577. https://doi.org/10.1016/j.gim.2022.08.029

di Pellegrino, G., Fadiga, L., Fogassi, L., Gallese, V., & Rizzolatti, G. (1992). Understanding motor events: A neurophysiological study. *Experimental Brain Research 91*(1), 176–180. https://doi.org/10.1007/BF00230027

Gardiner, K., & Costa, A. C. S. (2006). The proteins of human chromosome 21. *American Journal of Medical Genetics Part C: Seminars in Medical Genetics, 142*(3), 196–205. https://doi.org/10.1002/ajmg.c.30098

Legerstee, M., Bowman, T., & Fels, S. (1992). People and objects affect the quality of vocalizations in infants with down syndrome. *Early Development and Parenting, 1*(3), 149–156. https://doi.org/10.1002/edp.2430010304

Maenner, M. J., Warren, Z., Williams, A. R., Amoakohene, E., Bakian, A. V., Bilder, D. A., Durkin, M. S., Fitzgerald, R. T., Furnier, S. M., Hughes, M. M., Ladd-Acosta, C. M., McArthur, D., Pas, E. T., Salinas, A., Vehorn, A., Williams, S., Esler, A., Grzybowski, A., Hall-Lande, J., … Shaw, K. A. (2023). Prevalence and characteristics of autism spectrum disorder among children aged 8 Years - Autism and Developmental Disabilities Monitoring Network, 11 Sites, United States, 2020. *Morbidity and Mortality Weekly Report. Surveillance Summaries, 72*(2), 1–14. https://doi.org/10.15585/mmwr.ss7202a1

McGuire, D., & Chicoine, B. (2006). *Mental wellness in adults with Down Syndrome: A guide to emotional and behavioral strengths and challenges.* Woodbine House.

McGuire, D., & Chicoine, B. (2021). *Mental wellness in adults with Down Syndrome: A guide to emotional and behavioral strengths and challenges* (2nd ed.). Woodbine House.

Medlen, J. (1999). More than Down syndrome: A parent's view. *Disability Solutions, 3*(5/6), 1–7.

Reilly, C. (2009). Autism spectrum disorders in Down syndrome: A review. *Research in Autism Spectrum Disorders 3*(4), 829–839. https://doi.org/10.1016/j.rasd.2009.01.012

Sparrow, S. S., Cicchetti, D. V., & Balla, D. A. (2005). *Vineland Adaptive Behavior Scales* (2nd ed.). Pearson Publishing.

CHAPTER FOUR

DS-ASD AND PRIMARY CARE: PEDIATRIC AND ADULT

Noemi Alice Spinazzi, MD, FAAP (PART I: Pediatric)
Mary Stephens, MD, MPH (PART II: Adult)

PART I:

PEDIATRIC PRIMARY CARE FOR PATIENTS WITH DS-ASD

Noemi Alice Spinazzi, MD, FAAP

DOWN SYNDROME AND AUTISM— PHENOTYPE, SCREENING, AND RECOGNITION

Autism spectrum disorder (ASD) is common in people with Down syndrome (DS). Different studies estimate that autism co-occurs with Down syndrome at a frequency of 4%–39% (Capone et al., 2005; DiGuiseppi et al., 2010; Hepburn et al., 2008; Lowenthal et al., 2007; Moss et al., 2013), with meta-analysis data showing that 16%–18% of individuals with DS are on the autism spectrum (Richards et al., 2015). ASD appears to be more common in males with Down syndrome, with multiple studies suggesting a male prevalence (Hepburn et al., 2008; Oxelgren et al., 2017; Spinazzi, Santoro et al., 2023). This is consistent with ASD in the general populations (Loomes et al., 2017; Russell et al., 2011). Much like in the general population, ASD can be missed in girls, as symptoms could be masked by slightly better language skills and/or prosocial behavior (Hull et al., 2020). While autism is indeed common in people with DS, diagnosis is often delayed or missed due to diagnostic overshadowing. The core features of autism often look different in children with DS-ASD compared to autistic children without Down syndrome (Carter et al., 2007; Channell et al., 2019; Molloy et al., 2009; Oxelgren et al., 2019). As a primary care provider (PCP), you are likely to care for a child with DS-ASD over the course of your career; being on the frontlines of care, you may be the first to recognize signs and symptoms of autism and other neurodevelopmental conditions in a patient with DS. Caregivers may suspect co-occurring autism or may just notice that their child is a little different from other children with DS; they will likely share their concerns with their child's primary care provider, and it is crucial not to dismiss them (Spinazzi, Velasco, et al., 2023). Here are some common features of autism seen in children with Down syndrome that can clue you into the presence of this additional diagnosis.

Stereotypy is defined as the "frequent repetition of the same, typically purposeless movement, gesture, posture, or vocal sounds or utterances" (Merriam-Webster, n.d.). [Author's note: while the definition describes the movements as purposeless, stereotypy can serve many functions for autistic children, including stimulation and regulation (McCarty & Brumback, 2021)]. Stereotypy is commonly seen in people with DS-ASD and can include repetitive hand movements; twirling of strings, beads, or cables; rocking; spinning in place; repetitive sounds made with the tongue or throat; as well as some self-injurious behavior including hitting oneself and head banging (Capone et al., 2005; Ortiz et al., 2017; Spinazzi, Velasco, et al., 2023). Notably, stereotypy is commonly seen in DS alone as well, but it is typically less complex and easier to redirect (Channell et al., 2015; Kraijer & de Bildt, 2005).

Rigid and abnormal play can be noted in children with DS-ASD and often persists beyond the early years (Spinazzi, Velasco, et al., 2023). Toddlers and preschoolers with DS-ASD may prefer cause-and-effect toys that light up and make music, while finding toys such as dolls, stuffed animals, and cars less interesting. With a doll, they may throw it or use it to twirl, instead of rocking it or pretending to feed it. They may line up toys, sort them, move them in and out of a container, or throw them. Many children with DS-ASD will mouth toys well beyond toddlerhood. It is important to compare the play style with the child's chronological and developmental age, as some of these types of play can be typical for a developmentally very young child. The manner of play can also be rigid—the child may play in the same way with the same toy over and over, and struggle to deviate from the routine. A child with DS-ASD who has been taught pretend-type play through repeated practice may appear to be engaging in symbolic play, but a closer look will reveal little creativity or deviation from the practiced routine. During play, a child with DS-ASD will often struggle with imitation (Ortiz et al., 2017), and it will feel harder for the examiner to engage them in play for a sustained period. If a toy is withheld from the child, a child with DS-ASD is more likely to walk away, as opposed to using eye gaze, gestures, and vocalizations to ask for it back.

Communication is one of the most impaired aspects of development for a child with DS-ASD (Magyar et al., 2012; Molloy et al., 2009; Spinazzi, Velasco, et al., 2023). This is an area where diagnostic overshadowing can hinder early recognition of ASD in a child with DS, given the near universal delays in communication seen in children with DS. A child with DS-ASD will acquire language very slowly and will likely use words to label things, as opposed to requesting or calling attention to them. If they have mastered a word or sign, they may be able to repeat it consistently yet struggle to use it spontaneously to communicate with a peer or adult. Unlike kids with DS-only, a child with DS-ASD will also have limited use of communicative gestures, including shrugging and pointing. It is important to ask how a child asks for things they want — if they ask verbally, if they point, or if they simply rely on routine to have their needs met. For example, a toddler with DS-only may point to the fridge, or to a food they want, or sign or say "eat"; a child with DS-ASD, on the other hand, may go directly to the fridge to take what they want, or sit at the table and wait for the parent to feed them, or take the parents' hand and place it over the desired object. It is important to note that children with DS-ASD will often learn to use communication strategies to request food long before they generalize this skill to ask for other things, such as going outside or obtaining a preferred toy. Pointing is a very important communicative gesture that tends to be acquired later by children with DS-ASD, if at all. There are two types of pointing: pointing to request items and pointing to share interests. Children with DS will often begin using pointing for both functions around the same time, while children with DS-ASD may begin to point to request but may take a lot longer to point for the sake of joint attention. Furthermore, when a child with DS-ASD points, they will often do so without integrated eye contact (Ortiz et al., 2017).

Indeed, eye contact is different in people with DS-ASD than in children with DS-only (Ortiz et al., 2017; Spinazzi, Velasco, et al., 2023). The presence of eye contact in a child with DS does not rule out autism. Most children with DS-ASD will briefly make eye contact, especially upon first greeting someone, as well as throughout an interaction to "check in"; however, the eye contact is less sustained, and may shift to gazing at one's mouth or other parts of one's face. Furthermore, many children with DS-ASD will not use eye gaze communicatively and will not use a "3 point gaze" to draw their interlocutor's attention to a shared interest in the room.

Children with DS-ASD often struggle with sensory integration difficulties, another potential clue to an additional diagnosis (Spinazzi, Velasco, et al., 2023). Children with DS-ASD will often struggle with crowded places, loud noises, and experiences such as haircuts and blood draws. They can be very sensitive to touch-type activities, such as touching shaving cream or playdough, and be averse to having dirty or sticky hands. They can have difficulties tolerating tooth brushing or showering. They can have significant food sensitivities, including aversions to specific textures and flavors. Much like every other symptom of ASD discussed in this chapter, sensory issues are commonly seen in DS alone, so their presence does not always imply a dual diagnosis of autism.

Children with DS-ASD can struggle with increased impulsivity, inattention, and anxiety (Capone et al., 2005; Carter et al., 2007; Moss et al., 2013; Oxelgren et al., 2017; Spinazzi, Velasco, et al., 2023). They can have meltdowns and may be more difficult to soothe, as it can be more difficult to identify the cause of their distress. This is compounded by the communication difficulties described above.

A percentage of children with DS-ASD present with a regression of skills in their preschool years (Capone et al., 2006; Castillo et al., 2008; Warner et al., 2014, 2017). The age of regression is older than children with idiopathic autism who present with a developmental regression. Regression in the early childhood years as a presentation of ASD is different from regression in the teenage years, a clinical entity known as Down syndrome regression disorder or Down syndrome disintegrative disorder characterized by a loss of previously acquired adaptive, cognitive, and social functioning (Rosso et al., 2020; Santoro et al., 2023; Walpert et al., 2021).

A physician caring for an individual with DS should become familiar with the phenotype of children with DS-ASD and observe each child carefully (Bull et al., 2022). This may require making modifications to the visit, including allowing additional time, devoting one to two visits specifically to autism screening, and using toys during the encounter to better understand how the child interacts with playthings and with the examiner. It is very important to observe the child away from screens, which can pacify a fearful or active child during a visit but will also strip the examiner of the ability to watch the child interact and communicate. Always heed parental concerns: caregivers are likely to have spent time with other children with DS and their families and may have noticed "differences" in their child that can be attributed to autism symptoms. The following list includes some helpful questions that a primary care provider can integrate into their developmental screening for children with Down syndrome.

- Do you have any concerns about your child's behavior or development that have made you wonder if your child may be different from other children with Down syndrome?
- How does your child communicate with you what they want or need? Do they point to request something they want?
- How do they let you know that they are hungry? Sleepy? That they want a specific toy, food, or activity?
- Does your child look at you in the eye when you are talking to them? Do they answer when you call their name?
- If your child sees something interesting, such as a plane in the sky, a train or truck going by, or a dog in the street, what do they do? Do they try to call your attention to the thing that is interesting? Do they show you things by bringing them to you or holding them up for you to see, not to get help, but just to share?
- If you point to something, such as a toy or person across the room, does your child turn to look at it?
- Is your child sensitive to particular textures? Do they struggle with activities such as toothbrushing or haircuts? Do they appear to get upset by noise or crowds, or by people laughing or speaking loudly?
- Have you noticed any behaviors that your child does repetitively and without a clear purpose?
- What are your child's favorite toys? How does your child play with cars/dolls/stuffed animals? Does your child roll the ball back and forth a few times?

- Does your child use words spontaneously to communicate them, or do they mostly repeat them or use them to label things (if the child says a few words)?

Formal screening tools should be used to help identify children with DS who may have ASD as well. The Modified Checklist for Autism in Toddlers, Revised with Follow-Up (MCHAT-R/F) is a short, 20-item screener freely available online that relies on caregiver report. The MCHAT-R/F has been studied in DS and DS-ASD up to age six years and it has been found to be sensitive (81.8%, 95% CI: 55.0–96.4%) though not specific (46.8%, 95% CI: 33.2–60.7%); its sensitivity improves when combined with results from the Social Communication Questionnaire (SCQ; DiGuiseppi et al., 2010). Despite its limitations, the MCHAT-R/F is a practical and useful first-line formal screener for all children with DS in the primary care office. Because it can lead to false positive results (especially in children with significant vision and hearing impairments, and in children with more significant developmental delays), the MCHAT-R/F should not be used as a solo tool to diagnose autism, and it should be accompanied by informal observation of the child and parent interview as outlined above. For those providers who have access to behavioral health integration, or who are trained in the SCQ and/or brief level-2 screening tools such as the Screening Tool for Autism in Toddlers & Young Children (STAT), Childhood Autism Rating Scale (CARS), or the Rapid Interactive Screening Test for Autism in Toddlers (RITA-T), these can be helpful additional tools in the evaluation of a patient. When a primary care provider suspects a potential dual diagnosis of DS-ASD, and/or if the parent expresses concern for DS-ASD, it is important to refer the patient for a formal diagnostic evaluation. For some providers who practice in under-resourced and/or rural areas where telehealth evaluations are the only available avenue for evaluation, this diagnostic modality can be acceptable; however, if an in-person evaluation can be accessed, this is recommended because of the potential for diagnostic overshadowing when evaluating a child with Down syndrome for autism. As the primary care provider reviews the formal evaluation, they may see results from diagnostic tests such as the Autism Diagnostic Observation Schedule, Second Edition (ADOS-2), Autism Diagnostic Interview-Revised (ADI-R), Social Communication Questionnaire (SCQ), Social Responsiveness Scale (SRS), and the Aberrant Behavior Checklist-Community (ABC-C). It is important to review the evaluation report to ensure that formal tools were used and detect incomplete or inappropriately shallow evaluations. More information on diagnostic tools used when evaluating individuals with Down syndrome for autism can be found in chapter five.

When autism is suspected, it is important to include a thorough medical evaluation that includes testing of the individual's hearing and vision, as well as basic labs including thyroid function tests and a complete blood count. Additional testing should include review of the newborn screen and lead level testing. If the individual is presenting with a developmental regression in early childhood, a full neurologic evaluation should be pursued. Similarly, if the regression is accompanied by abnormal and apparently involuntary movements, a seizure disorder should be ruled out with electroencephalography (EEG). Behavioral concerns should also prompt screening for celiac disease. A medical evaluation can occur concurrently with neuropsychological evaluations outlined above.

If the primary care physician refers for an autism evaluation based on significant clinical concern, and the evaluator does not diagnose the child/young adult with autism, there are several steps that the primary care provider should take. First, the provider should request a copy of the evaluation for their review, to ensure it was thorough and that the evaluator was familiar with the unique phenotype of individuals with DS-ASD. If the parent's and provider's concerns persist, a second opinion should be pursued. The primary care provider should continue to evaluate for other mental health issues that can present similarly to ASD, including:

- Severe sensory integration issues
- Severe attention deficit hyperactivity disorder (ADHD)
- Obsessive-compulsive disorder (OCD)
- Stereotypic movement disorder (SMD)
- Severe anxiety
- Post-traumatic stress disorder (PTSD)
- Verbal apraxia
- Severe intellectual disability

Notably, these conditions can present with features of autism but can also co-occur with an autism diagnosis in a person with Down syndrome. Many of the supports and interventions discussed throughout this chapter and this book can benefit children with Down syndrome who do not have a confirmed autism diagnosis, especially if they are experiencing similar challenges around behavior, communication, and sensory processing dysfunction.

If an adolescent or young adult undergoes a developmental regression and newly exhibits an autism phenotype, they should be evaluated for Down syndrome regression disorder, a condition characterized by a subacute loss of milestones that can respond to psychiatric and neuroimmunomodulatory treatments (Santoro et al., 2023).

The Down Syndrome Medical Interest Group-USA (DSMIG-USA) has developed a one-page graphic using the acronym LEAD (Listen, Evaluate, Advocate, and Distribute) to guide primary care providers in their interactions with children with possible DS-ASD and their families. As you discuss the possibility of a dual diagnosis of DS-ASD with a family, remind parents that an autism diagnosis does not change *who* the child is; rather, it helps us understand how to best support them and can be crucial to unlocking additional resources and supports.

Listen

- To the patient's parents, therapists, educators, and your own voice if the child is presenting differently from others with DS
- Review red flag checklists https://www.autismspeaks.org/down-syndrome-and-autism-spectrum-disorder-ds-asd
- Understand that an additional diagnosis of ASD can allow access to more school- and community-based services

Evaluate

- Beware of "diagnostic ovreshadowing"
- Observe the patient's communication, social skills, and rigid/repetitive behaviors
- Administer the M-CHAT R/F and, when available, the Social Communication Questionnaire
- Refer your patient for a formal autism evaluation

Advocate

- Refer families to autisim centers of excellence, DS clinics (directory available at: www.globaldownsyndrome.org), or university centers on disabilities (directory available at: www.aucd.org) for specialized care and support
- Support families as they interface with school districts and insurance plan to obtain evidence-based treatments for ASD, including occupational, behavioral and speech therapy, and augmentative communication
- Connect families to ds-asd-connection.org and, when available, local support organizations

Distribute

- Share information about DS+ASD
  - links above for DS-ASD connection, autism speaks
  - Information pages on NDSS and NDSC websites
- Inform families of evidence-based behavioral treatments for ASD
- Recommend books and podcasts
  - When Down Syndrome and Autism Intersect: A Guide to DS-ASD for Parents and Professionals
  - A New Course: A Mother's Journey Navigating Down Syndrome and Autism
  - The LowDOWN Podcast

PROVIDING MEDICAL CARE TO INDIVIDUALS WITH DS-ASD

The primary care provider plays a crucial role in the life of a child with DS-ASD. They can provide a trusted medical home where the child can receive developmentally informed medical care, and the parents can feel safe and supported as they share their successes and challenges in raising their child. When evaluating a child with DS-ASD, there are some adaptations to the visit that can be helpful. A child with DS-ASD may have difficulty waiting for long periods of time; to improve their visit experience, schedule the visit at a time when they are less likely to wait to be seen and can be ushered into a quiet room as soon as they arrive. Remind parents to bring highly preferred activities to the visit, to distract and entertain the child with DS-ASD while they are waiting to be seen. Some children may need to feel comfortable in the office before being able to participate in vital sign checks and may be more successful with blood pressure checks and height/weight measurements at the end of the appointment, rather than at the beginning. The staff in charge of rooming the patient should ask the parent how the child communicates best. It is helpful to use a gentle tone of voice, allow for adequate processing time, and offer a lot of praise during vitals. The physical exam can be challenging for some children with DS-ASD; encourage parents to practice parts of the exam at home, to help with desensitization. Visuals, including pictures and videos (ideally in the form of a social story) can also orient the child to what is expected to happen during the visit, and will work best if reviewed daily for several days ahead of the visit. Incorporating sensory supports into the exam can help the child overcome some of their anxiety; examples include making the room darker, speaking in a soft voice, gently squeezing the child's arm, or rhythmically patting their back or leg. Safe positioning of the child on the parent's legs can help with the ear exam. When appropriate, prioritize the parts of the exam that are most relevant to the visit's chief complaint; however, while the provider should be thoughtful about avoiding parts of the exam that are stressful and not necessarily salient to the visit, they should also ensure that a complete physical examination is performed at least once a year, including a full check of the skin and genitalia.

The American Academy of Pediatrics guidelines for Health Supervision for Children and Adolescents with Down Syndrome (Bull et al., 2022) apply to persons with DS-ASD as well. Additional care coordination and support may be necessary to support children with DS-ASD with the recommended screenings.

The American Academy of Pediatrics (AAP) recommends audiologic evaluation starting at six months of life, to be performed every six months until ear-specific information can be obtained, at which point screenings can occur yearly (Bull et al., 2022). Children with DS-ASD may struggle with behavioral testing due to difficulties following directions and tolerating headphones. Preparing for the procedure through play, use of visuals and gradual desensitization to headphones can help a child with DS-ASD successfully participate in behavioral audiologic screening. Helpful information, such as the presence of otoacoustic emissions (OAEs) and tympanometry, can be obtained even when the child cannot fully cooperate with behavioral testing, and the primary care provider should refer for audiologic screening universally, as recommended by the guidelines. A minority of children with DS-ASD will continue to be unsuccessful with behavioral testing and will require a sedated auditory brainstem response (ABR) test. Evaluation for auditory neuropathy may be indicated in children with a history of prolonged hospitalizations, intensive care unit stay, significant prematurity, chemotherapy, and prolonged ventilation requirements. Adolescents and young adults with Down syndrome are at increased risk for early onset hearing loss, and will require ongoing screening of their hearing, as supported by published health care maintenance guidelines (Bull et al., 2022; Tsou et al., 2020).

The AAP health care guidelines recommend routine screening for ophthalmologic disorders and refractory errors in the first year of life, yearly for the first few years, and every two years thereafter (Bull et al., 2022). Once an initial ophthalmologic evaluation has been performed, subsequent screening can include in-office photoscreening, though ongoing ophthalmologic management is required if additional conditions such as strabismus, cataracts, nystagmus, or keratoconus are identified. A child with DS-ASD may have difficulties participating in a visual evaluation, though cycloplegic refraction is an effective way to glean information about the child's visual acuity without requiring their full cooperation. Children with DS-ASD may have difficulties getting used to the feeling of glasses on their faces and may require additional assistance with desensitization to wear their spectacles successfully. A child with DS-ASD may have poor eye contact, and a thorough evaluation will need to differentiate difficulties with eye contact attributable to autism from significant refractory errors or cortical visual impairment, especially in a child with a history of prolonged hospitalizations, intensive care unit stay, significant prematurity, and prolonged ventilation requirements.

Recommended yearly screenings for thyroid disease, anemia, as well as symptom-based screening for celiac disease (Bull et al., 2022) require blood draws at least once a year, which can be particularly distressing for a child with DS-ASD. This may be due to a combination of heightened anxiety, difficulties with receptive language and understanding the rationale for the blood draw, sensory processing difficulties, as well as compounded trauma from previous phlebotomy events where the child may have been restrained. Children with existing thyroid disorders, diabetes, a recent history of leukemia, inflammatory diseases managed with immunomodulatory medications, as well as those taking medications such as coumadin, atypical antipsychotics, and antiepileptics will likely require even more frequent blood tests, creating more opportunities for successful desensitization (if done in a well-coordinated manner) or for re-traumatization and worsening anxiety (if the child has to be restrained or held down during phlebotomy). Desensitization protocols, sensory accommodations, behavioral reward strategies, visual aids and social stories can all help make blood draws more successful. (More information on desensitization strategies can be found in chapter nine.) Premedication with anxiolytic medications such as lorazepam or hydroxyzine can also assist a child with DS-ASD during phlebotomy.

All children, regardless of whether they have Down syndrome, require dental care from when the first few teeth erupt and throughout their lives. Individuals with DS have specific dental, oral, head, neck, and orthognathic characteristics that impact their oral health (Macho et al., 2014); despite this, they often experience barriers to accessing adequate dental care (Lewis et al., 2005). Maintaining gingival and periodontal health is critical for prevention of cavities, infections, tooth pain and loss, and for supporting comfortable chewing of food. Children with DS, and especially those with DS-ASD, can react adversely to the sensations triggered by toothbrushing, flossing, and care at the dentist's office, which can make prevention and treatment of dental disease challenging (Mubayrik, 2016). To address this, consistent desensitization, such as with the use of an electric toothbrush, distraction, video modeling and reward systems, can all assist with achieving successful oral health routines at home, and can facilitate dental visits. (More information about how to successfully tackle the dental visit is available in chapter seven.) Unfortunately, it is not uncommon for children with DS-ASD to require oral rehabilitation under general anesthesia.

Sleep apnea is common in individuals with Down syndrome and can often go undetected without dedicated screening (Ng et al., 2007; Shott et al., 2006); the AAP recommends universal screening with polysomnogram (also known as a sleep study) by age four. The procedure involves tolerating multiple sensors on the face and body and requires a child to fall asleep in an unfamiliar environment; both can be particularly challenging for a child with DS-ASD. Techniques such as social stories with visuals, video modeling, and desensitization in the weeks leading to the sleep study can prepare the child and increase the likelihood that the study will be successful. Child life specialists can support a patient undergoing a sleep study, and the primary care provider can advocate for their involvement.

Children with Down syndrome often require frequent appointments to manage multiple medical conditions; because patients with co-occurring ASD will experience additional challenges as they interact with the health care system, the role of the primary care provider in coordinating care is crucial. This includes combining procedures that require sedation, such as hearing tests, eye exams under anesthesia, bloodwork, and imaging such as echocardiograms, to minimize anesthesia events and increase adherence to health care maintenance guidelines. The primary care provider of a child with DS-ASD should inquire about care coordination needs at every visit. Routine screenings should not be deferred due to behavioral concerns or expected poor tolerance of things like glasses, hearing aids, or continuous positive airway pressure (CPAP) equipment.

There is evolving knowledge of medical issues that can be associated with a diagnosis of DS-ASD (Spinazzi, Santoro, et al., 2023). There is significant evidence that infantile spasms have a strong association with a later diagnosis of autism (Katz et al., 2020; Spinazzi, Santoro, et al., 2023). If available, it will be beneficial to refer a child with DS who has been diagnosed with infantile spasms to a high-risk developmental follow-up program where the patient can be monitored for signs of autism. It is also helpful to discuss this well-described association with the child's infant development specialist working with the child through early intervention services, so that they can focus on social-emotional development and total communication as early as possible. While it may not be helpful to discuss the association between infantile spasms and ASD at the time of seizure diagnosis, this is something that should be addressed once the seizures are under better control, as part of an overall discussion on how to support the child's development after suffering from such a significant illness.

There is some evidence that individuals with DS-ASD are more likely to experience constipation and gastroesophageal reflux (GERD; Spinazzi, Santoro, et al., 2023). This is consistent with increased incidence of these conditions in individuals with idiopathic ASD (Afzal et al., 2003; Buie et al., 2010). Constipation and GERD can be uncomfortable, and discomfort can lead to alterations in mood and behavior. Thus, a physician should screen their patients with DS-ASD consistently for these conditions, and make sure that they are adequately and consistently treated.

Behavioral feeding difficulties are common in children with DS-ASD (Spinazzi, Santoro, et al., 2023) and may present in early childhood as aversion to specific flavors or textures (including mixed textures) and/or prolonged need for supplementation with formula, either orally or through a feeding tube. Children with DS-ASD may take longer to learn to feed themselves with utensils and may continue to throw utensils or resist hand over hand assistance for longer than expected based on other skills. The primary care provider should routinely screen for feeding difficulties in a child with DS-ASD through a thorough dietary recall, to identify patients at increased risk for nutritional deficiencies who would benefit from targeted supplementation. Close monitoring of height, weight, and body mass index (on both the Down syndrome–specific (Zemel et al., 2015) and the Center for Disease Control growth charts) is indicated in children with DS-ASD with feeding challenges. Prompt referral to feeding therapy is recommended for children with DS-ASD experiencing feeding aversions and behavioral feeding difficulties; the primary care provider should counsel families about the importance of consistent application of therapeutic interventions and encourage them to persist even when facing frustratingly slow progress.

Puberty can bring on some challenges for individuals with DS-ASD, including some increases in behavioral dysregulation. Premenstrual dysphoria (PMD) may present as increases in aggression or self-injury in a child with DS-ASD. Furthermore, a young woman with DS-ASD may have difficulties tolerating the sensation of a sanitary pad in her underwear. Desensitization and visual supports can be helpful tools for the young person with DS-ASD and their family. For young women with DS-ASD who struggle with management of their menses, the use of hormonal contraceptives can make periods more predictable and can, if desired, suppress menses altogether. Medications that can suppress menses in some women include the oral contraceptive pill, taken continuously (skipping of the placebo week); the medroxyprogesterone injection, though this is a less preferred option due to the associated weight gain and decreased bone density; and hormonal intrauterine devices, which will last several years though may require placement under anesthesia and are initially associated with spotting. Combined estrogen-progestin oral contraceptives can also be helpful in young women with PMD symptoms. For individuals who struggle with the sensation of a sanitary pad, reusable "period underwear" that absorbs menstrual blood may be better tolerated. The primary care provider will usually be the first to hear about challenges related to puberty and menses and plays a crucial role in supporting families through this time of physical and emotional transitions. (Education around pubertal changes is available online on the UCSF Benioff Children's Hospital Oakland Down syndrome clinic website, https://sites.google.com/view/charlies-clinic/home). Excellent books on this topic include Terri Couwenhoven's books *A Girls' Guide to Growing Up: Choices & Changes in the Tween Years* (Couwenhoven, 2011); *The Boys' Guide to Growing Up: Choices & Changes During Puberty* (Couwenhoven, 2012); and *Teaching Children with Down Syndrome about Their Bodies: A Guide for Parents and Professionals* (Couwenhoven, 2007).

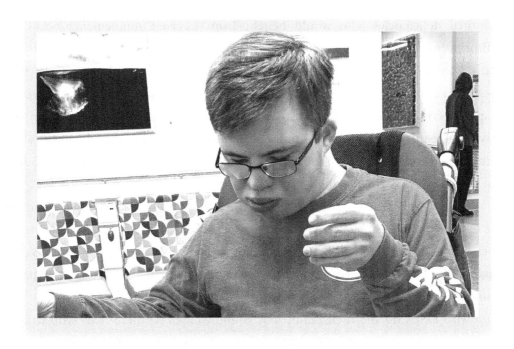

BEHAVIORAL AND DEVELOPMENTAL IMPACT AND GUIDANCE

Children with DS-ASD are most significantly impacted in four categories: (1) their ability to communicate; (2) their ability to master functional skills, including toilet training and other self-care skills; (3) their sensory processing difficulties, which impact their behavior and their ability to self-regulate, and (4) their ability to stay safe due to increased likelihood of non-self-directing behavior. Each of these areas of challenge should be supported through in-depth evaluation and skilled therapeutic support. As the primary care provider, you are a very powerful ally, and you play a crucial role in supporting a family as they advocate for evaluations, goals, services, and accommodations through their child's insurance and school district.

Communication Challenges

Most children with DS-ASD will experience significant communication challenges, including difficulties with receptive as well as expressive (spoken and gestural) language. It is important to emphasize the importance of total communication (verbal, gestural, and visual) from early on; in fact, when caring for a child with Down syndrome, the primary care provider should emphasize the importance of total communication from infancy to all families, as we cannot predict which children will experience greater challenges with expressing themselves, and early exposure to a communication-enriched environment will support their overall development. Further, the primary care provider should debunk the myth that exposure to sign language or other forms of total communication will hinder the acquisition of verbal language, and instead educate families that augmentative communication of all forms enhances expressive language development while also supporting working memory and behavioral regulation.

Many children with Down syndrome, including those with DS-ASD, experience verbal apraxia—a difficulty with motor planning that results in additional difficulties with verbal speech, "decreased intelligibility with increased length of utterance, inconsistency of speech errors, decreased ability to perform voluntary tasks as compared to automatic tasks, and difficulty sequencing oral movements and speech sounds" (Kumin, 2006, p. 12). A child with DS-ASD and apraxia requires intensive, individualized speech therapy using techniques that target motor planning difficulties. Unfortunately, many parents are told that apraxia cannot be diagnosed until a child has "enough verbal speech to allow for a valid evaluation," thus creating a catch-22 that hinders access to services. Identifying speech and language pathologists with experience caring for children with Down syndrome and/or children with apraxia can help overcome some of these barriers.

Regardless of the presence of apraxia, parents can advocate for speech therapy services from the district to be delivered in a one-to-one setting, away from distractions, or in a very small group setting. Intensive speech therapy support is typically needed for a child with DS-ASD to make meaningful progress in their expressive communication. It is also important to request an evaluation for alternative and augmentative communication services early on—ideally as soon as the child qualifies for special education services, to be performed by a skilled evaluator. Parents may be discouraged from pursuing this support, and the primary care provider can be a trusted advisor in this process, including by connecting a family with their local parent training and information center (PTI: https://www.parentcenterhub.org/find-your-center/) for advocacy support. Behavioral techniques can be used to encourage the use of verbal, gestural, and visual communication; as such, formal behavioral support, in the form of Applied Behavioral Analysis (ABA) or other evidence-based therapy, is crucial for supporting communication development for a child with DS-ASD.

The primary care provider can support families in creating communication-enriched environments in their home by emphasizing the importance of total communication in the life of a child with DS-ASD and connecting them with resources that can help parents learn basic sign language. The UCSF Benioff Children's Hospital Oakland Down syndrome clinic (Charlie's Clinic), in collaboration with Dr. Bettina Larroudé, EdD, CCC-SLP, has developed an ASL toolkit that is freely available for families to download at https://sites.google.com/view/charlies-clinic/home. Simple picture/photo grids, placed in salient locations in the house, can help a child with DS-ASD communicate their wants and needs; sample grids are also available on the Charlie's Clinic's website. The primary care provider should also refer a child with DS-ASD for additional speech therapy support as well as evaluations for augmentative and alternative communication (AAC) through insurance, especially if the family is encountering obstacles in obtaining this service through the school district, or if the patient is about to age out of school-based services.

Developing Independence with Self-Care Skills

Children with DS will typically take longer than their neurotypical peers to become independent with self-care skills, also known as "activities of daily living" (ADLs); their peers with DS-ASD may experience even greater difficulties. Examples of self-care skills include self-feeding; managing hygiene tasks such as toothbrushing, hair combing, washing one's hands and face, and bathing/showering independently; eliminating in the toilet and no longer using a diaper; dressing oneself independently and choosing correct outfits for weather. Obstacles to achieving independence include difficulties with receptive language; sensory integration challenges that can make certain activities (hair combing, tooth brushing, etc.) more overwhelming; and poorer imitation skills. There are many adaptations and supports that can assist a child with DS-ASD in achieving greater independence with ADLs. ABA therapy, as well as other forms of behavioral support that incentivize imitation and motivate a child to perform a skill, help children with DS-ASD in mastering a variety of self-care skills through repetition and consistent reward structures. Visual supports, including visual task analysis and video modeling, capitalize on the strong visual processing skills typical of children with DS, ASD, and DS-ASD. They break down complex tasks into individual steps that a child can more easily follow and master, and they orient the child with poor working memory to the next step in the task. Families can access information about these visual supports through online resources, including those on the Charlie's Clinic website, and they can partner with their child's behavior specialist and educators to develop effective tools that are appropriate for their child's developmental level. Many children with DS-ASD will have greater success with toilet training when done on a schedule, especially early on, instead of relying on the child recognizing and communicating their own internal cues that they need to evacuate their bladder or bowel. More information on toilet training is available in Dr. Lina Patel, PsyD and Terry Katz, PhD's book *Potty Time for Kids with Down Syndrome: Lose the Diapers, Not Your Patience* (Katz & Patel, 2020).

Addressing sensory challenges is also very important when supporting a child with DS-ASD in their journey toward independence. This requires a thorough sensory evaluation, to understand areas of challenge, and to develop a desensitization plan that is individualized to the child's needs. The primary care provider should refer the child to an occupational therapist with experience treating sensory integration difficulties. School accommodations catered to the sensory needs of a student with DS-ASD can have a profound impact on attention, self-regulation, and behavior.

The individualized educational plan (IEP) is a powerful legal document where goals related to self-care and independence can be developed; services and supports should be put in place to enable a student with DS-ASD to make meaningful progress in this and other areas of their education. Chapter eleven discusses best educational practices when working with a student with DS-ASD and provides tips on how to advocate for adequate structure and support for your dually diagnosed patients.

Safety

Children with DS-ASD have higher rates of co-occurring ADHD and anxiety (Capone et al., 2005; Carter et al., 2007; Moss et al., 2013; Oxelgren et al., 2017; Spinazzi, Velasco, et al., 2023), and even those who do not have formal diagnoses will often engage in behaviors that can put their safety at risk. Examples of these non-self-directing behaviors include:

- Elopement
- Self-injury
- Mouthing non-food items beyond the early childhood years, which can result in infection, poisoning, and choking

- Reaching for sharp or hot objects, such as scissors, knives, the stove, etc.
- Playing with strings, cords, and other rope-like objects—another choking hazard
- Climbing on tall surfaces without awareness of height, then jumping off recklessly

In addition to these non-self-directing behaviors, individuals with DS-ASD may be more likely to engage in aggressive behaviors toward others, especially if they feel threatened, anxious, or overwhelmed. They may also flop on the floor in the middle of the street or in a busy parking lot. As they grow older, they may learn to unbuckle themselves from their car safety restraint system, try to open car doors or windows, or lunge forward toward the driver.

Addressing safety at every visit is of paramount importance when caring for a child with DS-ASD. Safety at home may include adding specialized locks on every entrance door of the house, including the door to the garage, as well as on gates that separate one's property from the street; door alarms should be installed to alert an adult that their child has opened a door; swimming pools must be enclosed by tall gates to prevent accidental drownings. Children with DS-ASD who elope should wear a form of identification on their person at all times—examples include a medical ID bracelet; an identification tag that can be secured on the laces of the person's shoes; or even writing one's name, address, and emergency contact on shoes or clothing, especially if the individual's sensory challenges prevent them from tolerating a medical ID bracelet. Demographic information can even be applied to the child's skin via temporary tattoos.

Newer technology, including shoe insoles that are equipped with GPS tracking devices or other geotagging devices, can help locate a child with DS-ASD who elopes. If the child elopes while at school, a functional behavioral assessment should be immediately requested; the child may be better served in a school that has a secure campus, and the child will likely need one-on-one support to prevent elopement by noticing early signs of dysregulation and promptly enacting their individualized behavior intervention plan. A primary care provider can recommend in-home care services, emphasizing the need for protective supervision due to the presence of non-self-directing behaviors. When filling out disabled parking placard applications, the primary care provider can explain that the child has Down syndrome, autism, and behavioral dysregulation that causes individual to run into traffic without awareness of safety, emphasizing the need to park close to one's destination to minimize the risk of being run over by a vehicle. An older child who no longer fits in a commercially available stroller should be prescribed an adaptive stroller that can allow for safer transfers in the community, and the primary care provider is often the medical professional best positioned to write this durable medical equipment prescription.

Car safety is also very important, and the primary care provider can prescribe appropriate passenger safety restraints, including large medical seats such as the Carrot 3 Child Restraint, IPS car seat, Roosevelt, Special Tomato Car Seat, Spirit, Spirit Plus or Wallaroo, or specialized vests that can keep the child safely positioned, such as the Chamberlain, EZ-On Vest, and Moore Support Vest. For more information on this topic, see the Indiana University School of Medicine's Automotive Safety Program website (https://preventinjury.pediatrics.iu.edu/adaptive-needs/child-restraint-options).

A child who engages in self-injurious behavior may benefit from soft helmets if they bang their head or hit their head repeatedly, especially if with a closed fist; or may need hard splints such as a T-guard to keep them from biting their hands. All behaviors have a purpose, and if a self-injurious behavior is helping a child regulate themselves through sensory input, it is important to offer safer replacement behaviors; for example, a child who bites themselves or others may benefit from chewy toys that can satisfy their need to bite without causing injury.

ABA therapy and other therapeutic supports can target self-injury and aggression in their treatment plan. This often involves supporting the use of verbal, signed, or augmentative communication instead of resorting to aggressive or self-injurious behavior. Recognizing and addressing sensory triggers will decrease self-injury. Sensory supports such as weighted blankets or vests, joint compression, tight hugs, and other calming techniques can be included in an individualized "sensory diet" and used throughout the day to fulfill the child's sensory cravings. Noise-canceling headphones can facilitate community outings. At times, it may be necessary to remove the child from an overstimulating situation to prevent self-injury.

For children with behavioral difficulties that jeopardize their safety or the safety of those around them, psychotropic medications often play a part in management, though there are few rigorous studies assessing their efficacy in this patient population (Palumbo & McDougle, 2018). There are many classes of medication that can be considered for a child with DS-ASD and behavioral dysregulation. Alpha-2 agonists such as guanfacine and clonidine can help with self-injurious behaviors and aggression (Capone et al., 2016); they can cause some sedation, especially early on in treatment, and they require monitoring of blood pressure, which can be challenging for children with DS-ASD who are anxious with vital sign checks. Antihistamines like hydroxyzine can be used as needed to help a child with DS-ASD who is acutely dysregulated; like other antihistamines, individuals should be monitored for signs of a paradoxical reaction. Children with clear impulsivity can benefit from stimulants, with a preference for methylphenidate over amphetamine salts; notably, children with DS and DS-ASD can be particularly sensitive to this class of medication and require close monitoring. Children who are anxious can benefit from selective serotonin reuptake inhibitors, and should be closely monitored for signs of akathisia, which can cause their behavior to worsen. Atypical antipsychotics, such as risperidone and aripiprazole, are generally effective at decreasing self-injurious and aggressive behaviors, though parents should be counseled on the risk for rapid weight gain and metabolic syndrome and the need for bloodwork every six months (Bacanli, 2016; Palumbo & McDougle, 2018). Medication should always be used in combination with the therapeutic modalities listed throughout this chapter. Children with Down syndrome can be more sensitive to psychotropic medications, so it is important to start at a low dose and increase slowly to an effective dose, monitoring for side effects. The primary care provider may need to initiate medication management while the child waits to establish care with psychiatric providers due to nationwide personnel shortages (see chapter six for more information).

THE IMPACT ON THE FAMILY

Raising a child with DS-ASD can be challenging, and families have reported that they feel isolated, as they do not feel like they belong in either the ASD or the Down syndrome community (Spinazzi, Velasco, et al., 2023). Sources of stress include the child's behavioral challenges, which can limit caregivers' ability to gather with families, travel, and be out in the community; the child's ongoing need for assistance with self-care activities, often beyond what is expected for other individuals with Down syndrome; and difficulties with communication, which impair the caregiver's ability to understand the child's needs and triggers. Caregivers must advocate hard and often for their child to receive adequate services, which can lead to caregiver burnout. The primary care provider plays a very important role in supporting the whole family unit, including parents and siblings (Soccorso et al., 2023). This includes screening caregivers frequently for depression, anxiety, and burnout, and encouraging caregivers to seek support for themselves, in the form of support groups, mental health services, spiritual support, etc. The primary care provider should remind caregivers to take care of themselves, including encouraging caregivers to eat regular meals, exercise whenever possible, and sleep, as caregivers may often be so busy caring for the individual with DS-ASD that they will forego their own basic care needs. The primary care provider should refer parents to the Down Syndrome-Autism Connection, an online support organization that welcomes caregivers of individuals with DS-ASD and their families (https://ds-asd-connection.org/). Caring for a child with DS-ASD can impact a family's finances, and the primary care provider should screen families for connectedness with available government benefits, including respite care and in-home care services. Whenever available, a social worker should partner with the family to help connect with available resources and support. Caregivers of a child with DS-ASD experience less frustration when they interact with medical providers who are informed about the dual diagnosis, and if you are a primary care provider reading this chapter, you have already taken a huge step toward meaningfully supporting the whole family unit of an individual with DS-ASD.

TAKE-HOME POINTS: PEDIATRIC CARE

Autism commonly co-occurs in children with DS, and the primary care provider is uniquely positioned to recognize signs of ASD and promptly refer for formal evaluation. Children with DS-ASD will benefit from adaptations in the medical visit, though they should continue to receive all medical care that is standard for individuals with DS. They should be screened for conditions that can more often co-occur in DS-ASD, including digestive issues and behavioral feeding difficulties.

Children with DS-ASD may struggle with communication, sensory integration, independence with self-care, and their ability to be safe at home and in the community. Behavioral, sensory, and communication interventions can help a child with DS-ASD thrive. A good educational plan that recognizes the impact of autism on the child's learning and development is paramount. Psychotropic medications are often used when managing a child with DS-ASD. The PCP should prescribe durable medical equipment that can help keep the child safe.

The dual diagnosis of DS-ASD impacts the whole family unit, and the primary care provider should screen routinely for caregiver well-being and connect households with social support.

ADULT PRIMARY CARE FOR PATIENTS WITH DS-ASD

Mary Stephens, MD, MPH

TRANSITION TO ADULT PRIMARY AND SPECIALTY CARE

While planning may have begun in the early to mid-teens, the transition to adulthood and aging out of the school system can still be a challenging time. Given the loss of school-based services and pediatric insurance coverage benefits including wraparound behavioral health services, and often longtime health care providers, it has been likened to falling off a "cliff" (Steinway et al., 2017). Limited evidence around health care transition for adults with DS suggests that this process can be very challenging and gaps in service exist leading some services for complex young adults with special health care needs to be delivered in both the pediatric and adult health systems (VanZant & McCormick, 2021; Varshney et al., 2022).

This is also an exciting and challenging time for those with DS-ASD! On a very positive note, some young adults may thrive out of the demands of school and rigid scheduling. It is a time for ongoing skill acquisition, development, and desire for independence. For the parents and caregivers, however, these benefits can sometimes create some downsides and challenges.

Tools to help patients, caregivers, and health care providers navigate transition are available and include resources from Got Transition, a federally funded national resource center on health care transition from pediatric to adult care (www.gottransition. org). Caregivers should be aware that adult primary health care providers may be more comfortable managing medical comorbidities than in pediatric health care systems. When planning for the health care transition, consider starting with the primary care provider first to see what they are willing to manage. Although thyroid medication may have been managed by the endocrinologist in the past, this is something that most primary care providers will take over. For patients with celiac disease who are well controlled, there may be no need to find an adult gastroenterologist. Similarly, for patients with anxiety, depression, and complex behavioral symptoms, the adult provider may be willing to continue prescribing and managing those medications for patients, at least until an adult psychiatrist is identified.

Young Adults 21–40

As the diagnosis of DS-ASD is a relatively recent phenomenon, there is less medical literature and research solely focused on the medical care of adults with DS-ASD. Looking at the health care experiences of those with ASD and intellectual disability, adults may be at greater risk for health problems than expected based on their age, and specifically have a higher risk of seizure disorders, autoimmune conditions, sleep disorders, gastrointestinal conditions, and heart disease (Bishop-Fitzpatrick & Rubenstein, 2019). It's unclear in terms of heart disease if the relatively protective benefit of having Down syndrome protects against the increased heart disease risk. Barriers to care cited by adults with autism with and without disabilities include fear and anxiety, need for additional processing time, sensory issues, and difficulty communicating with health care providers (Raymaker et al., 2017).

Based on adult guidelines for adults with DS, routine screening in this age group should include thyroid bloodwork (TSH) every one to two years. Screening for diabetes, typically a blood test called a HbA1c, should begin in the 20s for those with risk factors and be repeated every two to three years. For those without risk factors such as overweight or obesity, consider starting in the 30s. Monitor for signs of celiac disease (loose stools, cramping, and constipation) and screen with blood tests if they are present (Tsou et al., 2020).

Evidence-based reviews from the Down Syndrome Medical Interest Group-USA (DSMIG-USA) adult health work group focus on additional areas of importance for the care of adults with DS and include the following (Capone et al., 2018, 2020):

- While the risk of atlantoaxial and hip instability decreases over time, there may be an increased risk of early neck and hip arthritis that clinicians should be aware of.
- The risk of hearing impairment approaches 70% in adults with DS, and there is an ongoing need for testing, treatment, and speech therapy.

- While we have a lot to learn about overweight and obesity, the 20s can be a particularly challenging time for young adults with DS, and patients and caregivers need to think about strategies to mitigate this. In practical terms, what nonfood rewards can be put in place to support positive behaviors? Who is tracking what the young adult with DS eats in the community with support staff? How can we best partner with patients to educate them and help foster healthy nutritional choices? How can we promote enjoyable physical activity?

- As young adults age out of pediatric systems and caregivers may shift from parents to siblings or staff, patients need to continue to be monitored based on established guidelines for congenital heart disease and/or acquired heart valve disorders. General medical history must transition with the patient and new caregivers must be aware of prior diagnoses and treatments.

- Dysphagia or trouble swallowing remains more common in adults with DS along with reflux/GERD. Families and caregivers should alert the medical team about coughing or other mealtime symptoms, spit-ups, new tooth grinding, or recurrent pneumonia. Referral to speech and occupational therapy may be a consideration although one might have to look a little harder to find adult therapists with the skills to meet the needs of the patient.

- Adults with DS remain at increased risk of obstructive sleep apnea (OSA). Although no formal screening guidelines exist for adults, symptoms of OSA can include both symptoms related to sleep like snoring and gasping and daytime symptoms including irritability, decline in performance and daytime sleepiness. Home sleep studies that feel less intrusive to patients may be an option to consider for making the diagnosis. Modalities other than CPAP or BIPAP are emerging, such as the hypoglossal nerve stimulator, which may make treatment a possibility for adults with DS-ASD when it was not before (Li et al., 2019; Liu et al., 2022).

As the increased risk of autism in individuals with Down syndrome has only been more recently recognized, young and middle-aged adults with DS may have not been diagnosed in childhood. Caregivers and health care professionals should consider this diagnosis, particularly in individuals who struggle with communication and challenging behaviors. A retrospective review of developmental history, observations in school and the community, and reports from family, caregivers, and therapists may support the diagnosis. Formal diagnostic or neuropsychological testing may be harder to find in adult health care systems, but potential resources include Down syndrome clinics, offices of vocational rehabilitation, autism centers of excellence, and academic medical centers. While the absence of a diagnosis of autism should not preclude clinicians from addressing communication challenges or behavioral issues, a formal diagnosis may be worthwhile pursuing as it may open the door to additional services and help individuals with DS-ASD get the care and support they need.

A Practical Approach in the Office

The health care provider very often may be new both to you and the individual with DS-ASD. Try to engage them in strategies for success. Let them know—or ask them up-front, if possible—the following:

- Does the patient do better with the history or physical first?
- Does the patient need to be present for the entire visit? While even for a telehealth appointment the patient needs to be present for some portion of the visit, can they leave after the physical portion while the paperwork and counseling is done? While certainly we want the patient to be engaged and learn new skills in the health care setting and the health care provider to talk/communicate with them directly, an incremental approach may work better for all involved. For example, does the visit have to start with vital signs if blood pressure is particularly challenging for the patient?
- Focus on the comfort of the patient. Do headphones, fidget toys, taking a walk, listening to music, or stimming help the patient stay calm and focused and able to participate in the visit? Let the provider know when these behaviors are "ok" or when they mean the patient is starting to show signs of distress, and it's time to shift gears or end the visit.
- Prioritize what needs to be accomplished in the visit and what can wait. Practical experience suggests that recovering from a "bad" encounter with a patient takes a lot longer than ending a visit early and trying on a better day, different time of day, or via telehealth.
- Allow time for processing and communication and remember to charge up communication devices and bring them to the visit if they help the patient. If the diagnosis of DS-ASD was made later, has use of an augmentative and alternative communication (AAC) system been considered?

While it's appropriate and may be important to share information specific to DS-ASD with health care providers if they don't have a lot of experience caring for someone with DS-ASD, as a health care provider, one must be cautious about diagnostic overshadowing and attributing all symptoms/behaviors to the diagnosis of DS-ASD and not thinking broadly. Especially when seeing a patient with new or troubling behaviors, think about a head-to-toe approach in addition to appropriate evaluations suggested by age and diagnosis.

- Don't forget ear wax and oral health. Screen for hearing loss and make sure the patient is connected to a source of dental care. (See chapter seven for Strategies for Successful Dental Health Care.)
- Refer to an eye specialist every one to two years to evaluate for common eye problems such as cataracts and an increased risk of keratoconus.
- Is the scalp healthy and/or are there signs of folliculitis, hidradenitis, or yeast infections elsewhere? Caregivers can bring up these concerns or document with pictures if the patient is unlikely to tolerate an exam where they must lift or remove clothing.
- For women, how are things when they have their period? Hormonal changes can contribute to behavior changes but think about sensory issues due to bleeding, pads, and cramps. Menopause may be earlier in individuals with DS but are missed periods a sign of a thyroid problem?
- How are things with bowels and bladder? Constipation can be a primary issue or secondary to celiac. Constipation can contribute to new incontinence of bladder during the day or night. It can be difficult to tell if someone is constipated and an X-ray of the abdomen may be necessary to look at stool burden. Other signs may be loss of appetite or fecal smearing. New incontinence or loss of bowel and bladder control can also be a sign of atlantoaxial instability, although this is much less common in this age group than in children.
- Look at feet and bones and joints. Could the patient benefit from inserts for flat feet or physical therapy for knee pain due to hypermobility?
- Don't forget immunizations! Consider spacing them out so the patient does not have to receive more than one vaccine at a time. Would they do better in the health care provider's office, a local pharmacy, or even in their car? Do the patient's comorbidities mean they qualify for early pneumococcal immunization? Some health care providers who care for individuals with

DS recommend early pneumococcal immunization in general given the risk of pneumonia in adults with DS. Giving variable immune response to vaccination, others advocate for checking hepatitis B titers in adults. Future schedules for COVID vaccination may suggest more frequent boosters given risk factors for severe disease and variable immune response to vaccination.

- Many patients with DS-ASD have restricted diets and/or pica (chewing on ice, clay, soil, paper, other household objects). For this reason, clinicians should consider screening for anemia (CBC, B12, Folate, ferritin and iron studies, Vitamin D) and excluding elevated lead levels.

- Consider treatment of reflux in patients with decreased appetite, spitting, or mouthing behaviors. For patients with a restricted diet, consider difficulty swallowing or dysphagia as a possible cause. Evaluation by a speech therapist with or without a formal swallowing study may both lead to a diagnosis of swallowing dysfunction but also be of a therapeutic benefit in expanding the diet of an individual with restrictive patterns of eating. Nutritional consultation may be of great benefit as well in terms of broadening the diet of individuals with DS-ASD.

- Consider evaluation by neurology for partial seizures in individuals who have staring episodes or periods of being disconnected.

- Mental health and mood disorders may occur at higher frequencies in adults with DS-ASD. While making the diagnosis may be more challenging in individuals with DS-ASD, clinicians should keep these diagnoses on their radar and explore family history and recent life changes that may impact the individual. Both medication and other therapeutic approaches may significantly improve the well-being of both individuals and caregivers. The approach to medications is discussed earlier in this chapter and in chapter five of this book.

- While more challenging to obtain in adults, a functional behavioral analysis, consultation with a behavioral therapist, or participation in social skills groups may be helpful.

- As discussed earlier in the chapter, unexplained functional regression after an appropriate medical and mental health workup may prompt further evaluation for Down syndrome regression disorder.

- Finally, it's important to consider an approach that includes meeting the patient where they are. Are the concerning behaviors, changes, and actions related to a typical desire for greater independence as individuals grow and age? Conversely, are the demands being placed on the individual too much for where they are at the moment, and could they benefit from less stimulation and simpler, more predictable routines?

Most patients in the US and abroad do not have easy access to health care providers with experience caring for individuals with DS-ASD. Although not specific to DS-ASD, general tools that may be helpful and that are available online without cost are:

www.aaspire.org—a toolkit for providers focused on best practices for individuals with ASD.

https://iddtoolkit.vkcsites.org/—a toolkit for providers focused on best practices for individuals with intellectual and developmental disabilities. (Note: As of this time, guidance related to the care of individuals with Down syndrome has not been updated since the release of the new adult health care guidelines.)

Adults with DS-ASD can continue to acquire new skills important to their medical care. While they may not have been able to have blood drawn or been given a vaccine as a young child or teen without sedation or restraint, it doesn't mean that they can't learn those skills as an adult. Practice sessions, social stories, online videos, and desensitization can all allow the patient to grow. Allowing the patient to select music they might like; separating from the primary caregiver; having the caregiver be present; bringing a favorite sibling or staff; being able to communicate "no" or "enough"; using a premedication such as an oral benzodiazepine; or selecting the time of day or focus of the visit may all be helpful strategies. While sedation services are not as readily available in adult medical practice, the health care provider can try to "maximize the sedation" when it does occur. For example, for patients who require sedation for dental, PCPs can coordinate lab draws, vaccines, and so on. For patients who require sedated medical procedures, coordinate multiple specialty providers so that an ultrasound of the heart, pap smear if appropriate, IUD for menstrual management, and endoscopy can be performed at the same time.

All adults, patients, families, and other caregivers should engage in regular conversations about lifespan planning and end of life care goals and wishes when appropriate. While there are limited resources on how to best do this with individuals with intellectual disabilities or ASD in general, conversations with a primary care provider are often a safe place to start, as they have experience and training with these topics and can advocate for the patient. Palliative care clinicians are other valuable partners. Resources focused on individuals with DS or other intellectual disabilities can further guide these discussions.

Older Adults—40 Plus

As early dementia is common in Down syndrome, routine screening is recommended to begin at age 40 using the National Task Group-Early Detection Screen for Dementia (NTG-EDSD), although some experts recommend regular screening as early as age 35 (Alzheimer's Association, 2022; Iulita et al., 2022). Symptoms of cognitive decline before the age of 40 in the individual with DS-ASD are unlikely to represent dementia and other causes should be thoroughly investigated. Even with decline after age 40, identifying other comorbidities that may be treatable is critical to the well-being of the individual with DS-ASD. Health care providers should consider common causes of cognitive decline and change in behavior that they routinely evaluate for in older adults including urinary tract infection, vitamin B12 deficiencies, hearing and vision loss, and mood disorders such as depression, anxiety, or OCD, as well as polypharmacy. In individuals with DS-ASD, also consider things that might be more common to them specifically, such as constipation and painful skin conditions like hidradenitis or yeast infections in the armpits and groin.

TAKE-HOME POINTS: ADULT CARE

- Don't forget to consider that the diagnosis of autism may have been missed in individuals with DS during childhood, and making the diagnosis can lead to better support and care of the individual.
- Adults with DS-ASD may benefit from adaptations in the medical visit, but don't forget that they are still capable of learning and may acquire new skills over time, such as being able to tolerate blood draws and immunizations without drama or sedation. As they age, however, expectations may also need to change if there is a functional decline. Consider telehealth as a way to allow adults to more comfortably access care and allow for one-on-one time for both patients and caregivers.
- As technology has advanced, and especially if DS-ASD has been unrecognized earlier in childhood, consider evaluation or reevaluation for assistive technology to decrease communication barriers and foster independence.
- Primary care providers may be able to prescribe psychotropic medications if necessary to help address challenging behaviors in addition to recommending other therapeutic modalities.
- As individuals with DS-ASD age, they may face transitions in caregivers as well as functional decline. It's important for families and nonfamily caregivers to communicate and plan for these inevitable changes to best support the individual with DS-ASD.

ADDITIONAL RESOURCES

Academic Autism Spectrum Partnership in Research and Education. https://aaspire.org

Alzheimer's Disease & Down Syndrome. https://ndss.org/resources/alzheimers

Alzheimer's Disease and Dementia. https://alz.org/alzheimers-dementia/what-is-dementia/types-of-dementia/down-syndrome

Global Down Syndrome Foundation's Medical Care Guidelines for Adults with Down Syndrome. https://www.globaldownsyndrome.org/wp-content/uploads/2020/10/Global-Down-Syndrome-Foundation-Medical-Care-Guidelines-for-Adults-with-Down-Syndrome-v.1-10-20-2020.pdf

Jenny's Diary. Learning (Intellectual) Disability and Dementia. https://www.learningdisabilityanddementia.org/jennys-diary.html

NTG-EDSD Screening Tool | Dementia and ID or DD | The NTG. https://www.the-ntg.org/ntg-edsd

REFERENCES

Afzal, N., Murch, S., Thirrupathy, K., Berger, L., Fagbemi, A., & Heuschkel, R. (2003). Constipation with acquired megarectum in children with autism. *Pediatrics*, *112*(4), 939–942. https://doi.org/10.1542/peds.112.4.939

Alzheimer's Association. (2022, October 2). *Down syndrome and Alzheimer's Disease*. https://www.alz.org/alzheimers-dementia/what-is-dementia/types-of-dementia/down-syndrome

Bacanli, A. (2016). Aripiprazole use in children diagnosed with Down syndrome and comorbid autism spectrum disorders. *Journal of Child and Adolescent Psychopharmacology*, *26*(3), 306–308.

Bishop-Fitzpatrick, L., & Rubenstein, E. (2019). The physical and mental health of middle aged and older adults on the autism spectrum and the impact of intellectual disability. *Research in Autism Spectrum Disorders*, *63*, 34–41. https://doi.org/10.1016/j.rasd.2019.01.001

Buie, T., Campbell, D. B., Fuchs, G. J., III, Furuta, G. T., Levy, J., Vandewater, J., Whitaker, A. H., Atkins, D., Bauman, M. L., Beaudet, A. L., Carr, E. G., Gershon, M. D., Hyman, S. L., Jirapinyo, P., Jyonouchi, H., Kooros, K., Kushak, R., Levitt, P., Levy, S. E., … Winter, H. (2010). Evaluation, diagnosis, and treatment of gastrointestinal disorders in individuals with ASDs: A consensus report. *Pediatrics*, *125*(1), 1–18. https://doi.org/10.1542/peds.2009-1878C

Bull, M. J., Trotter, T., Santoro, S. L., Christensen, C., & Grout, R. W. (2022). Health supervision for children and adolescents with Down syndrome. *Pediatrics*, *149*(5), 1–24. https://doi.org/10.1542/peds.2022-057010

Capone, G. T., Brecher, L., & Bay, M. (2016). Guanfacine use in children with down syndrome and comorbid attention-deficit hyperactivity disorder (ADHD) with disruptive behaviors. *Journal of child neurology, 31*(8), 957–964

Capone, G. T., Chicoine, B., Bulova, P., Stephens, M., Hart, S., Crissman, B., Videlefsky, A., Myers, K., Roizen, N., Esbensen, A., Peterson, M., Santoro, S., Woodward, J., Martin, B., Smith, D., & Workgroup, D. S. M. I. G. D. (2018). Co-occurring medical conditions in adults with Down syndrome: A systematic review toward the development of health care guidelines. *American Journal of Medical Genetics Part A, 176*(1), 116–133. https://doi.org/10.1002/ajmg.a.38512

Capone, G. T., Goyal, P., Ares, W., & Lannigan, E. (2006). Neurobehavioral disorders in children, adolescents, and young adults with Down syndrome. *American Journal of Medical Genetics. Part C, Seminars in Medical Genetics, 142*(3), 158–172. https://doi.org/10.1002/ajmg.c.30097

Capone, G. T., Grados, M. A., Kaufmann, W. E., Bernad-Ripoll, S., & Jewell, A. (2005). Down syndrome and comorbid autism-spectrum disorder: Characterization using the Aberrant Behavior Checklist. *American Journal of Medical Genetics Part A, 134*(4). 373–380. https://doi.org/10.1002/ajmg.a.30622

Capone, G. T., Stephens, M., Santoro, S., Chicoine, B., Bulova, P., Peterson, M., Jasien, J., Smith, A. J., & Workgroup, D. S. M. I. G. (2020). Co-occurring medical conditions in adults with Down syndrome: A systematic review toward the development of health care guidelines. Part II. *American Journal of Medical Genetics Part A, 182*(7), 1832–1845. https://doi.org/10.1002/ajmg.a.61604

Carter, J. C., Capone, G. T., Gray, R. M., Cox, C. S., & Kaufmann, W. E. (2007). Autistic-spectrum disorders in Down syndrome: Further delineation and distinction from other behavioral abnormalities. *American Journal of Medical Genetics. Part B, Neuropsychiatric Genetics, 144*(1), 87–94. https://doi.org/10.1002/ajmg.b.30407

Castillo, H., Patterson, B., Hickey, F., Kinsman, A., Howard, J. M., Mitchell, T., & Molloy, C. A. (2008). Difference in age at regression in children with autism with and without Down syndrome. *Journal of Developmental and Behavioral Pediatrics, 29*(2), 89–93. https://doi.org/10.1097/DBP.0b013e318165c78d

Channell, M. M., Hahn, L. J., Rosser, T. C., Hamilton, D., Frank-Crawford, M. A., Capone, G. T., Sherman, S. L., & Down Syndrome Cognition Project. (2019). Characteristics associated with Autism Spectrum Disorder risk in individuals with Down syndrome. *Journal of Autism and Developmental Disorders, 49*(9), 3543–3556. https://doi.org/10.1007/s10803-019-04074-1

Channell, M. M., Phillips, B. A., Loveall, S. J., Conners, F. A., Bussanich, P. M., & Klinger, L. G. (2015). Patterns of autism spectrum symptomatology in individuals with Down syndrome without comorbid autism spectrum disorder. *Journal of Neurodevelopmental Disorders, 7*(1), 1–9. https://doi.org/10.1186/1866-1955-7-5

Couwenhoven, T. (2007). *Teaching children with Down syndrome about their bodies, boundaries, and sexuality: A guide for parents and professionals.* Woodbine House.

Couwenhoven, T. (2011). *The Girls' Guide to Growing Up: Choices & Changes in the Tween Years.* Woodbine House.

Couwenhoven, T. (2012). *The Boys' Guide to Growing Up: Choices & Changes During Puberty.* Woodbine House.

DiGuiseppi, C., Hepburn, S., Davis, J. M., Filder, D. J., Hartway, S., Lee, N. R., Miller, L., Ruttenber, M., & Robinson, C. (2010). Screening for autism spectrum disorders in children with Down syndrome: Population prevalence and screening test characteristics. *Journal of Developmental & Behavioral Pediatrics, 31*(3), 181–191. https://doi.org/10.1097/DBP.0b013e3181d5aa6d

Hepburn, S. L., Philofsky, A., Fidler, D. J., & Rogers, S. (2008). Autism symptoms in toddlers with Down syndrome: A descriptive study. *Journal of Applied Research in Intellectual Disabilities, 21*(1), 48–57. https://doi.org/10.1111/j.1468-3148.2007.00368.x

Hull, L., Petrides, K. V., & Mandy, W. (2020). The female autism phenotype and camouflaging: A narrative review. *Review Journal of Autism and Developmental Disorders, 7*(4), 306–317. https://doi.org/10.1007/s40489-020-00197-9

Iulita, M. F., Garzón Chavez, D., Klitgaard Christensen, M., Valle Tamayo, N., Plana-Ripoll, O., Rasmussen, S. A., Roqué Figuls, M., Alcolea, D., Videla, L., Barroeta, I., Benejam, B., Altuna, M., Padilla, C., Pegueroles, J., Fernandez, S., Belbin, O., Carmona-Iragui, M., Blesa, R., Lleó, A., ... Fortea, J. (2022). Association of Alzheimer Disease with life expectancy in people with Down syndrome. *JAMA Network Open, 5*(5) 1–15. https://doi.org/10.1001/jamanetworkopen.2022.12910

Katz, T., & Patel, L. (2020). *Potty time for kids with Down syndrome: Lose the diapers, not your patience.* Woodbine House.

Katz, D. J., Roche, K. J., & Skotko, B. G. (2020). Epileptic spasms in individuals with Down syndrome: A review of the current literature. *Epilepsia Open, 5*(3), 344–353. https://doi.org/10.1002/epi4.12412

Kraijer, D., & de Bildt, A. (2005). The PDD-MRS: An instrument for identification of Autism Spectrum Disorders in persons with mental retardation. *Journal of Autism and Developmental Disorders, 35*, 499–513. https://doi.org/10.1007/s10803-005-5040-0

Kumin, L. (2006). Speech intelligibility and childhood verbal apraxia in children with Down syndrome. *Down Syndrome Research and Practice, 10*(1), 10–22. https://doi.org/10.3104/reports.301

Lewis, C., Robertson, A. S., & Phelps, S. (2005). Unmet dental care needs among children with special health care needs: Implications for the medical home. *Pediatrics, 116*(3), 426–431. https://doi.org/10.1542/peds.2005-0390

Li, C., Boon, M., Ishman, S. L., & Suurna, M. V. (2019). Hypoglossal nerve stimulation in three adults with Down syndrome and severe obstructive sleep apnea. *The Laryngoscope, 129*(11), 402–406. https://doi.org/10.1002/lary.27723

Liu, P., Kong, W., Fang, C., Zhu, K., Dai, X., & Meng, X. (2022). Hypoglossal nerve stimulation in adolescents with down syndrome and obstructive sleep apnea: A systematic review and meta-analysis. *Frontiers in Neurology, 13*, 1–10. https://doi.org/10.3389/fneur.2022.1037926

Loomes, R., Hull, L., & Mandy, W. P. L. (2017). What is the male-to-female ratio in autism spectrum disorder? A systematic review and meta-analysis. *Journal of the American Academy of Child and Adolescent Psychiatry, 56*(6), 466–474. https://doi.org/10.1016/j.jaac.2017.03.013

Lowenthal, R., Paula, C. S., Schwartzman, J. S., Brunoni, D., & Mercadante, M. T. (2007). Prevalence of pervasive developmental disorder in Down's syndrome. *Journal of Autism & Developmental Disorders, 37*(7), 1394–1395 https://doi.org/10.1007/s10803 007 0374 4

Macho, V., Coelho, A., Areias, C., Macedo, P., & Andrade, D. (2014). Craniofacial features and specific oral characteristics of Down syndrome children. *Oral Health and Dental Management, 13*(2), 408–411.

Magyar, C. I., Pandolfi, V., & Dill, C. A. (2012). An initial evaluation of the Social Communication Questionnaire for the assessment of autism spectrum disorders in children with Down syndrome. *Journal of Developmental and Behavioral Pediatrics, 33*(2), 134–145. https://doi.org/10.1097/DBP.0b013e318240d3d9

McCarty, M. J., & Brumback, A. C. (2021). Rethinking stereotypies in autism. *Seminars in Pediatric Neurology, 38*, 1–16. https://doi.org/10.1016/j.spen.2021.100897

Merriam-Webster. (n.d.). Stereotypy. In *Merriam-Webster.com dictionary*. Retrieved July 21, 2023, from https://www.merriam-webster.com/dictionary/stereotypy

Molloy, C. A., Murray, D. S., Kinsman, A., Castillo, H., Mitchell, T., Hickey, F. J., & Patterson, B. (2009). Differences in the clinical presentation of Trisomy 21 with and without autism. *Journal of Intellectual Disability Research, 53*(2), 143–151. https://doi.org/10.1111/j.1365-2788.2008.01138.x

Moss, J., Richards, C., Nelson, L., & Oliver, C. (2013). Prevalence of autism spectrum disorder symptomatology and related behavioural characteristics in individuals with Down syndrome. *Autism, 17*(4), 390–404. https://doi.org/10.1177/1362361312442790

Mubayrik, A. B. (2016). The dental needs and treatment of patients with Down syndrome. *Dental Clinics of North America, 60*(3), 613–626. https://doi.org/10.1016/j.cden.2016.02.003

Ng, D. K., Chan, C. H., & Cheung, J. M. (2007). Children with Down syndrome and OSA do not necessarily snore. *Archives of Disease in Childhood, 92*(11), 1047–1048.

Ortiz, B., Videla, L., Gich, I., Alcacer, B., Torres, D., Jover, I., Sanchez, E., Iglesias, M., Fortea, J., & Videla, S. (2017). Early warning signs of autism spectrum disorder in people with Down syndrome. *International Medical Review on Down Syndrome, 21*(1), 3–11. https://doi.org/10.1016/j.sdeng.2017.01.001

Oxelgren, U. W., Åberg, M., Myrelid, Å., Annerén, G., Westerlund, J., Gustafsson, J., & Fernell, E. (2019). Autism needs to be considered in children with Down Syndrome. *Acta Paediatrica, 108*(11), 2019–2026. https://doi.org/10.1111/apa.14850

Oxelgren, U. W., Myrelid, Å., Annerén, G., Ekstam, B., Göransson, C., Holmbom, A., Isaksson, A., Åberg, M., Gustafsson, J., & Fernell, E. (2017). Prevalence of autism and attention-deficit-hyperactivity disorder in Down syndrome: a population-based study. *Developmental Medicine and Child Neurology, 59*(3), 276–283. https://doi.org/10.1111/dmcn.13217

Palumbo, M. L., & McDougle, C. J. (2018). Pharmacotherapy of Down syndrome. *Expert Opinion on Pharmacotherapy, 19*(17), 1875–1889.

Raymaker, D. M., McDonald, K. E., Ashkenazy, E., Gerrity, M., Baggs, A. M., Kripke, C., Hourston, S., & Nicolaidis, C. (2017). Barriers to healthcare: Instrument development and comparison between autistic adults and adults with and without other disabilities. *Autism: The International Journal of Research and Practice*, *21*(8), 972–984. https://doi.org/10.1177/1362361316661261

Richards, C., Jones, C., Groves, L., Moss, J., & Oliver, C. (2015). Prevalence of autism spectrum disorder phenomenology in genetic disorders: a systematic review and meta-analysis. *The Lancet Psychiatry*, *2*(10), 909–916. https://doi.org/10.1016/S2215-0366(15)00376-4

Rosso, M., Fremion, E., Santoro, S. L., Oreskovic, N. M., Chitnis, T., Skotko, B. G., & Santoro, J. D. (2020). Down syndrome disintegrative disorder: A clinical regression syndrome of increasing importance. *Pediatrics*, *145*(6), 1–9. https://doi.org/10.1542/peds.2019-2939

Russell, G., Steer, C., & Golding, J. (2011). Social and demographic factors that influence the diagnosis of autistic spectrum disorders. *Social Psychiatry and Psychiatric Epidemiology*, *46*(12), 1283–1293. https://doi.org/10.1007/s00127-010-0294-z

Santoro, J. D., Filipink, R. A., Baumer, N. T., Bulova, P. D., & Handen, B. L. (2023). Down syndrome regression disorder: updates and therapeutic advances. *Current Opinion in Psychiatry*, *36*(2), 96–103.

Shott, S. R., Amin, R., Chini, B., Heubi, C., Hotze, S., & Akers, R. (2006). Obstructive sleep apnea: Should all children with Down syndrome be tested? *Archives of Otolaryngology Head & Neck Surgery*, *132*(4), 432–436. https://doi.org/10.1001/archotol.132.4.432

Soccorso, C., Milliken, A., Hojlo, M., Pawlowski, K., Weas, S., Sideridis, G., & Baumer, N. (2023). Quality of life and family impact in Down syndrome, Autism Spectrum Disorder, and co-occurring Down syndrome and Autism Spectrum Disorder. *Journal of Developmental & Behavioral Pediatrics*, *44*(3), e185–e195. https://doi.org/10.1097/DBP.0000000000001171

Spinazzi, N. A., Santoro, J. D., Pawlowski, K., Anzueto, G., Howe, Y. J., Patel, L. R., & Baumer, N. T. (2023). Co-occurring conditions in children with Down syndrome and autism: a retrospective study. *Journal of Neurodevelopmental Disorders*, *15*(1), 1–8. https://doi.org/10.1186/s11689-023-09478-w

Spinazzi, N. A., Velasco, A. B., Wodecki, D. J., & Patel, L. (2023). Autism Spectrum Disorder in Down syndrome: Experiences from caregivers. *Journal of Autism and Developmental Disorders*, 1–10. https://doi.org/10.1007/s10803-022-05758-x

Steinway, C., Gable, J., & Jan, S. (2017). *Transitioning to adult care: Supporting youth with special health care needs.* Policylab: Evidence to Action Brief. https://policylab.chop.edu/sites/default/files/pdf/publications/Transitions_Of_Care.pdf

Tsou, A. Y., Bulova, P., Capone, G. T., Chicoine, B., Gelaro, B., Harville, T. O., Martin, B. A., McGuire, D. E., McKelvey, K. D., Peterson, M., Tyler, C., Wells, M., & Whitten, M. S. (2020). Medical care of adults with Down syndrome: A clinical guideline. *The Journal of the American Medical Association (JAMA)*, *324*(15), 1543–1556. https://doi.org/10.1001/jama.2020.17024

VanZant, J. S., & McCormick, A. A. (2021). Health care transition for individuals with Down syndrome: A needs assessment. *American Journal of Medical Genetics Part A*, *185*(10), 3019–3027. https://doi.org/10.1002/ajmg.a.62403

Varshney, K., Iriowen, R., Morrell, K., Pillay, P., Fossi, A., & Stephens, M. M. (2022). Disparities and outcomes of patients living with Down Syndrome undergoing healthcare transitions from pediatric to adult care: A scoping review. *American Journal of Medical Genetics Part A, 188*(8), 2293–2302. https://doi.org/10.1002/ajmg.a.62854

Walpert, M., Zaman, S., & Holland, A. (2021). A systematic review of unexplained early regression in adolescents and adults with Down syndrome. *Brain Sciences, 11*(9), 1–21. https://doi.org/10.3390/brainsci11091197

Warner, G., Howlin, P., Salomone, E., Moss, J., & Charman, T. (2017). Profiles of children with Down syndrome who meet screening criteria for autism spectrum disorder (ASD): a comparison with children diagnosed with ASD attending specialist schools. *Journal of Intellectual Disability Research, 61*(1), 75–82. https://doi.org/10.1111/jir.12344

Warner, G., Moss, J., Smith, P., & Howlin, P. (2014). Autism characteristics and behavioural disturbances in ~500 children with Down's syndrome in England and Wales. *Autism Research, 7*(4), 433–441. https://doi.org/10.1002/aur.1371

Zemel, B. S., Pipan, M., Stallings, V. A., Hall, W., Schadt, K., Freedman, D. S., & Thorpe, P. (2015). Growth charts for children with Down syndrome in the United States. *Pediatrics, 136*(5), e1204–e1211. https://doi.org/10.1542/peds.2015-1652

CHAPTER FIVE

THE DS-ASD DIAGNOSTIC EVALUATION PROCESS: WHAT TO EXPECT

Rudaina Banihani, MD

George Capone, MD

Paige Church, MD

Kathleen Lehman, PhD

Lina Patel, PsyD

Maria Stanley, MD

Once autism screening has been completed by your primary care provider (see chapter four), it will be important to ensure that the individual is also up to date on medical care recommended for persons with Down syndrome. Certain medical issues for individuals with Down syndrome, such as vision or hearing problems, sleep apnea, or problems with thyroid function, can cause symptoms that overlap with symptoms of autism spectrum disorders. Both the American Academy of Pediatrics' (AAP) Health Supervision for Children and Adolescents with Down Syndrome, and Medical Care of Adults with Down Syndrome: A Clinical Guideline provide guidance for primary care doctors about needed health screenings and preventive care for individuals with Down syndrome (Bull et al., 2022; Tsou et al., 2020). The AAP HealthyChildren.org website has checklists for families with these recommendations, titled "Children with Down Syndrome: Health Care Information for Families." (https://www.healthychildren. org/English/health-issues/conditions/developmental-disabilities/Pages/Children-with-Down-Syndrome-Health-Care-Information-for-Families.aspx). The Global Medical Care Guidelines for Adults with Down Syndrome provides similar guidance for the care of adults (https://www.globaldownsyndrome.org/medical-care-guidelines-for-adults/; Tsou et al., 2020). Primary care doctors or Down syndrome specialists can also screen for medical issues contributing to the individual's developmental or behavioral concerns. Once these medical issues have been evaluated, if questions about autism persist, the next step will be to get a referral for diagnostic evaluation.

A range of specialists may be able to make a diagnosis and determine whether the individual meets the diagnostic criteria for autism spectrum disorder. If you have access to a Down Syndrome Clinic or provider with expertise in Down syndrome, they may help direct you to options. Family-to-Family (F2F) health information centers are another resource in the US. These are centers in every US state, the District of Columbia, five US territories, and three serving tribal communities that are staffed with knowledgeable family members that can help connect you within your community. To find the F2F in your state, go to https://familyvoices.org/affiliates. Other families/caregivers in your community who care for individuals with DS-ASD may also be useful in providing resources. The individual's health insurance provider and available community resources influence what options are available and how long you may have to wait for an evaluation where you live. Finally, your state and your insurer may determine who can make a diagnosis for purposes of accessing treatment services.

SPECIALISTS WHO CAN MAKE AN AUTISM DIAGNOSIS

- **Interdisciplinary Team:** Interdisciplinary team assessments include one (or more) of the following: psychologist, developmental-behavioral pediatrician, speech/language pathologist, occupational therapist, audiologist, special educator, social worker or family navigator, and/or nurse. The goal is to provide a comprehensive look at the individual's strengths and concerns and evaluate for other medical, mental health, or developmental issues. These teams are often located at academic medical centers (large teaching hospitals) and sometimes are a part of Down Syndrome Clinics (see National Down Syndrome Society: https://ndss.org/resources/healthcare-providers; Global Down Syndrome Foundation: https://www.globaldownsyndrome.org/research-medical-care/medical-care-providers/; Down Syndrome Medical Interest Group-USA: https://www.dsmig-usa.org/clinic-directory-map).
- **Psychologist:** Psychologists with specialized training to evaluate for autism spectrum disorders can provide diagnostic assessments.
- **Developmental-Behavioral Pediatrician:** Specialty-trained pediatricians can provide autism diagnostic assessments.
- **Psychiatrist:** Some psychiatrists have the training to administer diagnostic assessments for autism.
- **Primary Care Provider:** Some primary care providers (pediatricians, family medicine physicians, or pediatric nurse practitioners) with additional training in specialized assessments can make a diagnosis, especially for very young children.

If there are choices of who will be doing the diagnostic evaluation, consider the following:

- Does the provider have experience or expertise working with individuals with Down syndrome and DS-ASD?
- If the individual receives a diagnosis of autism, will the results of this assessment allow them to access autism treatment services?
- What resources does the evaluator(s) provide for families/caregivers if given a diagnosis? Are there social workers, family navigators, or others who can

help with understanding support services that may be available in the setting of a new autism diagnosis?

- How long will the individual have to wait for an assessment? If the wait is long, are there other options for what to do or resources that can be accessed while waiting for an assessment?
- Does the individual's health insurance cover the provider/provider group? If not, what are the financial costs of the assessment?

What to Bring to the Assessment

1. The individual being evaluated: Ideally, the assessment will be arranged at a time when the individual is healthy, rested, and well-fed. If the individual is ill, recovering from surgery, or the visit is scheduled at naptime, check with the provider doing the evaluation to explore rescheduling to another time.
2. Knowledgeable parent or caregiver: the evaluator(s) will likely need to ask questions that are best answered by someone who knows the individual well. Information about the person with DS from the early years to the time of the evaluation will be needed.
3. Any prior developmental or cognitive evaluations, including the most recent early intervention Individualized Family Service Plan (IFSP), or school Individualized Education Plan (IEP), or adult Service Plan (SP) evaluation report. Having the most recent evaluations from therapists (occupational therapist, physical therapist, speech-language pathologist) or behavioral health specialists involved in the individual's care would also be helpful.
4. Glasses, hearing aids, and/or speech generating device/"talker" if used.
5. While not required, videos of the individual with DS when they were younger or current videos in other settings, such as at school or a social function, are also helpful for the evaluator to understand the individual and presenting symptoms.
6. Other things that may help make this a comfortable experience for the individual may include a water bottle, a fidget or other favorite toy, a favorite blanket, or using a headset connected to calming music.

THE DIAGNOSTIC EVALUATION

An autism diagnostic evaluation includes a variety of components to help provide an understanding of the individual across a range of areas. The evaluation usually includes a medical/developmental history and physical exam, developmental observation, screening, and diagnostic testing, and putting the pieces together to make a diagnosis.

Developmental And Behavioral Observation/Informal Assessment

Evaluators/clinicians get important information from observing an individual in a relaxed environment, such as a playroom or a waiting room with access to toys and/or other engaging objects, and/or evaluation team members/individuals. This setting places "no demands" on the individual, and the clinician will be able to observe their spontaneous play and communication skills.

During the interview with the parents/caregivers, the clinician will observe how the individual communicates and interacts with others. The evaluator/clinician will watch how the individual with DS uses words, signs, pointing, or other gestures to request, comment, or protest during social interactions. The evaluator will watch how the individual responds to his/her/their name and play with toys/objects. Looking at all these activities and behaviors helps with understanding the individual's social communication skills. The presence of motor mannerisms ("stereotypies"), such as hand flapping or looking at hands in unique ways, will be noted. These mannerisms can be seen when a person is excited but can also occur if they are distressed.

Informal Interaction: The clinician/evaluator will try to interact with the individual. One of the easiest ways to do this is by using a toy/object, such as a cause-and-effect toy or bubbles. This may lead them to show behaviors associated with autism. The clinician/evaluator will also use this opportunity to evaluate their ability to request or initiate social interaction using eye contact, vocalizations, gestures, and/or body language. How often the individual tries to get another person's attention (parent/caregiver or clinician/evaluator) is important. Individuals with DS-ASD may make fewer attempts to get someone's attention. The clinician/evaluator may also use the above strategies but may direct them toward another person, often referred to as a "communication partner."

Diagnostic Testing

A trained clinician/evaluator will use diagnostic testing tools to help discriminate between typical behaviors, DS phenotype (typical behaviors for people with DS), and ASD-specific behaviors. This can be a difficult task and ultimately relies on the clinician's judgment based on all the information gathered from the assessment. Currently, the Autism Diagnostic Observation Schedule, Second Edition (ADOS-2) diagnostic test (Lord et al., 2012) is the recommended assessment tool to differentiate between ASD and non-ASD profiles, though other assessment tools may be used (see table 5.1).

Diagnostic Tools to Identify Autism Spectrum Disorder

There are different ways to evaluate ASD in children and adults. Screening tools are the first step in the process (see chapter four). Screening tools evaluate individuals for the possibility of ASD, using tools that compare an individual's development to the general population (not individuals with already identified developmental differences, like DS). Screening tools should not be used to diagnose but rather to determine whether the likelihood of autism is significant enough that a full diagnostic evaluation is warranted.

However, community providers sometimes use screening tools to make a diagnosis. It is important to be aware that making a diagnosis using a screening tool may lead to delays in getting treatment, as many insurance companies and service providers require a full diagnostic evaluation. A more detailed way of assessing for ASD is a developmental assessment or a much more detailed tool that has been studied to identify the presence or absence of ASD specifically.

Diagnostic tools are often chosen based on an individual's needs and abilities, as well as any previous recent assessments that have been done. The assessments may include parent/caregiver questionnaires and interaction with the individual. Many of these tests can include activities that look like play. In a person/individual with a dual diagnosis of DS-ASD, a single diagnostic tool to differentiate between the two diagnostic profiles is nonexistent.

The full diagnostic assessment may include a specific autism diagnostic assessment tool, a cognitive assessment, a speech-language evaluation, and/or an assessment that looks at the person's adaptive skills, as described in Tables 5.1, 5.2, and 5.3 below.

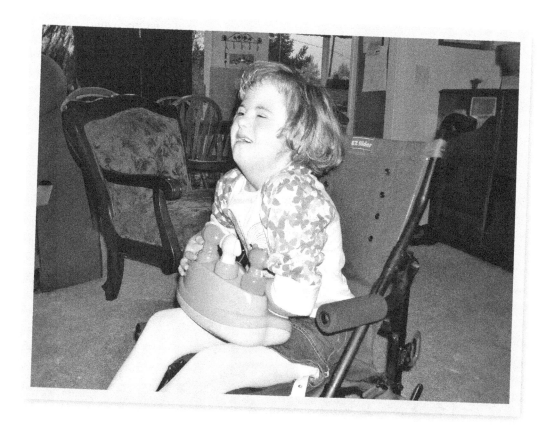

Table 5.1: Autism Spectrum Disorder Diagnostic Tools

Tool	Ages	How It Works	Comments & Considerations
The Autism Diagnostic Observation Schedule - **2nd Edition (ADOS-2)** (Lord et al., 2012)	12 months to adulthood	Standardized and semi-structured set of activities to allow the provider to observe communication, social interactions, play, and behavior.	Considered the "gold standard" for ASD evaluations across ages and language abilities. It should not be used in isolation but as supportive evidence to complement the patient's history and the clinician's observations. Not validated for individuals with DS but can be combined with additional cognitive developmental tools to interpret symptoms. It has been used in multiple publications for diagnosing ASD in DS (DiGuiseppi et al., 2010)

Tool	Ages	How It Works	Comments & Considerations
The Childhood Autism Rating Scale-2nd Edition **(CARS2-ST or CARS2-HF)** (Schopler et al., 2010)	Developmental age of 2 years & older	Structured tool based on observations and parent/caregiver information.	It should not be used in isolation but as supportive evidence to complement the patient's history and clinician's observations. Offers modifications for communication limitations and cognitive differences. Test research includes persons with DS. Used in DS-ASD publications (Davis et al., 2018; Dressler et al., 2011; Ferreira-Vasques & Lamônica, 2015; Ghosh et al., 2008; Kent et al., 1998, 1999)
The Autism Diagnostic Interview-Revised **(ADI-R)** (Rutter et al., 2003)	Developmental age of 2 years to adolescence	Standardized semi-structured interviews with family members.	Lengthy (90–120 minutes long) Most often used in research settings vs clinical visits Parallels the ADOS Used in DS-ASD publications (Bruining et al., 2014; Castillo et al., 2008; DiGuiseppi et al., 2010; Doran et al., 2012; Godfrey et al., 2019; Hepburn & MacLean, 2009; Hepburn et al., 2008; Molloy et al., 2009; Oxelgren et al., 2017; Starr et al., 2005; Sung et al., 2013)

Developmental and Cognitive Measures

An evaluation of an individual's cognitive ability is not required to diagnose ASD in individuals with Down syndrome. Still, it is helpful to ensure that the presenting concerns are more related to an autism spectrum disorder and not simply related to the person's intellectual ability. It is important to know whether all developmental skills are at approximately the same level (which would be more indicative of intellectual disability) or if social and communication skills are significantly different from other developmental skills. Cognitive assessment of individuals with DS is challenging, as many tests were only created based on typically developing individuals. Table 5.2 below describes developmental and cognitive diagnostic tools that may be used in a comprehensive evaluation in publications that evaluate ASD in the DS population.

Table 5.2: Developmental and Cognitive Measures

Tool	Ages	Overview	Comments & Considerations
The Bayley Scales of Infant and Toddler Development-4th Edition **(Bayley-4)** (Alfonso et al., 2022)	0–42 months	Standardized assessment of cognitive, language, and motor skills.	Uses norms for children with Down syndrome. The cognitive subscale can be used in isolation. It may be used with older ages to obtain an estimate of cognitive function based on age equivalents, but this can be misleading because the individual may have variable skills and may not be functioning at that age level in all areas. Previous versions of Bayley have been used in multiple publications as part of DS-ASD comprehensive assessment (Capone et al., 2005; Carter et al., 2007; Ji et al., 2011)
Mullen Scales of Early Learning-GS Edition (Mullen, 1995)	0–68 months	Characterizes a child's cognitive and developmental profile.	Commonly used in the evaluation of children with neurodevelopmental conditions and has been used in Down syndrome (Chiodo, 2002; Doran et al., 2012; Godfrey et al., 2019; Hahn et al., 2020; Hamner et al., 2020; Hepburn & MacLean, 2009; Hepburn et al., 2008). Similar issue with the Bayley when using it with older ages. It has not been updated since it was created in 1995.

Tool	Ages	Overview	Comments & Considerations
The Stanford-Binet Intelligence Scales-5th Edition (SB-5) (Madaus et al., 2008)	2–85+ years	Standardized assessment of cognitive abilities.	Provides overall composite score plus information about verbal and nonverbal reasoning. Assesses variations in abilities across cognitive domains. Can give a shortened version (just two subtests) to get an abbreviated IQ. Has been used in multiple publications as part of DS-ASD comprehensive assessment (Castillo et al., 2008; Doran et al., 2012).
The Differential Ability Scales-2nd Edition (DAS-2) (Elliott, 1997)	2½–17 years	Standardized assessment of cognitive abilities.	Special nonverbal composite can be used to reduce language demands. Used in a couple of publications as part of DS-ASD assessment (Cervantes & Matson, 2015; Hepburn & MacLean, 2009).
The Leiter International Performance Scales (Leiter-3) (Cornoldi et al., 2016)	3–75+ years	A nonverbal measure of cognitive abilities using gestures to explain directions.	The individual is not required to speak, read, or write. Gestures are used to administer. Used in publications as part of DS-ASD assessment (Channell, 2020; Channell et al., 2015; Glennon et al., 2020).

Tool	Ages	Overview	Comments & Considerations
Kaufman Brief Intelligence Test-2nd Edition (KBIT-2 Revised) (Kaufman & Kaufman, 1990)	4–90 years	Standardized assessment of cognitive abilities.	Provides an overall composite and additional information on verbal and nonverbal reasoning. Difficult to use at younger ages due to the difficulty level of the lowest item on each subtest. Used in publications as part of DS-ASD assessment (Channell et al., 2019; Davis et al., 2018).

Language Development

An evaluation of language development in an individual with DS may be included in a comprehensive assessment for ASD. It is not required to determine a diagnosis of ASD, but it may provide more information for interventions and support. It may help to determine the specific ADOS module to administer. Table 5.3 includes additional language assessment tools that may be used in comprehensive evaluation in publications that evaluated ASD in the DS population.

Table 5.3: Language Measures

Tool	Ages	Overview	Comments & Considerations
The Preschool Language Scale-5th Edition **(PLS-5)** (Zimmerman et al., 1979)	0–7yrs, 11mo	Assesses language abilities.	Provides information on overall receptive and expressive language skills.

	2½–90+ years	Assesses receptive English vocabulary.	This correlates with cognitive ability.
The Peabody Picture Vocabulary-5th Edition (PPVT-5) (Dunn, 2019)			PPVT-4 has been used as part of DS-ASD assessment (Channell et al., 2015).
The Expressive Vocabulary Test-3rd Edition (EVT-3) (Williams, 2019)	2½–90+ years	Assesses expressive English vocabulary.	Provides information on general language, word knowledge.

Adaptive Measures

These measures provide information on an individual's functional daily living skills, specifically what they can do without the support of others. It is useful in accessing support services as well as in developing plans for teaching skills. These measures rely on a detailed report from a caregiver or support person. Table 5.4 includes additional adaptive assessment tools that may be used in a comprehensive evaluation in publications that evaluated ASD in the DS population.

Table 5.4: Adaptive Measures

Tool	Ages	Overview	Comments & Considerations
The Vineland Adaptive Behavior Scale-3rd Edition (Vineland-3) (Sparrow et al., 2016)	0–90 years	Assesses functional skills of communication, daily living, socialization, and motor skills.	It can be administered as an interview or using a parent/caregiver form. It has been used in multiple publications as part of the assessment in DS-ASD (Castillo et al., 2008; Davis et al., 2018; Dressler et al., 2011; Ghosh et al., 2008; Hepburn & MacLean, 2009; Hepburn et al., 2008; Ji et al., 2011; Molloy et al., 2009; Sung et al., 2013).

Tool	Ages	Overview	Comments & Considerations
The Adaptive Behavior Assessment System-3rd Edition (ABAS-3) (Harrison & Oakland, 2015)	0–89 years	Assesses functional skills across conceptual, social, and practical domains.	Includes five rating forms. Used in multiple publications as part of the assessment in DS-ASD (Kirchner & Walton, 2021; Oxelgren et al., 2017; Wester Oxelgren et al., 2019).

Autism-Specific and Behavioral Measure

Table 5.5 lists caregiver report measures which may be included in a comprehensive evaluation. Although some of these tools may be used as screeners (see chapter four), they may add additional information to help the evaluator determine the diagnostic criteria. In addition, more general information about behavioral and emotional functioning may help determine if additional diagnoses are present or if the behavior is better explained by other diagnoses (see the subheading, "What if the ASD Diagnosis was not given because the criteria for ASD were not met?" following the summary of this section).

Table 5.5: Autism-Specific & Behavior Measures

Tool	Ages	Overview	Comments & Considerations
The Social Communication Questionnaire (SCQ) (Oosterling et al., 2010)	4 years and older (requires developmental age of 2 years old)	A standardized parent questionnaire to obtain more information about communication skills and social functioning.	Based on the ADI-R and ADOS, and is the most researched with individuals with Down syndrome (Channell, 2020; Channell et al., 2015, 2019; Davis et al., 2018; Derks et al., 2017; DiGuiseppi et al., 2010; Hepburn & MacLean, 2009; Kirchner & Walton, 2021; Magyar et al., 2012; Maljaars et al., 2012; Naerland et al., 2017; Richards et al., 2017; Sappok et al., 2015, 2017; Warner et al., 2014, 2017; Wester Oxelgren et al., 2019). Overall, the scale shows good concurrent validity with other ASD measures.
The Social Responsiveness Scale-2nd Edition (SRS-2) (Bruni, 2014)	4–18 years	Parent and teacher questionnaire provides information about social communication, social motivation, and behaviors observed in children/ adolescents with ASD.	Information about social motivation is a distinguishing feature in children with DS-ASD. Used in multiple publications in that regard as part of the assessment in DS-ASD (Channell, 2020; Channell et al., 2015, 2019; Glennon et al., 2020).

Tool	Ages	Overview	Comments & Considerations
The Child Behavior Checklist (CBCL) (Achenbach, 1994) & **The Adult Behavior Checklist (ABCL)** (Achenbach et al., 2003)	1½–18 years & 18–59	Standardized questionnaires that provide a broad spectrum of information on behavioral and emotional difficulties	Often used in research and clinical settings. Not specific to ASD, but helpful in a comprehensive evaluation to consider diagnoses instead of or in addition to ASD (Griffioen et al., 2020; Pourbagheri et al., 2018).
Aberrant Behavior Checklist (ABC) (Bravo Oro et al., 2014)	5 years to adulthood	Assesses the severity of maladaptive behaviors on five subscales: Irritability, Lethargy/Social Withdrawal, Stereotypy, Hyperactivity, and Inappropriate Speech	The ABC was able to identify individuals with DS and co-occurring ASD. Also able to differentiate between a dual diagnosis of DS and other behavior disorders. The ability to differentiate between these subgroups is beneficial for clinicians. Used as part of DS-ASD assessment in multiple publications because of that (Capone et al., 2005; Carter et al., 2007; Ji et al., 2011; Marshburn & Aman, 1992; Ono, 1996; Rojahn & Helsel, 1991; Rojahn et al., 2013; Sung et al., 2013; Yang & Zhao, 2014).

Putting the Pieces Together

The clinician/evaluator formulates an overall clinical impression by combining information from the history, observation, and diagnostic assessment tools. The clinician/evaluator will identify the individual's strengths and challenges and their impact on the individual's overall level of functioning. Significant challenges in social and communication skills and atypical behaviors that impact the individual's functioning suggest an ASD profile. Once a diagnosis is confirmed, an appropriate intervention targeting the individual's challenges and supporting their strengths can be initiated (see chapter ten).

What If the ASD Diagnosis Was Not Given Because the Criteria for ASD Were Not Met?

Individuals with DS (without ASD) can also have mood instability, irritability, anxiety, sensory seeking/avoiding, self-injury, and decreased social engagement, which are regarded as "autistic-like" behavior (Capone et al., 2008). Consider the case where the diagnosis of ASD is not confirmed using an ADOS. In that case, another autistic-like condition may be diagnosed: atypical attention deficit disorder, social anxiety disorder, stereotypic movement disorder, obsessive-compulsive disorder, disruptive mood dysregulation disorder, or mixed expressive-receptive language disorder. In persons with these conditions, repetitive behaviors or stereotypies, unusual attention, and sensory seeking or aversion may sometimes be intense. When the social environment permits (stable, familiar), these individuals can usually demonstrate and use social communication and other key social skills, even when inconsistent.

Regardless of diagnosis, individuals with DS and "autistic-like" behavior may demonstrate an unusual behavior symptom profile. Regarding academics and social-adaptive function, individuals with DS and "autistic-like" behavior have significant struggles, no different from many children who meet the full criteria for ASD. They require the same comprehensive approach to evaluation, diagnosis, and management as any other child with DS; rather than feeling disappointed or discouraged by "not having ASD," parents and professionals need to determine the proper developmental or psychiatric diagnosis or diagnoses to support the individual's specific educational, life skills, and emotional needs. Many educational and behavioral strategies for individuals with DS-ASD may also be recommended for individuals with an autistic-like condition. They may include behavior management with parent/caregiver training, functional communication strategies, creating a stable/predictable environment, avoidance of unpleasant stimuli, preferred sensory activities, relaxation techniques, and medications for important target symptoms, including sleep (see chapters eight and ten).

CONCLUSION

Evidence exists for the coexistence of DS and ASD. Early intervention is key in optimizing the developmental path for individuals with dual diagnoses. The goal of identification is to support development by introducing appropriate interventions. Due to the overlapping symptoms of the two conditions, identification is very often delayed. Autism spectrum disorder–specific screening instruments that have been used and/or are suitable for an individual with DS should be used if autism is suspected through history and observation, even though screening tools may have significant limitations. Screening should then lead to a referral for a full diagnostic evaluation. The ADOS-2—considered the gold standard diagnostic observation instrument—can be successfully administered once the individual's developmental age/level is measured or determined (through caregiver interview and review of records).

Nevertheless, the overall approach in evaluating an individual with DS and social communication impairments should be weighted on the **"best clinical estimate,"** defined by history, observation, and examination. Much work is needed to better define the developmental paths of individuals with a dual diagnosis of DS-ASD throughout their life span. Understanding changes in social, communication, and behavioral characteristics over time will allow more precise and earlier identification of ASD in DS.

Finally, it is important to recognize that the clinical presentation of DS-ASD evolves over time in some individuals with less overt symptoms. We recommend closely monitoring the social and communication development of the individual with DS. This leads to earlier identification of conditions such as ASD, which are responsive to intervention.

REFERENCES

Achenbach, T. M. (1994). Child behavior checklist and related instruments. In M. E. Maruish (Ed.), *The use of psychological testing for treatment planning and outcome assessment* (pp. 517–549). Lawrence Erlbaum Associates, Inc.

Achenbach, T. M., Dumenci, L., & Rescorla, L. A. (2003). *Ratings of relations between DSM-IV diagnostic categories and items of the CBCL/6-18, TRF, and YSR.* University of Vermont, Research Center for Children, Youth, & Families.

Alfonso, V. C., Engler, J. R., & Turner, A. D. (2022). *Essentials of Bayley-4 assessment.* Wiley.

Bravo Oro, A., Navarro-Calvillo, M. E., & Esmer Sanchez, M. (2014). Autistic Behavior Checklist (ABC) and its applications. In: V. B. Patel, V. R. Preedy, & C. R. Martin (Eds.), *Comprehensive guide to autism* (pp. 2787–2798). Springer.

Bruining, H., Eijkemans, M. J., Kas, M. J., Curran, S. R., Vorstman, J. A., & Bolton, P. F. (2014). Behavioral signatures related to genetic disorders in autism. *Molecular Autism, 5*(1), 11–23. https://doi.org/10.1186/2040-2392-5-11

Bruni, T. P. (2014). Test review: Social responsiveness scale–second edition (SRS-2). *Journal of Psychoeducational Assessment, 32*(4), 365–369. https://doi.org/10.1177/0734282913517525

Bull, M. J., Trotter, T., Santoro, S. L., Christensen, C., & Grout, R. W. (2022). Health supervision for children and adolescents with Down syndrome. *Pediatrics, 149*(5), 1–24. https://doi.org/10.1542/peds.2022-057010

Capone, G. T., Goyal, P., Grados, M., Smith, B., & Kammann, H. (2008). Risperidone use in children with Down syndrome, severe intellectual disability, and comorbid autistic spectrum disorders: A naturalistic study. *Journal of Developmental and Behavioral Pediatrics, 29*(2), 106–116. https://doi.org/10.1097/DBP.0b013e318165c100

Capone, G. T., Grados, M. A., Kaufmann, W. E., Bernad-Ripoll, S., & Jewell, A. (2005). Down syndrome and comorbid autism-spectrum disorder: Characterization using the Aberrant Behavior Checklist. *American Journal of Medical Genetics Part A, 134*(4). 373–380. https://doi.org/10.1002/ajmg.a.30622

Carter, J. C., Capone, G. T., Gray, R. M., Cox, C. S., & Kaufmann, W. E. (2007). Autistic-spectrum disorders in Down syndrome: further delineation and distinction from other behavioral abnormalities. *American Journal of Medical Genetics. Part B, Neuropsychiatric Genetics, 144*(1), 87–94. https://doi.org/10.1002/ajmg.b.30407

Castillo, H., Patterson, B., Hickey, F., Kinsman, A., Howard, J. M., Mitchell, T., & Molloy, C. A. (2008). Difference in age at regression in children with autism with and without Down syndrome. *Journal of Developmental and Behavioral Pediatrics, 29*(2), 89–93. https://doi.org/10.1097/DBP.0b013e318165c78d

Cervantes, P. E., & Matson, J. L. (2015). Comorbid symptomology in adults with autism spectrum disorder and intellectual disability. *Journal of Autism and Developmental Disorders, 45*(12), 3961–3970. https://doi.org/10.1007/s10803-015-2553-z

Channell, M. M. (2020). The Social Responsiveness Scale (SRS-2) in school-age children with Down syndrome at low risk for autism spectrum disorder. *Autism & Developmental Language Impairments, 5*, 1–12. https://doi.org/10.1177/2396941520962406

Channell, M. M., Hahn, L. J., Rosser, T. C., Hamilton, D., Frank-Crawford, M. A., Capone, G. T., Sherman, S. L., & Down Syndrome Cognition Project. (2019). Characteristics associated with autism spectrum disorder risk in individuals with Down syndrome. *Journal of Autism and Developmental Disorders, 49*(9), 3543–3556. https://doi.org/10.1007/s10803-019-04074-1

Channell, M. M., Phillips, B. A., Loveall, S. J., Conners, F. A., Bussanich, P. M., & Klinger, L. G. (2015). Patterns of autism spectrum symptomatology in individuals with Down syndrome without comorbid autism spectrum disorder. *Journal of Neurodevelopmental Disorders, 7*(1), 1–9. https://doi.org/10.1186/1866-1955-7-5

Chiodo, A. A. (2002). *Assessment of Down syndrome children: Mullen scale of early learning.* Carlos Albizu University.

Cornoldi, C., Giofrè, D., & Belacchi, C. (2016). *Leiter-3 Leiter International Performance Scale Third Edition Standardizzazione Italiana.* Organizzazioni Speciali.

Davis, M. A. C., Spriggs, A., Rodgers, A., & Campbell, J. (2018). The effects of a peer-delivered social skills intervention for adults with comorbid Down syndrome and autism spectrum disorder. *Journal of Autism and Developmental Disorders, 48*(6), 1869–1885. https://doi.org/10.1007/s10803-017-3437-1

Derks, O., Heinrich, M., Brooks, W., Sterkenburg, P., McCarthy, J., Underwood, L., & Sappok, T. (2017). The Social Communication Questionnaire for adults with intellectual disability: SCQ-AID. *Autism Research: Official Journal of the International Society for Autism Research, 10*(9), 1481–1490. https://doi.org/10.1002/aur.1795

DiGuiseppi, C., Hepburn, S., Davis, J. M., Filder, D. J., Hartway, S., Lee, N. R., Miller, L., Ruttenber, M., & Robinson, C. (2010). Screening for autism spectrum disorders in children with Down syndrome: Population prevalence and screening test characteristics. *Journal of Developmental & Behavioral Pediatrics, 31*(3), 181–191. https://doi.org/10.1097/DBP.0b013e3181d5aa6d

Doran, E., Osann, K., Spence, M. A., Flodman, P., & Lott, I. T. (2012). Behavioral phenotype in Down syndrome with autism: Differences from autism alone. *Annals of Neurology 72*(S16), 198. https://doi.org/10.1002/ana.23709

Dressler, A., Perelli, V., Bozza, M., & Bargagna, S. (2011). The autistic phenotype in Down syndrome: differences in adaptive behaviour versus Down syndrome alone and autistic disorder alone. *Functional Neurology, 26*(3), 151–158.

Dunn, D. M. (2019). *Peabody picture vocabulary test* (5th ed.). Pearson.

Elliott, C. D. (1997). The Differential Ability Scales. In D. P. Flanagan, J. L. Genshaft, & P. L. Harrison (Eds.), *Contemporary intellectual assessment: Theories, tests, and issues* (pp. 183–208). The Guilford Press.

Ferreira-Vasques, A. T., & Lamônica, D. A. (2015). Motor, linguistic, personal and social aspects of children with Down syndrome. *Journal of Applied Oral Science, 23*(4), 424–430. https://doi.org/10.1590/1678-775720150102

Ghosh, M., Shah, A. H., Dhir, K., & Merchant, K. F. (2008). Behavior in children with Down syndrome. *Indian Journal of Pediatrics, 75*(7), 685–689. https://doi.org/10.1007/s12098-008-0129-z

Glennon, J. M., D'Souza, H., Mason, L., Karmiloff-Smith, A., & Thomas, M. S. C. (2020). Visuo-attentional correlates of Autism Spectrum Disorder (ASD) in children with Down syndrome: A comparative study with children with idiopathic ASD. *Research in Developmental Disabilities, 104*, 1–11. https://doi.org/10.1016/j.ridd.2020.103678

Godfrey, M., Hepburn, S., Fidler, D. J., Tapera, T., Zhang, F., Rosenberg, C. R., & Raitano Lee, N. (2019). Autism spectrum disorder (ASD) symptom profiles of children with comorbid Down syndrome (DS) and ASD: A comparison with children with DS-only and ASD-only. *Research in Developmental Disabilities, 89*, 83–93. https://doi.org/10.1016/j.ridd.2019.03.003

Griffioen, R. E., van der Steen, S., Verheggen, T., Enders-Slegers, M. J., & Cox, R. (2020). Changes in behavioural synchrony during dog-assisted therapy for children with autism spectrum disorder and children with Down syndrome. *Journal of Applied Research in Intellectual Disabilities, 33*(3), 398–408. https://doi.org/10.1111/jar.12682

Hahn, L. J., Hamrick, L. M., Kelleher, B. L., & Roberts, J. E. (2020). Autism spectrum disorder-associated behaviour in infants with Down syndrome. *Journal of Health Science & Education, 4*(2), 180–193.

Hamner, T., Hepburn, S., Zhang, F., Fidler, D., Robinson Rosenberg, C., Robins, D. L., & Lee, N. R. (2020). Cognitive profiles and autism symptoms in comorbid Down syndrome and autism spectrum disorder. *Journal of Developmental and Behavioral Pediatrics*, *41*(3), 172–179. https://doi.org/10.1097/DBP.0000000000000745

Harrison, P. L., & Oakland, T. (2015). *Adaptive behavior assessment system* (3rd ed.). Western Psychological Services.

Hepburn, S. L., & MacLean, W. E. (2009). Maladaptive and repetitive behaviors in children with Down syndrome and autism spectrum disorders: Implications for screening. *Journal of Mental Health Research in Intellectual Disabilities, 2*, 67–88. https://doi.org/10.1080/19315860802627627

Hepburn, S. L., Philofsky, A., Fidler, D. J., & Rogers, S. (2008). Autism symptoms in toddlers with Down syndrome: a descriptive study. *Journal of Applied Research in Intellectual Disabilities, 21*(1), 48–57. https://doi.org/10.1111/j.1468-3148.2007.00368.x

Ji, N. Y., Capone, G. T., & Kaufmann, W. E. (2011). Autism spectrum disorder in Down syndrome: cluster analysis of Aberrant Behaviour Checklist data supports diagnosis. *Journal of Intellectual Disability Research*, *55*(11), 1064–1077. https://doi.org/10.1111/j.1365-2788.2011.01465.x

Kaufman, A. S., & Kaufman, N. L. (1990). *Kaufman Brief Intelligence Test*. American Guidance Service.

Kent, L., Evans, J., Paul, M., & Sharp, M. (1999). Comorbidity of autistic spectrum disorders in children with Down syndrome. *Developmental Medicine and Child Neurology, 41*(3), 153–158. https://doi.org/10.1111/j.1469-8749.1999.tb00574.x

Kent, L., Perry, D., & Evans, J. (1998). Autism in Down's syndrome: Three case reports. *Autism, 2*(3), 259–267. https://doi.org/10.1177/1362361398023004

Kirchner, R. M., & Walton, K. M. (2021). Symptoms of autism spectrum disorder in children with Down syndrome and Williams syndrome. *American Journal on Intellectual and Developmental Disabilities*, *126*(1), 58–74. https://doi.org/10.1352/1944-7558-126.1.58

Lord, C., Rutter, M., DiLavore, P., Risi, S., Gotham, K., & Bishop, S. (2012). *Autism diagnostic observation schedule (ADOS-2)* (2nd ed.). Western Psychological Corporation.

Madaus, G. F., Lynch, C. A., & Lynch, P. S. (2008). Stanford-binet intelligence scales. *Educational Measurement: Issues and Practice, 11*(3), 5–11.

Magyar, C. I., Pandolfi, V., & Dill, C. A. (2012). An initial evaluation of the Social Communication Questionnaire for the assessment of autism spectrum disorders in children with Down syndrome. *Journal of Developmental and Behavioral Pediatrics*, *33*(2), 134–145. https://doi.org/10.1097/DBP.0b013e318240d3d9

Maljaars, J., Noens, I., Scholte, E., & van Berckelaer-Onnes, I. (2012). Evaluation of the criterion and convergent validity of the diagnostic interview for social and communication disorders in young and low-functioning children. *Autism: The International Journal of Research and Practice, 16*(5), 487–497. https://doi.org/10.1177/1362361311402857

Marshburn, E. C., & Aman, M. G. (1992). Factor validity and norms for the aberrant behavior checklist in a community sample of children with mental retardation. *Journal of Autism and Developmental Disorders, 22*(3), 357–373. https://doi.org/10.1007/BF01048240

Molloy, C. A., Murray, D. S., Kinsman, A., Castillo, H., Mitchell, T., Hickey, F. J., & Patterson, B. (2009). Differences in the clinical presentation of Trisomy 21 with and without autism. *Journal of Intellectual Disability Research, 53*(2), 143–151. https://doi.org/10.1111/j.1365-2788.2008.01138.x

Mullen, E. M. (1995). *Mullen scales of early learning.* AGS.

Naerland, T., Bakke, K. A., Storvik, S., Warner, G., & Howlin, P. (2017). Age and gender-related differences in emotional and behavioural problems and autistic features in children and adolescents with Down syndrome: a survey-based study of 674 individuals. *Journal of Intellectual Disability Research, 61*(6), 594–603. https://doi.org/10.1111/jir.12342

Ono, Y. (1996). Factor validity and reliability for the Aberrant Behavior Checklist-Community in a Japanese population with mental retardation. *Research in Developmental Disabilities, 17*(4), 303–309. https://doi.org/10.1016/0891-4222(96)00015-7

Oosterling, I., Rommelse, N., de Jonge, M., van der Gaag, R. J., Swinkels, S., Roos, S., Visser, J., & Buitelaar, J. (2010). How useful is the Social Communication Questionnaire in toddlers at risk of autism spectrum disorder? *Journal of Child Psychology and Psychiatry, and Allied Disciplines, 51*(11), 1260–1268. https://doi.org/10.1111/j.1469-7610.2010.02246.x

Oxelgren, U. W., Myrelid, Å., Annerén, G., Ekstam, B., Göransson, C., Holmbom, A., Isaksson, A., Åberg, M., Gustafsson, J., & Fernell, E. (2017). Prevalence of autism and attention-deficit-hyperactivity disorder in Down syndrome: a population-based study. *Developmental Medicine and Child Neurology, 59*(3), 276–283. https://doi.org/10.1111/dmcn.13217

Pourbagheri, N., Mirzakhani, N., & Akbarzadehbaghban, A. (2018). A comparison of emotional-behavioral problems of siblings at the age range of 3-9 year old children with autism and Down syndrome. *Iranian Journal of Child Neurology, 12*(2), 73–82.

Richards, C., Powis, L., Moss, J., Stinton, C., Nelson, L., & Oliver, C. (2017). Prospective study of autism phenomenology and the behavioural phenotype of Phelan-McDermid syndrome: comparison to fragile X syndrome, Down syndrome and idiopathic autism spectrum disorder. *Journal of Neurodevelopmental Disorders, 9*(1), 37–52. https://doi.org/10.1186/s11689-017-9217-6

Rojahn, J., & Helsel, W. J. (1991). The Aberrant Behavior Checklist with children and adolescents with dual diagnosis. *Journal of Autism and Developmental Disorders, 21*(1), 17–28. https://doi.org/10.1007/BF02206994

Rojahn, J., Schroeder, S. R., Mayo-Ortega, L., Oyama-Ganiko, R., LeBlanc, J., Marquis, J., & Berke, E. (2013). Validity and reliability of the Behavior Problems Inventory, the Aberrant Behavior Checklist, and the Repetitive Behavior Scale-Revised among infants and toddlers at risk for intellectual or developmental disabilities: A multi-method assessment approach. *Research in Developmental Disabilities, 34*(5), 1804–1814. https://doi.org/10.1016/j.ridd.2013.02.024

Rutter, M., LeCouteur, A., & Lord, C. (2003). *Autism Diagnostic Interview - Revised (ADI-R).* Western Psychological Services.

Sappok, T., Brooks, W., Heinrich, M., McCarthy, J., & Underwood, L. (2017). Cross-cultural validity of the social communication questionnaire for adults with intellectual developmental disorder. *Journal of autism and developmental disorders, 47*(2), 393–404. https://doi.org/10.1007/s10803-016-2967-2

Sappok, T., Diefenbacher, A., Gaul, I., & Bölte, S. (2015). Validity of the social communication questionnaire in adults with intellectual disabilities and suspected autism spectrum disorder. *American Journal on Intellectual and Developmental Disabilities, 120*(3), 203–214. https://doi.org/10.1352/1944-7558-120.3.203

Schopler, E., Van Bourgondien, M. E., Wellman, G. J., & Love, S. R. (2010). *The childhood autism rating scale (CARS-2)* (2nd ed.). Western Psychological Services.

Sparrow, S. S., Cicchetti, D. V., & Saulnier, C. A. (2016). *Vineland adaptive behavior scales* (3rd ed.). Pearson.

Starr, E. M., Berument, S. K., Tomlins, M., Papanikolaou, K., & Rutter, M. (2005). Brief report: Autism in individuals with Down syndrome. *Journal of Autism and Developmental Disorders, 35*(5), 665–673. https://doi.org/10.1007/s10803-005-0010-0

Sung, M., Ooi, Y. P., Law, G. C., Goh, T. J., Weng, S. J., & Sriram, B. (2013). Features of autism in a Singaporean child with Down syndrome. *Annals of the Academy of Medicine, Singapore, 42*(5), 251–252.

Tsou, A. Y., Bulova, P., Capone, G. T., Chicoine, B., Gelaro, B., Harville, T. O., Martin, B. A., McGuire, D. E., McKelvey, K. D., Peterson, M., Tyler, C., Wells, M., & Whitten, M. S. (2020). Medical care of adults with Down syndrome: A clinical guideline. *The Journal of the American Medical Association (JAMA), 324*(15), 1543–1556. https://doi.org/10.1001/jama.2020.17024

Warner, G., Howlin, P., Salomone, E., Moss, J., & Charman, T. (2017). Profiles of children with Down syndrome who meet screening criteria for autism spectrum disorder (ASD): a comparison with children diagnosed with ASD attending specialist schools. *Journal of Intellectual Disability Research, 61*(1), 75–82. https://doi.org/10.1111/jir.12344

Warner, G., Moss, J., Smith, P., & Howlin, P. (2014). Autism characteristics and behavioural disturbances in ~500 children with Down's syndrome in England and Wales. *Autism Research, 7*(4), 433–441. https://doi.org/10.1002/aur.1371

Wester Oxelgren, U., Myrelid, Å., Annerén, G., Westerlund, J., Gustafsson, J., & Fernell, E. (2019). More severe intellectual disability found in teenagers compared to younger children with Down syndrome. *Acta Paediatrica, 108*(5), 961–966. https://doi.org/10.1111/apa.14624

Williams, K. T. (2019). *Expressive vocabulary test* (3rd ed.). Pearson.

Yang, W. Z., & Zhao, Y. J. (2014). Clinical report: A female with Down syndrome and autism. *Hong Kong Journal of Paediatrics 19*(3):185–187.

Zimmerman, I. L., Steiner, V. G., & Pond, R. E. (1979). *Preschool language scale.* Psychological Corporation.

CHAPTER SIX

GUIDELINES AND INDICATIONS FOR MEDICATION USE

Nicole Baumer, MD, MEd

George Capone, MD

There are currently no approved psychiatric or behavioral medication approaches to reduce core symptoms of ASD (deficits in social communication/ interaction, restricted/ repetitive interests/behaviors) or to enhance cognition in Down syndrome. However, individuals with Down syndrome (DS), autism spectrum disorder (ASD), and especially those with both (DS-ASD) may have behavioral symptoms and psychiatric conditions that can greatly interfere with health, safety, community participation, learning, response to therapies, and can impact quality of life and burden on caregivers. Individuals with DS-ASD may display problematic behaviors, such as irritability, aggression, self-injurious behavior, tantrums, impulsivity, hyperactivity, anxiety, obsessions, compulsions, mood disorders, and sleep problems, which may be potential targets of using medication as an intervention. With proper treatment of these problematic behaviors, there may be improved access and response to behavioral and educational therapies, and improvement in overall adaptive functioning. Pharmacological treatment is complex, and use of pharmacological treatments is often a journey. This chapter will review commonly used psychiatric or behavioral medication treatments and the symptoms that can be targeted, medical literature of current research in psychiatric or behavioral medication treatment of DS, ASD, and DS-ASD, and practical approaches when using these medications.

CLINICAL TRIAL RESEARCH AND FOOD AND DRUG ADMINISTRATION APPROVAL OF MEDICATIONS

Prescription drugs are regulated and approved by the United States Food and Drug Administration (FDA). Most drugs that are approved by the FDA are studied in large, clinical trials. A randomized controlled trial (RCT) is considered the most rigorous and reliable way to see whether a drug works. In these studies, participants are randomly assigned to either receive the experimental drug or to receive a placebo, or an inactive drug. Usually neither the researcher nor the participant knows which group they are in during the study, in order to minimize bias. The effects are then compared in the two groups. Often, multiple trials are completed to measure how well a drug works, and to make sure the drug is safe in a particular population before the FDA will approve it. Many medications have not been explicitly and directly studied in RCTs, but may still have some scientific evidence, such as in open-label trials or case reports, to support their use. Therefore, many commonly used medications are prescribed and used "off-label," which means that the FDA did not specifically approve the medication for that particular use or in that specific study population.

Two medications, risperidone and aripiprazole, have been approved by the FDA to treat irritability and aggressive behaviors in persons with ASD and/or IDD. These medications are atypical antipsychotic drugs which block dopamine receptors. They have been FDA-approved as they have the most scientific evidence supporting their use specifically in people with ASD with IDD. Risperidone is the most extensively studied and was approved in 2006, and aripiprazole was approved in 2009. Risperidone has been shown to be effective in treating agitation, aggression, motor stereotypies, hyperactivity, and impulsivity. When risperidone and aripiprazole were compared to each other, studies either showed no significant difference, or slight increase in effectiveness but also side effects with risperidone. Both medications have been less well studied in adults.

Most drugs that are commonly used have not been directly studied in people with DS, or in those with DS-ASD. Given the scarcity of evidence and experience with psychiatric or behavioral medication treatment in DS and DS-ASD, most clinicians make decisions that are learned from experience in other populations. Most prescribing is off-label with clinical decisions about medication made on a case-by-case basis depending on various factors, such as medical history, behavioral profile, and known side effect profiles. Some clinicians may not be comfortable with off-label prescribing for people with DS-ASD, especially given their potential health complexity. As a result, families may have difficulty finding providers with the expertise to treat these behaviors and psychiatric conditions.

PSYCHIATRIC AND BEHAVIORAL MEDICATION RESEARCH STUDIES IN DOWN SYNDROME

There are currently no psychiatric nor behavioral medication approaches to enhance cognition in people with DS and IDD. There are a few randomized controlled trials (RCT) available that target individuals with DS, particularly those trials testing cognitive-enhancing drugs (Hefti & Blanco, 2017). While the rationale for recommending acetylcholinesterase inhibitors (AChE) (donepezil, galantamine, rivastigmine) and/or glutamate antagonists (memantine) in adults with DS and early dementia (Prasher, 2004), is sound, the results of several RCTs have been disappointing (Boada et al., 2012; Hanney et al., 2012; Kishnani et al., 2009). Antioxidant supplementation for dementia has also shown a lack of benefit (Lott et al., 2011). In children with DS, there is a colorful history of using various vitamins, supplements, and metabolic precursors in attempts to improve cognitive outcomes with no success (Ellis et al., 2008; Roizen, 2005; Salman, 2002). A large RCT using the AChE donepezil and a smaller study using the dual-cholinesterase inhibitor rivastigmine have also failed to demonstrate benefit in children and adolescents (Kishnani et al., 2010; Spiridigliozzi et al., 2016). Co-occurring behavioral and psychiatric disorders are common, estimated in 20%–35% of people with DS, and are common targets of psychopharmacological treatments (Dykens et al., 2015), and are likely more common in those with DS-ASD. Experience using psychotropic medications has been reported in adolescents and adults with DS. There are several small case series reporting clinical experience using psychotropic medications (lithium; anticonvulsant mood stabilizers; benzodiazepines; tricyclic antidepressants; selective serotonin reuptake inhibitors; and first and second generation antipsychotics) for the treatment of mood-anxiety disorders, obsessive-compulsive disorder, agitation, functional decline and psychosis in adults with DS (Akahoshi et al., 2012; Palumbo & McDougle, 2018; Sutor et al., 2006; Walker et al., 2011). Unfortunately, there are no RCTs specifically testing psychotropic medication for behavioral or psychiatric indications in children or adults with DS. There are two studies in children with DS targeting symptoms of inattention, hyperactivity, impulsivity, and disruptive behavior (Capone et al., 2016; Roche et al., 2021), and another targeting DS-ASD (Capone et al., 2008), as seen in table 6.1.

Table 6.1: Psychopharmacological Research Studies in Down Syndrome

Atypical Antipsychotics:

The effectiveness of risperidone in treating disruptive behaviors and self-injury was investigated in an open-label study in 23 participants with DS-ASD whose mean age was 7.8 (±2.6) years (Capone et al., 2008). Most participants had severe intellectual disability (ID). The study used the Aberrant Behavior Checklist-Community (ABC-C), which is a 58-item rating scale used to assess maladaptive behaviors across five original dimensions or subscales: Irritability, Hyperactivity, Lethargy/Withdrawal, Stereotypy, and Inappropriate Speech. Participants showed significant improvement in all five subscales following treatment with risperidone. The mean duration of treatment was 95.8 ± 16.8 days, and the average total daily dosage was 0.66 ± 0.28mg/day.

The Hyperactivity, Stereotypy and Lethargy subscale scores showed the most significant reduction followed by Irritability, and Inappropriate Speech. Children with disruptive behavior and self-injury showed the greatest improvement. Sleep quality also improved for 88% of the subjects with preexisting sleep disturbance. Subjects for whom a follow-up weight was available showed an average weight increase of 2.8 kg or 6.1 lbs during the treatment period. Low-dose risperidone was otherwise well tolerated, though concerns about weight gain and metabolic alterations were discussed. The ABC-C findings supported clinical impressions of improvement on important target behaviors such as aggression, self-injury, stereotypy as well as social withdrawal.

Alpha$_{2A}$-adrenergic agonists:

Capone et al. (2016) conducted a single open-label trial which supported the use of guanfacine in DS and attention deficit hyperactivity disorder (ADHD). All 23 of the participants in the trial had ADHD and disruptive behavior. Guanfacine was hypothesized to reduce hyperactivity, impulsivity, aggression, and related disruptive behaviors. Guanfacine was initiated at bedtime in every participant, then adjusted as required targeting daytime symptoms. Five participants received only bedtime dosing, 13 received twice daily, and five received thrice daily dosing. After 4 to 6 months of treatment, significant decreases were observed on the parent-reported ABC-C Hyperactivity and Irritability scales as well as the composite score. The ABC-C findings supported clinical impressions of improvement on target behaviors. Prior sleep disturbance was reported in 16 participants and improved in 14 (88%). Treatment emergent side effects (daytime sedation, dry mouth, lower blood pressure) were acceptably low.

Psychostimulants:
Methylphenidate was studied in a small retrospective observational study in DS and ADHD and was found to be effective in 76% of cases, and most common side effects were loss of appetite and difficulty falling sleep, with 57% experiencing side effects, most which were not severe enough to interrupt treatment (Roche et al., 2021).

PSYCHIATRIC AND BEHAVIORAL MEDICATION RESEARCH STUDIES IN AUTISM SPECTRUM DISORDER

Compared to people with DS, many more different pharmacological agents have been studied in those with ASD. This includes research studies investigating drugs targeting core symptoms of ASD based on proposed pathophysiological processes (Howes et al., 2018; Thom et al., 2021). While some of these have shown promise for treating core impairments in ASD (e.g., vasopressin, oxytocin, memantine for social impairment; folinic acid for language impairment), at this time there is insufficient evidence to recommend their routine clinical use (Thom et al., 2021).

Psychiatric and behavioral medication treatments are very commonly used in children and adults with ASD. A large, national population-based study looking at managed health plan claims revealed that more than half of children and adults with ASD in the US received a prescription for a psychotropic medication (Feroe et al., 2021). Research studies have demonstrated effectiveness of many pharmacological agents used to treat co-occurring behavioral and psychiatric conditions in ASD (Howes et al., 2018; Persico et al., 2021; Thom et al., 2021). There are far more RCTs in children and adolescents than in adults, however, these studies have not included individuals with DS-ASD, as presented in table 6.2.

Table 6.2: Psychiatric and Behavioral Medication Research Studies in Autism Spectrum Disorder

Atypical antipsychotics:

As previously mentioned, two medications, risperidone and aripiprazole have been approved by the FDA to treat irritability and aggressive behaviors in children with ASD. These medications have been shown to decrease repetitive behaviors and stereotypy when compared to placebo, and to improve obsessive-compulsive and anxiety symptoms. However, these were not the primary targets of the studies, and participants were enrolled into the clinical trial based on high levels of irritability, not repetitive behaviors, or anxiety, or obsessive-compulsive symptoms.

Alpha$_{2A}$-adrenergic agonists:

Guanfacine and clonidine, have been used to target behavior, attention deficits, hyperactivity, impulsivity, aggression, as well as sleep symptoms. They have also been studied and shown to be effective in children with ASD. Benefits have primarily been observed in those with co-occurring attention deficit hyperactivity disorder (ADHD).

Psychostimulants:

Methylphenidate has been the most studied stimulant for children with ASD who also have high levels of ADHD symptoms. While methylphenidate has been shown to be an effective treatment for ADHD symptoms in children with ASD, the response rates are less than in those who have ADHD without ASD, and they experience greater severity of common side effects, such as irritability, emotional outbursts, and insomnia. There is very little evidence to guide treatment of ADHD symptoms in adults with ASD, who may respond less well to stimulants. With regards to core symptoms, subanalyses of studies of methylphenidate in children with ASD and ADHD symptoms revealed dose-dependent improvements in joint attention and self-regulation in those on methylphenidate compared to placebo. However, it wasn't clear whether these results were mediated by improvement in the ADHD symptoms, and there is no current evidence to suggest that methylphenidate would be useful for social communication skills in those with ASD who do not have high levels of ADHD symptoms. Amphetamine mixed salts have been far less studied in children with ASD than methylphenidate-based stimulants.

Other Non-Stimulant ADHD Medications:

Atomoxetine, which is a non-stimulant medication for ADHD has also been used in ASD, with two studies showing improvement in symptoms of hyperactivity but not inattention. The most common side effects with atomoxetine are nausea, fatigue, and sleep difficulty. Amantadine, which is a N-methyl-D-aspartate (NMDA) receptor blocker has also been studied in ASD, and may be effective at reducing hyperactivity, inattention, and irritability in children and adolescents with ASD. Insomnia and somnolence have both been reported as side effects.

Selective serotonin reuptake inhibitors (SSRIs):

There are few rigorous studies investigating the role of SSRIs in treating mood and anxiety disorders in ASD and much of their use is largely extrapolated from the general population. In studies in ASD, fluoxetine seems to be the best tolerated, and there is some data to support use in adults for repetitive behaviors (Howes et al., 2018). For depression, only fluoxetine was studied in adults with ASD, with no change in depressive symptoms relative to placebo. There have been a few smaller studies of SSRIs for treatment of anxiety and OCD symptoms in adults with ASD, including fluoxetine and fluvoxamine. Fluoxetine has been shown to improve obsessions and possibly compulsions; fluvoxamine reduced both obsessions and compulsions in a small study. Different SSRIs have not been studied head-to-head against each other.

Anxiolytics:

Buspirone, an "atypical" anxiolytic has been used to treat generalized anxiety disorder in the general population and has been tested in some studies in ASD. Some studies show that at low doses it may be efficacious for anxiety and irritability, and possibly restrictive/repetitive behaviors, but there seems to be large interindividual variability and difference in dose tolerability.

Acute anxiolytics such as benzodiazepines have not been well studied in ASD compared to other drug classes.

Antiepileptic medications and mood stabilizers:

Antiepileptic medications and mood stabilizers have also been studied in ASD to address irritability and behavioral symptoms. Valproate, levetiracetam, topiramate, lamotrigine, carbamazepine, oxcarbazepine, and lithium have been studied yielding mixed results with great interindividual variability among both responders and nonresponders, and variability in severity and frequency of side effects. (Note: See also section on Epilepsy below.)

Cannabidiol (CBD):

Irritability was studied in a 12-week crossover design of CBD and whole-plant cannabis extract in 150 individuals with ASD, ages 5–21 years. CBD was not associated with improvement in disruptive behaviors compared to placebo; however improvement was seen with whole-plant cannabis extract (Aran et al., 2021).

TREATMENT APPROACH AND CONSIDERATIONS IN DS-ASD

Many parents and primary care pediatricians will prefer to utilize low-risk, developmentally based interventions, or other techniques in young children before considering the use of medications. Only when developmental progress becomes stifled and chronic behavioral problems ensue will most parents avail themselves to try "whatever may help," including medications. It seems unfortunate that so many choose this entry into medications, as a last resort, for it is likely that prompt management of physiological-based behavioral symptoms may permit educational interventions and behavioral strategies to proceed more successful early on. Given the scarcity of evidence and experience with psychopharmacological treatment in DS, but especially in those with DS-ASD, most clinicians make decisions that are extrapolated from experience in other populations. In general, in children with DS, as well as in those with DS-ASD, problem behaviors are common, and most often occur within a setting of atypical cognitive-language function, and inconsistent progress achieving or demonstrating developmental skills.

Differences in patterns of symptoms are often observed in different age groups. Externalizing symptoms (such as disruptive behavior, aggression, hyperactivity, and impulsivity) tend to be more common in younger children, whereas older children and adolescents may manifest more internalizing symptoms (social withdrawal, apathy, depressed mood). Repetitive motor behaviors and sensory aversions may appear or intensify over time. Some degree of peculiar sensory responding, anxiety, and sleep disturbance are often present. In adolescents, once puberty begins, it is not unusual for new onset psychiatric symptoms affecting mood, repetitive thoughts/action, attention/ cognitive organization, sociability, motivation/initiative, or sleep to present anew. While symptoms of mood, anxiety, or thought disorder can be seen across all levels of cognitive function, psychiatric symptoms are more readily noticed in those with higher cognitive-language function and lower social-adaptive skill. Adolescence tends to be a vulnerable time due to both physiological changes, as well as rapid transition across family-social-educational-workplace settings. Parental expectations for behavioral self-regulation and appropriate social function are often a high priority at this time, yet not all younger adults are able to meet these demands easily.

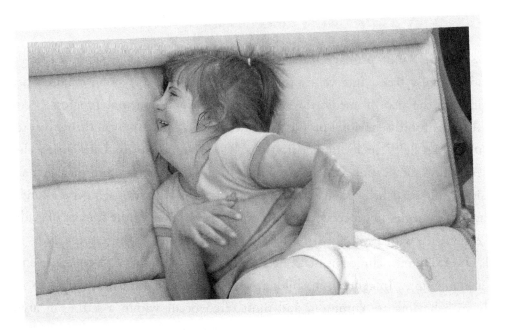

Psychosocial and environmental stressors can also impact symptoms and behaviors. Significant transition or loss of services, such as in early adulthood when school services come to an end and adult programming and services have not yet been established, can be a vulnerable period for emergence of mood and behavioral problems. The extended period of self-isolation due to the SARS-2/COVID-19 pandemic is another example of this. Distinguishing the physiologic component of psychiatric symptomatology within the setting of problem behavior is often difficult, yet critical because it helps to prioritize and set realistic expectations for pharmacologic, behavioral, and educational treatments going forward.

One of the most elusive, but fundamentally important goals of pharmacotherapy in DS-ASD is to improve physiologic regulation, sleep-wake cycles, activity-impulsivity, attention, and emotional self-regulation. Improvements in behavioral self-regulation with concurrent reduction in the intensity, severity, or duration of maladaptive behaviors often occurs once impulse control, overactivity, sleep disturbance, anxiety-mood state, and cognitive disorganization are addressed. In many individuals, successful management of these physiologically based behavioral symptoms may permit subsequent neuromaturation to proceed, so that learning, communication, and social function are able to progress. In the following sections, we provide a symptom-based approach to pharmacological treatment in DS-ASD.

CO-OCCURRING PSYCHIATRIC CONDITIONS AND TARGET SYMPTOM TREATMENT APPROACHES FOR DS-ASD

Irritability, Aggression, Self-Injurious Behavior

It is not uncommon for children with DS-ASD to show irritability, aggression, and self-injurious behaviors (skin picking/scratching, biting, head banging). Medication choice should be selected based on target symptoms with priority given to those most functionally impairing or most likely to result in harm or other safety concerns. These symptoms can be treated with many different pharmacological options. For example anticonvulsant mood stabilizers (oxcarbazepine, lamotragine, or valproic acid and derivatives) or atypical antipsychotics (AAP) (risperidone, aripiprazole, or quetiapine) for irritability, self-injury, mood dysregulation and sleep, or $alpha_{2A}$-adrenergic agonists (guanfacine or clonidine) for hyperactivity, impulsivity, restlessness, and sleep disturbance. Depending on symptom severity and complexity it is often wise to start with clonidine or guanfacine given at bedtime and morning to mitigate problems with sleep, hyperactivity, and impulsivity. Each of these medications are also available in extended release formulations to reduce the need for repeat dosing during the day. When titrated slowly upward, effects on blood pressure (BP), dry mouth, constipation, and daytime sedation can be minimized. Additionally, ensuring fluid and salt intake to avoid dehydration particularly during the summer, and use of a bowel regimen as needed for constipation can mitigate these side effects.

Antipsychotic medications can be quite effective when irritability, aggression, or self-injury are severe. Initiation of risperidone at bedtime and/or daytime can result in rapid de-escalation of symptoms in the short term. Slow upward titration allows daytime sedation to be avoided in most patients. Over the long-term these medications are associated with potentially serious side effects (see table 6.3). Therefore, while these medications may be the most efficacious, their clinical use requires discretion due to potential side effects, in those with higher risk of obesity and consequent health concerns (type-2 diabetes, hyperlipidemia, sleep apnea). It remains a challenge for clinicians to monitor any real benefit from these medicines in exchange for an acceptable level of risk due to unwanted side effects. Sometimes the trade-off between improved emotional-behavioral control and some degree of weight gain is deemed acceptable. In some cases, adding medication such as metformin can mitigate weight gain and elevated blood sugars.

Attention, Hyperactivity, Impulsivity

Children with DS-ASD can also have co-occurring ADHD. Early signs of ADHD can manifest in young children prior to 3–5 years, but may be regarded as "developmentally consistent" with overall cognitive function. However, as a child gets older, if these symptoms persist or intensify parents or teachers will often request an evaluation to seek further clarification. ADHD is diagnosed by the presence of inattention, impulsivity and/or motor hyperactivity disproportionate to developmental level, resulting in significant academic or social impairment. When all these symptoms are present, we diagnose the condition as ADHD (combined); when hyperactivity and impulsivity predominate, we diagnose the condition as ADHD-HI, when inattention and problems focusing predominate, we would diagnose it as ADHD-I. Difficulty obtaining a child's cooperation and oppositional-resistant behavior may emerge despite good language comprehension. Since ADHD, particularly hyperactivity/impulsivity symptoms, place any child with DS at especially high risk for elopement, accidental injury, and even maltreatment, these symptoms deserve careful consideration even in the youngest children (Capone et al., 2006).

Clinical practice suggests that some children with DS or ASD (and DS-ASD) may not tolerate stimulant medications such as methylphenidate and its derivatives at commonly prescribed doses and may demonstrate a greater degree of common side effects, and less improvement in symptoms compared to those with ADHD alone. Additionally, whenever anxiety, perseveration, repetitiveness, or agitation are already present, stimulant medications can exacerbate these features. For these reasons, alpha agonists are commonly used as first-line treatment. These medications can be sedating, and therefore beneficial when sleep is also disrupted, particularly as psychostimulants can contribute to insomnia and further sleep difficulty. Generally, guanfacine is considered less sedating than clonidine, a factor to be considered when selecting a first-line treatment for ADHD-HI. The later introduction of a low-dose psychostimulant in the daytime for improved attention at school is then often well tolerated. Physicians may require this type of explicit guidance on the rational use of polypharmacy when prescribing and monitoring psychostimulants used in combination with alpha agonists.

Mood Disorders

Mood disorders are very common in children and adults with DS and DS-ASD with symptoms including depressed mood, crying, decreased interest, psychomotor slowing, fatigue, appetite/weight change, and sleep disturbance commonly observed. In some females these symptoms are exacerbated just prior to onset of menses. Poor concentration, agitation, or reduced speech are also common in depression in DS, while feelings of worthlessness or guilt are less commonly present. In severe cases, self-care routines may deteriorate, requiring greater assistance or frequent prompting from caretakers. Profound loss of previously acquired skills is sometimes dramatic, but often improves with successful medication management and improved sleep (Mircher et al., 2017; Walton & Kerr, 2015).

Mood dysregulation can also present with fluctuations between "elated-giddy" and "sad-irritable," which may suggest disruptive mood dysregulation disorder (DMDD), a mixed-mood state, or a bipolar I disorder when cycles of predominately activated-elevated mood (mania) alternate with irritability-low mood (depressive) over a period of many days, weeks, or even months.

Mood (and anxiety) disorders are often treated with SSRIs, such as fluoxetine, sertraline, and citalopram. It is generally observed that children with DS and ASD may have increased sensitivity to side effects of SSRIs, and thus it is recommended that dosing be initiated at low doses with slow titration and close monitoring for side effects. In cases of mood dysregulation disorder or bipolar disorder/mania, use of SSRI antidepressants at typical adult dosages can destabilize or worsen mood fluctuation, thus an atypical antipsychotic or anticonvulsant mood stabilizer is the preferred choice initially. Symptom stabilization is achieved once the correct diagnostic formulation allows for proper medication management.

Anxiety Disorders

In addition to use of SSRIs as above for treatment of anxiety symptoms, buspirone may be used for anxiety and as it tends to have less weight gain associated with it, may be more desirable and better tolerated in children with DS. The antihistamine hydroxyzine can also be used in low doses to treat daytime situational anxiety or to improve sleep at night. Heightened anxiety can also be associated with a major depression or may become exacerbated in some females prior to onset of menstruation. Sometimes a low-dose oral estrogen contraceptive in conjunction with an SSRI is helpful.

Acute anxiolytics such as benzodiazepines have not been well studied in DS or ASD compared to other drug classes. Lorazepam is often used as an emergency room intervention for acute agitation, for pre-procedure calming, such as before dental work or blood draws. Generally, prolonged use of benzodiazepines and other GABA agonists for sleep are not recommended, due to concerns about dependence and potential impact on cognition. However, for severe anxiety which includes agitation and panic with autonomic symptoms (gagging, vomiting, fainting, or incontinence), a low dose of clonazepam in conjunction with an SSRI can be particularly helpful for some adolescents and adults.

Obsessive and Compulsive Behaviors

Obsessive-compulsive behaviors typically involve repetitive thoughts or verbalization and seemingly nonpurposeful, patterned routines. Obsessive thoughts can be difficult to ascertain in people with intellectual disability (ID) and limited expressive language skills. Repetitive, compulsive actions or movements are easier to appreciate. People with DS may have co-occurring obsessive-compulsive disorder (OCD), characterized by strong compulsions to perform certain actions, and resultant anxiety or agitation when these activities are interrupted or prohibited. These behaviors may include ordering and tidiness compulsions, especially rearranging personal belongings or opening/closing doors, cabinets, blinds, and light switches. Hoarding of seemingly worthless objects (clips, pens, papers, etc.), and repetitive list-making is commonly seen. Verbal perseveration on past events or relationships, movie characters, or the need to ask repeatedly about upcoming events can be challenging for caretakers.

SSRIs at higher dose than typically used for mood disorder are generally required to reduce OCD-related symptoms. However, SSRIs may not be tolerated due to emergent side effects such as abdominal cramping, headache, or behavioral activation. It may be necessary to combine an SSRI with a low-dose benzodiazepine (clonazepam) for perseveration, anxiety, and panic. Other approaches include switching to a SNRI (serotonin and norepinephrine reuptake inhibitor, such as venlafaxine), using an older tricyclic antidepressant (e.g., clomipramine), or adding an atypical antipsychotic (Sutor et al., 2006). It is probably not realistic to strive for zero-tolerance of repetitive behaviors as they can represent a manifestation of the behavioral phenotype common in many children and adults with DS (Capone et al., 2006; Evans & Gray, 2000; Glenn et al., 2015).

Repetitive Movements and Stereotypy

Stereotypies, including repetitive, rhythmic, or shaking movements, body rocking, shaking, flapping, vocalizations, and repetitive play are common in children with DS, and especially in those with DS-ASD. While no medication is FDA-approved to treat stereotypies, many children appear to improve some when antipsychotic medications are used to treat other symptoms (Capone et al., 2006, 2008).

Thought Disorder and Psychosis

Disorganized thought processing, inattention, delusional thinking, paranoia, episodic panic and agitation, self-talk, or actual hallucination can lend complexity to the interpretation of psychiatric symptoms and their treatment in people with intellectual disability. Anxiety and verbal perseveration may be prominent features in some individuals, but when delusions, hallucinations, or paranoia are present a psychosis or psychotic-like disorder may be diagnosed. Psychosis may occur in the setting of a major depression accompanied by some loss of previously established skills. Typically, it is beneficial to start with an atypical antipsychotic such as risperidone, aripiprazole, or olanzapine given at bedtime to help improve both disordered sleep and daytime symptoms. If psychotic disorganization improves but mood or anxiety or compulsive features persist, an SSRI can be added.

It is important not to ascribe increased self-talk, which can occur during times of stress or isolation, as prima facie evidence of a psychosis, as self-talk is common in persons with intellectual disability (ID) and can serve as an adaptive strategy (self-coaching, calming) in times of stress (Capone et al., 2006).

Neuromotor Function

It is not unusual for young adults to demonstrate some reduction in initiative or spontaneity, often with slowing of motor activities. This is common around the time of transition from school to community-based adult program and may be part of an adjustment process. However, when neuromotor symptoms persist, intensify, or become functionally impairing, it may signal the onset of a psychiatric condition or catatonia. In some persons catatonic features include fluctuating motor tone, neuromotor rigidity, stereotypies, hand/arm posturing, specific mannerisms, or other odd movements. In such cases, a benzodiazepine such as lorazepam or clonazepam can help to reduce catatonic symptoms. When severe, functionally impairing catatonia is present, a trial of high-dose lorazepam is indicated, and electroconvulsive therapy should be strongly considered for those persons failing pharmacology trials (Ghaziuddin et al., 2015).

Sleep

In addition to obstructive sleep apnea (OSA), other types of sleep disturbance are seen in children with DS that are associated with ADHD and behavior problems and executive function (Esbensen & Hoffman, 2018; Soltani et al., 2023). Difficulty initiating sleep onset may be due to alerting nighttime activities, lack of bedtime routine, anxiety-fearfulness, behavioral resistance, or excessive daytime napping (see chapter eight on sleep problems). Difficulties remaining asleep (maintenance) or repeated awakenings during the night may be due to untreated sleep apnea, periodic limb movement disorders, or the "restless" sleep pattern sometimes seen in conjunction with psychiatric symptoms (ADHD, ASD, anxiety, mood disorders). Some of the medications under consideration for psychiatric symptoms have sedating properties that make their use at bedtime convenient for improving sleep onset or maintenance and could be used strategically for this purpose, despite some concerns about worsening gas exchange during OSA (Taranto-Montemurro et al., 2019). A few studies even suggest improvement in apnea-hypopnea index when using the antidepressant mirtazapine.

Sleep-related problems due to obstructive sleep apnea may also result in nighttime awakening. OSA is typically associated with snoring, increased airway resistance, respiratory pauses or gasping, leading to an arousal in an effort to relieve the obstruction. When moderate or severe and untreated, chronic OSA will impact daytime behavior. When frequent awakening, daytime yawning, excessive fatigue, and napping are present prior to initiating medications, this should raise the suspicion of OSA. If after initiating treatment with an SSRI/SNRI a poor or only partial response is noted, ongoing sleep disturbance may be a contributing factor. Frequently, some improvement in sleep consolidation is required before complete recovery of psychiatric symptoms is to be realized. (Capone et al., 2013).

Epilepsy

Epilepsy is more common in Down syndrome, ranging from 1%–13%, and typically occurring in specific time periods: infancy/early childhood (most commonly infantile/epileptic spasms); in early adulthood; and after the fifth decade of life, also called "late onset myoclonic epilepsy in Down syndrome" (LOMEDS), which is associated with Alzheimer's disease. Those with DS-ASD may be at higher risk for epilepsy than those with DS alone. Infantile spasms may be a specific risk factor for ASD in DS. Diagnosis, classification, and treatment approaches for epilepsy in DS and in DS-ASD do not differ from the general population, primarily because there is not enough evidence to support a different epilepsy treatment approach for DS or ASD. It should also be noted that most antiepileptic medications have not been studied specifically in DS, but many have been studied in children generally. A comprehensive review of epilepsy diagnosis and management is beyond the scope of this chapter. However, epilepsy is an important consideration for pharmacological treatment in DS-ASD

Epilepsies are described and classified according to specific features, such as the seizure type (manifesting as motor symptoms, staring off, sensory symptoms, and the impact on the person's awareness or consciousness during an event), as well as the nature

of the seizure onset and brain region(s) involved (focal onset arising from a specific area of the brain, or generalized onset arising from all areas of the brain). All major seizure types have been described in DS. Pharmacological treatment is the primary way of treating epilepsy, and different types of antiseizure medications work better for different types of seizures. Additional considerations for treatment choice include the side effect profile, convenience of use, and cost. There are "narrow spectrum" antiseizure medications that typically work for a specific type of seizure, such as a partial, focal, absence, or myoclonic seizure, as well as "broad spectrum" antiseizure medications that can be used for a wide variety of seizure types, including generalized seizures. Recommendations for antiseizure medications are typically based on research studies from the general population, and not necessarily a population of individuals with ID or ASD.

Specifically for individuals with DS-ASD, there are some considerations that may be helpful when choosing antiseizure medications. Some medications used to treat seizures may also be helpful for psychiatric symptoms commonly associated with ASD, such as irritability, mood dysregulation, and aggression. These may include carbamazepine and oxcarbazepine for focal/partial seizures, and valproate and lamotrigine for a broad range of seizure types. Some antiseizure medications have particular adverse effect profiles that must be weighed against the individual's specific profile. For example, some antiseizure medications have a greater potential for negative cognitive effects (phenobarbital, phenytoin, topiramate, zonisamide), or psychiatric or behavioral side effects (levetiracetam). Careful coordination and assessment of drug interactions is also needed when using antiseizure medications along with other psychopharmacological treatments for behavioral and mental health symptoms. For further reading on epilepsy treatment in neurodevelopmental disabilities, please see Frye, et al. (2013), Watkins et al. (2022), and Canitano et al. (2022).

Rational Polypharmacy

Choosing a medication that may have a dual effect on multiple targets can be very helpful, and in some cases can avoid polypharmacy. For example, the use of an antiepileptic medication with mood-stabilizing properties may be a good first choice for someone with both seizures and mood concerns. Additionally, an alpha agonist may be beneficial for someone with sleep disturbance and ADHD symptoms.

In cases with very complex psychiatric symptomatology, rational polypharmacy may be required. In urgent situations, it makes sense to target the most functionally impairing symptoms first to afford prompt symptom relief.

Generally, antidepressant/antianxiety medications can be used in conjunction with an atypical antipsychotic or anticonvulsant mood stabilizer with good safety, tolerability, and efficacy. Importantly, the order in which medications are introduced, based on target symptom prioritization, seems to be important for producing the best response. It appears for instance that many antidepressants work best for mood, anxiety, and OCD when sleep disorders are treated at the outset. However, obtaining a sleep evaluation or any recommendation for airway management using Positive Airway Pressure (PAP) may be difficult to achieve prior to alleviating psychiatric symptoms. Therefore, pending improvements in anxiety, irritability, mood, and maladaptive behaviors using medication, it then may be possible to obtain a diagnostic polysomnogram (PSG) to determine if OSA is present and requires specific treatment.

Alpha agonists can be used in conjunction with psychostimulants to manage ADHD. Whenever anxiety, perseveration, repetitiveness, or agitation is already present, stimulant medications can exacerbate these features. For these reasons, alpha agonists are commonly used as first-line treatment. The later introduction of a low-dose psychostimulant in the daytime for improved attention at school is then often better tolerated.

Table 6.3: Overview of Medication Classes, Target Symptoms, Common Side Effects, and Treatment Considerations

Medication Class	Target Symptoms	Common Side Effects / Considerations
Alpha Agonists		
Clonidine*# Guanfacine*#	Hyperactivity/Impulsivity Inattention Aggression Sleep	Drowsiness, dizziness, lowered blood pressure and heart rate, constipation, dry mouth #clonidine more sedating than guanfacine

Stimulants		
Methylphenidate* Dexmethylphenidate* Mixed amphetamine salts* Dextroamphetamine*	Hyperactivity/Impulsivity Inattention Alertness	Decreased appetite, insomnia, emotional problems/anxiety, agitation/irritability, tachycardia Start with lowest possible starting dose; escalate to effect/tolerability
Nonstimulants		
Atomoxetine Bupropion*	Hyperactivity/Impulsivity Inattention	Drowsiness, GI symptoms, worsening depression, suicidality
Selective Serotonin Reuptake Inhibitors (SSRIs)		
Fluoxetine Citalopram Sertraline Paroxetine	Mood Disorder Anxiety Obsessive-compulsive behaviors Premenstrual dysphoria Repetitive behaviors Social withdrawal Sleep	Drowsiness, GI symptoms, worsening depression, suicidality Note: Black box warning
Older Antidepressants		
Clomipramine (TCA) Trazodone (SRI) #	Mood Disorder Anxiety Obsessive-compulsive behaviors Sleep	Trazodone often used alone for sleep
Atypical Antipsychotics (AAP)		
Aripiprazole# Risperidone # Olanzapine# Quetiapine*# Ziprasidone# Lurasidone#	Psychosis Irritability Aggressive behavior Self-injurious behavior Behavioral disorganization Sleep Repetitive behaviors Restricted interests	Increased appetite, weight gain, sleepiness, involuntary movements/extrapyramidal symptoms, diabetes/high cholesterol, high prolactin

Typical Antipsychotics (AP)		
Perphenazine# Haloperidol#	Psychosis Irritability Aggressive behavior Self-injurious behavior Behavioral disorganization Sleep	Sleepiness, involuntary movements
Anticonvulsants (AED)		
Valproate* Carbamazepine* Oxcarbazepine* Lamotrigine* Levetiracetam*	Mood lability Irritability Self-injury Bipolar (manic-depressive) Seizures	Need to monitor blood levels (liver, blood counts, chemistries), behavior problems, rash
Anxiolytic		
Buspirone Gabapentin#	Anxiety Sleep	Nausea, headache, dizziness/light headedness
Benzodiazepines		
Lorazepam# Clonazepam# Diazepam	Acute anxiety/panic Agitation Seizures/epilepsy Sleep Pre-procedure sedation	Sleepiness Dependency Cognitive blunting
Antihistamine		
Hydroxyzine# Diphenhydramine#	Anxiety Sleep	Dry mouth

Table Legend:

*Available as long-acting formulation
Helpful for sleep

CONCLUSION

Here, we have reviewed currently available research studies of pharmacological treatment in DS and ASD. However, most medication recommendations are extrapolated from research and experience from other populations, and not specifically studied in DS or DS-ASD. We have provided a practical pharmacological treatment approach for management of symptoms such as aggression, impulsivity, anxiety, sleep, and problem behaviors that interfere with health, safety, learning, and community participation for those with DS-ASD. The decision whether to trial a certain medication class in any individual should consider the severity, intensity, and urgency of symptom management. It is difficult to predict how an individual will respond to taking any medication, and positive responses can be subtle. Additionally, when positive or negative responses do occur, it can be difficult to know if those changes are the result of the medication itself, another intervention, or expected variation in baseline behavioral status. Sometimes, the only way to know if a medication is helpful or effective is to try to lower the dose or stop the medication and observe for reemergence of the target symptoms. It is encouraging to note that in some cases, successful management of physiological-based behavioral symptoms allows educational interventions and behavioral strategies to proceed more successfully. For these reasons, it is helpful to work with a medical provider who has experience with children or adults with DS, intellectual disability, or ASD.

KEY POINTS

1. There is very little research of medications specifically in children or adults with DS and with DS-ASD.
2. There are currently two FDA-approved medications that target irritability and aggression in Intellectual and Developmental Disability (IDD) and ASD.
3. Most medication use in DS is extrapolated from other populations.
4. Medications are chosen based on target symptoms and side effect profile.
5. Medications should be used in conjunction with educational, behavioral, and other therapeutic intervention strategies.

REFERENCES

Akahoshi, K., Matsuda, H., Funahashi, M., Hanaoka, T., & Suzuki, Y. (2012). Acute neuropsychiatric disorders in adolescents and young adults with Down syndrome: Japanese case reports. *Neuropsychiatric Disease and Treatment, 8*, 339–345. https://doi.org/10.2147/NDT.S32767

Aran, A., Harel, M., Cassuto, H., Polyansky, L., Schnapp, A., Wattad, N., Shmueli, D., Golan, D., & Castellanos, F. X. (2021). Cannabinoid treatment for autism: a proof-of-concept randomized trial. *Molecular Autism, 12*(6), 1–11. https://doi.org/10.1186/s13229-021-00420-2

Boada, R., Hutaff-Lee, C., Schrader, A., Weitzenkamp, D., Benke, T. A., Goldson, E. J., & Costa, A. C. S. (2012). Antagonism of NMDA receptors as a potential treatment for Down syndrome: a pilot randomized controlled trial. *Translational Psychiatry, 2*(7), 1–11. https://doi.org/10.1038/tp.2012.66

Canitano, R., Palumbi, R., & Scandurra, V. (2022). Autism with epilepsy: A neuropsychopharmacology update. *Genes, 13*(10), 1–10. https://doi.org/10.3390/genes13101821

Capone, G. T., Aidikoff, J. M., Taylor, K., & Rykiel, N. (2013). Adolescents and young adults with Down syndrome presenting to a medical clinic with depression: Co-morbid obstructive sleep apnea. *American Journal of Medical Genetics Part A, 161*(9), 2188–2196. https://doi.org/10.1002/ajmg.a.36052

Capone, G. T., Brecher, L., & Bay, M. (2016). Guanfacine use in children with Down syndrome and comorbid Attention-Deficit Hyperactivity Disorder (ADHD) with disruptive behaviors. *Journal of Child Neurology, 31*(8), 957–964. https://doi.org/10.1177/0883073816634854

Capone, G. T., Goyal, P., Ares, W., & Lannigan, E. (2006). Neurobehavioral disorders in children, adolescents, and young adults with Down syndrome. *American Journal of Medical Genetics Part C: Seminars in Medical Genetics, 142C*(3), 158–172. https://doi.org/10.1002/ajmg.c.30097

Capone, G. T., Goyal, P., Grados, M., Smith, B., & Kammann, H. (2008). Risperidone use in children with Down syndrome, severe intellectual disability, and comorbid Autistic Spectrum Disorders: A naturalistic study. *Journal of Developmental and Behavioral Pediatrics, 29*(2), 106–116. https://doi.org/10.1097/DBP.0b013e318165c100

Dykens, E. M., Shah, B., Davis, B., Baker, C., Fife, T., & Fitzpatrick, J. (2015). Psychiatric disorders in adolescents and young adults with Down syndrome and other intellectual disabilities. *Journal of Neurodevelopmental Disorders, 7*(1), 1–9. https://doi.org/10.1186/s11689-015-9101-1

Ellis, J. M., Tan, H. K., Gilbert, R. E., Muller, D. P. R., Henley, W., Moy, R., Pumphrey, R., Ani, C., Davies, S., Edwards, V., Green, H., Salt, A., & Logan, S. (2008). Supplementation with antioxidants and folinic acid for children with Down's syndrome: randomised controlled trial. *The BMJ, 336*(7644), 1–7. https://doi.org/10.1136/bmj.39465.544028.AE

Esbensen, A. J., & Hoffman, E. K. (2018). Impact of sleep on executive functioning in school-age children with Down syndrome. *Journal of Intellectual Disability Research, 62*(6), 569-580. https://doi.org/10.1111/jir.12496

Evans, D. W., & Gray, F. L. (2000). Compulsive-like behavior in individuals with Down syndrome: its relation to mental age level, adaptive and maladaptive behavior. *Child Development, 71*(2), 288–300. https://doi.org/10.1111/1467-8624.00144

Feroe, A. G., Uppal, N., Gutiérrez-Sacristán, A., Mousavi, S., Greenspun, P., Surati, R., Kohane, I. S., & Avillach, P. (2021). Medication use in the management of comorbidities among individuals with Autism Spectrum Disorder from a large nationwide insurance database. *JAMA Pediatrics, 175*(9), 957–965. https://doi.org/10.1001/jamapediatrics.2021.1329

Frye, R. E., Rossignol, D., Casanova, M. F., Brown, G. L., Martin, V., Edelson, S., Coben, R., Lewine, J., Slattery, J. C., Lau, C., Hardy, P., Fatemi, S. H., Folsom, T. D., MacFabe, D., & Adams, J. B. (2013). A review of traditional and novel treatments for seizures in autism spectrum disorder: findings from a systematic review and expert panel. *Frontiers in Public Health, 1*(2013), 1–26. https://doi.org/10.3389/fpubh.2013.00031

Ghaziuddin, N., Nassiri, A., & Miles, J. (2015). Catatonia in Down syndrome; A treatable cause of regression. *Neuropsychiatric Disease and Treatment, 11*, 941-949. https://doi.org/10.2147/NDT.S77307

Glenn, S., Cunningham, C., Nananidou, A., Prasher, V., & Glenholmes, P. (2015). Routinised and compulsive-like behaviours in individuals with Down syndrome. *Journal of Intellectual Disability Research, 59*(11), 1061–1070. https://doi.org/10.1111/jir.12199

Hanney, M., Prasher, V., Williams, N., Jones, E. L., Aarsland, D., Corbett, A., Lawrence, D., Yu, L. M., Tyrer, S., Francis, P. T., Johnson, T., Bullock, R., & Ballard, C. (2012). Memantine for dementia in adults older than 40 years with Down's syndrome (MEADOWS): a randomised, double-blind, placebo-controlled trial. *The Lancet, 379*(9815), 528–536. https://doi.org/10.1016/S0140-6736(11)61676-0

Hefti, E., & Blanco, J. G. (2017). Pharmacotherapeutic considerations for individuals with Down syndrome. *Pharmacotherapy: The Journal of Human Pharmacology and Drug Therapy, 37*(2), 214–220. https://doi.org/10.1002/phar.1880

Howes, O. D., Rogdaki, M., Findon, J. L., Wichers, R. H., Charman, T., King, B. H., Loth, E., McAlonan, G. M., McCracken, J. T., Parr, J. R., Povey, C., Santosh, P., Wallace, S., Simonoff, E., & Murphy, D. G. (2018). Autism spectrum disorder: Consensus guidelines on assessment, treatment and research from the British Association for Psychopharmacology. *Journal of Psychopharmacology, 32*(1), 3–29. https://doi.org/10.1177/0269881117741766

Kishnani, P. S., Heller, J. H., Spiridigliozzi, G. A., Lott, I., Escobar, L., Richardson, S., Zhang, R., & McRae, T. (2010). Donepezil for treatment of cognitive dysfunction in children with Down syndrome aged 10–17. *American Journal of Medical Genetics Part A, 152A*(12), 3028–3035. https://doi.org/10.1002/ajmg.a.33730

Kishnani, P. S., Sommer, B. R., Handen, B. L., Seltzer, B., Capone, G. T., Spiridigliozzi, G. A., Heller, J. H., Richardson, S., & McRae, T. (2009). The efficacy, safety, and tolerability of donepezil for the treatment of young adults with Down syndrome. *American Journal of Medical Genetics Part A, 149A*(8), 1641–1654. https://doi.org/10.1002/ajmg.a.32953

Lott, I. T., Doran, E., Nguyen, V. Q., Tournay, A., Head, E., & Gillen, D. L. (2011). Down syndrome and dementia: A randomized, controlled trial of antioxidant supplementation. *American Journal of Medical Genetics Park A, 155*(8), 1939–1948. https://doi.org/10.1002/ajmg.a.34114

Mircher, C., Cieuta-Walti, C., Marey, I., Rebillat, A. S., Cretu, L., Milenko, E., Conte, M., Sturtz, F., Rethore, M. O., & Ravel, A. (2017). Acute regression in young people with Down syndrome. *Brain Sciences, 7*(6), 1–9. https://doi.org/10.3390/brainsci7060057

Palumbo, M. L., & McDougle, C. J. (2018). Pharmacotherapy of Down syndrome. *Expert Opinion on Pharmacotherapy, 19*(17), 1875–1889. https://doi.org/10.1080/14656566.2018.1529167

Persico, A. M., Ricciardello, A., Lamberti, M., Turriziani, L., Cucinotta, F., Brogna, C., Vitiello, B., & Arango, C. (2021). The pediatric psychopharmacology of autism spectrum disorder: A systematic review - Part I: The past and the present. *Progress in Neuro-Psychopharmacology and Biological Psychiatry, 110.* https://doi.org/10.1016/j.pnpbp.2021.110326

Prasher, V. P. (2004). Review of donepezil, rivastigmine, galantamine and memantine for the treatment of dementia in Alzheimer's disease in adults with Down syndrome: implications for the intellectual disability population. *International Journal of Geriatric Psychiatry, 19*(6), 509–515. https://doi.org/10.1002/gps.1077

Roche, M., Mircher, C., Toulas, J., Prioux, E., Conte, M., Ravel, A., Falquero, S., Labidi, A., Stora, S., Durand, S., Mégarbané, A., & Cieuta-Walti, C. (2021). Efficacy and safety of methylphenidate on attention deficit hyperactivity disorder in children with Down syndrome. *Journal of Intellectual Disability Research, 65*(8), 795–800. https://doi.org/10.1111/jir.12832

Roizen, N. (2005). Complementary and alternative therapies for Down syndrome. *Mental Retardation and Developmental Disabilities Research Reviews, 11*(2), 149–155. https://10.1002/mrdd.20063

Salman, M. (2002). Systematic review of the effect of therapeutic dietary supplements and drugs on cognitive function in subjects with Down syndrome. *European Journal of Paediatric Neurology, 6*(4), 213–219. https://doi.org/10.1053/ejpn.2002.0596

Soltani, A., Schworer, E. K., & Esbensen, A. J. (2023). The mediatory role of executive functioning on the association between sleep and both everyday memory and ADHD symptoms in children and youth with Down syndrome. *American Journal of Intellectual and Developmental Disability, 128*(1), 82–95. https://doi.org/10.1352/1944-7558-128.1.82

Spiridigliozzi, G. A., Hart, S. J., Heller, J. H., Schneider, H. E., Baker, J. A., Weadon, C., Capone, G. T., & Kishnani, P. S. (2016). Safety and efficacy of rivastigmine in children with Down syndrome: A double blind placebo controlled trial. *American Journal of Medical Genetics Part A, 170*(6), 1545–1555. https://doi.org/10.1002/ajmg.a.37650

Sutor, B., Hansen, M. R., & Black, J. L. (2006). Obsessive compulsive disorder treatment in patients with Down syndrome: A case series. *Downs Syndrome Research and Practice, 10*(1), 1–3. https://doi.org/10.3104/case-studies.299

Taranto-Montemurro, L., Messineo, L., Sands, S. A., Azarbarzin, A., Marques, M., Edwards, B. A., Eckert, D. J., White, D. P., & Wellman, A. (2019). The combination of atomoxetine and oxybutynin greatly reduces obstructive sleep apnea severity: A randomized, placebo-controlled, double-blind crossover trial. *American Journal of Respiratory and Critical Care Medicine, 199*(10), 1267–1276. https://doi.org/10.1164/rccm.201808-1493OC

Thom, R. P., Pereira, J. A., Sipsock, D., & McDougle, C. J. (2021). Recent updates in psychopharmacology for the core and associated symptoms of Autism Spectrum Disorder. *Current Psychiatric Reports, 23*(79). https://doi.org/10.1007/s11920-021-01292-2

Walker, J. C., Dosen, A., Buitelaar, J. K., & Janzing, J. G. (2011). Depression in Down syndrome: A review of the literature. *Research in Developmental Disabilities, 32*(5), 1432–1440. https://doi.org/10.1016/j.ridd.2011.02.010

Walton, C., & Kerr, M. (2015). Down syndrome: systematic review of the prevalence and nature of presentation of unipolar depression. *Advances in Medical Health and Intellectual Disabilities, 9*(4), 151–162. https://doi.org/10.1108/AMHID-11-2014-0037

Watkins, L. V., Linehan, C., Brandt, C., Snoeijen-Schouwenaars, F., McGowan, P., & Shankar, R. (2022). Epilepsy in adults with neurodevelopmental disability - what every neurologist should know. *Epileptic Disorders, 24*(1), 9–25. https://doi.org/10.1684/epd.2021.1366

CHAPTER SEVEN

STRATEGIES FOR SUCCESSFUL DENTAL CARE

Lauren A. Lewis, DDS

As a pediatric dentist who subspecializes in patients with special needs, I frequently hear from parents about the stress and worry they feel about their child's oral health and dental care. There are ample accessible resources elsewhere to help parents understand the developmental oral factors associated with Down syndrome and/or autism; therefore, in this chapter I will instead discuss dental care and oral health care both in the home and at the dental office. My focus in this chapter will be on developing your child's success as a dental patient and as a participant in oral health care at home, which are incredibly vital to every person's overall health.

For many parents, the search for medical specialists to aid in your child's care began at birth or shortly thereafter. At that point, your child had no teeth, so finding a dental provider was far from thought. But now your child has teeth—probably many of them and possibly even some adult teeth. Regardless of where your child is now in terms of dental development, if you don't have a dentist, now is the time to find one! If you do have a dentist, I hope you will learn something new about your child's experience in the dental office.

FINDING A GOOD FIT

The earlier you can introduce your child to dental care, the less likely your child is to need more extensive treatment later, and the easier it is for him or her to attain a level of comfort in the dental chair. For those of you with young children, I recommend starting your search by looking for a pediatric dentist in your area. Many pediatric dentists have experience treating individuals with intellectual and developmental disabilities (IDD), as well as medically compromised patients.

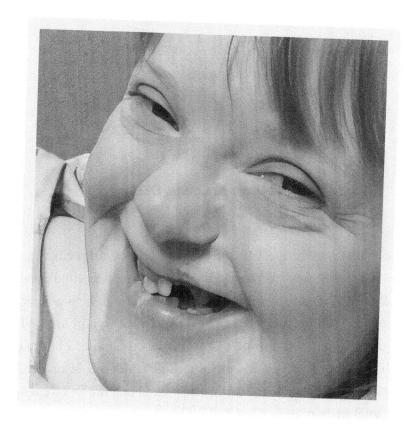

The American Academy of Pediatric Dentistry (www.aapd.org) or your state pediatric dental association is a good place to start to look for a dentist. If circumstances have delayed your ability to seek dental care for your child, please don't be discouraged. If your child is still a minor, I would again recommend looking for a pediatric dentist. If your child is an adult, you may have to look for an adult or general dentist who is familiar with treating patients with special needs, or a university- or hospital-based dental clinic. The Special Care Dentistry Association (www.scdaonline.org) is a good starting point when looking for general dentists experienced in serving patients with IDD. There are also pediatric dentists who may have age limitations for typically developing children, but who are willing to continue to see patients with IDD through adulthood. A DS-ASD parent forum may also be a good resource to guide you to the dental practices in your community that have a good reputation for care of patients with IDD.

Once you have found a dental provider for your minor or adult child with DS-ASD, you should call to schedule a consultation visit. The first visit is very important for you, your child, and the dentist. The dental team will collect a thorough medical history, including dental history, surgical history, medications taken, and allergies. They will also want to gather information about the individual's home dental care, behavior at other medical or previous dental visits, any sensory challenges, and more, to set the entire experience for success. The dentist will want to observe your child's comfort level and behavior during this visit and may not provide any dental treatment. You should have a conversation about your treatment goals and the dentist should share their treatment philosophy. If your child has been to the dentist before, it would be extremely helpful for the prospective dentist to receive any previous dental records, including X-rays, prior to the first visit. This material will allow the new dentist to understand the successes or areas of improvement of past appointments and will understand any previous treatment that may have been completed.

Topics that are helpful to consider before visiting a dentist:

- How does my child cooperate with dental hygiene practices at home?
- What home oral health care am I able to accomplish and/or need help with?
- How successful have any previous visits to the dentist been?
- What are my goals for my child's dental care?
- Are aesthetics important to me or my child?
- How do I feel about sedation options for my child?
- How do I feel about stabilization options for my child?
- How would my answers to these questions change in an emergency dental situation?

Building a relationship between patient, family, and dentist takes time, so patience from all participants is required. The goal is your child's success with in-office dental care and home oral health care.

GOALS OF THE DENTAL TEAM

Considerations for dental treatment for patients with Down syndrome are well studied and include medical, dental developmental, orthodontic, and surgical factors. There are many commonalities in caring for patients with Down syndrome that help create a specialized standard of care for providers. These commonalities also provide dentists with guidance and historical data to provide care with predictable outcomes. In addition to physical factors, cognitive and behavioral variability are considerations that need to be addressed.

In patients with autism, there are fewer known correlations between autism and dental developmental anomalies. Most anatomical variations in children with autism are related to co-diagnoses. Behavioral and sensory challenges are often the biggest factors in providing dental care in patients with autism.

When treating children diagnosed with DS-ASD, the nuances of both conditions must be considered. The dentist must become knowledgeable about each patient's unique medical and developmental status to develop a plan of oral health care for them. Most importantly, however, the dentist needs to be able to understand the cognitive, sensory, and behavioral needs for each patient with DS-ASD to provide optimum care.

BEHAVIOR AND SENSORY TRIGGERS

The hallmarks of dental care for any child with special needs are trust and predictability. Sharing any known behavioral and sensory triggers will help your child's dental team cater their care to your child. There are many alternatives to sensory challenges in the dental office. For example, if you know your child doesn't like loud sounds, then instead of using an electric toothbrush and suction, your dental team can use a manual toothbrush and wet gauze to provide a noise-free solution. There are many workarounds that the dental team can use to help your child have a pleasant experience. Once that trust and predictability are well established, then many patients with IDD gain familiarity and confidence and are then able to move past some of their sensory challenges to allow for more comprehensive care.

Referring to the example above, once your minor or adult child has experienced multiple successful dental office visits where a manual toothbrush has been used for ten seconds intervals, the dentist may then be able to introduce the electric toothbrush for one ten second interval. If trust and predictability are there, then your child may understand that no matter what, the noise and sensation are only there for ten seconds and then there will be a reprieve. The dentist will read your child's verbal or nonverbal cues to determine whether the time is right to add ten more seconds with the electric toothbrush. This technique is called *desensitization* and is a highly effective technique for pediatric dentists and their patients with special needs. I will discuss it further in the upcoming section on behavior management.

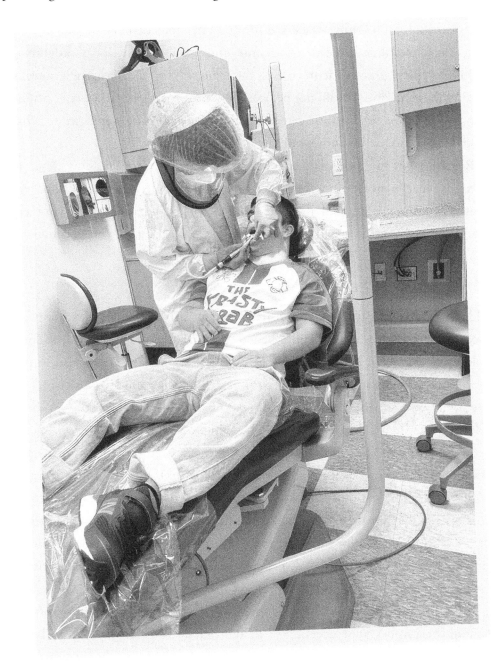

THE DENTAL JOURNEY BEGINS

Once you have consulted with and aligned your treatment goals with your dental provider, the dental journey can begin. This journey will be dependent on your agreed-upon goals as well as the dental needs of your child, and it may need to be modified to accommodate changes over time. If your child has no pressing dental needs, then they will be placed on a preventive track (i.e., routine in-office dental care that will likely include exams, cleanings, fluoride treatments, and possibly X-rays or photographs). If your child has more pressing dental needs, then you will be guided through options for addressing those needs. It would not be possible for me to discuss treatment options for cavities, gum disease, orthodontic care, and other more advanced topics in this chapter because those recommendations would be patient specific.

Regardless of the type of care your child needs or their age, how that care is delivered is what is most important. There are many different behavior management options that are available, and the ones chosen will be determined by your child's comfort level, the dentist's capabilities and comfort level, and your child's dental needs.

BEHAVIOR MANAGEMENT

Wouldn't it be amazing if your child visited the dentist for the first time, hopped into the dental chair, laid back, held still, opened their mouth, and allowed the dentist to complete any treatment necessary? The reality is that a standard dental visit can make any patient—with or without special needs—feel vulnerable and anxious. Think about all the adults in your life who have been visiting the dentist for years, maybe even decades, and yet they still have anxiety about going to their biannual appointment!

In this next section, I will discuss some of the most common behavior management techniques that are used to support individuals with IDD, including those with DS-ASD. Not all dental offices provide all these options, so it is important to know what is offered by your dentist and to let the dentist know what you are comfortable with. It is also important for the dentist to let you know how they feel treatment can be provided safely for your child. Every dentist has different success rates with each of these methods, so it is important to respect the recommendations of the dentist, as well. If the recommendations of the dentist don't fit within your comfort zone, then you should reconsider your selection of dental practice. When it comes to behavior management, trust from parent to dentist and from dentist to parent is essential when utilizing the methods below.

DESENSITIZATION

For those patients who find it challenging or outright frightening to visit the dentist, there is a method called desensitization that is used by many dentists to gain trust, decrease anxiety, and build confidence for patients to be able to tolerate (and maybe even like!) going to the dentist. Desensitization often requires shorter, more frequent visits and the utmost patience on the part of the dental team and the family. It is used to gradually accommodate an anxious patient to a procedure by repetitious, predictable, and progressively small steps over multiple appointments to accomplish the totality of the procedure.

With desensitization, the goal at each visit is for the patient to leave feeling more comfortable, confident, and successful. What is accomplished at the desensitization visits varies greatly. For some patients, desensitization may start with just sitting in a chair in the waiting room and meeting the dentist. For these patients, it may take several visits just to feel comfortable enough to come back into the treatment area. For others, coming into the treatment area may not cause anxiety, but seeing the dental instruments or hearing the sounds of treatment being provided elsewhere in the area may be triggering.

Patients who are verbal may be helpful in sharing any worries so that the dental team can help address these fears most effectively. For those patients who are nonspeaking, caregiver support with alternate communication methods is crucial to providing help in understanding patient cues. The important part of these visits is that each one should accomplish more than the last and draw attention to and celebrate the new accomplishment. Accomplishments don't have to be huge each time. In fact, at the beginning, the accomplishments tend to be very small and could be misconstrued as insignificant. For example, perhaps your child touched their hand to the dental mirror in one visit then the goal of the next visit could be to allow the dental mirror to touch their chin. We still didn't use the mirror in the mouth, for which it is intended, but we got a physical step closer. As the desensitization series of appointments progress, the accomplishments oftentimes become more significant. Referring to the dental mirror example, maybe it took us three visits to even be able to touch the dental mirror to the patient's mouth, but once the patient allowed the mirror in their mouth, we were able to use two new instruments directly in the mouth without having to introduce a new tool to their hand and chin multiple times first.

Desensitization should be person-centered and work as slowly or as quickly as the patient requires and desires. Some of my patients have taken a year or more to gain the comfort to sit in a dental chair and have their teeth brushed. Other patients have only needed one or two desensitization visits before building enough trust to have a complete examination, cleaning, or treatment. Again, patience, predictability, and frequency of visits are of utmost importance in successful desensitization.

Desensitization is ideally done with patients who are new to the dental environment or at least new to a particular dental practice. It is still possible for patients who may have had unpleasant dental experiences to have treatment completed with alternative behavior management options, such as sedation or stabilization. It is important to note that there are a few contraindications to using desensitization. For example, the safety of the patient, caregivers, and dental team must be maintained at all times. Therefore, desensitization is not usually indicated for patients who may be combative. Desensitization is also not indicated in patients experiencing pain or a dental emergency. In these cases, the goals of the dentist and family may need to temporarily shift to address the pain or emergency, and the behavior management techniques may need to pivot to maintain patient health and safety.

DISTRACTION

Drawing a patient's attention to something other than the dental procedure may provide a distraction from the potentially anxiety-producing procedure that may be occurring. Playing music or having a screen with videos, TV shows, or movies to watch, or music to listen to, may provide comfort and distraction. If you think this method would be helpful for your child, then discuss which distraction options your dental team may have in their office or ask what you could bring from home, such as a favorite toy or their iPad.

ADVANCED BEHAVIOR MANAGEMENT OPTIONS

If desensitization and/or distraction are not able to be utilized, then more advanced behavior management options may need to be considered. Below are some examples of *advanced behavior management options* that you may want to consider prior to visiting the dentist in case they are recommended.

PROTECTIVE STABILIZATION

Protective stabilization is a behavior management method in which the objective is to reduce unwanted patient movements in order to protect the patient, parent, caregiver, and/or dental team from injury during dental procedures. It can be performed by human helpers such as parents holding their child's hands or the dental team stabilizing the child's head. Alternatively, protective stabilization can be performed using a stabilization device. If a stabilization device is used, *informed consent* must be given by the parents or consenting guardian.

Stabilization devices are a topic of debate for many parents; therefore, your dentist's philosophy on using them should be discussed at your initial visit. One common stabilization device is called a *papoose*. An obvious indication for using a papoose could be when urgent care is needed with an upset or uncooperative patient who requires stabilization for completion of treatment in order to maintain safety for the patient, parent, and dental team. Using a papoose for routine care should be implemented only when other less restrictive behavior management options are not feasible, or they have been exhausted. There are some patients who feel more content in the papoose (i.e., the tightness, squeezing, and movement restriction may provide relief for some). If your child is one who likes a weighted blanket or who is calmed by hugs or pressure, then your child may like the papoose. I highly recommend having a conversation about how your dentist uses protective stabilization in their practice. Make a plan depending on your comfort level with the different stabilization options, for routine dental situations as well as emergent ones.

SEDATION

For patients who may have anxiety or exhibit a lack of cooperation that other behavior management modifications, such as desensitization or distraction, cannot address, then sedation may be considered. A patient's medical history including medications and allergies are vital factors in determining whether sedation in a dental office would be a wise option. Like protective stabilization, sedation is an important topic of discussion to have with your dentist. Because sedation often requires a higher level of education and certification, you should understand what your dentist's capabilities and preferences are regarding sedation. For children with Down syndrome (with or without autism), sedation in an office is often not recommended due to potential airway concerns. If in-office sedation is recommended for your child, you should consult with your child's physician to consider whether in-office sedation is safe for your child.

There are different types of sedation to consider and discuss with the dentist and primary care physician:

- *Laughing gas* (nitrous oxide) is not a sedative when used alone. It is merely an anxiety reducer that is inhaled, and it only works while it is being inhaled.

- *Conscious sedation* is a medication or local anesthesia that promotes relaxation and serves to increase comfort and decrease panic, anxiety, discomfort, and pain during dental procedures.

- *General anesthesia* is a state of unconsciousness rendered by a medical professional (anesthesiologist, dental anesthesiologist, or nurse anesthetist) in either an office or hospital setting. The laws regarding general anesthesia administered in dental offices vary from state to state. For children with Down syndrome who require general anesthesia, a hospital setting will likely be recommended due to other systemic factors. Before recommending general anesthesia, a dentist should weigh the risk versus benefit and ensure that no lesser behavior management modalities could help achieve the desired result. In other words, general anesthesia should only be used if no other behavior management options are possible.

HOME CARE

Now that we have talked about dental care in the dentist's office, let's discuss dental care at home. After all, what the dental team can accomplish in their office only happens a couple of times per year. Oral home care ideally happens every single day. Let's make sure you have some home oral health care tools and skills to optimize the care you can provide to your minor or adult child which they may learn to practice on their own.

If you aren't a trained dental professional, then providing home oral health care to someone else can be awkward. Many parents and caregivers share with me how challenging brushing teeth is at home. Some of the challenging aspects that I hear repeatedly are the following: he doesn't hold still; she doesn't like flavors; he doesn't like textures; she doesn't open her mouth. I'm going to address some of these challenges and offer some tips. Remember to share your personal challenges with your dental team. As the team gets to know your child, they will be able to offer some personalized tips to help, as well.

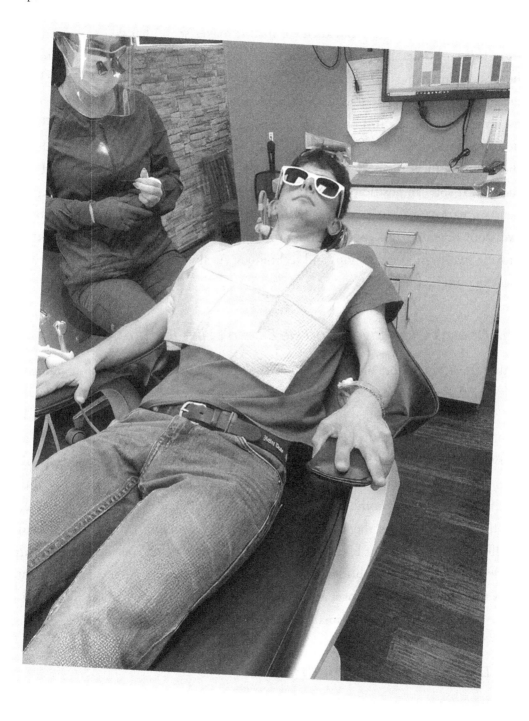

He Doesn't Hold Still

Think about your child's experiences in the dental office. Does it take a team to help your child get their teeth cleaned? If so, then it makes sense that you may need some extra help at home. This doesn't mean you need to hire a hygienist to come to your house every morning and every evening. However, if you have an extra helper at home, great! If not, you can use stable objects to support your efforts. For example, you can have your child sit (or if possible, lay down) in a nonstressful space at home. There is no law that says you must brush your teeth in the bathroom. Perhaps the couch with the TV in front of them, lying on the bed, or sitting at the dinner table would work the best. If you can position yourself behind your child, you can lay their head against your stomach, torso, or lap. The physical support will help you have better control over your brushing and your motions. You may find helpful videos on YouTube that provide step-by-step suggestions and techniques. As always, please use discretion when accessing internet resources.

She Doesn't Like Flavors and He Doesn't Like Textures

If they don't like flavors or textures, then don't use toothpaste. We are so ingrained in thinking that toothbrushing has to be done just one way—and with toothpaste! Don't get me wrong, a soft-bristled toothbrush with a fluoridated toothpaste is the ideal, but sometimes ideal isn't always possible. If you've tried multiple toothpaste flavors and you've tried gels and pastes but can't seem to find a palatable toothpaste for your child, then try using a fluoridated, alcohol-free mouth rinse. Pour a little mouth rinse into a small cup and dip the toothbrush into the cup, shake off any excess, and brush. (Never dip the toothbrush into the mouth rinse bottle.) If the mouth rinse flavor or texture is still too much, then just brush with water. Remember to tell your dentist about this challenge. You could also bring your child's toothpaste or mouth rinse to the dental visits for the dentist to approve, and maybe even use, during the first few dental visits while your child is getting acclimated to toothbrushing.

She Doesn't Open Her Mouth for Me

Talk to your dentist about this challenge. There are many tricks to help your child open wide enough for you to reach in. There are soft props that you can use and secret reflex spots in the mouth that trigger instant opening. If this is your challenge, it's important for a professional to show you safe ways to help your child open their mouth for you at home. The techniques won't feel natural to you at first, so you'll need some patience and practice to learn them.

The Challenging "Trifecta"

If your child has the "trifecta" (doesn't sit still, doesn't like tastes and textures, and doesn't open their mouth), then discuss with your dentist which of these three challenges would be best to work on first. The theme for all these challenges is to discuss them with your dentist and dental team and reinforce the need for you to find a dental practice as soon as you can so that you have support in how you care for your child's mouth at home. It is my belief that every child can have some level of oral health care completed at home—you just need the right tips and tricks. Most parents think they're doing a worse job than they actually are. So have faith that if you're doing something, then you're helping your child more than you realize.

CONCLUSION

My goal in authoring this chapter was to provide guidance and offer hope to parents of minor and adult children with DS-ASD—guidance in how to select a dental provider and what questions to ask yourself and the dental team, and hope that no matter where you are in your child's dental health journey, you now have some insight into how to navigate oral health care in the dental office and at home.

I hope you also noticed that the consistent thread throughout this chapter is communication. It is imperative that you and your child have a trusting relationship with your dental team. This relationship, like many others, is built on clear, open, and honest communication, so have the conversations that will enable you and your child's dental team to work together to achieve optimum oral health for your child.

I wish you and your child a wonderful dental experience.

SUGGESTED RESOURCES

The American Academy of Pediatric Dentistry (www.aapd.org)

List of State Pediatric Dental Associations (https://www.aapd.org/about/state-and-district-chapters/)

The Special Care Dentistry Association (www.scdaonline.org)

CHAPTER EIGHT

BEHAVIORAL TREATMENTS FOR SLEEP PROBLEMS IN INDIVIDUALS WITH DS-ASD

Terry Katz, PhD
Ann Reynolds, MD

Parents often assume that sleep difficulties are "part of life," especially if they have a child with co-occurring diagnoses of Down syndrome and autism spectrum disorder (DS-ASD). In some respects, this is correct. Many families of children diagnosed with autism spectrum disorders do experience difficulties with sleep, and some evidence suggests that children with DS-ASD have an even greater incidence of sleep difficulties than do children with Down syndrome alone. So, while it is common for children with DS-ASD to have a sleep disturbance, this does not mean that sleep problems are insurmountable. On the contrary, there are many strategies that may improve a child's sleep.

It is hard to overestimate the importance of good sleep; improvements in sleep often lead to improvements in physical and emotional health as well as improvements in learning. We are continually learning more about the consequences of poor sleep. Difficulties with sleep have been linked to poor physical health including the risk of obesity, diabetes, and heart disease. Individuals with DS-ASD may be particularly at risk for health difficulties that are tied to poor sleep. A lack of sleep affects our ability to remember information, concentrate, make good decisions, and process information. A lack of adequate sleep is called a "sleep debt," and studies show that we do not get used to or adapt to insufficient sleep. The longer we go without adequate sleep, the worse we perform on tests of cognitive functioning. Sleep deprivation is as much a risk when driving as that of alcohol consumption. Sleep also affects our emotional state. Research indicates that poor sleep is related to depression, anxiety, and hyperactive behavior. Further, there is evidence to suggest that better sleep may result in positive behavioral changes during the day such as improvements in activity level and attention. Some research even suggests that sleep promotes the processing of negative experiences in a helpful way.

SLEEP BASICS

Knowledge of the mechanics of sleep will help you understand the basis for effective strategies that improve sleep. While our understanding of sleep is not complete, researchers have learned a great deal about how we fall asleep, what happens while we are sleeping, and what to expect as we grow and develop. This information has helped scientists identify problems in sleep and ways to help promote healthy sleep.

While researchers have learned a great deal about sleep, there is still much to learn. We have some knowledge about what happens when we don't get enough sleep, yet we lack a complete understanding of why we sleep. Until scientists were able to measure electrical current in the brain (in the 1930s), it seemed impossible to study what happens when we sleep. Studies using electroencephalograms (EEGs) have helped us learn that sleep is divided into two major states: Non-REM and REM sleep. REM stands for rapid eye movement sleep. Non-REM sleep is also called "quiet sleep" and includes "slow-wave sleep."

When we first start to fall asleep, we experience a stage called "alpha sleep." During this stage we are still awake, but relaxed and calm. This relaxed wakefulness sets the stage for non-REM sleep which consists of stages that involve deeper and deeper sleep. *Stage 1* of non-REM sleep typically lasts only a few minutes and is a light sleep. Our body temperature drops, we become more relaxed, and we are easily roused. We then move to *Stage 2*. During this stage we are firmly asleep, but we are also easily awakened. Approximately half the night is spent in Stage 2 sleep, and this phase usually occurs during transitions to other sleep stages. *Stage 3* is referred to as deep sleep or slow-wave sleep. During deep sleep our breathing slows, our temperature drops even more, and it is much more difficult to wake up. Researchers have determined that deep sleep is a time for body renewal and repair. When we are sleep deprived, we typically move into the deeper stages of sleep quickly and spend more time in these stages. Researchers have interpreted this to mean that deep, slow-wave sleep helps us feel restored and refreshed.

We typically move through one or two cycles of non-REM sleep before moving into REM sleep. While non-REM sleep is described as "quiet" and includes a slowing of bodily functions, REM sleep is "active." Rapid eye movement is characteristic of REM sleep, and this is the time when we dream. Our breathing and heart rate increase and are comparable to the rates we experience when we are awake. Surprisingly, the part of our body responsible for the "fight or flight" response is twice as active during REM sleep as it is when we are awake. While our mind is quite active, however, our body is hardly moving; in fact, muscles that are not needed for breathing, eye movements, or hearing are basically paralyzed during this stage of sleep. There is some indication that REM sleep may help with learning and memory. We enter REM sleep about 3–5 times a night, or approximately every 90 minutes. People who have repeatedly been awakened from REM sleep do not do as well at learning a new task as those who are repeatedly awakened from non-REM sleep. There is thus some evidence to suggest that REM sleep helps with our cognitive and emotional well-being, while non-REM sleep helps with our physical well-being.

Throughout the night we move through the different stages of sleep. Some changes occur in the length of a full sleep cycle and in the amount of time we spend in each stage as we grow and develop. Most of our deep sleep occurs in the first half of the night, with longer periods of REM sleep occurring during the latter part of the night. As we move from one stage to another, we experience changes in our brain wave patterns. It is not unusual to move about and shift in our bed during these transitions; we may also briefly awaken and make sure that "all is well." Such arousals occur most frequently when we are moving in and out of REM sleep. These changes in arousal and brief awakenings occur in all children and adults, and they are not considered interruptions in sleep unless we cannot return to sleep afterwards. For many individuals this is a time when some sleep disturbance may occur, and an awareness of this process may point to effective ways to improve the quality of one's sleep.

In addition to understanding what happens while we sleep, it is useful to look at the mechanisms that help us fall asleep at night and those that help us to awaken and be alert during the day. There are two physiological or biological mechanisms that control our sleep/wake cycle: *circadian rhythms* and *homeostasis*.

"Circadian" comes from the Latin phrase "about a day." We all have biological cycles that occur approximately every 24 hours. In addition to our sleep/wake cycle, many other biological functions have a daily rhythm; some of these physiological processes involve body temperature, the release of hormones, digestion, and elimination. These processes work in concert to help us move through the sleep and wake cycle. For example, we typically fall asleep when our body temperature drops, and we wake up as it starts to rise. The production of various endogenous hormones, such as melatonin and cortisol, has also been linked to our sleep/wake cycle.

Our circadian cycles are all somewhat longer than 24 hours, lasting closer to 25 hours in length. This tendency toward a 25-hour cycle helps explain why it is easier to stay up later than it is to fall asleep earlier than our natural sleep time. There are a number of cues, however, that help us maintain a 24-hour cycle. Sleep researchers call these cues *zeitgebers*, which means "time givers" in German. Some *zeitgebers* include light, social demands, and ambient temperature. Exposure to light in the morning and darkness in the evening helps us maintain a 24-hour cycle. For this reason, individuals who are blind have circadian rhythm disturbances and sleep problems. A decrease in temperature is another signal that it is time to go to sleep. Social cues also help us stay on a 24-hour schedule. We respond to cues from others about our sleep/wake cycle.

When we are with people who are sleeping or getting ready for bed, we sense a need to do the same. There is also no social reinforcement to be awake when others are sleeping.

In addition to circadian rhythms, we also have homeostatic drives. These drives help us maintain a physiological equilibrium. Homeostatic drives help explain why we typically eat when we are hungry or drink when we are thirsty. We all have a homeostatic drive to sleep, and we become sleepier after an extended period of wakefulness. The longer we are awake, the stronger our drive to sleep becomes. We also experience a drive to sleep when we have accumulated a sleep debt. Ideally, our homeostatic drive and circadian rhythms work in concert to help us stay awake and alert during the day and fall asleep at night. Understanding our homeostatic drive for sleep and circadian rhythms helps us understand why we might have trouble falling asleep at certain times. For example, the hour before our regular bedtime is often called the "forbidden zone" because it is extremely difficult to fall asleep during this time. Even though our sleep drive is strong, our circadian rhythms make it difficult to fall asleep during this time. For the same reason, it is hard to fall asleep in the morning even if we have had a night of little or no sleep.

HOW DO I KNOW WHETHER AN INDIVIDUAL HAS A SLEEP PROBLEM?

Determining whether an individual has a sleep problem is not always as clear-cut as it may seem. Different people need different amounts of sleep. Some of us are truly "short sleepers" who need less sleep than the amount typically recommended, and others are "long sleepers" who need more. Furthermore, our sleep needs change as we grow and develop. A young child, for example, needs more sleep than an adolescent. One way to help determine if someone is getting enough sleep is to examine their behavior during the day. Are they sleepy or tired during the day? Do they fall asleep at unusual or inconvenient times? Is it hard for them to awaken in the morning? Do they have behavioral difficulties (such as hyperactivity or irritability) that might be explained by a lack of sleep? Answering these questions helps us determine whether an individual has a sleep problem. Presented below is a table that provides information about children's sleep patterns at different ages.

The National Sleep Foundation website describes the recommended number of hours of sleep based on age. It is important to note that there is a wide range of hours that may be appropriate. For example, it is recommended that preschoolers ages 3–5 get somewhere between 8 and 14 hours of sleep each day. While the recommended range is 1–13 hours, it may be appropriate for some toddlers to get 8 hours of sleep and for others to get 14 hours of sleep. Again, some people are considered short sleepers, and do not need as much sleep as others who may need more sleep.

Table 8.1: Sleep Patterns at Different Ages

Descriptive Category	Age Range	Recommended	May Be Appropriate	Not Recommended
Newborn	0–3 months	14–17 hours	11–13 hours or 18–19 hours	Less than 11 hours; more than 19 hours
Infant	4–11 months	12–15 hours	10–11 hours or 16–18 hours	Less than 10 hours; more than 18 hours
Toddler	1–2 years	11–14 hours	9–10 hours or 15–16 hours	Less than 9 hours; more than 16 hours
Preschool	3–5 years	10–13 hours	8–9 hours or 14 hours	Less than 8 hours; more than 14 hours
School Age	6–13 years	9–11 hours	7–8 hours or 12 hours	Less than 7 hours; more than 12 hours
Teenager	14–17 years	8–10 hours	7 hours or 11 hours	Less than 7 hours; more than 11 hours
Young Adult	18–25 years	7–9 hours	6 hours or 10–11 hours	Less than 6 hours; more than 11 hours
Adult	26–64 years	7–9 hours	6 hours or 10 hours	Less than 6 hours; more than 10 hours
Older Adult	> 65 years	7–8 hours	5–6 hours or 9 hours	Less than 5 hours; more than 9 hours

Adapted from the National Sleep Foundation (2020): *How many hours of sleep do you need?* https://www.thensf.org/how-many-hours-of-sleep-do-you-really-need/

Understanding an individual's preferences for bedtime and wake time may also help us identify specific problems. Some people naturally tend to be early risers (larks) while others naturally become energized late in the evening (owls). There are also developmental differences, as adolescents tend to prefer later bedtimes. There is research indicating that children on the autism spectrum sleep less than their peers who are not on the spectrum. It is not clear if this is because autistic children have more sleep problems or whether they may need less sleep than children who are not on the spectrum.

Some sleep habits may pose more difficulties for parents and other family members than for the individual with DS-ASD. For example, a young child might not be at all upset about needing to fall asleep with a parent by their side, but this may cause difficulties for their parents. The same may be true for the length of time it takes an individual to fall asleep and the time at which they wake up in the morning.

Some of the first questions that parents and professionals should ask when assessing an individual's sleep include the following:

- Does the individual maintain a regular sleep schedule (school and non-school days)?
- How long does the individual sleep each night on average?
- Does the individual have any problems at bedtime?
- Does the individual have any problems falling asleep?
- Does it take the individual more than 20–30 minutes to fall asleep at night?
- Does the individual snore or have any problems breathing during the night?
- Does the individual have seizures that are not well controlled?
- Does the individual have any unusual/repetitive behaviors during the night?
- Does the individual need assistance to wake up in the morning?

·   Does the individual seem sleepy or overtired during the day?

If the answers to these questions lead to any cause for concern, further evaluation of the individual's sleep may be warranted.

HOW ARE SLEEP PROBLEMS FORMALLY EVALUATED?

The first step in evaluating an individual's sleep should include a thorough medical history to determine whether there may be a medical cause for any sleep difficulties. Medical problems that cause pain or discomfort may disrupt sleep. Medical problems that may affect sleep include reflux, constipation, abdominal pain, hunger, wheezing/coughing, seizures, eczema/itchy skin, headaches, dental pain, and joint pain. Medications need to be considered as some make it more difficult to fall asleep at night. It is necessary to determine whether asthma, sinusitis, allergies, or nasal congestion are affecting sleep and whether an individual is snoring or gasping for breath at night. This may indicate that an individual is experiencing poor air movement/oxygenation while sleeping. This may cause fragmented sleep, which has physical and behavioral implications. Snoring and breathing issues are especially important to assess when evaluating children with DS-ASD because of the prevalence of disordered breathing while sleeping in children with Down syndrome. Talk with a health care provider if your child is snoring two to three nights per week or more. There is mounting evidence that disordered breathing while sleeping has a negative impact on daytime behavior and attention. A thorough medical history will also include questions about nutrition as there is evidence to suggest that low iron stores may be related to restless leg syndrome or periodic limb movement disorder. Finally, psychiatric conditions including anxiety and depression should be ruled out as they can contribute to difficulty sleeping. (See chapter four for more details about medical conditions that might affect sleep in individuals with Down syndrome and ASD.)

After a comprehensive medical evaluation has been completed, the next step is to obtain a good understanding of an individual's sleep history. This includes learning about the development of an individual's sleep habits. Has the individual always had difficulty sleeping or is this a new problem? When did the difficulties begin? Did they coincide with changes in the environment, family situation, schooling, work, daily routines, or with age? Learning about an individual's daily routines, amount of exercise, exposure to outdoor light, dietary habits, dinner routine, and evening schedule is helpful. Noting if, when, and for how long an individual naps should also be considered as well as whether the individual ever falls asleep while riding in the car, at school, or during other activities. Specific information about bedtime routines, aspects of the bedroom environment, and what happens after saying "good-night" also needs to be reviewed. It may be helpful to complete a sleep diary that documents bedtime, how long it takes to fall asleep, the number and length of nighttime awakenings, and morning wake-up time. Information about daytime activities, naps, and use of medications are also frequently noted in a sleep diary.

For many individuals, this is all the information that is needed to assess their sleep difficulties and develop an effective treatment plan. At times there will be a need for further assessment. If there are concerns that medical conditions may be affecting sleep, children may need to complete an evaluation in a sleep laboratory. In-home sleep studies may also be an option for moderate to severe obstructive sleep apnea. They may allow for more sleep time but do not collect as much information (Revana et al., 2022). A sleep study or polysomnogram (PSG) provides information about how much time it takes an individual to fall asleep, how much sleep they get during the night, progression through the sleep stages, amount of time in each sleep stage, whether sleep apnea is present (and if so the severity), whether there are periodic limb movements that occur while sleeping, and whether there are any EEG abnormalities that might suggest the presence of seizures. Preparation for a sleep study involves placement of electrodes and sensors on an individual's head, face, and body that allow monitoring of movement and physiological functions. Many individuals can successfully complete a sleep study with little difficulty; others may need time and careful preparation before entering a sleep laboratory. The use of teaching/personalized stories about the study, systematic desensitization, and creative use of distracters and tangible rewards may help many individuals successfully complete these studies. (See chapter nine for more detailed desensitization strategies.) You may want to work with a behavioral specialist, occupational therapist, or Child Life specialist to help with preparation for the study.

SLEEP PROBLEMS AND INTERVENTION STRATEGIES

Parents of children with autism spectrum disorders and Down syndrome report that their children demonstrate a range of sleep-related problems including difficulty falling asleep, going to bed at a late time, sleeping for only a short amount of time, frequent night waking, and early morning rising. Other difficulties commonly noted include sleep-disordered breathing, excessive daytime sleepiness, teeth-grinding, parasomnias, restless sleep, and daytime sleepiness. Sleep-related breathing disorders are frequent in adults and children with Down syndrome. While these concerns cover a wide range of sleep difficulties, they do not include all sleep problems that may be encountered. The *International Classification of Sleep Disorders* is used for diagnosis and coding of sleep problems and includes over 80 different sleep disorders. We will limit the discussion in this chapter to sleep difficulties that are commonly problems in autistic individuals and individuals with Down syndrome. Many of these difficulties are shared by children, teens, and adults, and the strategies we discuss will be helpful for individuals of all ages.

Difficulty Falling Asleep at Bedtime

This is a common problem experienced by many individuals, especially those with autism spectrum disorders. Research indicates that up to 80% of autistic people have difficulty with sleep. The National Institute of Health notes that 76% of children with Down syndrome experience difficulties falling asleep and staying asleep. Research also indicates that up to 75% of adults with Down syndrome have difficulties with sleep. When someone takes more than 20 minutes to fall asleep once they are in bed, it may be helpful to consider strategies to help them fall asleep more quickly. Parents will often observe that their children will resist or refuse to go to bed. Once their children are in bed there may be frequent curtain calls ("can I have one more drink of water… *pleeease!*"), and a longtime settling. For many families, these difficulties are frustrating and chronic. Some individuals, especially teens and young adults, may not protest going into bed but may lie in bed awake for a long period of time before actually falling asleep. A variety of techniques may be effective in helping individuals fall asleep with less difficulty. A number of these techniques also help with other sleep problems which we will discuss subsequently. These strategies are often referred to as "sleep hygiene" or "sleep habits" because they help promote healthy sleep. Please see below for strategies that may help an individual fall asleep more readily at bedtime.

Daytime Activities: The first step toward improving sleep is examining daytime habits and making changes that may promote sleep at the end of the day. The main areas we examine include exercise, light, food, daytime sleep, and bedroom use.

Exercise: Exercise early in the day helps promote sleep. Among its many benefits, exercise helps promote healthy sleep. Ideally, exercise should happen at the same time each day. Exercise should not, however, occur too close to bedtime as physical activity is often stimulating and arousing and may thus make it more difficult to fall asleep. Generally, it is best to avoid any arousing or stimulating activities in the late evening.

Light: Individuals should be exposed to as much light as possible during the day. Exposure to daytime light (especially natural light) helps suppress our melatonin levels and primes us to respond well to a decrease in light as evening falls. While we want lots of exposure to light during the day, we want very little exposure to light starting about an hour before bedtime.

Food: Caffeine acts as a stimulant that promotes alertness and interferes with sleep. Take time to look at the foods that an individual is eating to make sure that they are not getting caffeine late in the day. While most of us realize that coffee contains caffeine, some may not realize that it is also present in chocolate and some clear drinks. Not all chocolate contains the same amount of caffeine as this varies by the amount of cocoa solids in the product. An ounce of dark chocolate contains approximately 12 milligrams of caffeine. Dark chocolate generally contains more caffeine than sweet chocolate or milk chocolate. White chocolate does not have any caffeine. A careful inventory of foods that may contain caffeine may therefore be informative. Caffeine remains active in our bodies for long periods of time. The half-life for caffeine in adults is approximately six hours. This means that if someone drinks a beverage that contains 100 milligrams of caffeine, they will still have 50 milligrams in their body six hours later. The exact half-life of caffeine in children is not known, but some researchers hypothesize that it may be longer for children.

Daytime Sleep: When thinking about daytime habits, consider the timing of naps. Generally, naps should be completed by 4:00 p.m. Sleeping later than that may interfere with an individual's sleep drive and make it harder to fall asleep at bedtime. Sometimes it is helpful to carefully track naptime and bedtime to find the right balance between a nap that is needed in the afternoon and a bedtime that works for everyone in the family. This may sometimes be a trial-and-error process. We worked with one family, for example, that found that waking up their child at 3:30 p.m. resulted in a difficult afternoon and evening while waking them up at 3:45 p.m. resulted in a happier rest of the day and no subsequent difficulties with falling asleep at night.

Bedroom Use: Review how an individual's bedroom is being used during the day. To promote strong sleep associations, we recommend that an individual's bedroom only be used for sleep. The use of a child's bedroom for time-out may result in negative and anxious associations while the use of a child's bedroom for play may result in excited and playful associations. Ideally, the child's bedroom is only associated with sleep, which may help a child fall asleep more readily. If it is not possible to keep a bedroom only for sleep, try to make sure that the bed itself is reserved for sleep and physically mark an area of the bedroom that is reserved for play. If it is hard to keep the bed just for sleep, try changing the bedding at bedtime each night.

Evening Activities: Evening activities also play a role in regulating an individual's sleep. Moving toward calming, relaxing, and relatively easy activities in the hour before bed is often helpful. Try to avoid roughhousing and intense physical play before bedtime. Any activities that are stimulating and exciting should be avoided. For instance, a favorite behavior such as watching a portion of a movie repetitively can also be overstimulating and interfere with going to sleep. It may be necessary to rearrange schedules so that these fun activities occur at other times during the day. Developing set routines in the evening may also help promote successful sleep.

Try to keep the lights down low and avoid exposure to light about an hour before bedtime. Exposure to light, especially blue light will lower our endogenous melatonin levels and thus our sleep. Melatonin, often called the hormone of darkness, is released by the suprachiasmatic nucleus (SCN) in our pineal gland in the brain. Melatonin levels go down with exposure to light. Even a brief exposure to light may suppress our melatonin levels. Blue light interferes the most with sleep and this is the primary light that is emitted from our electronic devices. It is best to stop using any electronic devices about an hour before bed. This is often easier said than done for most of us and if it is too hard to eliminate the use of electronic devices, make sure that the devices are set to a night mode that filters out blue light. There are also apps that you can install on a device to filter out the blue light. It may also be helpful to wear yellow or orange glasses that filter out the blue light emitted from electronic devices.

In addition to monitoring the light from any electronic devices, consider an individual's exposure to white light the hour before bedtime. For example, a bath in the evening may help an individual relax, but the exposure to the bright lights in the bathroom may interfere with melatonin production. It may help to use lower watt light bulbs or red light instead of white light during bath time. When compared to other types of light (such as blue light), red light will not interfere with melatonin production. You can use red light bulbs or red night-lights in the evening and during the night. Some families we have worked with have found that using a string of red Christmas lights in their child's bedroom as well as in the bathroom instead of white light resulted in a significant improvement in their child's sleep.

Sleep Environment

The child's sleep environment should also be considered. Is the child's bed and bedroom comfortable? The following factors should be considered when evaluating whether your child's bedroom is helping or hindering sleep.

Lights should be off, if possible, but some children do need a night-light. Some children have developed routines in which they have become used to having an overhead light or desk light on while they try to fall asleep. Families may find that using light bulbs with progressively lower wattage may decrease their children's dependence on light at night. Also consider the output from hall lights and digital clocks as well. Once again, consider the use of red night-lights or other red lights if a light is needed during the night. You may want, for example, to use red night-lights in the hallway and bathroom for middle of the night trips to the toilet.

Sounds should be kept to a minimum. Think about where an individual's room is placed relative to the rest of the household. Are they able to hear distracting or potentially stimulating noises? If so, it may be beneficial to move a child's bedroom to a quieter, less central location. Some individuals respond well to the use of a "noise machine," which produces calming white noise or nature sounds that mask distracting household noises. If a noise machine is used, care should be taken to make sure that it stays on all night so that there is no change in the child's sleeping environment throughout the night.

Tactile sensations should also be considered. Try to attend to a child's preference for certain textures in bedding and pajamas. Individuals may also respond to different amounts of pressure on their body. While some individuals might prefer little input, others are comforted by deep pressure. Some individuals respond well to the use of a weighted blanket or sleeping bag. Be sure to discuss the appropriate weight for a weighted blanket with your child's medical provider. Sleep sacks may work for younger children and zippered bedding may be a good option for older children, teens, and adults. For individuals who sleep well with lots of input, but who also are warm during the night, it may be helpful to consider a cooling mattress and/or cooling pillow.

We have worked with many families who have benefitted from having their child sleep in a medical safety bed. These beds allow a child to sleep in a safe and comforting way. There are many different types of medical safety beds, and some provide additional sensory input and comfort for a child. Often consideration of this type of bed is necessary to help keep a child safe during the night. This may be especially true for children who are at risk of elopement and for those who may engage in unsafe behaviors if they leave their bedroom during the night. Some of the families we have worked with have noted that in addition to providing a safe environment during the night, the medical safety bed promoted better sleep.

Consistency

Consistency is the basis for effective sleep habits. Try to keep daytime, evening, and bedtime routines the same whenever possible. While today's busy families cannot always maintain a consistent schedule, it helps, for example, to have dinner at about the same time every evening. If possible, maintain the same bedtime and wake times every day of the week, including weekends. Avoid varying bedtime and wake times by more than one hour. The more consistent our daily schedule, the more our bodies and minds become conditioned to expect sleep to begin at a certain time and respond accordingly.

Families should carefully consider when to put their children to bed. It helps to have gathered some information about when an individual is falling asleep (versus the time of night that the individual is put to bed) and how much sleep they get each night. Some children may not need as much sleep as other children their age and for these children an early bedtime may be counterproductive. They may also have biological clocks that tend toward a late bedtime. This is especially true for teens and young adults who go through a normal developmental phase in which they have a naturally occurring delayed sleep time. Finally, avoid having an individual go to bed during a time that has often been referred to as the "forbidden zone." This is the time during which we are all more alert and have great difficulty falling asleep. This time usually occurs about an hour before an individual's usual time to fall asleep. You may have experienced this as a "second wind," or a time when you suddenly have more energy than you had earlier in the evening. If you have ever tried to go to bed during this time (perhaps because you knew you needed to get up extra early the next morning), you may remember how difficult it was to fall asleep. A child who has been struggling to fall asleep may fall asleep more readily when bedtime is moved to a later hour by avoiding this period of alertness. Often it works best to have an individual go to bed at the time they are generally falling asleep. For example, if an individual is going into bed at 9:00 p.m. but falling asleep at 11:00 p.m., you can try having that person go to bed at about 10:45 p.m. Hopefully that person will then fall asleep at about 11:00 p.m.

Once good bedtime routines and sleep habits have been established, it is often possible to gradually move the bedtime to an earlier time. We usually suggest moving bedtime back by about 15 minutes every few days. While this method often works, we do occasionally work with individuals who still take two hours to fall asleep even if their bedtime is moved to a later time. If that is the case, other strategies will be needed! As is true for many interventions, there is some trial and error involved in finding the best way to help someone sleep better. It is often helpful to work with a sleep behavior specialist if you continue to struggle to improve a loved one's sleep.

Consistent bedtime routines are a cornerstone of good sleep. An effective bedtime routine helps our minds, and our bodies know that it is, in fact, time for sleep. A bedtime routine should consist of a small number of calming and easy activities that help prepare us for sleep. Once you develop a set of activities that are easy and relaxing for your child, go through the routine in the same order each night. It often helps to include calming sensory strategies in a bedtime routine. Look carefully at the activities that typically occur before bed and determine whether these activities should be part of an actual bedtime routine. For example, bath time is often calming for children, but some children react negatively to this. It may be helpful to consider adding sensory or behavioral strategies that will make bath time less stressful. Sometimes bath time is exciting and stimulating. While the activity is positive, the child may become aroused and then have trouble calming down for sleep. In this case, it may help to move bath time earlier in the day. We often find that working on strategies for toothbrushing also helps make bedtime less stressful. One easy trick that often works is to finish up toothbrushing right after dinner so that a child has time to recover from any upset from this task.

Many children with DS-ASD respond positively to the use of visual schedules. A visual schedule depicts the activities involved in a bedtime routine. If, for example, a child's bedtime routine includes brushing teeth, bathing, putting on pajamas, and singing songs, a visual schedule would include a picture for each of these activities. Parents may use photographs, picture icons, or written lists to represent each activity. Some children also respond well to the use of objects rather than pictures. We recommend teaching children to learn to move through their schedule on their own with support from their parents. Try to keep the visual schedule in a central location. Bedtime routines should take approximately 30 minutes or less and involve only a few activities. The idea is to gradually move closer and closer to the bedroom and to engage in progressively relaxing and sleep-promoting activities. A visual schedule increases the consistency and predictability of bedtime routines and may thus reduce a child's anxiety. Use of visual schedules also promotes independence and mastery. Autism Speaks has an excellent toolkit about using visual schedules. They also have a sleep toolkit with visuals you can use to make a bedtime visual schedule (see the suggested resources section at the end of this chapter).

Once children are in bed, they need to fall asleep independently. Make sure that anything a child uses to fall asleep at the beginning of the night will be available throughout the night. You may recall that earlier in this chapter we discussed how we all go through brief periods of arousal throughout the night. If nothing changes after falling asleep at the beginning of the night, we should have no difficulty remaining asleep throughout the night. If, however, changes do occur, it is much more likely that we will become alert during these brief periods of arousal. Thus, in addition to falling asleep on their own, children should fall asleep in the same place that they will sleep throughout the night. Children who are allowed to fall asleep in one place (such as the couch or a parent's bed) and who are then moved to their own bed later in the evening often wake up during the night.

Many children resist falling asleep on their own. They may be anxious, afraid of the dark, or have significant separation anxiety. In addition to the sleep habits suggestions that we have already outlined, an anxious child may also benefit from bedtime relaxation techniques. These simple techniques include taking deep breaths or alternatively squeezing and relaxing one's muscles.

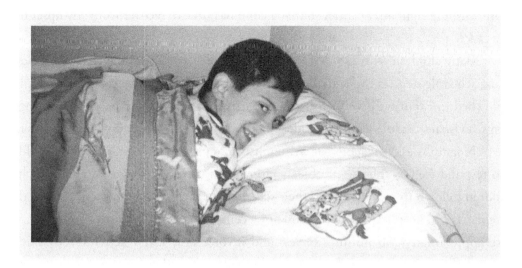

Children who have become dependent on sleeping with another person may be particularly resistant to learning to sleep alone. A variety of strategies may help. Some parents will try the "cold turkey" or "crying it out" approach. Parents who use this method decide that they will say good night to their children and then leave the room with the expectation that their children will fall asleep without any help. Parents who use this method resolve not to return to their children's bedroom "no matter what." While this approach has been well researched and has been found to be effective and efficient, it is emotionally difficult for many parents and children. If a parent is not able to ignore their child's cries, they will inadvertently be reinforcing crying. The child will learn that if they cry loud enough and long enough, their parent will come to them. This method may also be especially difficult for children who tend to be anxious and have difficulty with changes to their routine. It is important, therefore, to determine before you start whether you can consistently ignore your child's cries even if they cry for a very long time. Fortunately, it is not the only way to teach children to sleep independently, and a gradual approach may work well for many families. One such approach involves having parents say goodnight and leave their child's room and then periodically check back in with their children. The goal is to gradually increase the length of time between visits and to keep all interactions "brief and boring." Children may also learn to fall asleep independently without their parents leaving the room. Parents may stay near their children's bed while their children fall asleep. The plan is for parents to gradually move farther and farther away from their children's bed until they are out of the room. We have found that the third method (often called fading parental presence) works best for most of the families that we work with. Some families can start by staying close to their child's bed without touching them; other families need to continue to cuddle with their child at bedtime and stop when the child is drowsy but not yet asleep. They can then gradually increase the amount of time between ending a cuddle and letting a child fall asleep without cuddling. It is often helpful to pair progress in learning to sleep alone with rewards in the morning. These may include engaging in a special activity or earning stickers or a small present.

Co-sleeping (when parents and children sleep together) is a family decision, and we respect parents who have made this choice. There are often practical, cultural, financial, and medical reasons that families decide to co-sleep. Many families, however, have resorted to co-sleeping as a way of helping their children get some sleep and would prefer to have their children sleep in their own beds. Teaching children to sleep alone in their own beds in a separate bedroom from their parents involves the same gradual approach that we discussed above. Parents may gradually move their children farther and farther away from them in the family bed and then have their children sleep in a bed near them. The child's bed may then be gradually moved to another bedroom. It is often easier for parents and children to start this process by moving together to the child's bedroom and for parents to then move farther and farther away from their child. Few children object to this initial change (if they are still sleeping with their parents). Following this plan requires more transitions for parents but fewer transitions for children. For those families who are not sure whether they want to continue co-sleeping, it may be helpful to remember that all of us tend to sleep better, and with fewer interruptions, if we sleep alone rather than with another person.

Consider also whether an individual is falling asleep while watching television, listening to music, or engaging in any other activity that will stop after they fall asleep. Changes from how we first fall asleep at night (sleep onset associations) may result in night waking. For example, if someone is listening to music while they fall asleep, they will be more likely to wake up during the night if the music is turned off after they fall asleep. They may need to listen to this music during the night to fall back asleep. Listening to music before falling asleep or keeping the music on all night will be best. It is often difficult to keep the same calming music on all night. Turing off the music before falling asleep is often a better option. You can turn off the music when your child is drowsy but not yet asleep and gradually turn off the music a little earlier to give them time to settle and fall asleep without any music on.

Helping children fall asleep on their own and in a consistent location also helps minimize *night waking*. In addition to helping your child learn to fall asleep independently, you should develop a plan so that you have a consistent way of responding if your child wakes up during the night. If feasible, talk with your child about your expectations for sleeping through the night. Visual aids (such as a stop sign on the door) may be helpful, and teaching stories are another useful technique. You should respond to your child's distress (especially if they are anxious) and doing so before he or she becomes more upset is helpful. You should also, however, take care to ignore the inconsequential shifting and stirring that takes place during the night. It is fine to comfort a child who needs reassurance, but as with all interactions that occur after you say goodnight, they should be kept to a minimum.

The ***bedtime pass*** is another technique that helps with night waking and difficulties falling asleep independently. This is a technique that was developed by Patrick Friman, PhD and his colleagues. The bedtime pass is a small card that has an attractive picture on one side and the words "bedtime pass" on the other. When children are given this card at bedtime, they are told that they can use the pass to check in with their parents and this is often comforting to the child. They are also told that they will receive a reward if they still have the pass in the morning. Children who do want to see their parents during the night will need to forfeit their pass (and a reward) for that night. Even when using a bedtime pass, do your best to keep all interactions with your child "brief and boring" during the night. A quick "I love you; it's time to go back to bed" will be best. Using a meaningful picture (including a picture that represents a child's special interest) on the pass may be quite effective; some children become attached to the pass itself because of the strong positive value attached to the picture. Your child may want to help you design the pass. Some children benefit from using more than one pass when they first start this program. The Autism Speaks Sleep Toolkit has a nice teaching story about using a bedtime pass.

Please be aware that changes in your response to your child's night waking may result in them testing to see if you are going to consistently follow through on the new routine. This is also true if you make changes to how your child falls asleep at the beginning of the night (especially if you stop sleeping with your child). After your child spends some time testing to make sure that there isn't anything they may do to change the situation ("maybe if I just keep crying…"), the situation will improve. Being consistent will be helpful. Try to come up with a plan that will allow you to respond consistently to your child. For some families, that means a slow, gradual approach that will not result in any crying or challenging behaviors. It is also important to consider safety issues if your child is waking up during the night. All doors and cabinets should be locked, and any dangerous materials should be kept well out of reach. It may also be necessary to put a bell on your child's door so that you may be alerted if he or she leaves the bedroom. As we discussed earlier, you may also want to consider the use of a medical safety bed.

Early morning awakening is different from waking in the middle of the night and then returning to sleep at some point. Some children wake up earlier than their parents would like because of their need for less sleep or their tendency to be early morning risers. One strategy that might help delay early rising is delaying bedtime. The elimination of naps for children who still take them may also help delay the start of the day for some children.

Some children simply need less sleep and are ready to go much earlier than their parents. These children need to learn how to entertain themselves safely and quietly. Parents and children can work together to develop a morning schedule and a basket of toys and activities for morning time. Some children also respond well to visual cues about when they are allowed to go to their parents or other family members. A light with a timer may be used to cue children that it is permissible to leave the room only when the light is on. Parents may be able to gradually set the timer to go off at later times in the morning. Rewards for playing quietly and staying in one's room are often effective as well. As always, safety issues should be considered. As early morning awakening may be a sign of depression or anxiety, a child's mood should be assessed if this represents a change in behavior.

Nightmares are common and typically occur during REM sleep and in the latter part of the night. When children wake up from nightmares, they will typically remember at least part of what they have dreamt. Stress and anxiety have been linked to an increase in nightmares, so helping children learn to relax and be less anxious through simple relaxation techniques often results in fewer nightmares. It is advisable to provide some comfort to children who awaken from bad dreams, while helping them return to sleep in their own bed. Parents should try to maintain the sleep routines that have been established, and if necessary, talk about the nightmare in the morning. Some children respond very well to a technique called imagery rehearsal therapy (IRT). Children are asked to describe their bad dreams in as much detail as possible. They may make a drawing of the bad dream and then crumple it up or tear it up. Next, they will describe a new, positive dream with as much detail as they can. They will practice saying/repeating their new, positive dream during the day and before bed. They may also make a drawing of the good dream and put it up in their room near their bed. Then, if they do have a bad dream, they can tell you their new positive dream. This will help decrease nightmares and help your child feel more confident about conquering their fears.

Parasomnias are common in childhood and tend to run in families. Some children cry out during the night but are not actually awake. These children may be experiencing night terrors, which are also called non-REM parasomnias. Other types of parasomnias include sleepwalking, sleep talking, and confusional arousals. Night terrors and nightmares are often confused with one another but are quite different and respond best to different strategies.

Night terrors are characterized by loud, piercing screams. Children experiencing night terrors are not actually awake. Night terrors typically occur during the first third of the night and are more common during the deep sleep phases of non-REM sleep. Children do not respond to attempts to provide comfort during these times. In fact, children may appear more agitated if others try to interact with them during a night terror. Remember that children are asleep during these episodes, and they typically do not recall much if anything about the incident. If they remember anything, it is typically a single image but not a dream sequence. Some of these images may be quite frightening to a child and may include monsters or dangerous people. The fact that children are usually moving during these episodes tells us that they are not in REM sleep (when almost all movement is suppressed) and are not, in fact, dreaming. There is some evidence to suggest that night terrors are more common in younger children; they frequently stop by the time a child enters adolescence. Confusional arousals are another type of parasomnia; children frequently sit up during these episodes and appear to be in a confused state. At times, forcing a child from a confusional arousal may result in some aggressive behavior. These types of arousals usually occur in children under the age of five and are like night terrors as the child typically does not remember the event. Sleepwalking is somewhat common in school-aged children and occurs more frequently in boys than in girls.

There is some evidence to suggest that sleep fragmentation and sleep deprivation may increase night terrors. Children who are not sleeping well may thus have more night terrors. Noises or movement nearby may also be triggers. Improving a child's sleep habits may thus decrease the frequency of night terrors. During the time a child is experiencing a parasomnia, ensure their safety, but do not awaken the child or try to stop the event. Even if your child is sleepwalking, all you need to do is help him or her get back to bed and provide comforting, soothing statements. Although parasomnias may improve with age and better sleep habits, be sure to let your physician know about these difficulties. In some instances, poor sleep due to obstructive sleep apnea (OSA) or restless legs syndrome (RLS)/Periodic Limb Movement Disorder may be the cause of the night terrors and should be treated. Differentiating parasomnias from nocturnal seizures can be challenging.

Some sleep researchers consider *teeth-grinding*, or sleep-related bruxism, to be a type of parasomnia. It is not clear what causes teeth-grinding; stress and anxiety may be contributing factors, so relaxation techniques may reduce this behavior. There is also some indication that dental problems and the shape of the jaw may contribute to this problem, and consultation with a dentist is often advised. Dental guards or splints (if tolerated) decrease teeth-grinding and lessen the physical impact of this behavior. Teeth-grinding only at night should be differentiated from teeth-grinding during the day.

As children transition to adolescence, they commonly begin to develop later bedtime schedules and consequently experience delays in their circadian rhythms. The same good sleep habits that we have outlined above will help these adolescents maintain typical sleep schedules. In more extreme cases, an individual may develop a delayed sleep phase (DSP) disorder. If allowed to follow their own preferences, individuals with DSP will fall asleep late at night and then sleep until late in the morning. They do not experience any difficulties falling or staying asleep if they are able to follow their own schedule. Thus, if there are no pressing reasons to change the schedule of an individual with DSP, treatment is not necessary. Most individuals, however, do need to conform to a traditional school and work schedule. Families may also want everyone in the household to follow a similar day/night schedule so that they can spend time together. Treatment for delayed sleep phase disorder involves gradually and systematically changing an individual's bedtime. Consultation with a health care provider or sleep specialist is often helpful when making significant changes to an individual's sleep/wake schedule.

While teens and young adults may be more likely to have a phase delay (they are going to sleep later and waking up later than others), there is some research to indicate that autistic adults with intellectual disability may be more likely to have advanced phase disorder. (This means that they are going to sleep earlier and waking up earlier than others.) This is also seen in a small number of adults without intellectual disability. Advanced phase disorder is also best managed by consulting with a health care provider or sleep specialist.

Narcolepsy is another sleep disorder that involves excessive daytime sleepiness. While many think of this disorder as occurring in adults, it has been diagnosed in children as young as five years of age. Individuals with a diagnosis of narcolepsy will have extreme and sudden urges to sleep. They may suddenly fall asleep at any time during the day, even while they are eating, talking, or engaging in positive interactions. A tell-tale sign of narcolepsy is cataplexy. This involves the loss of muscle control during the day and often occurs during times of intense emotions, including positive emotions. Individuals with narcolepsy may also experience temporary paralysis as they fall asleep or when they are first awakening. Diagnosis of narcolepsy involves a nighttime and daytime sleep study. Currently, treatment involves medication and good sleep habits. Consultation with a sleep specialist is recommended.

Sleep-Related Breathing Disorders are some of the most common difficulties for children with DS-ASD. Obstructive sleep apnea (OSA) is a serious disorder that has important behavioral and medical implications. OSA can affect cardiovascular and metabolic functioning and has been found to affect attention, tasks of executive functioning, and irritability. Individuals with OSA have a narrowing of the airways which makes it difficult to breathe. As the size of a person's breath decreases, levels of oxygen drop while levels of carbon dioxide increase. These changes (difficulty breathing as well as changes in levels of oxygen and carbon dioxide) result in disrupted sleep as the individual awakens and gasps for air. Once the individual has obtained enough good breaths, he or she returns to sleep. This happens repeatedly throughout the night resulting in poor sleep and sleepiness during the day. This in turn may lead to difficulties in activity level, attention, memory, processing speed, and learning as well as other behavioral problems. The changes in oxygen and carbon dioxide levels are also physically stressful and may lead to heart and lung issues. Diagnosis of OSA is confirmed with polysomnography. Research indicates that OSA is very common in individuals with Down syndrome; estimates range from 50% to 79% in children with Down syndrome and 65% to 100% in adults with Down syndrome. There are many factors that may relate to so many people with Down syndrome having OSA. These include anatomical characteristics of people with Down syndrome, hypotonia, increased mucosal secretions, as well as a high incidence of upper respiratory tract infections and gastroesophageal reflux. There is also evidence that as an individual gets older, other factors such as hypothyroidism and obesity increase and that this in turn increases the risk for OSA. The American Academy of Pediatrics (AAP) Health Supervision Guidance for Children and Adolescents with Down Syndrome recommends screening for Sleep-Disordered Breathing at least by 6 months of age and at every health supervision visit after that. Every child should also get a polysomnogram between 3 and 5 years of age (Bull et al., 2022).

Most individuals with OSA may use a device that provides positive airway pressure. This device provides air pressure to keep the airway open. Individuals wear a mask that connects via a hose to the machine that provides the pressure. One of the most common devices used for people with OSA is continuous positive airway pressure (CPAP). Respiratory technicians help individuals learn to use the device. Learning to wear a mask and use the machine may be initially challenging, but individuals with DS-ASD are able to learn to use these devices. Graduated exposure and desensitization techniques have been quite effective. It is often best to take a gradual approach in which children first learn to wear a mask without any airway pressure and then slowly learn to tolerate longer and increased amounts of pressure. Other strategies that have been effective include decorating masks or having other family members wear them as well. Individuals may be given masks before they have been evaluated for OSA so that they can begin the desensitization process. This is an effective strategy for children with DS-ASD since these children are particularly likely to require the use of a positive airway pressure device at some point in their lives. The use of continuous airway pressure has been linked to less fragmented sleep and improved learning, behavior, and physical health. (See Primary Care, chapter four.) There is also emerging evidence that hypoglossal nerve stimulation (an implant device that activates nerves that go to the tongue) may safely improve OSA in adolescents with DS (Caloway et al., 2020).

Sleep Movement Disorders include rhythmic movement disorder, restless legs syndrome (RLS), periodic limb movements in sleep (PLMS), and periodic limb movement disorder (PLMD).

Rhythmic Movement Disorder is characterized by repetitive motion of the head (including head banging), trunk, or limbs, usually during the transition from wakefulness to sleep. It may also arise during sustained sleep. Although the condition most often affects infants and toddlers in a transient and self-limited fashion, it may persist in children with autism and other developmental disabilities. Padding the sleep environment may be helpful.

Restless Legs Syndrome (RLS) is a sensorimotor disorder which involves an urge to move the legs that typically occurs in the evening and when the legs are not moving.

Periodic Limb Movements in Sleep (PLMS) are defined by repetitive stereotypic movements of the limbs during sleep.

Periodic Limb Movement Disorder (PLMD) also includes repetitive stereotypic movements but is associated with insomnia or daytime sleepiness as well.

Diagnosing RLS is difficult due to many individuals' inability to fully communicate their symptoms. A polysomnogram is necessary for making a diagnosis of PLMS or PLMD. Iron deficiency has been associated with RLS and PLMD in adults. Identification and treatment of iron deficiency in children with sleep disorders should be considered although more research is needed to determine the efficacy of this intervention. The AAP recommends that if a child with Down syndrome has sleep problems and a ferritin (iron stores) less than 50 mcg/L, the pediatrician may prescribe an iron supplement.

MEDICATION

In addition to addressing any medical issues and working on improving sleep habits, it may also be helpful to consider the use of medication to help with sleep. There is research to indicate that taking melatonin may help treat insomnia in autistic children. (Abdelgadir et al., 2018; Braam et al., 2009). It has also been used to reset individuals' biological clocks. Synthetic melatonin is available as a dietary supplement. While studies have not supported the use of melatonin to treat sleep disorders in children with typical development, it does appear to be safe and effective in individuals with an intellectual disability and ASD. However, there are no studies in children with Down syndrome. It is important to discuss the use of melatonin or any other supplement with your health care provider before use. Also, note that melatonin is not regulated by the government and there have been studies documenting the lack of consistency in the ingredients in over-the-counter melatonin. Try to find a brand that has an USP or NSF certification as this indicates at least some self-monitoring by the manufacturer of the melatonin. If melatonin use is not helpful, additional medications to treat sleep may also be considered. (See chapter six, Guidelines and Indications for Medication Use.)

CONCLUSION

We would like to conclude this chapter by emphasizing the importance of good sleep. In our research and clinical work, we have seen the ways in which poor sleep affects mood, behavior, and the ability to learn. We have learned a great deal from the families with whom we have worked, and we have been encouraged by the changes that we have been able to accomplish by working with them as a team. We have seen how addressing children's sleep difficulties can significantly improve their lives and the lives of their families. Parents of children with DS-ASD should remain optimistic that with proper intervention their children's sleep will likely improve.

SUGGESTED RESOURCES

Durand, Mark V. *Sleep Better!: A Guide to Improving Sleep for Children with Special Needs*, revised edition. Brookes Publishing, 2014.

This book describes sleep strategies for children with special needs.

Katz, T., and B. Malow. *Solving Sleep Problems in Children with Autism Spectrum Disorders: A Guide for Frazzled Families.* Independently published, 2020.

This book provides detailed information about many of the behavioral strategies described in this chapter.

Owens, J. A., and J. A. Mindell. *Take Charge of Your Child's Sleep: The All-in-One Resource for Solving Sleep Problems in Kids and Teens.* Marlowe & Company, 2005.

This is a review of common sleep problems and methods to address sleep difficulties in children and adolescents.

Autism Speaks Sleep Toolkit:

https://www.autismspeaks.org/tool-kit/atnair-p-strategies-improve-sleep-children-autism

Autism Speaks Visual Supports Toolkit:

https://www.autismspeaks.org/tool-kit/atnair-p-visual-supports-and-autism

National Sleep Foundation
2001 Massachusetts Ave, NW
Washington, DC 20036

Phone: 703-243-1697

https://www.thensf.org/

REFERENCES

Abdelgadir, I. S., Gordon, M. A., & Akobeng, A. K. (2018). Melatonin for the management of sleep problems in children with neurodevelopmental disorders: a systematic review and meta-analysis. *Archives of Disease in Childhood, 103*(12), 1155–1162. https://doi.org/10.1136/archdischild-2017-314181

Braam, W., Smits, M. G., Didden, R., Korzilius, H., Van Geijlswijk, I. M., & Curfs, L. M. (2009). Exogenous melatonin for sleep problems in individuals with intellectual disability: a meta-analysis. *Developmental Medicine and Child Neurology*, *51*(5), 340–349, https://doi.org/10.1111/j.1469-8749.2008.03244.x

Bull, M. J., Trotter, T., Santoro, S. L., Christensen, C., Grout, R. W., COUNCIL ON GENETICS, Burke, L. W., Berry, S. A., Geleske, T. A., Holm, I., Hopkin, R. J., Introne, W. J., Lyons, M. J., Monteil, D. C., Scheuerle, A., Stoler, J. M., Vergano, S. A., Chen, E., Hamid, R., Downs, S. M., … Spire, P. (2022). Health supervision for children and adolescents with Down syndrome. *Pediatrics*, *149*(5), 1–24. https://doi.org/10.1542/peds.2022-057010

Caloway, C. L., Diercks, G. R., Keamy, D., de Guzman, V., Soose, R., Raol, N., Shott, S. R., Ishman, S. L., & Hartnick, C. J. (2020). Update on hypoglossal nerve stimulation in children with down syndrome and obstructive sleep apnea. *The Laryngoscope*, *130*(4), 263–267. https://doi.org/10.1002/lary.28138

National Sleep Foundation. (2020, October 1). How much sleep do you really need? *Sleep and You.* https://www.thensf.org/how-many-hours-of-sleep-do-you-really-need/

Revana, A., Vecchio, J., Guffey, D., Minard, C. G., & Glaze, D. G. (2022). Clinical application of home sleep apnea testing in children: A prospective pilot study. *Journal of Clinical Sleep Medicine*, *18*(2), 533–540. https://doi.org/10.5664/jcsm.9650

CHAPTER NINE

GETTING THE MOST OUT OF YOUR DOCTOR VISITS: ADVICE FOR PARENTS AND HEALTH CARE PROVIDERS

Kimberly Bonello, Parent

Lina Patel, PsyD

Laura Pickler, MD, MPH

*The doctor of the future will give no medicine,
but will interest her or his patients in the care of the human frame,
in a proper diet, and in the cause and prevention of disease.*
—Thomas Edison (1847–1931)

BEFORE THE VISIT

Dr. Pickler:

Appointments with your child's medical provider will be much more productive for everyone involved if you do a little planning prior to making an appointment. If you don't already have a medical provider who sees your child regularly and knows your family, we highly suggest working toward this goal. It can be challenging to find a clinician who is a good fit for your child and family. Choices may be limited due to your insurance coverage, resources available in your area, practice location, desire to limit driving time, or other logistical considerations. As you are thinking about finding the right clinician for your child, you also should consider the health care system that supports the primary care office. You will be reliant on primary care and specialty care, which together need a system behind them to meet all your needs. A health care system should be connected electronically, which makes communication between you and your child's clinicians more efficient. You should have access to your child's medical record through a portal or similar password protected system where you can view records and lab results as well as send secure messages to your clinicians, care coordinator, or office staff. If an electronic portal is not available, be sure to keep a binder or notebook where you organize important information about your child. Your child's primary care clinician can help you know what is important to keep handy.

Every person deserves a Patient/Family-Centered Medical Home. A medical home is not a specific place or a doctor's office, but conceptually embodies a team approach to health care. These team members include the family, health care providers, educational services, community programs, insurance, and other payment sources.

According to the American Association of Pediatrics (AAP) National Resource Center for Patient/Family-Centered Medical Home, there are seven key components to a Medical Home (2022):

- Access to care
- Family-centered care
- Cultural responsiveness
- Continuity of care
- Comprehensive care
- Compassionate care
- Coordination of care

One key element in the medical home model of care is the presence of partnerships between the family and all professionals involved in the child's life that together provide a medical home throughout childhood and assist with transition to adult care. These partnerships include medical providers, but also acknowledge the additional resources that go into quality health care delivery such as school personnel, community therapists, and public health professionals. Also, the rejection of a medical home as a physical location or specific medical practice is important. The patient and family are at the center of the defining statement rather than a specific clinician's office. Each of the seven components of a medical home becomes linked to some extent to every medical provider of care for the patient with special health care needs as they manage chronic conditions. Familiarity with these components is the first step toward increasing the medical home approach in specialty care. There are specific resources for practices and families collected by the National Resource Center found online and cited at the end of this chapter. It is completely appropriate for parents to request and expect care to be provided according to the medical home model. Bear in mind, however, that this may look different for each individual family. Parents should feel empowered and encouraged to discuss what this means for their child with their child's primary care provider.

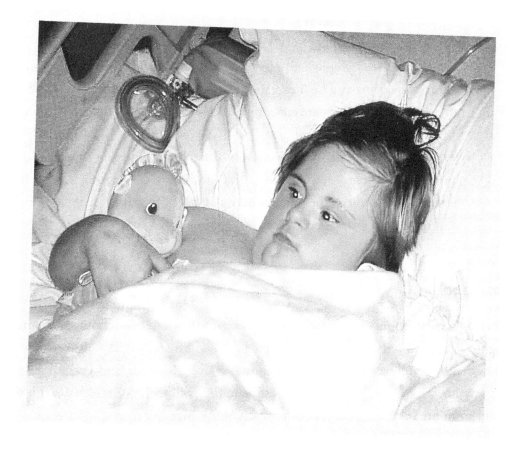

Once you have an established medical home, the following practical suggestions will be easier to implement:

- Make appointments that do not interfere with other activities, such as school or therapy sessions if at all possible.
- Consider whether it is better for your family to have multiple appointments in one day to minimize travel, or to only have one appointment in a day to minimize stress.

- Make a list of things you want to discuss. Keep in mind that if your list is long or the items are complex, you may not get every item addressed in one visit.

- Ask for extra time during an appointment when you schedule. If it is difficult to schedule extra time, consider requesting the last appointment of the day so that your doctor isn't rushed. Making sure that your doctor has enough time scheduled to meet your needs will limit the possibility of being kept waiting at the doctor's office.

- Be on time. No one likes to be kept waiting. If you are late, chances are that every family after you will also be seen late. Timeliness is considerate, not just to the doctor and his/her staff, but to every patient scheduled that day after you. Many offices are enacting policies that may ask you to reschedule if you are more than ten minutes late.

- If your child is agitated while you wait for your appointment to begin, let a nurse know. There are likely options for limiting or eliminating waiting time at the doctor's office. The practice may also have options for making the wait time more pleasant for everyone.

Kim Bonello:

As the mother of a young adult with DS-ASD, I have learned so much from my beautiful daughter, Emily, about how to be a good medical advocate for her as well as for myself and our entire family. I have made many mistakes over the years, and I've learned the hard way how to help streamline and coordinate Emily's medical care. I hope you will benefit from my experiences and decide which of my suggestions you will use on your family's journey with DS-ASD.

It might be helpful to remember that doctors and other health care providers are there to serve you and your child. A good doctor will not be offended if you request a second opinion. If it is not working well with a particular provider, please know that you are within your rights to seek a new provider. Being with the wrong doctor/provider will only cause you and your child undue anxiety, while finding the right doctor/provider will ease your mind and empower you to ask the questions you need to ask to ensure your child's long-term health and happiness.

With that said, I'd like to offer some suggestions to hopefully make your child's next appointment a little less stressful for both of you:

- Provide as much information as possible to the scheduler about what you want to accomplish during your child's doctor's visit so the doctor can be better prepared to address issues of concern.

- When visiting a new doctor or facility, ask the scheduler about location, parking, where to enter the building, and the check-in process so you can be prepared. Ask if they have a website where you can get all that information, as well as any needed forms you can fill out in advance. This will reduce stress for you and your child.

- Tell the scheduler about any special accommodations your child may need, such as wheelchair access, special or more private waiting areas, or immediate room placement to avoid overstimulation.

- To the extent that your child can understand, tell her about the appointment in advance, such as who will see her and why. For example, I tell Emily, "We are going to see Dr. Pickler [tomorrow, today, in a few minutes]. She will listen to your chest and back and will look in your ears and mouth." Whether there is a response or not, repeat this a few times before the appointment so there are no, or only a few, surprises.

- Work toward creating a medical home. Creating a medical home as Dr. Pickler described above will help with the constant requests to explain your child's medical issues. It will also help when filling out forms, as you can write, "See electronic medical record," instead of filling out multiple forms. If you see providers in multiple medical settings for different specialties, make sure that your providers are updating information from other specialists such as medications, or contact information of other clinicians. If it is an option to use a patient portal in the health care system where you receive care, this is an excellent way to improve communication between health care providers. Prior to every appointment, log in and make sure that the information in the patient portal is correct. Ask your provider to make updates and changes as they are needed. If there isn't an electronic portal available, keep a notebook of important information to have available for every appointment and keep it updated.

Dr. Patel:

Often, within our busy days, we only start thinking about a medical appointment when we are getting in the car to go to it. While it is important to attend a scheduled medical visit, getting there and working to ensure that the visit results in participation is key. To do this, it will be important to first understand your loved one's level of anxiety. Medical anxiety can be caused by several factors including comprehension issues, fear, infrequent exposure to that specific intervention, and historical experiences that were painful. Anxiety is the driving force for nonparticipation and can result in medical workups failing to be completed. In more extreme cases where medical intervention is urgent, medical trauma can also occur, which negatively impacts future participation in visits. Proactive strategies to prepare for the visit thus become key. There are several ways in which you can help your loved one with DS-ASD prepare for the visit. While not exhaustive, we will highlight several helpful strategies. You will need to determine how many you need to use depending on your loved one's typical level of distress. You will also have to take into consideration what your loved one's current skills are and if you feel that the strategy will make sense to the person or not.

Requests from the medical clinic or provider. It can sometimes be scary to ask for or direct professionals about what your loved one needs. It is important, however, to try to remind yourself that you are the expert when it comes to your loved one and that you bring valuable information to the table that can help make the visit more successful. Not all professionals can accommodate your requests, but it never hurts to ask! As such, we offer a few ideas of things that it may be helpful to request or discuss ahead of the visit. For example, you could request a picture of the provider that your loved one will see if you can't find one online. Frequent exposure to the picture ahead of the visit can help reduce anxiety about who they are meeting with and what will happen during the visit. A term that we often use in the medical community is "sensitive scheduling." This simply means that a visit can be scheduled at a particular time of day when your loved one is at their best. Perhaps your loved one does best early in the morning. Then you can request an appointment in the morning.

Perhaps your loved one does best when there are fewer people in the waiting room, and it is quieter. You can ask schedulers what time of day the lowest traffic is and perhaps schedule during that time. If your loved one takes medicine that helps calm them, perhaps scheduling the appointment shortly after medicine has been taken. Some places also can do something called "express rooming." This is a method by which a person can be sent to an exam room right when they have checked in so that they do not sit in a less predictable environment like a waiting room. Instead, they can wait in a calmer, quieter, space until it is time for the doctor to start the visit. Openly sharing information about your loved one and in what circumstances they do best can sometimes even result in learning about services that you didn't know existed. For example, some places can do "pre-visit tours" in which they will walk a person through the facility prior to the actual appointment so the person can become familiar with the environment and what will occur prior to being physically examined or any procedures being done. Other places have created a specific "low stimulation" exam room where lights can be dimmed, and noise level is low. Advocacy and open conversations are critical.

Social Stories. This is a picture book that tells a person what will happen at the visit. The story is written from a first-person point of view and shares what the expectations are for behaviors, participation, and coping strategies. Many social stories written by other families and professionals can be found online. You can also learn to write your own by visiting carolgraysocialstories.com/social-stories/what-is-it. Carol Gray is the original creator of the social story and has a clear format regarding what to include. You can also just write your own, based on what you feel would be the most helpful information in pictures and/or words for your loved one. The point of a social story is to expose the person to the needed information prior to the actual moment when anxiety kicks in and comprehension becomes too difficult.

Visual Schedules. A visual schedule breaks down each step of a visit into pictures or bite-sized pieces of information. Pictures or words are often attached to a board via Velcro so that each step can be removed as they occur. This tool is great to help a person see what they must do, how much they must do, progress toward being done (as the pictures or words are removed), and what preferred activity may come at the end. Many individuals may also already be familiar with visual schedules because they may use them in other settings such as school, home, work, or in the community.

First-Then Directives. A first-then directive is simply an instruction in which a person is told what hard task they will have to do "first" and then what preferred activity will come next. Like a visual schedule, a first-then directive helps a person know what they must do and what will immediately come next that is more preferred. For some individuals who have a higher level of distress, they may only be able to tolerate one step before they need something preferred. In this case, first-then directives, even verbally, can be very helpful. For example, you could say, "first look in ears, then break."

Visual Timers. Sometimes the most distressing part of a visit is not knowing how long a specific part of a visit will last. Visual timers can be a great resource for helping make the concept of time more concrete. A visual timer allows a person to see the passage of time visually, so that they know exactly how much longer they must engage in something distressing before time is up. This is also a tool that the person may already be familiar with in other settings.

Distractions. Individuals with Down syndrome and autism frequently engage in self-stimulatory behaviors (a repetitive movement that does not have a clear purpose) with a preferred object. This behavior is often noted as a self-calming activity and may increase when a person is particularly distressed. Bringing preferred objects to the visit can serve as a nice distraction. You can also give the object to the individual only after the doctor starts the exam, to increase the likelihood that the distraction will be helpful. First-then directives can be used to also help the person know when they will have access to the object ("First check ears, and then break with X").

Desensitization. Desensitization is a fancy word that just means that you take small steps to help someone get used to something that otherwise is distressing. For home practice, desensitization may mean practicing steps that you have access to. For example, you may practice the first step of a blood draw by using something you can find at home (perhaps a small scarf or hair tie) as a tourniquet for a prespecified amount of time. You may practice that every day for a short amount of time (i.e., count of 10), before you say, "all done," and allow your loved one access to something preferred. Once you notice that the "tourniquet" is no longer causing distress, then you can add a step and practice the pretend tourniquet and wiping the skin with an alcohol wipe. Once you see that your loved one is no longer distressed by these first two steps, then you could add another step. Obviously, in this example, you wouldn't be able to practice all the steps on your own. Because desensitization is a longer process and you may need access to medical space to engage in the practice, it will be helpful to ask your medical provider if they have someone on staff that can support the desensitization process. There are many community providers such as psychologists, behaviorists, occupational therapists, etc., that can also support this desensitization process.

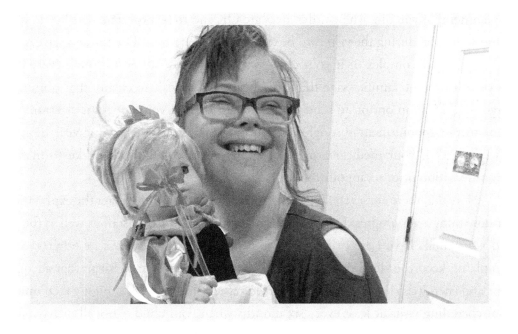

DURING THE VISIT

Dr. Pickler:

Once you have decided when and where your child will be seen, you have completed a great deal of work that will make the actual visit go well. Thinking through the logistics of the initial portion of the appointment is your next step. If you expect that your child will have behavior challenges, bring any items from home that will make it easier if you must wait to be seen that day. Examples may include snacks, a favorite toy, or a blanket. You might request to be put into a room right away so that your child is away from the noise and activity of the waiting area. Some children enjoy activities such as stringing beads, stacking blocks, or coloring while they wait. Whatever you decide will help your child be relaxed and comfortable during the initial process of checking in and waiting to be seen will greatly help when the doctor is in the room discussing your concerns.

Never underestimate the importance of a list. Grocery lists are important for efficiency when you are shopping and so are lists for your medical provider. If possible, prioritize the items you wish to discuss to avoid bringing up your most important concern when the doctor is thinking the visit is almost over. If you make a list, your doctor can know what things are most important to you. Keep in mind that the doctor may not have the same list that you do. He/she may not have prioritized items in the same order that you did. These differences are OK and to be expected. The key to good communication during the visit is to be clear about your needs. Do not be a slave to the list! If items are complex or if your child is sick, you may not get through every item on your list. Some families save their lists from visit to visit to ensure that nothing is forgotten. If it is an option to send your clinician a list of your concerns electronically prior to the appointment through a secure portal this may help your visit be more efficient. Ask if your medical provider has preferences for how they like to manage communication prior to appointments.

Note that there are several types of appointments that may dictate the expectations for how things will progress for the medical provider and his/her staff as well as for you and your child. If you are bringing in your child due to an illness or other specific complaint, keep your list brief. Try to focus on the reason for the visit so that adequate time and energy can be spent getting your child the help she needs. I highly recommend also scheduling visits at least every six months when your child is not ill or having an acute problem. This allows for time to receive information about the resources you need to successfully parent your child and to prevent things that may cause problems later. It also makes time for care coordination between the various providers with whom your child has interactions. More frequent visits help keep everyone up-to-date and provide opportunities to review items on your child's care plan. Most children and adults have a better experience during medical visits if there is a routine in place that is not forgotten between visits.

Due to important legal and regulatory changes during the early phases of the COVID-19 pandemic, video visits are much more commonplace and accepted among medical providers. Consider asking for a video appointment if your child is well and the purpose for the visit is to update information or for care coordination. Our experience with video visits for children with Down syndrome and autism has been positive. Make sure you are aware of the technical and internet bandwidth requirements for a successful video appointment. If a physical exam is needed at the visit, it is better to schedule an in-person appointment.

Kim Bonello:

Your child will learn from each doctor's visit, and it will get easier in time. Make simple accommodations to put your child at ease and lessen his or her anxiety. This may include turning off fluorescent lights, removing "crinkly" paper from the exam table, and closing the door if another child is fussing or crying. Bring quiet activities that you have saved just for the doctor's visit. Perhaps you can read a favorite book or bring a new coloring book and crayons to enjoy while you're waiting for the doctor to arrive.

Pay attention to your child's cues during the doctor's visit. If something is causing distress, be quick to react in order to head off a meltdown. Tell the doctor what works best for your child. Perhaps you might say, "Be swift about the exam and keep talking softly about what you are doing, but don't ask if you may look in her ears—just do it." Or you may say, "You need to warn her in advance about everything you are going to do and take your time and wait until she's ready to comply." It all depends on what your child needs, and you are the best expert on your child. Help the doctor out by telling him or her what works and what doesn't work. Also, if possible, you may want to request that anything really uncomfortable or painful such as shots be done toward the end of the visit.

From the time Emily was a child we tried to give her choices in any decision that she could understand. Examples include which arm she would have her blood pressure taken or where to have an immunization. Make sure to offer choices that are truly choices so that you don't create conflict. For example, ask her to choose a Band-Aid from available choices. Don't suggest a color that isn't available which then creates an opportunity for your child to be upset. If there is a color that your child prefers, bring a few in your purse until you know what is stocked at the clinic or hospital. These are examples of *respectful autonomy*. As your child gets older and you have a sense of how autonomy fits into his or her life, be intentional about adjusting your expectations over time so that your child can be as independent as possible. I believe in Emily so it's easy to advocate for her strengths and independence.

Know when it's time to end the visit, even if you haven't accomplished everything or asked every question you had written down. If you need to end the visit abruptly, make an appointment for a follow-up phone call or ask if you can send the doctor an email so you can finish asking your questions. Get as much of the physical exam done as quickly as possible just in case your child reaches his or her threshold for this visit and needs to leave. If you leave *before* a meltdown occurs, your child will learn to trust that future visits will be tolerable and that you care about their comfort.

When it comes to working with your child's doctor, be helpful and pleasant while he or she is examining your child. You catch more flies with honey than vinegar! If you need to become assertive to get your point across or to get what your child needs, absolutely be assertive. Remember, however, that your goal is to be assertive, not aggressive. Being aggressive will not serve your child in the slightest, but being positively assertive will pay off in a big way.

Dr. Patel:

Prior to your visit, you built your toolbox and practiced the parts that you were able to practice to help reduce anxiety. Now, during the visit, it is time to use the tools that you have practiced, but in the moment. The more that the tools you used prior to the visit look like and work in a similar fashion to the actual visit, the better. Gather your visual schedule, visual timer, distraction items, noise-canceling headphones, etc., and bring them to the visit. If the clinic had offered express rooming, remind staff when you check in. If they don't have express rooming and you have a loved one who becomes overstimulated or distressed in louder environments, call the clinic or doctor's office from your car when you arrive and see if they can call you to come in only once the exam room is ready or the doctor is ready for the visit. If your loved one becomes most distressed by vitals, see if it is safe to complete vitals at the end of the visit instead of the beginning of the visit to ensure cooperation and less distress for other aspects of the visit. Creative solutions are not always found unless we are willing to share what our loved ones need!

Most often, medical providers became medical providers because they wanted to help and not do harm. However, some providers may not have as much experience working with individuals with developmental disabilities. Therefore, it is important to remind yourself again that you are the expert when it comes to your loved one and that communication with the provider about what works well and what doesn't creates the best opportunities for successful and compassionate care. Communicate with your provider at the start of the visit what signs of distress look like for your loved one. For example, someone with Down syndrome and autism may increase their vocal stimming or get louder with their vocal stimming. While this may not be an obvious sign of distress to a less experienced provider, your communication of this may result in the provider offering to take a break before continuing the visit. Again, possibilities only arise when communication is clear. Since many individuals with Down syndrome and autism have a difficult time communicating their distress in a manner that is more easily understood by others, your sharing of information will be critical to the success of the visit.

AFTER THE VISIT

Dr. Pickler:

At the close of every visit, the parent and provider should both understand what needs to be done, who will do it, and in what time frame it will be completed. It is sometimes helpful to make a list so that everyone knows their role. A follow-up plan should be decided on. This can be done either in person or using the electronic medical record portal. Increasingly, technology is allowing families to manage aspects of their child's care electronically, such as by checking lab results or drafting written care plans.

If your practice does not already have a mechanism in place to communicate with a team member who has the role of case manager, explore with the practice whether they can assign this role to someone. This will greatly help with communication between visits and help your family get your needs for paperwork, equipment, and/or other authorizations met.

Occasionally, a family may desire to play a larger role in their child's medical home than is outlined above. For example, the family may want to organize quality improvement activities in the practice to help with making the practice more family-centered, assist other families in connecting with resources or community services, or provide support to other families who also have children with special needs. Most physicians who are committed to providing care in the medical home model will appreciate your efforts and find ways to encourage and support you. Even with electronic resources—which have become commonplace due to the COVID-19 pandemic—there are opportunities for families to have a role in practice improvement efforts.

Kim Bonello:

I always offer Emily a reward after she has visited the doctor. Sometimes I use a food reward, because there is a gelato stand in the lobby of her doctor's office and Emily loves gelato. But I also use other rewards, such as a promise to go home and watch a favorite movie and eat popcorn together, a new "stim" toy that she can add to her collection, or letting her decide what reward she would like that day. Rewards don't have to cost you anything. A "high five" or a heartfelt, "Thank you, Emily," can mean so much to her. She associates going to the doctor with a safe and rewarding experience at this point in her life, and this is what I call a major success!

Dr. Patel:

We have offered some strategies to manage health care visits and believe strongly that these suggestions can make a big difference. Sometimes, however, for a child with DS-ASD who has experienced significant trauma already in the health care setting, who has a level of anxiety that impacts their daily life in more than one way, or whose progress has been affected by multiple factors, it is critical that you seek out professional help. Speak to your primary care doctor and ask them to connect you with a behavioral specialist to specifically work on "desensitization." Other disciplines, like occupational therapists, audiologists, psychologists, and nurses may also be familiar with desensitization strategies and could serve as a resource.

SPECIAL TOPICS

TRANSITION TO ADULT CARE

Dr. Pickler:

Transition from pediatric to adult care for adolescents and young adults with Down syndrome and autism is a multifaceted process that is aimed at maximizing independence and self-advocacy in the areas of health and wellness. Given the complexity of transition for adolescents and adults with Down syndrome and autism, there has been demand for a framework to guide the transition for clinicians and the families they serve. The

National Center for Healthcare Transition, Got Transition, is a federally funded program with several goals aimed at improving the transition to adult health care experience for all youth and young adults. They have proposed and piloted a six-step process, titled "Six Core Elements." Each element is summarized in the table below.

Six Core Elements of Health Care Transition
Policy—no surprises for the patient or family
Tracking and Monitoring—who is ready and where are they in the process?
Readiness Assessment—used to help identify opportunities for increased independence
Planning—plan for success
Transfer of Care—to a new provider or an adult model of care with the same provider
Transfer Completion—close the loop and evaluate satisfaction

The authors of the Six Core Elements fully recognize that this process takes time. The ideal age to begin transition efforts varies between patients however the recommended start time is at age 12 years with a goal of completion soon after the patient's 21st birthday. It is never too late to begin the transition process. Health professionals, young adults, and their families all should have a high level of engagement in the transition process to ensure success. While we may begin encouraging independence at age 12 years, the actual timing for transferring care to adult providers can vary and must be a collaborative process with the clinician, patient, and family.

There is evidence measuring the Six Core Elements that shows positive outcomes with their use (Gabriel et al., 2017; Schmidt et al., 2020). Patients were shown to have better self-reported health, adherence of care, improved disease specific measures, and improved quality of life. The patient experience was also improved with better satisfaction and a reduction in barriers to care. A decrease in hospital admissions and emergency department visits has also been shown. A comprehensive and collaborative transition process is positive for everyone!

Kim Bonello:

Transition is important. I was afraid at first. We started off by going to one adult specialist. Every single doctor that we went to for adult care was well thought out and recommended by the pediatric provider. These were people that I trusted so I was able to trust the adult clinicians that they wanted to refer us to. Having a good team is at the top of my list for how to get started. It was obvious that the process was meticulously planned. My input as the parent was very important throughout the whole process. We discussed the transition ahead of time.

It is as important to prepare parents for medical transition as it is for our children. This is a big step! Adult health care providers and adult care pertains to the maturity of the body, not necessarily related to the developmental age of the patient. You need doctors and resources that are equipped and trained to provide care to your child's adult body.

I have a few suggestions for how to proceed with the transition process from the parent's perspective:

- Consider having an initial appointment on telehealth. This is a good way to meet the new adult provider in a comfortable and safe environment.
- Your adult child might need time to get used to going to a new location and seeing new people. We worked hard to make appointments successful in pediatric settings. Try to incorporate something your child likes into every in-person appointment. Consider letting your child look at the gift shop (not necessarily buying something every time), going to the coffee bar or promising something desired afterward (like a movie). Remember that the reward needs to be fairly immediate after the appointment to be effective as reinforcement. For example, buy the movie in advance and have it with you at the appointment so that your child knows it is there. Give the reward right after the appointment is over.
- Give *yourself* something to look forward to as well. When you've had a successful appointment, you deserve something for doing all of that work! You get to choose what it is but don't neglect yourself.
- You need to consider all the ways to create a medical home that were talked about at the beginning of this chapter for every new doctor.
- I advise you to space out the visits to a new doctor so that you aren't overwhelmed with a lot of new paperwork all at one time. Every new

appointment is a research project. You will need to go online to learn what paperwork to bring and what forms you need to fill out, plus maps so that you know where to go and figuring out parking.

- Recognize that there is grief associated with having to make a medical change. Take time to think about how you feel and seek support if you need it. It can be especially helpful if you can contact another parent who has gone through the transition to adult care. The Down Syndrome-Autism Connection group on Facebook has been particularly helpful for me. Being able to go online has been great and much more convenient than attending a meeting in person.

CONSIDERING VIDEO MEDICAL VISITS

Dr. Pickler:

The pandemic starting in 2019 challenged our health care system on many levels. However, concerns about infectious disease transmission spawned innovation for how direct patient care is provided. As can be imagined, relationships between clinicians and patients are best accomplished if both the patient and the clinician are able to see each other's faces. These challenges in combination with community restrictions and social distancing necessitated exploring telehealth modalities as a means for providing medical care. Some patients with Down syndrome and autism are unable to adequately wear a mask on their face and the already present anxiety around coming to the hospital can be significantly heightened by this practice. Simultaneously, regulatory restrictions that usually did not allow for home-based video services were lifted and a whole new intervention was born where patients could be in their homes and receive medical services virtually.

From the provider's perspective there are several things that contribute to successful virtual visits.

- Test technology in advance. Internet speeds can make or break an appointment. Be sure that there aren't too many other people streaming appointments at the same time in your home which can significantly reduce internet speeds. You may need to restart your device or download a specific app for the appointment, which is best done in advance.

- Log in a few minutes early. The extra time can be used to problem solve technology that doesn't work as you expect.
- Read the instructions from your provider's office carefully. They may ask for certain information such as current height, weight, or blood pressure to be obtained before the visit. There may be other things they want you to have handy as well, depending on what will be discussed during the visit.
- If the patient portal allows, submit all needed forms or questions you plan to ask during the visit in advance. This will help your provider be efficient when you are on video.
- In our experience a tablet or phone can sometimes be easier to manage than a laptop, particularly if the provider needs to see certain things that are not best observed at a desk or table. You may be asked to turn the camera to see your child to look more closely at their body or see them move. Your provider may also ask to see equipment or rooms where equipment is needed, such as the kitchen, bathroom, or your child's bedroom.

Kim Bonello:

One of the silver linings of the COVID-19 pandemic is the opportunity to have video visits with Emily's doctor. In fact, if she doesn't need a physical exam, we prefer video appointments. Your adult child might not always stay for the whole visit, but I try to have her stay on camera with me as long as possible so that she knows that she is having a doctor's appointment. It is important for Emily to see her doctor's face and hear their voice so that when she goes into the office, she is familiar with her doctor.

ORGANIZING GENERAL ANESTHESIA

Dr. Pickler:

A certain subset of patients with DS-ASD are greatly served by planning to have needed services or procedures that would otherwise be very distressing or significantly uncomfortable performed under anesthesia. A discussion with your doctor about organizing care in this way is important. The risks and benefits of general anesthesia should be carefully considered. Examples of procedures to be considered are:

- Dental work, deep cleanings, and X-rays (see chapter seven on Dental Care)
- Any blood monitoring (thyroid panels, medication monitoring labs, etc.)

- Eye health screenings
- Hearing screenings
- Immunization administration
- Gynecological exams
- X-rays, ultrasounds, MRIs, CT scans

Kim Bonello:

In the past on an annual basis, Emily's doctor and I scheduled one day to take care of all invasive and challenging procedures that are needed for the entire year. While it takes quite a bit of effort to coordinate the schedules of the dentist, ENT surgeon, radiology/lab, and other specialists, it is well worth it! Be aware that your child may tolerate different things over time as they grow up. You may not need to schedule anesthesia nearly as frequently or for the same things that you did in years past. Every procedure is an opportunity to make progress in this area. Make going to the hospital less overwhelming, by keeping your voice and body language calm and reducing the things that may cause anxiety. Try and make it a positive experience using rewards if that is important to your child. It can be a good time to give your child an opportunity to learn new skills. If your child has a certain provider they prefer or if the gender of the provider makes things easier, request this support.

In preparation for procedures under anesthesia, discuss with your child's surgical team options for pre-surgery medications that may help ease the anxiety of the entire experience. Perhaps your child would benefit from having a medication such as Versed, which not only relaxes but causes an "amnesia affect," so she will not even remember being brought back to the operating room. If your child will not willingly swallow a pre-surgery medication, ask for alternative methods of delivery, such as injection or a spray into the nasal passages. Pre-surgery medications have worked wonders for Emily and have saved me from watching her have panic attacks or become combative prior to surgery. I always ask the surgical team to have Emily go "under" with the mask *prior* to placing the IV. Emily does not cooperate with having an IV placed while awake, and this way she is unaware of its placement because she is already asleep.

It is also important to speak with the anesthesiologist about your child to ensure they are aware of individuals with Down syndrome are at risk for issues with cervical spinal instability due to lax ligaments. They should not hyperextend their necks when administering anesthesia.

Bear in mind that it can be difficult to get insurance companies to pay for anesthesia for procedures that are not usually done under anesthesia. In my experience, most insurance companies want you to try to do the procedure or appointment in the conventional way. If it is impossible to complete the procedure or exam any other way, then they will pay for anesthesia. Life is so much easier now that her medical care is more streamlined. Emily's anxiety has diminished, as has mine. Because we have chosen to have multiple procedures done under anesthesia as they are needed, Emily is no longer afraid of going to the doctor. It has all become very routine and she knows what to expect. It's important to laugh. Even if a situation doesn't seem funny at the time think about it later and find humor if you can. I've learned a lot and met some wonderful people. From one parent to another, I wish you all the best as you find the right medical providers who will work with you and help you coordinate a care plan that works well for your entire family.

ADDITIONAL RESOURCES

More information on the Patient/Family-Centered Medical Home: https://www.aap.org/en/practice-management/medical-home

Specific links for families: https://www.aap.org/en/practice-management/medical-home/tools-and-resources-for-medical-home-implementation/medical-home-resources-for-families-and-caregivers/

More information about transition from pediatric to adult care: https://www.gottransition.org/

REFERENCES

American Academy of Pediatrics National Resource Center for Patient/Family-Centered Medical Home. (2022, May 23). *What is a medical home?* American Academy of Pediatrics. *https://www.aap.org/en/practice-management/medical-home/medical-home-overview/what-is-medical-home/*

Gabriel, P., McManus, M., Rogers, K., & White, P. (2017). Outcome evidence for structured pediatric to adult health care transition interventions: A systematic review. *Journal of Pediatrics, 188,* 263–269. https://doi.org/10.1016/j.jpeds.2017.05.066

Schmidt, A., Ilango, S. M., McManus, M. A., Rogers, K. K., & White, P. H. (2020). Outcomes of pediatric to adult health care transition interventions: An updated systematic review. *Journal of Pediatric Nursing. 51,* 92–107. https://doi.org/10.1016/j.pedn.2020.01.002

CHAPTER TEN

UNDERSTANDING COMMUNICATION, BEHAVIOR, AND SENSORY STRATEGIES

Katarzyna Kowerska, MA, CCC-SLP

Lina Patel, PsyD

Teresa Unnerstall, BS Ed

Katie Frank, OT, PhD

Imagine that you are a child or adult with the dual diagnosis of Down syndrome and autism spectrum disorder (DS-ASD). You likely have some difficulty expressing your wants and needs to the people around you, and if the environment is loud or busy, you may experience feelings of anxiety and sensory overload. It stands to reason that you might try to "tell" others what is going on inside of you by behaving in ways that express your feelings of uncertainty and frustration. As a result, the behaviors you are using to communicate may confuse or upset the people who are trying to help you, and feelings of exasperation can escalate for everyone involved. What can be done to help individuals with DS-ASD and their caregivers avoid such conflicts? Thankfully, there are evidence-based strategies that parents and professionals can employ to support the individual with DS-ASD in their efforts to communicate and enjoy a more satisfying life.

Children and adults with DS-ASD frequently experience more significant challenges with communication, behaviors, and sensory issues than individuals with Down syndrome alone. In order to successfully support an individual with DS-ASD, it is imperative that parents and professionals understand the essential functions of all three. In this chapter, expert clinicians in communication, behavior, and sensory challenges offer a deep dive into these three key areas, explaining the relationship between the three and how they impact overall functioning and quality of life. Additionally, we will hear from a seasoned mother about her son's experiences with communication, behaviors, and sensory issues, and we will also offer approaches to successfully address them—for the individual's benefit, and yours as well.

COMMUNICATION, SPEECH, AND LANGUAGE

Katarzyna Kowerska MA, CCC-SLP

Communication, speech, and language development in individuals with DS-ASD are often significantly compromised, beginning in early childhood. Before further exploring why and how, however, it is important to understand the differences between these terms, as they are often used interchangeably, but have quite distinct meanings.

- **Communication** refers to the holistic concept of both understanding and producing messages intended to engage another person. Communication can encompass several modalities including speech, gestures, facial expressions, and body positioning, as well as use of signs and/or pictures.
- **Speech** is the process of using one's voice to make sounds, and then combining those sounds into words to produce a verbal message. Speech allows for a high degree of communicative specificity; however, it is also more difficult to master since it relies on consistent and effective collaboration between neurological and physiological systems of the body.
- **Language** refers to the use of arbitrary symbols (i.e., words, signs, pictures) to represent real objects or concepts, as a means of understanding (decoding) and expressing (encoding) ideas to others. Language can be expressed though speech, or other modalities like signs, or selecting pictures or words on a communication board or Speech Generating Device (SGD).

COGNITIVE IMPACTS ON COMMUNICATION—MEMORY, EXECUTIVE FUNCTION, AND ADAPTIVE BEHAVIOR

Communication is an incredibly complex task that requires constant coordination and understanding from a variety of sources to both take in information from the outside world and generate responses meant for others to receive. Cognitive skills play a large role in this process, and are involved in memory, executive function, and adaptive behavior, all of which contribute to communication skills.

Research has found that while cognitive impairments impacting communication are associated with both DS-only and DS-ASD, some findings suggest that the latter group is associated with the most impacted cognitive skills (Capone et al., 2005). Children with DS-ASD have significantly more impaired brain function than children with DS-only, with deficits in the core domains of social reciprocity and communication (Molloy et al., 2009). Additionally, individuals with DS-ASD have greater deficits in communication and exhibit more stereotypic behavior, anxiety, conduct problems, hyperactivity, and social withdrawal than individuals with DS alone (Capone et al., 2005).

Thoughtful consideration of the relationship between cognitive and language development is essential for developing an appropriate treatment approach. Furthermore, cognitive impairments of individuals who are dually diagnosed with DS-ASD should also be carefully explored when attempting to evaluate and propose communication treatment approaches for this unique and diverse group of individuals. It is important to understand the roles that the following concepts play in the development of cognition and language: memory, executive function, and adaptive behavior.

According to Wilkinson and Finestack (2021), individuals with Down syndrome experience difficulties in their short-term memory, impacting their capacity to acquire vocabulary; their executive function tends to present with weaknesses affecting their ability to plan and adapt to changing situations; and, deficits in their adaptive behavior skills can cause them to encounter difficulties with socialization and communication. To learn more about these important concepts (for example, the effects of hearing loss on communication), refer to Wilkinson and Finestack's book, *Multimodal AAC for Individuals with Down Syndrome.*

Teresa Unnerstall, Parent:

My son Nick was evaluated for a secondary diagnosis of autism at the age of 5. At that time, he was not put on the autism spectrum because his symptoms were conflicting. The report stated that Nick was highly social and made good eye contact and that his diagnosis of verbal apraxia of speech was the reason why his speech was delayed. Fast forward to age 12, my gut feeling was that the symptoms and behaviors were more than just Down syndrome. So, we had him reevaluated for autism. The evaluation and team were much more comprehensive and as I predicted, he got the secondary diagnosis of autism spectrum disorder, known as co-occurring DS-ASD.

The first step I took was to call an IEP meeting to get the secondary diagnosis in writing. Then, I requested that the school district's Board Certified Behavior Analyst (known as a BCBA) be brought on board to do classroom observations and a Functional Behavior Assessment (FBA). The FBA report indicated that Nick was not using his current Augmentative and Alternative Communication (AAC) effectively. In addition, the FBA revealed many triggers and setting events that were causing his behaviors. The IEP team collaborated to create a Behavior Support Plan (BSP) for Nick. This also included getting proper training for the staff and family to use the Picture Exchange Communication System (PECS) to truly give Nick a voice and provide him with sensory breaks and a sensory diet to help with regulation throughout the day across all environments.

The key to helping Nick was a cumulative effort by the entire IEP team and BCBA in the three areas of communication, behavior, and sensory regulation. One note here is to always rule out any health concerns first, as this can be a trigger for many behaviors. Putting these strategies of support together did not happen overnight. It's been a process over many years with expected hiccups along the way. Nick is now 28 years old and to be honest, it is still a work in progress. The good news is that many of the maladaptive behaviors we experienced in his teen years are no longer issues today. As you read through this chapter, we will be giving you specific examples and strategies in these three areas to help you understand how to best support individuals with co-occurring DS-ASD.

OTHER COMMUNICATION PRESENTATIONS: BEHAVIOR, SIGNS, AND USE OF VISUALS/PICTURES

In my work with families with children with DS-ASD, I consistently notice that despite children with DS-ASD presenting with substantial challenges in learning and using verbal language with adequate vocabulary, grammar, and speech intelligibility, they certainly show relative strengths in communicating their wants, needs, and mental states in other creative ways, often best understood mainly by familiar communication partners. Parents often become impressively attuned experts in interpreting their child's communicative behavior, while unfamiliar communication partners are mystified at the intricate and subtle dance between parent and child that is both very intimate and unique to each family.

Parents of children with DS-ASD report spontaneous use of conventional gestures (i.e., pointing, waving to greet, head shake "no," arms up to get picked up) with less consistency. The pointing gesture sometimes spontaneously develops in children with DS-ASD, but most often body movements that are communicative are more gross in nature (e.g., whole arm open palm movement in the direction of desired items vs. pointing) or a physical manipulation of a communication partner's body is reported (e.g., grabbing a parent's finger to turn on a toy, pushing a parent's body in the direction of a desired item).

More often parents report the use of idiosyncratic gestures or body movements "made up" by their child that become meaningful to the family with time, especially when paired with contextual knowledge of the child. Parents of children with DS as well as those of children with DS-ASD often serve as interpreters sharing things such as: this is how he asks for "iPad" and this means "hoodie sweater," while gesturing an arbitrary hand or body movement. Both children with Down syndrome and DS-ASD overuse gestures and sometimes sign approximations, with the first group sometimes pairing the movements with a verbal approximation and the latter group doing so with less regularity, per clinical observation and parent report.

Other behavior-based communication often seen by this author in the DS-ASD population include communicating protests using physical movement such as arching the back, moving their whole body away, pushing away the person/item, or throwing items. Standing near items or in places where desired activities often take place or items are kept (e.g., standing by the high chair, or by the door) as a means of requesting to "eat" or to "go outside" is also often reported by parents. If the child with DS-ASD has the motor capability to go and get things independently, this often is reported as a preferred means of communicating what he/she wants, suggesting that perhaps communicating a want or need to a caregiver using any means (aided or unaided) is much more elusive for this group of children. Parents also often share that their children bring them household items such as a remote or an empty cup or juice from the fridge as a request to "watch TV," "help," or "drink." Lastly, self-injurious behavior (SIB) may be used communicatively by children with DS-ASD to express frustration that their parent has not understood their request or anticipated their wants/needs. It also often indicates frustration when the child's request is declined by their parent (e.g., "you cannot have another cookie," "you cannot use the tablet, it needs to be charged"). In both cases, this frustration perhaps comes from a place of limited social-pragmatic understanding relating to a limited ability to understand that the parent may not have the same agenda that the child has.

If the use of signs is consistently taught by communication partners, it has been my observation that many individuals with DS may become adept at using approximated versions of signs for communication with familiar communication partners, both in isolation and simultaneously while verbalizing. While I have also observed children with DS-ASD be capable of learning to produce signs, often they require more substantial supports to learn rather than learning by copying another person, and their capacity for learning and using signs seems more limited. Parents of children with DS and DS-ASD often report that their children produce approximated versions of signs, which can be hard to understand by unfamiliar communication partners. More commonly, however, parents of children with DS-ASD also report that the meaning of the sign has become diluted and thus less clear for the communication partner. For example, the "more" sign was taught to mean "more" of the current activity (i.e., more music, more food, more drink), but over time has morphed in its meaning for the child, and now also means a request for gaining access to "music," "eat," or "drink," depending on the context, which is of course problematic for less familiar communication partners. Lastly, children with DS-ASD are reported by parents to know certain signs or words but not use them when making a request, or when responding to a question, or they may use the sign when asking for the item but do so out of a communicative context with a parent (i.e., when the parent is in another room not attending to the child).

Similarly, it has been my experience that given communication partner teaching, children with Down syndrome and DS-ASD can learn to use visuals such as pictures or symbols to augment verbal communication. However, as described above, this can also be challenging unless the underlying social-pragmatic fundamentals are addressed.

Difficulties with communication for children with DS and DS-ASD are reported by families to be very frustrating and can lead to a variety of behaviors including but not limited to flapping arms/hands, throwing the visual tools, flopping to the floor, and self-injurious behavior.

COMMON TREATMENT STRATEGIES TO ADDRESS COMMUNICATION CHALLENGES IN DS-ASD

If meaningful connection to others is what makes us feel more fulfilled in our lives, then certainly having effective communication is the conduit to this sense of belonging. Given the often pervasive, lifelong, and complex manner that communication deficits present in the DS-ASD population, perhaps the most important question to ask is, "What can be done to support the individual on their journey to be as independent in their communication as possible?" Increased independence in communication is associated with improved outcomes in academic, vocational, and independent living among other potentially valuable opportunities (Wilkinson & Finestack, 2021). Furthermore, early identification of challenges and implementation of high-quality, research-backed interventions should be prioritized to achieve the greatest potential, taking advantage of neural plasticity, which is optimal early in childhood. Interventions can help minimize autism symptoms, isolation, and communication challenges (Diniz et al., 2021). Additionally, focusing on the development of early expressive communication skills is important because the frequency of prelinguistic and early symbolic behaviors significantly predicts language growth in children with and without DS (Wilkinson & Finestack, 2021). Expanding research on individuals with DS and DS-ASD is a critical first step toward developing interventions that optimize spoken language outcomes (Cook et al., 2021).

While the suggestions included in this chapter might serve as a helpful perspective for families and clinicians and represent benefits of multimodal AAC interventions at large with some anecdotal observations included, certainly, more research needs to be done specifically with the DS-ASD population to determine with more specificity how to best support this unique and diverse group of individuals in their development of optimal communication skills. According to Cook et al. (2021), it is important for individuals with DS-ASD to receive "customized treatment and educational approaches distinct from intervention strategies for individuals with DS alone" (p. 2).

Since communication challenges associated with DS-ASD appear to be an amalgam of challenges associated with Down syndrome and autism (both along their respective spectrums), we can expect that no two individuals will present with the same exact combination of strengths and challenges, and therefore the treatment approaches must be thoughtfully customized to each individual in a dynamic manner over the course of the lifetime. Additionally, I have noted during my clinical experience observing how individuals with DS-ASD best learn and generalize communication skills in their daily lives, that a high level of caregiver involvement and training should be considered at every stage of treatment.

Treatment approaches that demonstrate strong balance between direct intervention with the individual with DS-ASD and the communication partner/caregiver (in the form of parent training) and that invest energy into collaboration with other invested individuals (siblings, teachers, therapists, vocational coaches, friends), are often reported to be optimal by clinical teams and families and result in more functional communication outcomes for children with DS-ASD. For this reason, the child's treatment team may not always be comprised of the same team members, and it may be most beneficial to work in focused bursts of care with highly qualified professionals, and then take a break from direct services to focus on continued implementation of learned skills in the daily context of life. The focus should always remain on improving communication skills with the most important people and contexts of the child's life, with a vision toward the future, as communication skills needed in adulthood will likely require daily practice, often for many years leading up to adulthood.

Given the social-pragmatic communication challenges most often associated with autism, and often to a higher degree in individuals with DS-ASD, it is crucial to address these fundamental prelinguistic elements of communication on which language and speech skills can be built. It is important to note that multimodal communication approaches that focus on teaching symbolic language (words, signs, visuals, SGDs) are only as effective as the fundamental communicative underpinnings in the child with DS-ASD. This means that if we do not work to address the social-pragmatic challenges, we may be puzzled as to the lack of functional progress in communication or end up with a child who verbalizes, signs, and engages with AAC tools, but not purposefully or effectively with others to communicate.

As mentioned earlier, if fundamental communication skills are adequate (i.e., children demonstrate an understanding of the give and take of communication with others, and they are able to appreciate the cause and effect of their actions on others and vice versa), multimodal communication approaches focusing on teaching language and speech should be included in the intervention for individuals DS-ASD.

DEFINING MULTIMODAL, AAC, AND TOTAL COMMUNICATION

- *Multimodal Communication* refers to the use of more than one modality (i.e., facial expressions, body language, speech, gestures, signs, pictures, SGD [Speech Generating Device]) when communicating. It represents a "whole" view of communication with flexibility to create a system that capitalizes on strengths to compensate for challenges. It values all modalities equally.

- *Augmentative and Alternative Communication (AAC)* refers to a variety of tools and strategies used by an individual to support their overall communicative effort. The word "augmentative" means to "add to" or "augment," and in this case, to add to a person's verbal communication efforts. The word "alternative" refers to "use instead of speech/verbal efforts." AAC tools and strategies can therefore be used not only instead of verbal communication but often *in addition to*, especially when verbal communication alone is insufficient due to limited intelligibility and/or consistency across contexts and communication partners.

  - There are many different types of AAC tools/strategies. Unaided AAC strategies do not involve any additional materials or equipment, and include things like facial expressions, gestures, signs, and body language. Aided AAC strategies take advantage of no-tech, low-tech, mid-tech, or high-tech visual, tactile, and/or voice output tools or materials to support the user in his or her communication efforts.

- ***Total Communication (TC)*** is also a term that has been used when referring to communication interventions and refers to a teaching philosophy for children with hearing loss. TC is typically used with individuals who use cochlear implants or hearing aids and focuses on incorporating all means of communication, including signs, conventional gestures, fingerspelling, body language, lipreading, and speech.

NONVERBAL VS. NONSPEAKING

Over the years, various terms have been used by the fields that support individuals for whom speech is challenging. Terms such as *non-vocal, non-oral*, and *non-speech* have been used in the past and have since declined in popularity for various reasons, including the fact that many people who use and need AAC supports are able to talk and make sounds. "Nonverbal" is another term that has been used; however, it too is flawed. The most literal definition of "verbal" refers to the idea of "using words," leaving room for assumptions that perhaps an individual who is "nonverbal" does not use, understand, or express words, or have ideas to communicate, which of course, is not accurate, and thus can lead to harmful assumptions, especially when taken out of context. Often, individuals who do not use speech to communicate are in fact able to use words in a variety of forms (e.g., written words, picture symbols, signs, speech generating devices) to understand language and express themselves.

The term "nonspeaking" is a relatively newer term that has slowly gained traction in the last decade with more clinicians, parents, and neurodivergent folks advocating for its use. Other terms that have also been used include *minimally speaking, unreliably speaking*, or *non-reliably speaking*. The term nonspeaking seeks to make the distinction that just because someone does not consistently or reliably communicate via speech, does not mean that they do not have words (Riggs, 2021; Zangari et al., 1994).

In summary, the ongoing conversation and debate about these terms which continues to take place on social platforms, points to the fact that the words we use to describe neurodivergent individuals' communication skills, influence people's perceptions of those individuals and should therefore be used with sensitivity and caution—and most importantly refrain from judgment.

Teresa Unnerstall, Parent: Communication and Nick

Along with DS-ASD, Nick also has verbal apraxia of speech which further complicates his ability to communicate verbally. He does use many meaningful words, but he is unable to carry a back-and-forth conversation. Nick's receptive language skills are strong, meaning he can comprehend information and understand spoken language and sign language. Nick uses Total Communication, including nonverbal (gestures, facial expressions, body language, and sign language), low-tech (photographs and PECS icons), and high-tech (AAC/Speech Generating Device).

When Nick was 12 years old, the BCBA noted that he was not using his AAC device effectively. Over the years, we have had several evaluations for AAC. At age 5 we tested a high-tech AAC device; however, Nick spent more time stimming on it by pushing the same button over and over. The determination at that time was to use actual photographs for Nick to express his needs and wants. Over the next few years, we began to phase in the Picture Exchange System (PECS) icons and pair them with the photographs.

After the FBA was done, the BCBA recommended that the IEP team and our family get formal training on how to use PECS. What we learned is that you need to start at phase one and make sure you reinforce within 5–10 seconds after the child gives you the PECS icon. Nick picked up on the power of pictures quickly and moved through the PECS phases making full sentences to express his wants and needs. In middle school, we had him reevaluated for AAC and he was successful at using higher-tech AAC with the program Touch Chat. I think he realized that the power of pictures gave him a voice and he no longer felt the urge to stim on the device.

The IEP team used SETT, an acronym for Student, Environments, Tasks, and Tools, to evaluate Nick for AAC. In the evaluation, the IEP team considered Nick's present performance level. Then we had to find the right display and access methods, how many buttons and pages he would be able navigate, the size and portability, and what tasks he needed to accomplish using a Speech Generating Device.

The speech generating program Nick uses is Touch Chat. There are many speech apps available to load onto a Speech Generating Device. To this day, Nick still uses all three modes of communication. These include no-tech (sign language, gestures, facial expressions, body language), low-tech (pictures, PECS icons), and high-tech AAC (Speech Generating Device). Using these modes of communication allows Nick to express his wants and needs more effectively.

EVALUATION OF COMPLEX
COMMUNICATORS: DS-ASD CONSIDERATIONS

Currently, there is no gold standard for evaluating communication skills in individuals with DS-ASD. Various formal/standardized evaluation measures are used by Speech-Language Pathology (SLP) professionals to determine an individual's level of speech and language impairment relative to the neurotypical population. Kumin (2012) suggested that these tests can present substantial difficulties for children with DS and DS-ASD, mainly because of the way standardized tests must be administered in order to maintain their validity. While these types of assessments may be effective at establishing academic eligibility (in the school setting) or speech and language diagnosis (in the medical setting), for the purposes of securing funding for supports and services, they can be rather lacking in their capacity to describe the strengths of the individual being evaluated and often fail at providing a rich representation of the whole child, especially to a parent who knows the child well. Informal and criterion-referenced assessment tools, on the other hand, are more flexible, dynamic, individualized, and continuous. These tools are designed to measure the child's current skills and the progress they are making over time. These types of tools can be more effective at giving insight into an individual's skills and are more practical in guiding goal development (Kumin, 2012), measuring functional progress, and in my experience, they are more meaningful to families and treatment teams of individuals with DS and DS-ASD. Other informal evaluation tools can include Parent-Child observations, checklists, developmental scales, and portfolio assessments (Kumin, 2012).

Informal assessments of individuals with complex communication profiles should include a variety of elements that attempt to paint a picture of the individual's communicative functioning across multiple communication modalities (i.e., behavior, verbal, gestures, signs, visuals/pictures) as well as various relevant communication contexts (i.e., home, school/work, community) and communication partners (i.e., family, teachers/therapists/colleagues, community members). Informal and/or criterion-referenced tools and resources that may be beneficial for evaluating communication skills in individuals with complex communication needs, including children with DS-ASD, include:

- Augmentative & Alternative Communication Profile (Kovach, 2009)
- Checklist of Communication Competencies, Revised (Bloomberg et al., 2009)
- Communication Matrix (CM) (Rowland, 2004)
- Functional Communication Profile, Revised (Kleiman, 2014)
- Social Networks: A Communication Inventory for Individuals with Complex Communication Needs and Their Partners (Blackstone & Hunt-Berg, 2012).
- SETT (Student, Environment, Tasks & Tools) Framework (Zabala, 2005)

Treatment teams and families often wonder if their child with DS-ASD is able to use symbols (sight words, signs, pictures/visuals) to communicate, especially when considering readiness for initiating use of AAC (Augmentative Alternative Communication) tools and strategies. While there certainly are many assessments that attempt to measure a person's ability to demonstrate that they can identify vocabulary when it is named (e.g., show me __, point to __) or demonstrate that they understand that a real apple can be represented by a drawing or photo of an apple, when asked to do so (i.e., "matching"), caution should be used when attempting to make determinations on AAC readiness based on these types of evaluation strategies.

In my experience, many complex communicators, including individuals with DS-ASD, may be good candidates for AAC even when they are not able to demonstrate their current language skills or their language learning potential using this "knowledge-testing" strategy. It is often more informative to spend time evaluating this symbol using skill within motivating and functional learning opportunities within natural contexts for communication (i.e., meals, recreation, social opportunities). This type of information gathering is more dynamic and flexible, and perhaps more meaningful if the goal is to determine what supports learning in the individual. Undoubtedly, this type of evaluation approach is much more time-consuming and laborious, and the reason why a dynamic or diagnostic speech-language therapy taking place over time is often a more sensible approach to evaluating not only the current skills but more importantly the learning potential of complex communicators (Kumin, 2012).

Another crucial element to consider when evaluating an individual with DS-ASD is their level of social awareness in their environment, especially when considering whether it would be beneficial to implement AAC tools and strategies such as signs, visuals, pictures, and SGDs. Communication, at the very basic level, necessitates that the individual is aware that his/her behavior has an impact on another person's behavior in a "cause-effect" manner. This premise facilitates neurotypical children to learn where to focus their attention for learning language and many other skills in early development, sometimes referred to as a "learning to learn" skill. In my experience, children with autism struggle to understand where to focus their learning efforts (i.e., looking, listening) to gain the crucial information provided by parents or therapists to learn to communicate regardless of communication modality. This means that unless we evaluate and address the underlying inherent social-pragmatic communication deficits in individuals with DS-ASD, our multimodal communication recommendations may not be as effective as we had hoped or as they could be.

In my practice, I have observed that children with DS-ASD often already use a variety of organic and often unique means to gain access to the things they are motivated by. The goals of therapy are to improve how children go about communicating what is important to them and to reduce frustration resulting from communication breakdowns. Communication breakdowns are moments when one person is sharing a message that their communication partner does not understand. While these happen to all of us occasionally, they happen to children and adults with DS and DS-ASD much more frequently, so the goals of therapy should include managing these communication breakdowns using AAC tools and strategies.

Additionally, AAC therapy goals should focus on supporting parents in recognizing moments when they are anticipating their child's wants and needs, and over time, improving communication dynamics at home relating to how much expectation and responsibility is on the child with DS-ASD and what strategies the parent uses to create more practice opportunities for communication, where maybe previously there were very few opportunities. In summary, when considering next steps after receiving your AAC tool, parents should think about not only what they would like their child to be doing differently, but first and foremost what the adults in the picture need to do differently daily to facilitate the change in the child, which will take much more practice and time.

BEHAVIOR STRATEGIES

Lina, Patel, PsyD

One of the biggest areas of discussion for caregivers of individuals with DS-ASD and the professionals supporting them is the topic of behavior. Behavior can be defined as how a person acts or responds in a given situation. Maladaptive, disruptive, or challenging behavior can then be defined as the communication of a mismatch between the individual and something in their environment, affecting their ability to appropriately respond. The factors impacting the behavior could be pain or discomfort related to medical issues, a skill deficit or delay in developing a needed skill (the person has not learned how to do something or does not have that specific skill), or even how a person responds to a challenging behavior when it occurs. These are factors that impact individuals with DS-ASD more often than those with Down syndrome alone. Furthermore, individuals with DS-ASD have more difficulty with communicating what is bothering them in a socially acceptable way, so they may use their behaviors to do so. Approaching challenging behaviors from this perspective, this is, that the person is trying to communicate something to us but doesn't have the right tools to do so, opens up a multitude of options to support that individual rather than simply thinking of that person as naughty or bad. In fact, if we proactively prepare ourselves by identifying what might be causing a behavior to occur, or what typically triggers our loved one, we can more effectively manage disruptive behaviors.

SETTING EVENTS

You may be asking yourself, "So, how do I do that?" The first step is to identify potential *setting events* that may trigger challenging behaviors. Setting events are things that can influence the likelihood of a challenging behavior happening, but long before the behavior actually occurs. For example, if a person has not been given a functional method for communicating their needs and wants, they could be at an increased risk for engaging in disruptive behaviors. If a person has sensory processing issues and their sensory needs are not being met, this could increase the likelihood of challenging behaviors occurring. If a person has difficulty with impulse control and is being asked to sit for an extended period of time, this could also increase the likelihood of a challenging behavior occurring. Setting events, therefore, are chronic issues and/or neurodevelopmental factors that can dramatically increase the likelihood of a challenging behavior occurring. Understanding this better prepares us to find a more meaningful solution to address problematic behaviors.

Common setting events in individuals with DS-ASD include sleep issues, constipation, Gastrointestinal (GI) issues, communication challenges, changes in routine, adding a new routine, not providing adequate transition time between tasks, rushing the individual, sensory processing issues, difficulty with motivation, and cognitive impairment. Since challenging behaviors occur within the context of a situation, but also in the context of development and these types of chronic issues, addressing the setting events can reduce behavioral problems from occurring in the first place. So, if things like chronic health issues, communication, and sensory issues are proactively (even before the behavior happens) addressed, the behavioral challenges are less likely to come up. As you will see in Nick's case, addressing his setting events dramatically decreased his challenging behaviors. Standard strategies to proactively address neurodevelopment can include using visual schedules and supports, allowing sufficient time for the individual to process information, and reducing the number of demands before giving a break.

Teresa Unnerstall, Parent: Setting Events and Nick

Here is an example of a behavior we targeted and a brief explanation of the functions of behavior:

The Haircut

- ***Setting Events (Antecedents):*** *Sensory defensive, non-preferred activity, not in control*
- ***Behaviors:*** *Biting medical alert bracelet, pinching himself and Dad, yelling, avoidance, and peeing himself*
- ***Reason for the Behavior:*** *Escape*
- ***Supports put into place:*** *Changing the time to first thing in the morning before stress chemicals build up, adding a small dose of anxiety meds, providing a visual schedule with highly preferred reward to follow, using desensitization techniques by doing small doses letting him hold trimmer feel the vibration, invested in high-quality trimmers.*

The behavior support plan (BSP) should be updated annually or as needed. Throughout a student's life, the IEP team, family members, and outside care providers should schedule planning meetings to determine what vision they see for the student. It's important to look at the child's strengths and barriers that they struggle with. This will determine a meaningful plan for work, social life, and place to live as an adult. Families can create a one page "About Me" profile sheet that can be a quick reference guide to share with the IEP team, aides/paraprofessionals, caregivers, medical professionals, therapists, and extended family and friends. It can be a great "at a glance" summary of the Behavior Support Plan.

One final note is that Nick's BSP is proactive, meaning that everyone who works with Nick knows his triggers. That way we can cut things off at the pass before escalation. This helps greatly to prevent meltdowns. The number of meltdowns has dropped drastically since Nick was in puberty. Part of this was hormonally related, but also due to having a BSP in place across all environments which is updated yearly. In addition, we now have a better understanding of Nick, and we can detect when he is getting overwhelmed, then redirect as needed.

THE ABCs OF BEHAVIOR AND APPLIED BEHAVIOR ANALYSIS

When a behavior is immediately triggered, we may not feel as prepared to address it in the moment. In fact, sometimes a caregiver or provider may inadvertently reinforce an undesired behavior, causing it to occur more frequently. For example, if a person hits to get our attention and we turn and then talk to the person or explain how hitting is not appropriate, we are increasing the likelihood of the person hitting again because hitting worked to get attention. A common method used to help people understand not only the immediate triggers to a behavior, but also the factors that can indirectly cause that behavior to occur more or less often is known as the "ABCs of behavior."

What does the acronym *ABC* stand for? The *A* stands for the word *antecedent*, which refers to what happened just before the behavior occurred or what may have triggered it. Antecedents can be positive or negative. Positive triggers result in behaviors that we want to see or that are desirable, while negative triggers lead to challenging behaviors. A positive antecedent can be a social story that helped a person understand what was expected of them or a visual timer helping the individual anticipate when a transition is coming. Some examples of negative antecedents that result in challenging behaviors include transitions, an overstimulating environment, and being told "no" to a preferred item or activity. The *B* stands for *Behavior* and refers to a description of anything that a person does in a given situation. Behaviors can also be positive or negative (problematic). Examples of positive behaviors are following directions or maintaining a calm body. Negative or problematic behaviors can include aggression, refusal, or self-harm. The *C* stands for *Consequence*, which is anything that happens as a result of the behavior. Consequences can either encourage that behavior to happen more often or it can decrease the likelihood of that behavior occurring. It is so important to understand how a consequence influences a behavior to ensure that you are not unintentionally increasing an undesirable or problematic behavior or decreasing a desirable one. Once you have identified the ABCs, then you can use your detective skills to determine the function of the behavior or why the behavior may have occurred. This is often referred to as the behavioral trigger. Understanding this trigger will then lead to successfully putting a targeted strategy in place to change the behavior.

There are common underlying behavioral triggers or functions of behaviors that have been identified over time. These include the following:

- Sensory: Some behaviors occur because they are satisfying or feel good.
- Escape: Some behaviors occur because the person wants to get away from something or avoid something.
- Attention: A person may engage in a certain behavior to get attention or a reaction from other people.
- Tangibles: Some behaviors occur so the person can get a tangible item or gain access to an activity that they like.

It is thought that all behaviors are connected to one of these underlying functions. When a challenging behavior occurs and a function is identified, then you can successfully implement a direct strategy to change the behavior. For example, if an individual hits and you determine that the function of the behavior is attention, you can implement a proactive (also called an antecedent) strategy to teach the individual how to gain your attention in a more socially appropriate manner (like tapping on the shoulder or vocalizing). For individuals with DS-ASD, you may need to practice this strategy for a longer period before it becomes muscle memory.

Sometimes, even after you have written down the ABCs and the behavioral trigger for a problematic behavior, you may still struggle with identifying a good strategy to address the behavior. It can be helpful to work with a psychologist or behavior analyst to identify triggers and learn how to manage them. A Board Certified Behavior Analyst (also called a BCBA) or a psychologist that specializes in behaviors can observe the behavior and collect data over a longer period of time, allowing for a more detailed evaluation of one or more challenging behaviors. A BCBA can specifically do what is called a Functional Behavioral Assessment (FBA), which is a lengthier process for gathering information about concerning behaviors, motivators, current skills, interests, needs, and environmental factors that may impact the behavior. BCBAs have received specialized training and board certification in behavioral analysis. FBAs can be conducted by a BCBA from a private company working with a family to address home and community needs or can be requested at school as a part of the IEP (Individualized Education Plan) process. There are times when a school district will utilize a school psychologist or staff member to collect the data for an FBA. It is best to request that a BCBA conduct the evaluation, as they have received specific training/certification to ensure the quality of the assessment. Once an FBA is complete, the information from the assessment can be used to create a behavioral plan with specific treatment goals.

Teresa Unnerstall, Parent: Behavior and Nick

Behavior challenges can impact individuals with co-occurring DS-ASD. Understandably so with deficits in verbal communication, often these behaviors are communicating an unmet need or struggle. My son Nick exhibited behaviors like throwing things and having an extreme aversion to haircuts early on. As he marched closer to puberty, the severity of these maladaptive behaviors led to physical aggression and meltdowns. Getting the evaluation and secondary diagnosis of autism with Down syndrome helped us to gain access to a BCBA to support him better. Here are some of the behaviors that we experienced and targeted with Nick:

- Elopement
- Sensory aversion (haircuts, nail trimming, medical procedures, etc.)
- Sleep
- Self-Stimulation (stimming)
- Obsessive Compulsive Disorder (OCD)/ Need for sameness
- Boundaries (personal and others)

- Property destruction
- Impulse control
- Aggression/Meltdowns
- Transitions
- Outburst that seems out of the blue
- Nudity
- Toileting incontinence/Fecal smearing (code brown)

While this list of behaviors can feel daunting, the good news is that getting a BCBA on board can help to target behaviors and bring in support to help individuals with DS-ASD and their families. The first thing we did was to request that a Functional Behavior Analysis (FBA) be done. This included classroom and home observations with data collection. It's important to do some detective work that can help to discover what is triggering the behavior as well as what function it is serving. Once the data is collected, look for any patterns, for example, a certain time of day, and the team can speculate what other setting events (antecedents) might be triggering a behavior.

After the FBA was completed, the Behavior Support Plan (BSP) was created. We utilized the school district BCBA and private Applied Behavior Analysis (ABA) therapy to not only support Nick with maladaptive behaviors, but also to teach him many independent living skills. Having more independent daily living skills will pay off as your child becomes an adult. It will allow them and their family to have more options for work, adult day programs, and housing.

The BCBA will write the behavioral plan, but someone called a Registered Behavior Technician (RBT) oftentimes will be the one that executes the plan under the direction and supervision of the BCBA. Targeted areas of intervention may be for communication and language, social skills, self-care, play and leisure, motor skills, and core skills needed for learning. It is important to know that FBAs in a school setting will only address behaviors and skills that are directly impeding the learning process in the educational setting. In other words, they will not be able to address things like self-care skills or play but may address communication skills that are impacting a person's ability to communicate needs in a socially appropriate way within the school setting.

There are many kinds of treatment interventions for managing challenging behaviors. Most are grounded in the principles of Applied Behavior Analysis (ABA). ABA is an evidence-based intervention for autism. This means that research has been conducted on this type of therapy specifically with individuals with autism and that there is a high success rate for making gains and sustaining those gains over time (some studies show up to 90% success rates when an individual receives 40+ hours of ABA per week). It has even been listed as an evidence-based "best-practice" treatment by the US Surgeon General and the American Psychological Association. It is important to note, however, that these studies did not evaluate the effectiveness specifically for individuals with DS-ASD. Given the common features between DS-ASD and ASD, it can be hypothesized that individuals with DS-ASD would also benefit. In fact, in our experience with DS-ASD, we have seen significant benefit and we recommend it quite often. Different families have different opinions on whether ABA is a good fit for their family. Some feel that the time commitment (anywhere from 10 to 40 hours per week depending on the recommendation of the BCBA) is too much. It may interfere with not only their ability to participate in a traditional school setting but may also result in some challenging behaviors due to fatigue. Others feel that it is too structured/rigid, trains children to be inflexible, and is difficult to translate into other settings where all environmental factors cannot be controlled. It is important to note that there are several versions of behavioral intervention that are based on the principles of ABA, which is only a theory/approach.

Many people get confused and refer to the most traditional form of ABA—*Discrete Trial Training*—as ABA itself. Discrete Trial Training (DTT) is only one type of ABA and involves structured teaching trials that systematically train a child to learn a new skill by breaking that skill down into smaller parts. Each part is taught through high levels of repetition. This is typically the version of ABA that most families do not like due to its intensity and level of structure. Other versions of behavioral intervention that are based on the principles of ABA but may be a better fit for some families have been created over the years. These also have strong evidence scientifically but may not be as well-known. One such intervention is called *Pivotal Response Treatment (PRT)*.

Although PRT is based on the principles of ABA, it is conducted in a more naturalistic setting. It targets what are known as "pivotal areas of development," such as response to multiple cues, social initiation, self-management, and motivation. The idea behind this intervention is that if these pivotal areas are targeted for intervention, they will have cascading effects on other areas of development too, such as communication, socialization, and behavior (https://www.autismprthelp.com/). The Early Start Denver Model (ESDM) is another program based on the principles of ABA. This is typically recommended for toddlers. ESDM focuses on building positive relationships through play to encourage language development, social skills, and cognitive skills (https://www.esdm.co/).

For those who do not want to use an ABA-based approach, there are alternative therapies available. One such therapy is called *Floor Time*. Floor Time (FT) is a developmental model that encourages development of self-regulation, engagement, communication, complex communication, and emotional development through play. While this intervention is often sought out by families, research on its effectiveness is limited (https://stanleygreenspan.com/).

Another non-ABA approach is called *Treatment and Education of Autism and Related Communication-Handicapped Children or TEACCH*. TEACCH is based on the unique learning profile of individuals with autism. It uses physical organization of the environment, visual schedules, work systems, and visual breakdown of more complex tasks to maximize strengths and support areas of difficulties for individuals with autism. TEACCH is frequently used in combination with other treatment interventions (https://teacch.com/about-us/).

Specific Behaviors

While this book will not be able to address all behaviors that occur at a higher frequency in those with DS-ASD, we will address a few specific areas of challenge that are sometimes more difficult to address. First, let us address stimming behaviors. Stimming behaviors are often thought to be a way in which individuals with DS and DS-ASD self-regulate. Therefore, we may notice that stimming behaviors increase when a person with DS-ASD is more distressed and may decrease when they are calm and better regulated. While both individuals with DS and DS-ASD can engage in stimming behaviors, individuals with DS-ASD are more likely to have difficulty disengaging from the stimming behavior even when given a direct, immediate task. This is often when it becomes problematic. Sensory strategies that are proactively implemented throughout the day can sometimes help decrease stimming behaviors when they are occurring at inopportune times by calming the nervous system. Structure, consistency, and predictability of routines can also decrease distress, additionally reducing the higher need for stimming. Because stimming behaviors are regulatory in nature, the goal is not to get rid of them completely, but to manage when they occur and their appropriateness.

The "Respect the Stim" Movement—Robin Sattel, MS

Everyone engages in "self-stimming" behaviors. For example, are your legs crossed as you're reading this? Are you bouncing your foot or tapping your pen? Why do we do this? Stimming can help to increase concentration, decrease boredom and anxiety, exert extra energy, and numerous other benefits. It is the same for individuals with DS-ASD; in fact stereotypic stimming behavior is a diagnostic criterion for autism spectrum disorder in the Diagnostic and Statistical Manual of Mental Health Disorders, Fifth Edition (DSM-5-TR) (American Psychiatric Association, 2022).

For many years, parents and professionals have attempted to restrict the stim, rather than respect the stim. Stimming behavior can make a person stand out in a crowd, and some parents may be embarrassed, irritated, or entirely frustrated by it. The recent "respect the stim" movement, however, poses the questions, "Why restrict it if it plays a functional role and it makes the child/adult feel more regulated and content? It's part of who they are, so why not respect it?" (The movement is gaining traction; you can even purchase Respect the Stim t-shirts on the internet.)

If the stimming behavior isn't dangerous or harmful, then perhaps limitations may not need to be placed on that behavior. If the behavior is less desired, the parent/caregiver may establish a set time and place for certain behaviors. Arguably, there may be some behaviors that should be extinguished for safety's sake, and there are behavior specialists who are trained to help with these types of issues. The movement says, "Let them be who they are," which can be liberating for the individual and the family; but it is something to consider on a person-by-person basis. Parents, work with the professionals in your child's life if you have concerns about stimming behaviors. Perhaps moving away from embarrassment and relaxing a bit around safe stimming behaviors can bring a measure of tranquility to everyone involved, especially to the person with DS-ASD who may have a strong need to stim.

Self-injury, defined as significant harm to one's body, is another behavior that occurs more frequently in individuals with DS-ASD compared to DS alone. It is unclear why some individuals with DS-ASD are more prone to self-injury. It can be speculated that more significant challenges in communication and increased risk for complex medical issues could be the culprit. Frustration with communication or pain associated with medical issues could increase the likelihood of self-injurious behaviors. Regular, proactive health evaluations and working on alternative methods for communication are helpful strategies to help reduce self-injury. Some individuals with DS-ASD may also benefit from an evaluation for medication with a psychiatrist.

PART III:

SENSORY CHALLENGES

Katie Frank, OT, PhD

No one has a perfectly functioning sensory system. We all have sensory preferences and sensory needs, each unique to how our central nervous system perceives and processes sensory information. Think about your sensory system being like electrical wiring. When there is a kink in a wire, it may cause lights to flicker. Sometimes we get a kink in our central nervous system, and that leads to mixed messages in our sensory system. Many times, we may not know what is causing that kink or how to stop our own internal lights from flickering. When sensory processing is compromised, the brain cannot do its most important job of organizing sensory messages. When this interferes with someone's ability to function in daily life and becomes a disruption, the person may wish to seek out therapy services to address the sensory processing disorder challenges.

Sensory processing challenges, which are relatively common among people with DS-ASD, do not just affect how a person moves and learns. These challenges also affect how the person behaves; completes tasks at home, school, or work; and interacts with others. Individuals with sensory processing challenges may experience touch, taste, sound, smell, movement, and other sensations differently from those without sensory processing challenges. Some may feel sensations more intensely, others feel them less so, and some just do not get sensory information "correct"; up may feel like down, or a penny may feel the same as a button. These sensory responses can lead to challenging behaviors (Will et al., 2019). When individuals with DS-ASD have sensory difficulties, those problems should be addressed to help them live each day feeling regulated.

SENSORY PROCESSING AND DS-ASD

Sensory processing difficulties are relatively common among individuals with DS-ASD, and certain difficulties are reported more often than others. However, it is important to remember that each person is unique, and it should never be assumed that one person with DS-ASD will have the same sensory problems as another.

Individuals with DS-ASD may experience sensory processing deficits which may make daily tasks like bathing, dressing, and eating a challenge. For example, a person may not tolerate lotion being applied to the skin, despite it being dry; some individuals may not like water touching their face, which makes bathing and hygiene a challenge; and individuals with DS-ASD may not like to wear socks, shoes, or other pieces of clothing because of the way they feel on the body. Transitioning from one season's clothing to the next can also be a challenge.

Many individuals with DS-ASD have sensory-related eating problems. For example, they are often reported to be picky eaters. Others may stuff their mouths full when eating. This may be due to proprioceptive deficits. For a person to chew, they must feel the food in their mouth, and they might only have this sensation if enough food is stuffed in the mouth full to the cheeks. Unfortunately, this is not safe because it can cause choking. Other feeding issues include the inability to feel thirst or to know when they are satiated, or full.

AUDITORY PROCESSING

Many people with DS-ASD have hearing loss or wax buildup in their ear canals, which can muffle sounds. Compounding these hearing problems, they often have difficulties with auditory processing. They often can be overwhelmed by loud or unexpected sounds yet prefer their music at a loud volume. In addition, because of slow auditory processing, they often perform best with visual cues or instructions alongside verbal cues, using simple, clear short sentences. It helps to allow for longer processing time before repeating the instructions, so you don't add undue stress or anxiety to the task.

Depth perception is also a challenge for many individuals with DS-ASD and can make it difficult for them to go up and down stairs or manage walking on uneven surfaces. People with DS-ASD also tend to have low muscle tone, which can affect how they interpret sensory input coming in through their muscles and joints (i.e., proprioceptive input; Bruni, 2016). Frequently, they require more proprioceptive input into their muscles and joints to help regulate their bodies. This also makes it challenging for them to regulate the amount of force they generate with their muscles; they often do something too hard (apply too much pressure to an object so it breaks) or not hard enough (apply insufficient pressure and have a hard time holding on to an object). This issue can impact the ability to apply the required pressure to adequately hold an eating utensil to independently eat, make, and cut a sandwich, and/or hold a pen/pencil/marker/brush with enough strength to write, draw, color, paint or brush their teeth or hair.

EVALUATING AND TREATING SENSORY PROCESSING

There is currently no gold standard assessment for diagnosing sensory processing disorders. However, an occupational therapist (OT) can help assess and treat people whose ability to function throughout the day is negatively affected by sensory processing issues. Occupational therapy is a health profession concerned with how people function in their respective roles and how they perform meaningful activities. OT views "occupation" as anything a person needs to do from the moment they wake up to the moment they fall asleep. OTs can assess what is interfering with a person's ability to engage in activities, including discerning whether the person has an impaired sensory system. OTs use formal and informal assessments as well as clinical observation and caregiver interviews to evaluate and assess for sensory processing deficits, and then use the results to create a treatment plan.

While all OT students receive education in sensory processing, not all practicing OTs are comfortable working with individuals with sensory dysfunction or have the equipment or support to provide these services. The other challenge is that pediatric and school-based therapists may address sensory needs, but who can an adult with sensory needs see for therapy? Many OT practitioners who do see adult clients work in rehab settings or other settings that are not well-equipped to address the needs of an adult with sensory processing deficits. It can be particularly difficult for adults with DS-ASD to find an OT who can help. These individuals may be permitted to be seen in a pediatric setting with clinicians who are skilled to address these needs, but many times insurance does not cover these services in that setting. Locating skilled therapists in your area to address sensory needs is unfortunately a huge challenge for many families.

Evaluation

When it comes to testing individuals with DS-ASD for sensory processing difficulties, there are just a few options. The only formal assessment that currently exists is the Sensory Integration and Praxis Test (SIPT), which is standardized for children ages 4 to 8 (Ayres, 1989). Lucy Jane Miller and her team from the STAR institute in Colorado are currently working on the development and standardization of a new formal assessment for individuals ages 3 and older. It is called the Sensory Processing Three Dimension Scale (SP3D). There is, however, a questionnaire called the Sensory Profile 2 (Dunn, 2014), which covers individuals from birth to age 14 and is available in English and Spanish. In addition, the original version of the Sensory Profile has an adolescent/adult version for ages 11 and older (Brown & Dunn, 2002). While parents/caregivers often complete this adolescent/adult questionnaire, it is standardized only when completed by the individual, which is challenging in the DS-ASD population. There are also a series of questionnaires as part of the Sensory Processing Measure-2 (Parham et al., 2021). This updated version covers a large span of ages (4 months to 87 years) and a variety of environments, including home and school. It is also available in both English and Spanish.

The second part of an evaluation process is to further assess motor skills. The Bruininks-Oseretsky Test of Motor Proficiency, second edition (BOT-2), is often used, but it is only standardized up to age 21 years, 11 months (Bruininks & Bruininks, 2005). The final aspect of the evaluation process is for the therapist to complete a detailed observation in a clinical setting and identify the person's strengths and weaknesses.

Treatment

There are many reasons why it is important to seek treatment for sensory processing deficits. First and foremost, sensory processing deficits are not outgrown; they grow and change with us. Treatment will help a person function more smoothly and can also help them to develop social skills. As stated earlier, individuals with sensory modulation deficits often have difficulty forming relationships with others. This is because they either respond to high sensory input with a fight or flight response (yelling, hitting, running away) when they are overstimulated, or they need *more* input (chewing on their fingers, flapping their hands) when they are understimulated. These reactions can be hard for others to understand and may make it hard for someone to want to be close to them because they do not understand and/or are confused by these behaviors.

Once their bodies feel regulated, people with DS-ASD are better able to learn because they are more emotionally stable. Finally, treating sensory processing deficits can play an important role in improving the quality of family relationships (Kranowitz, 2016).

Think about your body/sensory system as a teeter-totter (or, see-saw). There are times when your sensory system is over-responsive (you have received too much sensory input), perhaps because you are stuck in a loud or chaotic setting and just want to get out of there. In these cases, you are high up on the teeter-totter. There are other times when you are under-responsive (you do not have enough sensory input), perhaps because you have been sitting listening to a lecture for an hour and feel as if you are going to fall asleep. In these cases, you are low on the teeter-totter. When you are regulated, the teeter-totter is even. Our goal is to ensure the teeter-totter stays even.

SENSORY DIET

Treatment for sensory processing deficits is highly individualized. An OT can provide direct therapy in an outpatient setting, or direct (or consultative) therapy in a school setting. A therapist will create a sensory diet, which is a planned and scheduled activity program designed to meet a person's specific sensory needs. It can include a combination of alerting, calming, and organizing activities based on the person's needs in order to keep an optimal level of arousal and performance (i.e., an even teeter-totter). Some trial and error may be needed to determine the "best" sensory activities for each person.

Building and implementing a sensory diet should be more like choosing from a menu rather than following a recipe (Johnson, 2016). One main aim of a sensory diet is to prevent sensory and emotional overload by satisfying the nervous system's sensory needs (remember the teeter-totter image). For instance, if a sensory diet activity is done before another activity, it can help a person move through the transition or prepare for a change in routine more easily (Johnson, 2016). However, it can also be used as a recovery technique if the person does become overwhelmed. A sensory diet can be implemented at home and in the community (i.e., school, day program, or work). One key feature to remember, especially when considering behavior plans, is that sensory strategies should never be removed as punishment or given as a reward. If a person has a sensory diet, it is because it is needed for optimal performance, and their body begins to rely on it.

Activities in a sensory diet can be alerting, organizing, or calming, as highlighted below.

Alerting activities benefit people who are under-responsive and need a boost (i.e., the teeter-totter is low). Examples of alerting activities include:

- eating crunchy food
- taking a shower
- bouncing on a trampoline or therapy ball
- swinging in a circle
- swinging fast

Organizing activities help regulate a person's responses so he or she can be more attentive. Sensory cravers often benefit from these activities. Organizing activities include:

- eating chewy foods or chewing on a sensory chew necklace
- heavy work activities (i.e., proprioceptive input and other activities that include pushing and pulling, like vacuuming or pushing a grocery cart)
- vibration

Calming activities help decrease sensory over-responsiveness (i.e., the teeter-totter is high). These activities can include:

- sucking on hard candy
- doing heavy work (exercising, household chores, joint compression)
- twirling or swinging back and forth or forward and backward
- rocking in a rocking chair
- deep pressure/massage/compression
- using weighted products (blanket, lap pad, pillow, or neck wrap)
- playing with a fidget toy
- listening to a sound machine

Activities in a sensory diet should be offered periodically throughout the day (in order to keep the teeter-totter level). Sensory breaks can be short in length, often only for a few minutes. Sensory input should *not* be provided all day long. For instance, a weighted vest will often lose its impact after approximately 10 to 15 minutes (Ordre des Erothérapeutes du Quebec, 2008). Think about what happens when you put on jewelry: you may notice the necklace or ring initially, but at some point, you forget you are wearing it. It is the same with sensory input. There is a point when the body gets used to the sensation and tunes it out, making it no longer effective.

Teresa Unnerstall, Parent: Sensory Supports and Nick

Sensory supports:

- Provide noise-canceling headphones, motor breaks, and a designated area with various sensory toys, items, or other sensory input
- Provide flexible seating options with nubby cushions, footrests, standing desks, etc.
- Provide fidget toys, mini trampolines, and swings
- Keep bean bag chairs in the sensory area
- Offer weighted blankets, vests, and backpacks
- Ensure that you have sensory-friendly spaces available (i.e., reduce visual clutter in the classroom, install fluorescent light covers, etc.)

Another way to provide sensory diet activities is to incorporate them with life skills:

- Vacuuming
- Carrying and loading laundry baskets
- Recycling trash
- Loading and unloading the dishwasher
- Rolling garbage bins to curb
- Cleaning windows and dusting furniture
- Making the bed
- Setting the table

The last piece of the puzzle that we put in place was to address Nick's sensory needs. It was important to help Nick learn how to regulate his sensory needs. We taught Nick how to ask for a break when we noticed signs of stress, such as biting his medical alert bracelet. He used an "I need a break" icon card and his AAC device to communicate with us. One time, a baby was crying, and this was a huge trigger. His personal support worker pointed to Nick's AAC device and Nick hit the "Stop" button a few times. He was rewarded with praise and guess what? The baby stopped crying! Giving Nick the means to express himself when things were too much was a powerful tool for self-regulation.

It is important to understand, respect, and support your child's sensory needs. Enlist an occupational therapist to build in a sensory diet across all environments. Work with the IEP team, aides, family members, and caregivers to use proactive strategies so your child can learn, perform, and feel their best. Finally, watch for signs of stress build-up and diffuse before escalation.

CONCLUSION

Everyone has sensory processing differences. When these differences impair a person's ability to function day to day, we may want to consider therapy options to help. When people have a regulated sensory system, they are better able to pay attention, follow directions, and perform at an optimal level. This is true for all of us.

Children and adults with DS-ASD often experience challenges with communication, behavior, and sensory regulation and/or processing. It is essential to work with experts in these fields to collaboratively develop an ongoing working plan that best promotes how to best understand each individual, so they feel loved and supported. In addition to encouraging personal and educational success, staying flexible and open to developing new goals and strategies will help further continued growth and foster independent life skills. This can be a long and tiring journey, but over time, each small step made helps set the stage for new achievements and successes. Addressing the individual's strengths and challenges by implementing person-centered strategies will improve the quality of life and lend potential for increased independence for the individual as well as for their families and the professionals who serve them.

REFERENCES

American Psychiatric Association. (2022). *Diagnostic and statistical manual of mental disorders* (5th ed., text rev.). https://doi.org/10.1176/appi.books.9780890425787

Ayres, A. J. (1989). *Sensory Integration and Praxis Test: SIPT Manual.* Western Psychological Services.

Blackstone, S. W., & Hunt-Berg, M. (2012). *Social networks: A communication inventory for individuals with complex communication needs and their communication partners.* Attainment Company.

Bloomberg, K., West, D., Johnson, H., & Iacono, T. (2009). *The triple C: checklist of communication competencies* (Revised). Scope Vic, Limited.

Brown, C., & Dunn, W. (2002). *Adolescent/adult sensory profile.* Psychological Corporation.

Bruininks, R. H., & Bruininks, B. D. (2005). *Bruininks-Oseretsky Test of Motor Proficiency, Second Edition (BOT-2)* [Database record]. APA PsycTests. https://doi.org/10.1037/t14991-000

Bruni, M. (2016). *Fine motor skills in children with Down syndrome* (3rd Edition). Woodbine House.

Capone, G. T., Grados, M. A., Kaufmann, W. E., Bernad-Ripoll, S., & Jewell, A. (2005). Down syndrome and comorbid autism-spectrum disorder: Characterization using the aberrant behavior checklist. *American Journal of Medical Genetics, 134,* 373–380. https://doi.org/10.1002/ajmg.a.30622

Cook, A., Quinn, E. D., & Rowland, C. (2021). Exploring expressive communication skills in a cross-sectional sample of individuals with a dual diagnosis of autism spectrum disorder and Down syndrome. *American Journal on Intellectual and Developmental Disabilities, 126*(2), 97–113. https://doi.org/10.1352/1944-7558-126.2.97

Diniz, N. L. F., Parlato-Oliveira, E., Pimenta, P. G. A., de Araujo, L. A., & Valadares, E. R. (2021). Autism and Down syndrome: early identification and diagnosis. *Arquivos de Neuro-Psiquiatria, 80*(6), 620–630. https://doi.org/10.1590/0004-282X-ANP-2021-0156

Dunn, W. (2014). *Sensory Profile 2 manual.* Pearson.

Johnson, D. (2016). *Differentiating sensory from behavior* [Presentation]. https://summit-education.com/course/CSENDJ.1/differentiating-sensory-from-behavior#VIDEO/ONDEMAND.CSENDJ.1

Kleiman, L. I. (2014). *Functional Communication Profile-Revised.* Pro-Ed.

Kovach, T. M. (2009). *AACP: Augmentative & Alternative Communication Profile: A Continuum of Learning.* Pro-Ed.

Kranowitz, C. S. (2016). *The out-of-sync child grows up: Coping with sensory processing disorder in the adolescent and young adult years.* Penguin Random House.

Kumin, L. (2012). *Early communication skills for children with Down syndrome: A guide for parents and professionals* (3rd ed.). Woodbine House.

Molloy, C. A., Murray, D. S., Kinsman, A., Castillo, H., Mitchell, T., Hickey, F. J., & Patterson, B. (2009). Differences in the clinical presentation of Trisomy 21 with and without autism. *Journal of Intellectual Disability Research, 53*(2), 143–151. https://doi.org/10.1111/j.1365-2788.2008.01138.x

Ordre des Erothérapeutes du Quebec. (2008). *OEQ Position statement on the use of weighted covers.* OEQ. https://cotbc.org/wp-content/uploads/OEQPositionStatement_WeightedCovers.pdf

Parham, L. D., Ecker, C. L., Kuhaneck, H., Henry, D. A., & Glennon, T. J. (2021). *Sensory processing measure, second edition (SPM-2).* Western Psychological Services.

Riggs, C. (2021, November 29). Ask the expert: 'Nonspeaking' vs. 'Nonverbal' and why language matters. *The Guild for Human Services.* https://www.guildhumanservices.org/blog/ask-expert-nonspeaking-vs-nonverbal-and-why-language-matters

Rowland, C. (2004). Communication matrix (Revised). *Oregon Health & Science University.* https://documents.nationaldb.org/products/Parent-Comm-Matrix-Final.pdf

Wilkinson, K. M., & Finestack, L. H. (Eds.). (2021). *Multimodal AAC for individuals with Down syndrome.* Brookes.

Will, E., Daunhauer, L. A., Fidler, D., & Lee, N. R. (2019). Sensory processing and maladaptive behavior: Profiles within the Down syndrome phenotype. *Physical & Occupational Therapy in Pediatrics, 39*(2), 1–16. https://doi.org/10.1080/01942638.2019.1575320

Zabala, J. (2005). Ready, SETT, go! Getting started with the SETT framework. *Closing the Gap: Computer Technology in Special Education and Rehabilitation, 23*(6), 1–3.

Zangari, C., Lloyd, L., & Vicker, B. (1994). Augmentative and alternative communication: An historic perspective. *Augmentative and Alternative Communication, 10*(1), 27–59. https://doi.org/10.1080/07434619412331276740

CHAPTER ELEVEN

BUILDING STRONG RELATIONSHIPS WITHIN THE SCHOOL SYSTEM AND BEYOND

Julie Hearrell, MA Ed

Leah Martin, PhD

Robin Sattel, MS

Students with DS-ASD in the United States K–12 public school system have an interdisciplinary team (Individualized Education Program or IEP team) that includes parents, educators, and specialists who support them during their years at school. This or a similar system may also exist in other countries. Each person on the team plays a vital role as they collectively strive to provide a meaningful school experience that harvests all the best possible outcomes for the student's education and personal well-being. Ideally, the IEP team has worked to enhance relationships and build a strong foundation of trust throughout the student's journey from kindergarten through 12th grade, and possibly beyond through transition-type programs.

But what happens when the student's team doesn't work as a team at all? Chaos, stress, and lost opportunities can ensue, and as a result the student's progress and welfare can fall by the wayside. When listening to the experiences of seasoned parents who have had a child with DS-ASD move through the school system, we have heard successful stories about how the schools offered compassionate, dedicated, and skilled educators for their child. Conversely, we have heard stories of escalating contention between parents and educators that led them all to a place of shattered trust and radical differences of opinion. We have also heard of parents and educators coming to the ultimate impasse, resulting in long, drawn-out lawsuits brought by hurting and angry parents against educators, and even entire school districts. We have personally witnessed parents, teachers, and administrators who have been emotionally damaged in such cases, and we have felt compassion for all of them in their differing circumstances.

Is it possible to avoid this unfortunate scenario? We believe that in most cases, the answer is yes. Our proposed solution is two-fold. First, to build a strong foundation of mutual trust and respect that bolsters every member of the team, and second, to implement a person-centered approach in all aspects of the educational experience for the student with DS-ASD. In this chapter, we will be sharing some thoughts from a special educator who grew up with a brother with intellectual and developmental disabilities (IDD), a parent of a child with DS-ASD who is also a professional in the IDD field, and an advocate in the IDD field.

The aim of this chapter is not to provide answers to every situation that parents and educators may face within the educational setting. We recognize that school systems and regulations are quite different depending on what country, state, and school district that someone lives or works in. Experience has shown that even the best of teams can run into roadblocks at the administrative level and be faced with complex barriers for a student with DS-ASD that can seem insurmountable. In those difficult, seemingly impossible situations, we recommend finding a professional advocate (such as those provided at no cost by nonprofit organizations such as the Arc) or a disability attorney who can educate the team regarding steps that can be taken when it seems that individuals are not being provided services according to the regulations or laws of the governing body.

While we cannot address every type of school situation or dilemma, and do not claim to have answers to specific problems, we do aim to convey some strategies and tools for parents and educators that may facilitate more successful outcomes for the student. Our goal is to impart hope to parents and educators alike and affirm that it *is* possible to build positive school experiences for yourselves and the children you love and serve who have DS-ASD.

PART I:

BUILDING A FOUNDATION THAT CAN WITHSTAND THE STORMS

If you've ever been to Italy, you may have stopped by to see the world's finest example of what happens when you build a structure on a poor foundation. Construction of a free-standing bell tower began in the 12th century in Pisa, but by the time the second and third floors were being built, the entire structure began to sink on one side. This was due to a shallow three-meter foundation set into sandy silt and dense clay, which made for a weak and unstable base. The tower kept sinking into the ground over the centuries, leaning as much as 15 feet, or 5.5 degrees from perpendicular. It's now a tourist attraction that travelers to Italy can't miss. The Leaning Tower of Pisa is a perfect illustration that the foundation of a structure is critical to its stability, longevity, and integrity.

This history lesson can be extended to a powerful analogy that emphasizes the importance of trust between educators and parents in managing the educational goals of a student with DS-ASD. Even the most ideal relationships face times of distress and difficulty, often where the individuals involved can't seem to get on the same page about an issue they are facing. Imagine relationships that are *strained* trying to manage an issue or attempting to come to a consensus. A relationship that is built on a shaky foundation will eventually experience some damage under the tension and weight of the problems. Unless that relationship is based on a truly solid foundation of trust and respect, it is likely that the structure of that relationship will falter and won't stand up to the pressure of the elements. If it is built on the solid bedrock of trust, however, it will likely be able to withstand the pressures facing it.

Realistically, all members of the student's team should recognize that students with DS-ASD are complex individuals for many reasons, and educational differences of opinion are likely to arise. What matters in the long run is whether those differences are handled in a contentious way or in a diplomatic way by all stakeholders. The former leads toward an impasse; only the latter can put the team on the road toward success.

How can parents and educators work together to build the ideal interpersonal foundation? How can the team create the kind of solid foundation that, when disagreements arise or differences of opinions surface, they can be worked through and figured out peacefully? And not because team members always see things the same way, but because they have a foundation of common experience, mutual respect, and most of all, trust in one another that the best interests of the child are at the forefront of everyone's actions and intentions. The following section offers strategies for building this kind of foundational relationship between parents and educators. Once the work has been done to build it, the team will be positioned to withstand any of the proverbial storms that may lie ahead.

THE IMPORTANCE OF EMPATHY

As each school year begins, educators and parents are both presented with fresh opportunities to develop new relationships or build on existing ones. Those first introductions or initial meetings at the start of the school year are important ones; first impressions in any setting can set the tone for moving forward. In fact, every meeting and conversation has the potential to either build on this key relationship between parent and educator, or to erode the trust that is already there. With that in mind, a fundamental strategy to use in every interaction is for educators and parents to do their best to practice *empathy* as they approach each other in their advocacy for their child or student.

What is empathy? It is the ability to see things from another person's perspective and to understand where they are coming from. Empathy sometimes means imagining yourself in their shoes so that you can envision what they might be feeling or experiencing. Empathy allows us to give one another grace, to allow for imperfections, to assume the other person has good intentions, and to focus on the positive. This is not always easy! Because we are all human, we can get defensive and feel judged, and our first reaction against a perceived slight is often to take a stand and even "fight back." Empathy may come more naturally to some, and to others it's something that must be learned and practiced.

When educators and families come together at the table for IEP meetings or other conversations, there are often "unseen guests" that they bring with them. In other words, each person has their respective set of life experiences that has formed their opinions, their outlook, their style of advocacy, and potentially their ability to get through any given day. Parents of children with DS-ASD, for example, are likely to have experienced countless sleepless nights prior to a meeting with their child's teacher or team. They may be exhausted because their child's sleep patterns, like those of many individuals with DS-ASD, are disparate from typical circadian cycles. They may have had a stressful morning right before a conversation or a meeting because their child decided they didn't want to get on the bus that day, and it took "all hands on deck" to persuade them to get up from the middle of the driveway and into the car or school bus. Maybe the "unseen guest" is a previous experience the parent had with a different educator, in which they felt unheard, unappreciated, or simply misunderstood.

While these challenges often result in a powerful love and fierce commitment to protect and advocate for their child, they can also work against a parent making the great first impression they intended to make at their meeting with a teacher or administrator. The simple act of *acknowledging* these challenges puts educators in a position of empathy, sets the tone of the meeting with a measure of allowance and perspective, and shows the parent(s) that they are valued and respected. In this case, the meeting or conversation between the two has a much better chance of being productive and positive.

Educators, please *practice* empathy with these parents. (Don't worry, this advice goes in both directions.) Their child has diverse needs and behaviors than you may typically see in other students with Down syndrome alone or with autism alone. Try to put yourself in the parent's shoes. Would you function at the peak of your professional ability the morning after a sleepless and stressful night? Or if your child swiped their entire breakfast onto the floor, or had a bowel movement or meltdown just before the bus was to arrive? Would you come into this meeting with an open mind and willingness to trust if a previous educator had treated you dismissively?

Just as a novice pianist must practice diligently to develop their talent, educators must practice empathy in order to develop it and incorporate it into their character—or at least into their professional toolset. Be patient with parents. Be kind and offer compassion when you can. Experience shows that a small expression of empathy and acknowledgment of their reality will go a long way in a meeting with a parent.

Likewise, parents are not always aware that educators and service providers may bring "unseen guests" with them to the table, as well. It is not uncommon for teachers to experience extreme stress and burnout in their field. They may have students with intense behavioral needs that deplete their energy every day. They may have a schedule that allows for no breaks throughout their day, including little or no time for planning. This means they must complete all their lesson plans and paperwork during their personal time, leaving scant time for their own families or interests. Some educators have even experienced "second hand" trauma during their career, perhaps a result of witnessing the abuse or neglect of a student. It might even be the product of experiencing verbal abuse from a previous volatile parent.

Parents, try to remember that your child is one of several that educators are trying their best to serve, and they are trying to do their job in the most professional way possible. They may have several students with IEPs in their educational care, which means they have many goals they are required to work toward all at once. They may have issues going on in their personal lives or at work that you're not aware of, which are adding to their stress. Prior to meeting with them, or with the team, try to put yourselves in their shoes, with their heavy responsibilities on your shoulders.

Parents, we know that you are your child's best advocate, and perhaps in the past you've found yourself in a position where you have had to "stand up for them" or "fight for them" in their school setting. Our advice is to channel your fierce advocacy into a posture of empathy and respect instead of using a confrontational or aggressive demeanor. As parents, we do not want those who care for and work with our child with DS-ASD every day to resent our combative interactions with them in a way that can ultimately transfer to our child. A small measure of empathy will make a big difference in an educator loving our children instead of resenting them due to our style of "advocacy."

Empirical research has proven the assertion that empathy serves to strengthen parent-educator relationships. For example, a recent qualitative study found that when parents of children with severe disabilities and teachers found themselves thrown into the world of remote learning due to school closures during the COVID-19 pandemic, empathy was a key to success. Francis et al. (2022) indicated that at first, parents and teachers were both flustered and defensive, not sure how to navigate their new world of virtual learning. Then, as time went on, teachers started to empathize with the stresses and daily exhaustion that parents were experiencing. Parents began to empathize with the efforts that the teachers were making in the seemingly impossible scenario of remote learning for students with disabilities. "Mutual recognition of parent and teacher efforts and exhaustion resulted in a shift in perceptions, with [teachers] adopting a 'with not against' mentality—as evidenced by positive communication, instructional collaboration, and gratitude" (p. 9).

Through a change in their perspective, and putting themselves in each other's shoes, the parents and teachers came up with strategies like working around parent schedules, listening to one another's concerns, video conferencing, and more. The empathy they developed helped to build a positive relationship, and together they weathered the very tumultuous storm of virtual learning.

Some things can get in the way of empathy, such as fear of being judged or feeling threatened by what others might say. These reactions result in our walls being put up and communication being shut down—which is the exact opposite of productive teamwork. The benefits to practicing empathy in the parent-educator dyad include less stress, reduced negativity, a significant improvement in communication and collaboration, a healthy environment for voicing ideas and opinions, and the development of trusting relationships. Most of all, empathy is a *key building block* for the kind of trust that is required to work through developing and monitoring plans and goals for students with DS-ASD, as well as any issues or concerns that will surely present themselves somewhere along the way. It is one of the means to creating a great team that will work together toward the common educational goals for the unique student with DS-ASD.

We asked parents and educators, "What are some things you have done to build a strong foundation for positive, trusting relationships in the school setting?"

Parents said…	Educators said…
Worked hard to actively listen when others are talking instead of trying to format my response while they were talking.	Truly believed the parent is the expert on their child with DS-ASD. Had a teachable spirit and asked them for strategies.
Did a presentation about my son for peers and teachers at the beginning of each year.	Emphasized the positives and didn't focus on everything the student "can't" do. Parents loved to hear what their child CAN do.
Continually verbalized gratitude to the team and went over and above to help the teachers by bringing supplies and treats.	Invited families to the classroom several times over the course of the year to show the student's new skills and projects.
Followed through on suggestions to work on goals at home.	Created a portfolio to bring to the IEP meeting to celebrate my student's achievements with the family.

RESPECTFUL COMMUNICATION IS NONNEGOTIABLE

Communication and empathy ideally go hand in hand. After asking teachers and parents in the DS-ASD community about their experiences with building trust within the IEP team, *effective communication* was a significant recurring theme. This does not come as a surprise, since it aligns with recent empirical research that emphasized the critical nature of good communication strategies for building and maintaining strong parent-educator teams (Popovska et al., 2021). Keeping the lines of communication open, as well as creating meaningful opportunities for parents to engage in the education arena, have also been identified as requirements to developing this strong relationship (Gettinger & Guetschow, 1998; Leenders et al., 2019).

Why is communication so important? The ability to share our ideas and intent, our understanding of issues, and even our emotions, with others is an ongoing process that is part of everyday life and allows us to coexist in a meaningful way (Venter, 2019). Communication is interactive, iterative, and does not always require words. Communication can be nuanced and complex, which is why it is sometimes better to talk face-to-face in order to read nonverbal cues and body language. When communication is lacking between a parent and educator, misunderstandings are certain to occur, which can only impede the educational goals for the student.

There are times when parents and educators get into a habit of negative communications. In other words, the tone of the message can tend to focus only on what's going wrong. There are ways that both the parent and the educator can recognize whether their communication has fallen into this negative repartee. For example, some teachers have reported conversations with a certain parent in the past that have been stressful, and even hostile. Now, every time the teacher sees the parent arrive at school or gets an email from the parent in their inbox, the teacher automatically cringes with apprehension. An example from the parent perspective of being conditioned by negatively toned communication is when they get a phone call from the school. Inevitably, when they see that call coming in, they take a deep breath and brace themselves for what they naturally assume is a call about their child's challenging behaviors or being informed that—yet again—the student needs to go home early due to illness or some other reason.

Once recognized, a pattern or habit of communication that tends to have a negative focus can—and should—be turned around. The simple strategy of inserting positive anecdotes and feedback when addressing challenging matters makes a surprising difference in the way these interactions are received. Furthermore, make an effort to talk to each other in positive ways regularly, and don't wait until a challenging issue arises to communicate with one another.

Paying careful attention to the tone of messaging is also a key strategy in communicating. When the tone is celebratory and cooperative in nature, it makes discussing difficult matters more palatable when the time comes. Implementing these simple yet powerful techniques when communicating with each other may allow parents to answer phone calls from the school without dread and may prevent a teacher's heart from racing when they see that particular parent coming through the doors of the school.

To keep communication positive, but also realistic, teachers can make a habit of sending a message or photo announcing a happy, new development now and then. For example, "She met her communication goal by waving hello!" or something endearing their student did, such as, "He sat down next to a friend and shared his book; it was so sweet." Parents can reciprocate by sending quick notes about an achievement they have seen at home, such as, "Thank you for sharing your technique for helping my daughter wash her hands… it worked!" Partnering in a positive yet realistic way can mitigate knee-jerk defensiveness and help us assume the best of each other. *Remember: you can be an advocate without being an adversary.*

The following strategies are adapted from Davenport (2022) and can be helpful for developing good communication practices between parents and educators. There is common ground in wanting to be heard and understood, which makes *good communication* another important tool for building a solid foundation of trust among the team. Each person on the team—whether parent or educator—can ask themselves the following questions as a personal inventory of how well they communicate:

- *Do you pay attention to the person talking to you?* If not, then you may be telling them that you are truly disinterested in what they have to say. Don't be distracted by your phone, device, or even by other people. Set your phone aside when you're in a conversation and give your full attention to the person you're talking with.
- *Do you tend to speak in absolutes or use generalities?* Statements such as, "Your daughter **never** listens" tend to be indisputable. They put the person in a box and limit their true capabilities and character. If a parent heard this kind of statement, they would likely feel defeated and unsupported by their daughter's teacher. If a parent were to tell a teacher, "**No one** has **ever** understood my son," it might make the teacher feel either incapable

of understanding the student, or that the parent does not recognize or give credit for the ways in which the teacher *has* understood the student.

- *Do you assume you know what the other person means by what they say?* Assumptions can create problems, since not everyone can communicate perfectly what they want to convey. Give the person a chance to explain. Follow up with questions to clarify and confirm that you truly are understanding their intended meaning. You can paraphrase back to the person what you think is being said and ask if that is correct. Try not to develop a bad habit of interrupting the person you're conversing with. Interrupting them will unquestionably show them that you aren't interested in their explanation, and that your take on things is much more important to voice than hearing theirs. Frequent interruptions teach the other person to stop talking to you, which of course creates a massive roadblock to open communication and building trusting relationships.

- *Are you willing to compromise?* Relationships are made up of compromise. Sometimes what you think is important prevails in a decision, and other times you need to realize that your priorities may not be the most important for the overall goals of the team. Learn to meet halfway. When you encounter differing opinions, ask yourself if the issue is really so important that you need to stand by it at all costs. Do you make room for concession or collaboration?

- *Do you focus on the issue, and not the other person?* It is rarely a constructive process when the conversation becomes personal. Working together to determine how best to meet a student's needs requires brainstorming, collaboration, and respectful ideas—it does not require commentary such as, "you just don't want to work with my child," or "it would help if you weren't out to get me." Making it personal leads to unfair criticism and is destructive to a healthy working relationship.

- *Do you ask questions?* If the conversation doesn't seem to be going anywhere, perhaps try asking more questions to get to the bottom of what the person would like to convey to you. Generally, asking questions in a nonthreatening way and allowing time for the person to think about things before answering may provide the breakthrough you're looking for. Practice active listening, and follow up with additional, perhaps more probing, questions that are open-ended. This may signal to the other person that you really want to know their thoughts and opinions, and that you value their contribution.

Putting these strategies into practice may strengthen the relationship between parents and educators, and lead to more positive outcomes for the student with DS-ASD. With a solid foundation of trust among the team, a teacher may have a completely different reaction to seeing a parent coming toward their classroom. Instead of dreading what they were once certain would be a confrontational interchange, much better communication between them has perhaps created a feeling of trust that whatever the reason for the visit, the dialog between the two will be constructive, positive, and friendly.

Similarly, when parents see a call coming in from the school, they may not dread answering the call because, even though they know it might mean their child has had a challenging day, or that they may have to go pick them up early, at least they will be met with an understanding and empathetic teacher. The way the message is given means everything. Good communication builds upon empathy, and they work together to create a solid foundation of trust and collaboration for the benefit of the student. A strong partnership like this is what makes the difficult discussions easier to deliver, easier to receive, and more likely to work in collaboration toward the benefit of the student.

ACHIEVING PRODUCTIVE MEETINGS: WORDS AND TONE MATTER

Julie Hearrell, MA Ed

As a special education teacher, and later as a district-level educational coach, and now as a Goal Development Specialist in adult IDD services, building trusting relationships with parents has always been of utmost importance to me. I knew that every child's success was dependent on them having a collaborative team of adults who worked together to provide for their needs. I knew I had the opportunity each time I communicated with parents to either lead the conversation in a positive direction, or unintentionally turn down the wrong path. Early on, I found myself nervous to talk to parents, afraid I would mince words and end up on that "dark road." However, as the number of parent meetings increased, so did my level of confidence in using the right words to communicate information in a way that led to positive outcomes.

Over time, I developed strategies that became standard practice when engaging with parents in the school setting. These simple practices rarely failed to provide the framework for a collaborative and successful meeting.

Teacher-Led Meetings and Conversations

- I would gather my thoughts about what I wanted to communicate prior to the meeting or conversation. I would then jot down a few key words that I wanted to be certain to include in the conversation and would ensure that those words were positive and precise.
- I began every conversation with a student-centered approach, emphasizing the student's strengths and any celebrations, big or small.
- I acknowledged parents' efforts in supporting these strengths at home.
- I clearly stated the information I wanted to convey. I used the key words I had pre-chosen. I paid attention to my tone, always striving for kind and professional.
- I asked for questions, thoughts, and ideas from parents, assuring them their input was valued.

- I actively listened, paraphrased, and asked clarifying questions.
- I summarized any decisions made or goals set and included follow-up plans, when appropriate.
- I implemented the IEP, and whenever there were barriers to achieving certain goals or implementing strategies spelled out in the IEP, I communicated that to the parents and brainstormed with them. I didn't wait until the next IEP meeting to share concerns; instead I kept them informed of all my efforts so there weren't any unhappy or anger-provoking surprises.
- I shared my gratitude for their collaboration and commitment to their child's success.
- At the beginning of each year, I always extended the invitation for open communication with parents. I encouraged them to contact me any time they had questions, concerns, or celebrations they wanted to share. I also explained the district's "chain of command" and respectfully asked them to contact me first if concerns arose. I assured them I would always try to collaborate with them to address any concerns, but welcomed them to engage my principal, or other school leaders, at any time in the problem-solving process. As a result, many parents felt comfortable requesting collaborative meetings and/or conversations with me. I always accepted their invitation, but ensured it was at a time I could give them my focused attention. (I found that problem-solving conversations on the sidewalk while performing bus duty were rarely successful.)

I learned valuable lessons from parents who modeled excellent communication skills as they advocated for their child or themselves. Here are a few examples of collaborative practices I have observed from parents over the years:

Parent-Led Meetings and Conversations

- The parent began the conversation with a calm and friendly tone.
- They put their child at the center of the discussion and spoke only to their needs, resisting the temptation to talk about the needs and behaviors of other students.
- They were clear and concise with their words.
- They shared positive examples of success from their child's perspective.

- If the purpose of the meeting or conversation was to share a concern and advocate for their child, they still spoke with a respectful tone and approached the issue as a collaborative problem-solver.
- They asked clarifying questions and allowed me to ask questions as well.
- They offered ideas and possible solutions but also listened to alternative perspectives and suggestions.
- They were respectful of the time frame set for the meeting and were willing to continue the conversation at another time, if necessary.
- They ended our time together on a positive note and expressed appreciation for the collaborative time focused on their child.

Addressing Challenges

- If parents expressed that they believed the IEP was not being followed, I would set up a separate meeting and we would go over the IEP together. Sometimes they realized that my team and I really were working on the IEP, and other times I realized that we were missing something, and I was sincerely apologetic. At this point, since the conversation was respectful, we were able to discuss and agree on matters and move forward.
- If words and tone escalated, I would attempt to employ my de-escalation skills and offer empathy and positivity. If that did not help, I asked if we could continue the conversation at a time when everyone was calmer and ready to address the talking points.

Suggested Resource

An excellent resource for educators who wish to increase family engagement is the US Department of Education's Institute of Education Sciences publication, *Toolkit of Resources for Engaging Families and the Community as Partners in Education* (2016) found at https://ies.ed.gov/ncee/rel/Products/Publication/3767.

PART II:

A PERSON-CENTERED APPROACH —ONE SIZE NEVER FITS ALL

What is a person-centered approach, and why does it matter? A person-centered approach considers the student from a holistic perspective. It allows the team to view the student as a whole and unique person by asking two questions: *What is important to the student* and *what is important for the student*? Person-centered education considers the needs, wishes, and desires of the student and what is best for **them**, and ensures that the student remains the team's central focus.

Taking a person-centered approach can be quite liberating for the team if they like to try new approaches, but it can also cause each team member (parents, educators, and specialists alike) to reexamine long-standing beliefs and practices. For example, teachers may do things a certain way because "that's the way we've always done it," while parents may be on a completely different page. Many parents learn about concepts early on from their Down syndrome community and they are told that they "better brace" themselves for the school years. Parents get advice about *full inclusion* and how to *stand up* to educators. Both are fine concepts, of course, if they are appropriate or warranted.

What we have heard from many parents, however, is that when their child was diagnosed with autism in addition to Down syndrome, they experienced a paradigm shift on many levels. In general terms, what would work for most students with Down syndrome may not work well for a student with DS-ASD. At what point does the parent rebuff internal and external pressures so they can modify the ideals they so vehemently espoused when their child was younger? In the following section, we will look at IEP meetings and inclusion, two of the foremost pain points that parents and teachers have identified as causing division within the team.

IEP MEETINGS

What is an IEP?

In the United States, the Individuals with Disabilities Education Act (IDEA) mandated that eligible students with disabilities receive a "free appropriate public education" in the "least-restrictive environment." But, who decides what an appropriate education means for our students with DS-ASD? The process of defining this for each student is done by a team that develops an Individualized Education Program (IEP). Usually, the IEP team includes the student, their parent/guardian, and educators from the school. These educators can be teachers who have worked with the student, other providers such as therapists, and perhaps other school administrative staff. IEP meetings are conducted annually to develop goals for the student, and to discuss what individualized adaptations may be needed for the student's education.

A product of the IEP meeting is a definition of what an "appropriate education" looks like for the individual student. This includes where and how the education is received (Gilmour, 2018), such as full inclusion in the regular classroom, in a special education classroom or program, or perhaps a hybrid of the two. Additionally, it includes the supports the student will need, such as a paraprofessional. Keep in mind that "IDEA requires that the student be educated in regular classrooms unless their academic and behavioral needs cannot be met in that setting even with the use of supplemental aids and services" (Gilmour, 2018).

We can bring the concept of person-centeredness to IEP planning meetings by taking an individualized approach, which is, after all, the core aim of the Individualized Education Program. The IEP team members should focus on the student, first and foremost, and set high yet realistic goals and expectations. It is important to use the strategies we have learned regarding showing empathy and maintaining clear and respectful communication. It is also important to bring a spirit of collaboration to the table. Some parents bring chocolate or other treats to IEP meetings, just to set the tone and lay down a friendly foundation for jumping into IEP discussions and negotiations.

To be clear, IEP meetings can be intimidating for everyone. Problems and tensions within the team can arise when parents question whether the IEP is being followed and when teachers feel pressured or misunderstood around implementation of the IEP. There may be legitimate concerns on both sides, and they need to be addressed. The concern is whether breakdowns in communication and hurt feelings will derail the whole process, resulting in a stalemate. How can we maintain our focus on the child and how can we work as a team to accomplish our collective goals? Can parents and educators be strong advocates without being adversarial? It may take a lot of work and patience, but yes, they can.

Suggestions to Achieve Effective IEP Meetings

- Lead with an attitude of gratitude, and agree on meeting parameters, such as taking turns, not interrupting, and giving everyone equal time to share ideas.
- Use "I" statements, which feels less argumentative to the listener (*"I feel very uncomfortable and confused with what's happening right now. Can we back up a bit and start over?"*)

- Start by talking about the child's positive attributes and about goals they have achieved

  - *"I loved how Johnny sat next to his friend and engaged in parallel play, that was new!"*
  - *"Lisa's peer buddy can't stop talking about how much they love engaging with Lisa and about how 'cute' she is. It's a great opportunity for both of them!"*
  - *"Anita showed great interest in our cooking activity today; she participated in measuring ingredients (math skills) and pouring them in the bowl (fine motor skills). This shows tremendous growth, and we loved seeing her smile as she was doing it!"*

- Be positive and enthusiastic about potential goals.
- If a parent or educator is having a rough time, acknowledge it and affirm the person.
- Be an active listener, make eye contact, and be mindful of your words and tone.
- Educators should acknowledge the parent as the ultimate expert on the child.
- Communicate how the teacher's efforts can be reinforced at home, and how the parent's efforts can be reinforced in school.
- Ask questions and express concerns rather than make accusations or demands; come to a consensus as a group effort.
- Be flexible and understanding if there are extenuating circumstances for services being impeded for any reason—talk it out and come up with a plan to get things back on track.
- Parents, be gentle with yourselves. You are doing a great job.
- Teachers, be gentle with yourselves. You are doing a great job.
- Be gentle with each other. The old adage says "you catch more flies with honey than you do with vinegar," meaning you are more likely to get what you want and reach consensus by being sweet and respectful than by being acidic and militant.
- Thank each other for their time. If matters have not been resolved, give yourselves time to think and collect yourselves, and then schedule another time to meet.
- What other suggestions do *you* have?

INCLUSION

We all know that autism is a spectrum disorder, and the saying goes, "If you've met *one* person with autism, you've only met *one* person with autism." Of course, this is true of any disability, condition, or disorder. One person with DS-ASD is unique and different from the next, which is why a person-centered approach to education is so important. So, what about inclusion? The educational system in the United States is trending more toward full inclusion, and rightfully so since IDEA mandates it, unless the student's educational and behavioral needs cannot be met in that environment. Proponents of full inclusion in the regular education classroom may cite studies that demonstrate that full inclusion is the answer for everyone. However, there are others who feel that full inclusion does not necessarily work in all cases, and that there are pros and cons to consider (Francisco et al., 2020; Gilmour, 2018; Kauffman & Hornby, 2020; Mesibov & Shea, 1996).

Margaret Bray, mother of Alex, shared a few examples that demonstrate how strong relationships and good communication with school personnel, plus a person-centered approach to inclusion, have enriched Alex's educational and social experiences within the school setting:

"Alex has DS-ASD, and he attends our school district's [special education] 'LIFE' class. There are eight students in the LIFE class this year. They have their own 'specials' classes (physical education, music, and art), and then they are included with the general education class for lunch, field trips, and other subjects and events. Alex also receives speech, physical, and occupational therapies at school. His teachers and therapists provide me with a daily report that gives me important information about his day. For example, they report about how Alex was feeling that day, which therapies and classes he participated in, how he ate, about bathroom visits, whether they need anything from me, and any other notes they wish to share. The report gives me insight into his school day, which is so helpful to me as his mother. It also helps me to appreciate everything they are doing to educate and support my son.

Socially, Alex has become quite a star at school! There's a group of girls who sit with him at lunch and play with him at recess. He's popular with the school staff, as well, as he charms his teachers, paraprofessionals (classroom aides), and therapists on a daily basis.

School has become a happy and productive experience for Alex. I credit Alex for being so amazing, and I credit the school staff for valuing him as a student and me as a parent. Not only do they communicate clearly with me about his school day, most importantly, they have helped Alex to learn and grow in the environments that best support him, and they have helped him to develop his social skills and make real friendships. This is an educational success story!"

When a student has complex educational and behavioral needs—which includes many students with DS-ASD—taking a person-centered approach to inclusion may mean adjusting dreams and expectations for full inclusion. Kauffman et al. (2020) advocate for full inclusion in the general classroom for students with severe disabilities, but only when it is realistic, benefits the student educationally, and is determined by a consensus of a team with knowledge about the student and what is best for them. In other words, full inclusion is good *if it is appropriate* for the individual.

It must be acknowledged that full inclusion is not always appropriate for every student. Researchers have asserted that placing a person with IDD in the general classroom for the sake of prioritizing physical colocation can be a miscalculation, when access to the most effective instruction for the individual may be in a noninclusive setting (Kauffman et al., 2020). A realistic look at the individual student's instructional needs and abilities, behavioral needs, personal preferences, and interests, and even the parents' concerns for their child's dignity, should be assessed within the team when considering the location of educational services. The person-centered approach may nudge parents to consider partial inclusion, or low inclusion for a time, as deemed helpful by the team. This nudge can cause discomfort and strong emotions, or perhaps, feelings of relief.

Person-centered inclusion will look different for each student, as it should. Full inclusion can work for some students with DS-ASD, yet many of the parents we have worked with have accepted a blended approach that matches the student's educational needs and best interests at different points in their learning. Keep your focus on the student, try different types of inclusion, and experiment with different scenarios at school. Some parents may see it as a "failure" if their child is not fully included in the classroom. Our advice is to let that kind of thinking go, and don't be so hard on yourself. Partial inclusion, and even low inclusion, should not be seen as a failure if it's the best scenario in which your child with DS-ASD can learn, grow, interact with neurotypical peers, and have a meaningful day. If the team collaborates and finds that a hybrid or even a center-based program would be better, and your child is improving or thriving without full-time inclusion, take that as a win and celebrate that your child is succeeding. "Special education is, indeed, a service and not a place…*place* itself teaches nothing, is not a reliable predictor of instruction, and is no guarantee of instruction" (Kauffman et al., 2020, p. 31).

CONCLUSION

The quality of the relationship between parents and educators can make or break the educational experience for all involved. What does your team's foundation look like? Have you established open and honest lines of communication? Have you been able to put yourself in the other person's shoes by practicing empathy? If your "tower" seems to be precariously built on shifting sand, can you work together to restore the relationships and establish a brand-new foundation built on mutual respect?

At every step of the educational experience for the student with DS-ASD, we suggest approaching goals and decisions with a holistic view of that unique student. If there is disagreement, despite the efforts of open communication and empathy, consider using a mediator and set new standards of communication and interpersonal expectations. Do what it takes to come to a common and collaborative solution for the benefit of the student. As members of the student's team, both parents and educators must learn to adjust their *own* perspectives about inclusion, and other issues, to align better with a solution that will help the *student* be more successful. The educational experience is *not* about the parent, and it is *not* about the educator; it *is* about the exceptional student with DS-ASD.

REFERENCES

Davenport, B. (2022, May 13). Worried you're a bad communicator? 11 signs you need to step it up. *Live Bold & Bloom.* https://liveboldandbloom.com/05/self-improvement/poor-communicators

Francis, G. L., Raines, A. R., Reed, A. S., & Jerome, M. K. (2022). Parent-teacher interactions during COVID-19: Experiences of U.S. teachers of students with severe disabilities. *Education Sciences, 12*(7), 1–13. https://doi.org/10.3390/educsci12070488

Francisco, M. P. B., Hartman, M., & Wang, Y. (2020). Inclusion and special education. *Education Sciences, 10*(9), 238. https://dx.doi.org/10.3390/educsci10090238

Gettinger, M., & Guetschow, K. W. (1998). Parental involvement in schools: Parent and teacher perceptions of roles, efficacy, and opportunities. *Journal of Research & Development in Education, 32*(1), 38–52.

Gilmour, A. F. (2018). Has inclusion gone too far? Weighing its effects on students with disabilities, their peers, and teachers. *Education Next, 18*(4), 8–16.

Kauffman, J. M., & Hornby, G. (2020). Inclusive vision versus special education reality. *Education Sciences, 10*(9), 258. https://doi.org/10.3390/educsci10090258

Kauffman, J. M., Travers, J. C., & Badar, J. (2020). Why *some* students with severe disabilities are not placed in general education. *Research and Practice for Persons with Severe Disabilities, 45*(1), 28–33. https://doi.org/10.1177/1540796919893053

Leenders, H., de Jong, J., Monfrance, M., & Haelermans, C. (2019). Building strong parent-teacher relationships in primary education: the challenge of two-way communication. *Cambridge Journal of Education, 49*(4), 519–533. https://doi.org/10.1080/0305764X.2019.1566442

Mesibov, G. B., & Shea, V. (1996). Full inclusion and students with autism. *Journal of Autism and Developmental Disorders, 26*, 337–346. https://doi.org/10.1007/BF02172478

Popovska, N. G., Popovski, F., & Popovska, H. D. (2021). Communication strategies for strengthening the parent-teacher relationships in the primary schools. *International Journal of Research Studies in Education, 10*(14), 123–134. https://doi.org/10.5861/ijrse.2021.a076

Venter, E. (2019). Challenges for meaningful interpersonal communication in a digital era. *Theological Studies, 75*(1), 1–6. https://doi.org/10.4102/hts.v75i1.5339

CHAPTER TWELVE

MULTICULTURAL CONSIDERATIONS AND STRATEGIES FOR DS-ASD

Elina R. Manghi, PsyD, LMFT

POSTHUMOUS NOTE:

It is our distinct honor to include the late Dr. Elina Manghi's original chapter in this second edition of our book. Dr. Manghi's love and care for racially, ethnically, and culturally diverse families in Chicago (and beyond) was groundbreaking. The legacy and vision of Dr. Manghi remains alive at Grupo SALTO, practically unchanged since her passing in 2012. Grupo SALTO's mission is to provide state-of-the-art information, support, and services within a family framework with a high emphasis on cultural competency, as originally devised by Dr. Manghi. Grupo SALTO continues its unwavering commitment to bringing insight and hope to all aspects of life for families who have children with disabilities focusing on the autism spectrum.

"I am the proud mother of Faith, who has DS-ASD. I identify as Black/African-American. Navigating the system of special needs was very complicated for us. First Down syndrome, and then as years passed I, along with educators and some physicians, questioned whether something more than Down syndrome was going on. I went from feeling somewhat isolated to a deeper isolation. To receive a diagnosis of autism for a child with Down syndrome can be devastating for some parents, but for me it was more about understanding Faith better. I think that things are becoming better for families because more information is out there. My goal is to help families not feel so isolated."—Roxanne Hoke-Chandler

Autism spectrum disorder (ASD) is a neurodevelopmental disability characterized by differences in social and communication functioning and by restricted and repetitive behaviors and interests. (Long & Register-Brown, 2021). Further descriptions and diagnostic criteria can be found in the *Diagnostic and Statistical Manual of Mental Disorders* (5th ed., text rev.; DSM-5-TR; American Psychiatric Association, 2022). Recent epidemiological studies suggest that the incidence of autism is increasing.

According to the Centers for Disease Control and Prevention (CDC, 2023), the prevalence of autism in the United States, is now one in 36 children aged 8 years and was almost four times as more common among boys than among girls. Overall, ASD prevalence was lower among non-Hispanic White children and children of two or more races than among non-Hispanic Black or African-American, Hispanic. Non-Hispanic Asian or Pacific Islander was similar to that of other racial and ethnic groups (Maenner et al., 2023).

"More people than ever before are being diagnosed with ASD. It is unclear exactly how much of this increase is due to a broader definition of ASD and better efforts in diagnosis. However, a true increase in the number of people with an ASD cannot be ruled out. We believe the increase in the diagnosis of ASD is likely due to a combination of these factors" (CDC, 2023). Autism has now become a national health crisis (Mandy, 2022), surpassing all other childhood disorders as the fastest growing epidemic in the United States.

Despite the enormous amount of literature available on autism, surprisingly little is known about the specific manifestation of the disorder and the appropriate tools with which to diagnose it within minority communities. Little is known about parental knowledge of appropriate interventions, the use of available resources, and/or the effectiveness of interventions among minority families. For those minority families who have children with Down syndrome and autism (DS-ASD), the difficulties are even greater than in the nonminority population, even though autism occurs in all races and nationalities.

As has been discussed throughout this book, awareness, understanding, and knowledge regarding diagnosing DS-ASD remains a problem for many families. Recent empirical research (Spinazzi et al., 2023) sought to explore the experiences of caregivers of individuals with DS-ASD, including concerns they had prior to diagnosis, getting the second diagnosis, and through intervention. The researchers found that it took an average of 4.65 years among the sample of caregivers to receive the DS-ASD diagnosis from the time of their initial concerns. A common theme found among caregiver experience was that the concerns presented to their primary care professional were at first dismissed. Furthermore, 82% of respondents felt their primary care provider was not familiar enough with the dual diagnosis to provide them with any guidance on next steps to take. These contributed to the delay in obtaining the DS-ASD diagnosis (Spinazzi et al., 2023). Through our work, we can say that DS-ASD also occurs in multicultural families. This chapter will review the difficulties faced by any minority family in the United States having a child with DS-ASD. A discussion of the obstacles these families must overcome will be followed by lessons learned through the activities of Grupo SALTO, the largest support group for Latino families who have children with ASD. Strategies by which to engage minority families in training and appropriate delivery models will follow.

THE PROBLEM

Although minority populations have grown significantly in the United States, they have not been represented in autism research, because up to now, most research data has generally been limited to Caucasian subjects. According to one study, the reasons for the disparities in age of diagnosis for children of color with autism spectrum disorder (ASD) are multifactorial and may include intertwined sociodemographic influences related to financial and educational resources as well as language and cultural barriers (Tek & Landa, 2013).

Another study conducted a regression analysis to examine differences in autism identification among seven racial reporting categories (Travers & Krezmien, 2018) and found that minority students experience less access to services due to significantly lower rates of autism identification. In their review of nine empirical studies, Bishop-Fitzpatrick and Kind (2017) reported that seven of the studies found that access to general medical services or quality of care for children with autism differed among various racial groups. More research is needed concerning the reasons for the general delay in the diagnosis of autism and the differences among the respective ethnic groups in terms of access to treatment services.

For many minority groups, mental illness and/or developmental disabilities are hidden. This is likely to occur due to cultural factors such as the shame and disgrace associated with admitting to emotional problems and the tendency to handle problems within the family rather than seek outside resources. Therefore, many minority families tend to delay the search for treatment until their problems become severe, which can lead to a lack of early intervention and the diminished efficacy of treatment.

Another issue pertains to the inaccessibility and incompatibility of the mainstream service delivery system, as typified by:

a) inconvenient location of the facilities in the client's community with inadequate community outreach and organization efforts;

b) a serious shortage of bilingual/bicultural service providers and a lack of efficient interpretation services; and

c) the inability of mental health professionals to provide culturally sensitive, appropriate forms of treatment.

For example, many treatment and assessment methods for autism have not been translated from English into other languages. Consequently, communication difficulties and the lack of language-appropriate information concerning the nature of autism and the type of resources can discourage families from seeking formal services throughout the process of diagnosis and treatment.

The coordination of services and early intervention are critically important since they are systematically planned and tailored to the needs and strengths of individual children and their families. State and local public agencies must coordinate efforts to ensure that minority children receive services without charge, or, at least, on a sliding scale, as needed. Due to scarce funding and a lack of knowledge as to the prevalence of autism among minority individuals residing in the United States, the available services vary drastically from school to school, district to district, and state to state. Many children in need of services end up on long waiting lists or possibly receive no services at all.

The demand for health services is strongly influenced by knowledge and information regarding those services. Thus, minority parents who lack information regarding autism, its diagnosis, and treatment may not seek services at an early stage. Moreover, professionals who serve the needs of minority families may not be adequately trained to recognize autism in individuals with Down syndrome.

WHY MINORITY FAMILIES ARE UNDERSERVED

Although training initiatives for autism have started to address the needs of families affected by the disorder, there has not been a consistent effort to include minority families. The deficit is partially attributable to the lack of trained professionals who are bilingual and bicultural or can culturally deliver such services.

Services for minority children with autism vary in terms of profile and quality, and usually they are provided in English. This leaves the parents isolated and unable to learn the appropriate interventions, which are essential for the development of children with DS-ASD. Minority parents report that few bilingual personnel are available in many of the targeted schools, which makes it extremely difficult for them to communicate with the teachers and special education teams.

It has been recognized that minority children generally have lower rates of mental health service utilization (Garcia et al., 2016), prematurely terminate psychotherapy, and endorse unfavorable mental health-seeking attitudes (Atkinson et al., 1995; Matsuoka et al., 1997). For example, one study found that the proportion of Asian Americans who used mental health services was approximately one-third of what might be expected, considering their population ratio (Yang & WonPat-Borja, 2006). Families often delay using services until problems are very serious, so that more severe types of mental disorders are exhibited when treatment is finally used. Due to the severity of the problems when they enter treatment, the efficacy of treatment outcome may be diminished.

Commonly, cultural and financial barriers exist for minority families, given that many are immigrants with limited knowledge about the availability of resources, and have problems navigating the system. Moreover, the treatments that are available are too expensive for them to acquire without assistance. Therefore, given the absence of materials suited to the cultural needs of minority families, they will not be able to benefit from services and/or communicate with professionals who could otherwise help them. Other barriers identified in research include limited access to health services due to the lack of insurance coverage and/or a lack of knowledge regarding DS-ASD.

GRUPO SALTO

This section has been graciously updated by Matiana Ovalle, Executive Director, Grupo SALTO and Angelica Davila, a PhD student at University of Illinois Chicago (UIC).

In response to the needs of the Latino community in Chicago, Illinois, the authors, together with a team of professionals in social work (Irma Hernández, LCSW), speech and language therapy (Pamela Bondy, MS/CCC-L), and parent (José Ovalle), founded Grupo SALTO in 2004. Grupo SALTO has continued serving the needs of primarily Spanish-speaking Latino families who have children with ASD and other disabilities.

Monthly educational meetings include the dissemination of best-practice information regarding resources, trainings, interventions, and referrals for children with ASD. Additionally, we spend time with parents to help them learn the strategies that are necessary, so they take care of themselves and their neurotypical children, siblings of the person with a developmental disability. Free childcare is provided through volunteers so that parents can attend the educational sessions.

Grupo SALTO also provides a program of creative expression for children with ASD and their siblings. The program typically includes artistic components, such as visual art and music. The goal of the program is to expose children with ASD to the arts while preparing them for inclusion in community activities. Sibling groups are available to help neurotypical children address their concerns and questions in an environment that is safe and fun. A support group for teens with ASD is offered as well, thus providing opportunities to discuss life skills and the transition to adulthood.

Families that participate in the activities of Grupo SALTO not only report an increased knowledge of ASD but also enjoy the sense of community and empowerment that is part of their ongoing participation. Parents feel they are more able to speak out and educate community members about what it is like to have a child with autism. They also report a greater awareness and acceptance of other families who have children with disabilities. To that extent, they have been very supportive of Latino families with children with DS-ASD.

We, as a group, have earned the trust of our families by listening to their needs, by making the activities culturally meaningful, and by offering the services on Saturday mornings so that more family members are able to attend. Consequently, the growth of Grupo SALTO has been encouraged and facilitated. We provide snacks that are culturally acceptable, and we use visual tools, such as flyers, handouts, presentations, and other materials that are appropriate for our Spanish-speaking participants. We provide simultaneous interpretation when necessary, and we encourage parents to participate in different aspects of the organization based on their availability and willingness to contribute to the overall effort. We have been very successful in having moms and dads participate in the various aspects of training. In turn, this has helped strengthen marriages while challenging the stereotypes of gender. We strongly believe in teaching our families the power of advocacy and leadership.

INTERVENTION

It is well documented that children with autism, including those with DS-ASD, need intensive early intervention treatment. Moreover, autism treatment involves an interdisciplinary approach with comprehensive interventions, both at home and in school. Minority families who do not speak English do not receive adequate services due to that lack of trained, bilingual professionals who can share the cultural attributes of their communities.

The key to designing an effective mode of intervention for minority families is to first understand, respect, and appreciate their cultural diversity. Second, it is to make culturally relevant treatment approaches available to families with scant resources. Third, it is to use the families' strengths in helping them utilize the most effective strategies for handling autism within the home and within their children's own communities.

Accordingly, in response to the needs of the community, we created a plan to provide training to Latino families in Chicago who had children with ASD (including dual diagnoses such as DS-ASD). This training is sponsored by The Autism Program (TAP) (https://tap-illinois.org/) and is delivered through the Department of Disability and Human Development at the University of Illinois, in Chicago. We developed two aspects to this training:

1. ***Community Education and Training:*** We provide direct training to community agencies and professionals serving the needs of Latino families. Training activities include an overview of autism, the co-occurrence of other disorders (e.g., DS-ASD), and common interventions for the treatment of autism. Each agency and participating professional receives educational materials translated into Spanish for dissemination among the Latino community. A consumer satisfaction survey is used to assess the effectiveness of training.

2. ***Parent Education and Training:*** We provide parent training to Latino families who have children with ASD, including dual genetic disorders. Training is conducted in Spanish. At the end of the parent training, we evaluate the training and encourage parents to discuss the best ways to reach their respective communities. We assist parents who are unfamiliar with the assessment procedure to ensure that we obtain information regarding the training.

The parent training consists of ten weekly sessions offered at times that are convenient for families. Both parents and extended families are invited to attend the training sessions. The first three sessions are group-oriented, followed by six individual sessions, and then the last session, which is again given in the group context. In each cycle we train six families. We prefer to train families immediately after they receive the diagnosis of ASD; however, we also teach families who have never received this type of training despite having received the diagnosis of ASD in the past.

The group sessions are designed to teach the most effective interventions to support the best practices associated with learning, behavioral, and sensory challenges associated with ASD. Families get to know each other, and consequently they embark together on a path that will lead them to a better understanding and acceptance of their children's conditions. Cultural beliefs and barriers are discussed, as they are important elements in the success of any training. During the last group session, we assess progress, and we train parents to work with their children's school. Finally, we talk about the importance of taking care of oneself and explore the essential strategies for stress management.

The individual sessions are tailored to the specific needs of each family. During these sessions the parents can practice what they have learned during the group sessions. We use visual materials that are culturally appropriate. We teach parents how to implement behavioral interventions that are successful, and, of course, appropriate to the family's cultural beliefs. We help parents identify what prevents them from successfully applying appropriate interventions, and together with them we celebrate every success, no matter how small it might be.

Parents are encouraged to participate in the training sessions offered by Grupo SALTO as described above. The monthly sessions provide parents with another avenue by which to connect to a community of peers and at the same time continue their learning. We view parents as mentors who will not only help their own children but can also help other families that are just starting.

The role of the trainer is to help families attain a new perspective, and, at the same time, to promote creativity within the group. The trainer must therefore help the participants avoid failure. This is important because children who have ASD are constantly confronted by the experience of failure. When parents learn to recognize the signs and plan strategies that will help their children avoid repeated failure experiences, behaviors and family life will both improve. By learning to recognize what leads to their own experience of failure, parents will be more fully prepared to support their children to be successful. Additionally, the trainer facilitates connections among parents, helping them break the cycle of isolation.

CONTINUITY OF GRUPO SALTO DURING THE COVID-19 PANDEMIC

As of March 2023, Grupo SALTO finds itself in the process of returning to the same level of in-person activities that had been halted as a response to the COVID-19 pandemic. The group will move toward simultaneous in-person and virtual sessions. Despite the pandemic's effect on programming options, Grupo SALTO's membership has grown to approximately 750 Latino families who live in the Chicago metropolitan area, including some from other countries such as, Mexico and Colombia. The group's international members benefit through virtual programming. Some aspects of the program today are funded in whole or in part by TAP (The Autism Program of Illinois) and DHS (Department of Human Services). Matie M. Ovalle is the general coordinator.

Grupo SALTO continues its commitment of bringing insight and hope to all aspects of life for those families who have children with disabilities. Additional programs and training have been implemented to further inform and educate parents and caregivers, and are as follows:

1. **Youth Transition Training:** We provide training and support to parents and youth who are transitioning from middle school to high school, or who are transitioning out of high school.

2. **The Promotoras Program**: We continue to view parents as mentors for other parents. Therefore, we train parents on developing mentorship opportunities with new families in our program. The parent mentors serve as the *promotoras* who develop and foster peer-mentor relationships with the program's new families by educating them on challenges that can arise due to autism.

3. **IEP Training:** We focus on ensuring that parents are equipped with an understanding of the IEP process. Our goal is for parents to feel confident in their participation of the IEP process, and for them to become engaged advocates for their child.

4. **The Tu y Yo/Mentorship program**: We structured a social support group for teen youth and young adults with ASD. The group is meant to foster a welcoming and safe space for program participants to connect with peers as they explore their autistic identity. The program does not aim to change program participants but to build trust among each other and foster an outlet for them. The group is currently facilitated by Angelica Davila, Philip Marsh, Eileen Limón, Israel Sánchez, and Carlos and David Ovalle, all of whom are college graduates or current undergrad students with autism.

WHAT WE HAVE LEARNED

It is very important to avoid the bias of presupposition. This is particularly true, given the knowledge that minority families benefit from training and can be very successful in applying interventions that work for their children. However, they usually come to training with a lack of current knowledge regarding the management of ASD. They may believe there is little that can be done to improve their child's functioning (which might have been the case in their country of origin). Furthermore, due to language barriers they may have been unable to access current information. Many of our families may not have reliable access to the internet, or because of language barriers, they may not be able to adequately research the appropriate intervention based on the latest best practices.

We strongly believe the success of our training lies in the way we present our material, which is easily understood, visually accessible, provided in the family's first language, and accompanied by videos that demonstrate the concepts. The ability to conduct hands-on training also plays a role in the success of implementation. We ask both parents to work on creating visual schedules or a library of photos to use at home and in the community. We help them create behavioral plans with which to address particular challenges they are experiencing as families. We work closely with each family member to help all of them be successful in implementing the program. We create an emotional space where families can discuss their fears and concerns.

Factors that influence the success of training include the level of family stress, the family's attitude toward change, the strength of the parental relationship, and the trainer's ability to understand what cultural factors might obstruct the ability to apply the interventions presented. Occasionally, we have encountered families that were very resistant to the use of behavioral interventions. For example, many minority families view the use of rewards as bribery and a method that is not congruent with their belief systems. Unless the trainer can address this issue from a cultural perspective and show families the distinction between a reward and what would be considered bribery, the intervention will not be effective.

If the family is experiencing high levels of stress, which might not be related to their child's disability, it may be very difficult to learn and implement new techniques. Therefore, initially we assess and advise the family how to reduce stress, and then we focus on the intensive learning.

We carefully tailor our program to meet the needs of the community. Sessions are scheduled at times that are most convenient to families, in a central location that is readily accessible by public transportation. For some of the training sessions, we can provide childcare.

Initially, we had questions regarding the success of a training that included Latino parents whose children had either ASD or DS-ASD. However, we discovered that there were benefits to this arrangement. First, parents were able to understand that ASD can occur along with other conditions. Second, because the training focuses on the behavioral management or difficulties associated with ASD, the content of each session is clearly applicable to both groups. Third, parents have been able to express support for the parent of a child whose condition is more complex. Finally, an important discussion took place in which we addressed the difficulties of, a) someone who has readily been identified as having a disability due to obvious physical features, as is the case of children with Down syndrome; and, b) someone who has not been easily seen as an individual with a disability, due to the lack of obvious physical features.

We recently developed a program for Polish families who have children with ASD. The first family we trained had a 9-year-old child who had been diagnosed with DS-ASD. He had very poor communication skills and a series of sensory issues and was not toilet trained. We used a "train the trainer" model in which the author trained a Polish mental health provider to implement the ten-session program. The author presented the material in English, and the Polish mental health provider translated the content to the parent. We used visual systems to address the toileting and communication difficulties. The mother was very enthusiastic about trying the program, and she proved very successful in toilet training her child. With support, the teaching of basic behavioral principles, and use of visual systems, her child is beginning to communicate his needs. Temper tantrums have diminished significantly. Currently, we are completing the translation of the manual into Polish so that we can continue to assist the community.

The Asian American community is another underserved group in Chicago and elsewhere. We are developing a project to provide educational training regarding autism to Asian American frontline professionals in Illinois as well as to parents/families in appropriate languages (Chinese, Korean, and Lao). Additionally, through these training sessions we examine the unique needs of Asian American parents/families that might be affected by autism. Training and evaluation bring awareness to the importance of detection, diagnosis, and treatment for children with autism spectrum disorders, including DS-ASD within Asian American communities.

The approach we take in developing culturally appropriate interventions is always to be informed by the community about their needs, discover the best way to approach families, their understanding of services, their definitions of mental health issues, and how to empower them to get well within their own culture.

The following is a guide to working with three multicultural family groups. This guide is meant to be informative about some of the most salient values and beliefs of these ethnic groups but should in no way be considered exhaustive. There are many individual and family differences within each group, as determined by socioeconomic status, education, place of origin, etc. These guidelines have been adapted from the *Cultural Competence in Autism Training Manual* (Manghi et al., 2010).

CONSIDERATIONS IN WORKING WITH AFRICAN-AMERICAN FAMILIES

Values, Beliefs, and Life Ways

- Strong kinship bonds;
- Strong religious orientation;
- Large percentages of African-American families are headed by single parents;
- Adaptable family roles;
- Use informal support network (e.g., church or community);
- Distrust of government and social services;
- Most are assimilated into the Anglo-American culture;
- May lack knowledge about available services and how the system works;
- Natural remedies used frequently (e.g., prayers for the sake of healing);
- Seniors are highly respected, as aging represents respect, authority, and wisdom;
- May tend to keep things hidden within the family system; difficulty reaching out;
- Poverty impacts education, self-esteem, quality of life, and lifestyle throughout one's lifetime.

Intervention Tips

- Familiarity with Anglo-American communication patterns;
- Show respect at all times: a history of racism and sense of powerlessness impacts interactions;
- Prolonged eye contact may be perceived as staring and interpreted as confrontational or aggressive;
- Use community and/or religious leaders if assistance is needed;
- Do not use "street slang," which could be interpreted as disrespectful or offensive;

- Do not address by first name unless requested to do so, since it could be considered disrespectful;
- May not like to be asked questions about finances, past relationships, or marital status; initially it is more important to gain trust.

CONSIDERATIONS IN WORKING WITH LATINO FAMILIES

Values, Beliefs, and Life Ways

- The group has more importance than the self (collectivistic);
- Strong family unity; respect for and loyalty to the family;
- Strong spiritual and religious orientation;
- Distrust/fear of "government"; immigration status may impact interactions;
- Male-dominant (machismo); father/husband may be the primary authority figure;
- Age-dominant; respect for hierarchy;
- Live for the present/today, fatalistic; a perceived inability to control the future;
- Take care of their own;
- Negative view on asking for help; can take time before an agency is trusted;
- Modesty is important;
- Majority is Catholic; church is seen as a source for services and information;
- Strong belief in the importance of prayer;
- Very proud of heritage; never forget where they came from;
- Comfortable with physical contact (handshaking and hugging).

Intervention Tips

- Respect is basic for all communication;
- Like to be approached first; do not easily initiate conversation;
- Eye contact is perceived as a more confrontational body language than a sign of respect;
- Being ignored is a sign of disrespect and can be perceived as offensive;
- Being personal, warm, trustworthy, and respectful is valued;

- Avoid too much gesturing;
- Encourage the individual to ask questions;
- Make sure your questions have been understood, given the general reluctance to ask questions;
- Maintain an accepting attitude;
- Let them know their ideas, thoughts, etc., are valued;
- Less personal space is needed than with Anglo-Americans;
- Very expressive in their communication; seek physical contact; e.g., handshaking and hugging;
- Determine level of fluency in English; use an interpreter if necessary;
- Do not like to be asked about immigration status, religion, or financial sources.

CONSIDERATIONS IN WORKING WITH ASIAN FAMILIES

Values, Beliefs and Life Ways

- Need to maintain harmony within the group;
- The group has more importance than the self (collectivistic);
- Respect for hierarchy;
- Age-dominant;
- Male-dominant;
- Pressure to "keep face";
- Overt displays of emotion are considered shameful;
- May tend to keep things hidden within the family system; difficulty seeking services.

Intervention Tips

- Gather information regarding specific families' ethnic backgrounds, languages, immigration and refugee experiences, acculturation levels, and community support systems;
- Develop trust by establishing and adhering to rules of social conduct and proper social interaction;

- Attempt to maintain, and, if appropriate, reestablish traditional family structures according to cultural norms;
- Respect the family hierarchy;
- Use extended family members for support systems; lines between nuclear families and extended families are not as rigid in Asian families as they are in Western culture;
- Allow families and their individual members opportunities to "save face" whenever possible;
- Avoid creating situations that may lead to conflict and confrontation, and instead use indirect methods of communication, when appropriate, to make a point;
- Because Asians prefer to keep problems within the family, confidentiality is critical; families must be assured that their problems will not become public knowledge;
- Service providers must be active and offer tangible interventions for Asian American clients, as passivity in the worker may be viewed as a lack of expertise and authority; many Asian American families seek concrete, tangible solutions to their problems and are uncomfortable with process- and insight-oriented strategies.

FOR ALL FAMILIES REGARDLESS OF ETHNIC BACKGROUND

- Consider educational level—written and spoken words should be adapted to level of understanding;
- No cultural group is homogeneous; one must consider within-group differences;
- Individual and subgroup differences exist in every culture;
- Family, as defined by each culture, is usually the primary system of support and is the preferred intervention;
- Families/clients are the ultimate decision-makers for services and support for their children and themselves.
- Intervention Tips for Minority Families Who Have a Child with DS-ASD
- Develop interventions, such as visual systems, that are culturally appropriate;

- Gain an understanding of the family's definition of autism, and if necessary, offer a different way of viewing the disorder;
- Educate families about autism, its diagnosis, and treatment;
- Expand the family's support;
- Engage community support (e.g., church, school, park district, etc.);
- Encourage independence within the family's cultural comfort;
- Future planning: if appropriate, engage extended family and community support, and encourage communication between the family and other service providers;
- The provider may act as the bridge between cultural beliefs.
- None of the above interventions would be possible without a culturally competent organization to provide the corresponding services. Therefore, the organization that is culturally competent will have a defined set of values and principles, as demonstrated by behaviors, attitudes, policies, and structures that allow it to work effectively cross-culturally. Consequently, systems of care that can provide multicultural services value diversity (instead of simply tolerating it), and thereby adapt to the cultural context of the communities they serve. Cultural competence is a developmental process that evolves over time. What is important is that organizations incorporate diversity into all aspects of policymaking, administration, practice, and service delivery, systematically involving consumers, stakeholders, and communities (Cross et al., 1989).

CONCLUSION

In summary, to plan for culturally diverse families affected by DS-ASD, it is imperative that we look into culturally appropriate treatment models. Minority families are as eager to help their children with disabilities as mainstream families are. Inadequate schools, unresponsive medical systems, socioeconomic obstacles, inadequate training, and language-related issues combine to disturb the stability and sense of control that minority families could otherwise have (Montalvo & Gutierrez, 1990; Scheppers et al., 2006). The challenge is to develop and implement strategies that can address the specific needs of minority families who have children with DS-ASD. By facilitating services, understanding the cultural needs of each family, and providing the interventions that we know work, we will have children and adults with DS-ASD who are better adjusted and more productive members of society.

SUGGESTED RESOURCES

Black Down Syndrome Association (BDSA)

https://www.blackdownsyndrome.org/
The mission of the Black Down Syndrome Association (BDSA) is to connect Black families in the Down syndrome community with resources to improve their lives in a more meaningful way by addressing the many inequalities present that increase barriers to access, support, and education. We strive to fill the gap for the families we serve.

Substance Abuse and Mental Health Services Administration (SAMHSA)

"Racial/Ethnic Differences in Mental Health Service Use Among Adults" (brochure) https://www.samhsa.gov/data/sites/default/files/MHServicesUseAmongAdults/MHServicesUseAmongAdults.pdf

Grupo SALTO

https://gruposalto.org/
Grupo SALTO es un grupo de apoyo independiente para familias hispanas que tienen hijos con una discapacidad, especialmente el autismo.
La versión en español de la segunda edición del libro, *Bienestar mental en los adultos con síndrome de Down*, segunda edición, en formato PDF, por Dennis McGuire, PhD, y Brian Chicoine, MD.

The Spanish PDF version of the second edition of *Mental Wellness in Adults with Down Syndrome* by Dennis McGuire, PhD, and Brian Chicoine, MD.
https://www.down21.org/libros-online/bienestar-mental-en-los-adultos-con-sindrome-de-down-2-edicion.jpg.pdf

---

REFERENCES

American Psychiatric Association. (2022). *Diagnostic and statistical manual of mental disorders* (5th ed., text rev.). https://doi.org/10.1176/appi.books.9780890425787

Atkinson, D. R., Lowe, S., & Matthews, L. (1995). Asian-American acculturation, gender, and willingness to seek counseling. *Journal of Multicultural Counseling and Development 23*(3), 130–138. https://doi.org/10.1002/j.2161-1912.1995.tb00268.x

Bishop-Fitzpatrick, L., & Kind, A. J. H. (2017). A scoping review of health disparities in autism spectrum disorder. *Journal of Autism and Developmental Disorders, 47*(11), 3380–3391. https://doi.org/10.1007/s10803-017-3251-9

Centers for Disease Control and Prevention. (2023, April 4). *Data and Statistics on Autism Spectrum Disorder*. Centers for Disease Control and Prevention - Autism Spectrum Disorder (ASD). https://www.cdc.gov/ncbddd/autism/data.html

Cross, T., Bazron, B., Dennis, K., & Isaacs, M. (1989). *Towards a culturally competent system of care: A monograph of effective services for minority children who are severely emotionally disturbed.* Georgetown University Child Development Center, CASSP Technical Assistance Center.

Garcia, A., Kim, M., & DeNard, C. (2016). Context matters: The state of racial disparities in mental health services among youth reported to child welfare in 1999 and 2009. *Children and Youth Services Review, 66*, 101–108. https://doi.org/10.1016/j.childyouth.2016.05.005

Long, M., & Register-Brown, K. (2021). Autism Spectrum Disorder. *Pediatrics in Review, 42*(7), 360–374. https://doi.org/10.1542/pir.2020-000547

Maenner, M. J., Warren, Z., Williams, A. R., Amoakohene, E., Bakian, A. V., Bilder, D. A., Durkin, M. S., Fitzgerald, R. T., Furnier, S. M., Hughes, M. M., Ladd-Acosta, C. M., McArthur, D., Pas, E., Salinas, A., Vehorn, A., Williams, S., Esler, A., Grzybowski, A., Hall-Lande, J., … Shaw, K. A. (2023). Prevalence and characteristics of Autism Spectrum Disorder among children aged 8 Years — Autism and Developmental Disabilities Monitoring Network, 11 sites, United States, 2020. *Morbidity and Mortality Weekly Report Surveillance Summaries, 72*(2), 1–14. https://doi.org/10.15585/mmwr.ss7202a1

Mandy, W. (2022). Six ideas about how to address the autism mental health crisis. *Autism, 26*(2), 289–292. https://doi.org/10.1177/13623613211067928

Manghi, E., Montiel, F., & Philips, D. (2010). *Cultural competence in autism training manual.* Training program developed for the Autism Program of Illinois (TAP).

Matsuoka, J. K., Breaux, C., & Ryujin, D. H. (1997). National utilization of mental health services by Asian Americans/Pacific Islanders. *Journal of Community Psychology 25*, 141–45. https://doi.org/10.1002/(SICI)1520-6629(199703)25:2<141::AID-JCOP3>3.0.CO;2-0

Montalvo, B., & Gutierrez, M. J. (1990). Nine assumptions for work with ethnic minority families. In G. W. Saba, B. M. Karrer, & K. V. Hardy (Eds.), *Minorities and Family Therapy.* Haworth Press

Scheppers, E., van Dongen, E., Dekker, J., Geertzen, J., & Dekker, J. (2006). Potential barriers to the use of health services among ethnic minorities: a review. *Family Practice, 23*(3), 325–348. https://doi.org/10.1093/fampra/cmi113

Spinazzi, N. A., Velasco, A. B., Wodecki, D. J., & Patel, L. (2023). Autism Spectrum Disorder in Down syndrome: Experiences from caregivers. *Journal of Autism and Developmental Disorders,* 1–10. https://doi.org/10.1007/s10803-022-05758-x

Tek, S., & Landa, R. J. (2013). Differences in autism symptoms between minority and non-minority toddlers. *Journal of Autism Developmental Disorders, 42*, 1967–1973. https://doi.org/10.1007/s10803-012-1445-8

Travers, J., & Krezmien, M. (2018). Racial disparities in autism identification in the Unites States during 2014. *Exceptional Children, 84*(4), 403–419. https://doi.org/10.1177/0014402918771337

Yang, L. H., & WonPat-Borja, A. (2006). Psychopathology among Asian-Americans. In F.T.L. Leong, A.G. Inman, A. Elbreo, L.H. Yang, L. Kinoshita, & M. Fu (Eds.), *Handbook of Asian American Psychology* (2nd ed., pp. 379–406). Sage.

CHAPTER THIRTEEN

THE PARENTS' JOURNEY TO DS-ASD

Leah Martin, PhD
Robin Sattel, MS

Parents of a child with Down syndrome who find themselves on the path toward an autism diagnosis are already experts in hearing unexpected news, seeking resources, and rallying for the future. Every parent has a unique story to tell about how they discovered that their baby was born with Down syndrome. Although their stories stand on their own, they certainly share similarities with those of other parents, where experiences overlap and intertwine. This is why parents find abundant support, encouragement, and strength through their associations with other parents of children with Down syndrome. When they find out they are not alone in their experiences, in their emotions, or in their simultaneous love for their child and fear for what the diagnosis might mean, they are well equipped to move forward with hope to face a future they were not originally anticipating. Having someone to relate to makes all the difference in the world. The same thing is true for a parent who is seasoned in the world of Trisomy 21 but is now traversing the rocky road toward an autism diagnosis for their adorable, exceptional child with Down syndrome.

This chapter offers important information for parents and professionals related to receiving a single diagnosis of Down syndrome or autism from the parent perspective. This unique point of view can offer professionals valuable insight as they provide resources and support to families. We will also share critical information about the parents' journey to the diagnosis of DS-ASD, including the difficulties that parents often encounter in the process. While this may not be new information for parents, the familiar experiences may confirm their own, and even offer new perspectives on these topics. Finally, we will share information about the importance of self-care and the supportive role that grandparents and extended family members can play. As we examine the path to DS-ASD, we hope that parents will feel validated, and that professionals and others will gain new perspective and appreciation for the long, arduous journey it can be.

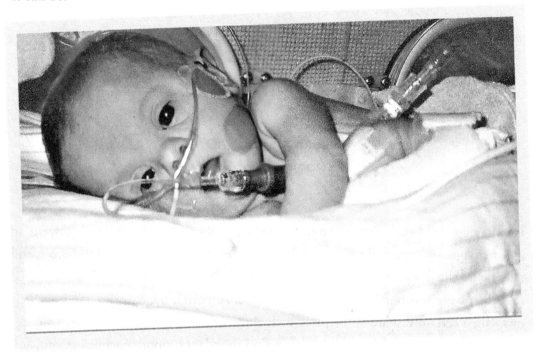

GETTING THE INITIAL DOWN SYNDROME DIAGNOSIS

Some parents receive a prenatal diagnosis of Down syndrome while others find out after the baby is born. Either way, there is a range of emotions that parents feel, both the day they find out about it and through the ensuing months and years. Professionals who deliver the diagnosis can make a tremendous difference, positively or negatively, in how a parent might accept it. Some parents are presented with the "bad news" of their baby having Down syndrome, as the medical professionals tell them how sorry they are about their baby's diagnosis. Imagine the tone that might set for those new parents. In more recent years, many health care providers have adjusted their delivery style to convey a more optimistic tone, which is placing new parents on a more hopeful path. Even so, many parents still report that they found out about their child's diagnosis in decidedly hurtful ways.

For example, one father was heartbroken when he learned his baby had Down syndrome. He remembered the doctor using inappropriate descriptors and blunt, callous language. He was angry that the doctor would talk about his baby that way and found it to be uncaring (Marsh et al., 2020). He remembered crying in his mother's arms and being reluctant to tell the extended family. Other experiences, gratefully, are more positive. When professionals make efforts to give new parents the diagnosis with realistic information accompanied with congratulations and helpful resources of people or organizations to reach out to for support, the parents don't feel as lost or hopeless.

Advice for Professionals: Delivering the Diagnosis

BE prepared prior to delivering a diagnosis

USE current and appropriate terminology

BE realistic but also supportive

PROVIDE resources that have great information and can help connect parents with a supportive community

CONGRATULATE new parents just as you would if their baby did not have any differences

BE happy for them — not sad for them

AFTER ALL, they have a beautiful infant in their arms to care for and love with all their hearts

Parents have said that finding out their child has a disability was "life-changing" to them, both in having to adjust their hopes and expectations of what they thought their child's future would be like, and in what they had envisioned for themselves as parents. There can be feelings of forfeited dreams and a loss of control over the future. One woman described her experience of the time she found out her child had Down syndrome, saying "my preoccupation, to be perfectly honest, was about me. It wasn't about my son. It was about what I was feeling. And I was feeling powerfully upset about this diagnosis because . . . it just completely turns your life upside down. I had plans" (King et al., 2006, p. 358). She was compelled to examine her values and decide what really mattered in her life. Lots of tears and grieving eventually broke through to a new and positive perspective for this mother. When new dreams are made, they can replace the old ones that were initially lost, giving parents a vision for their child's future.

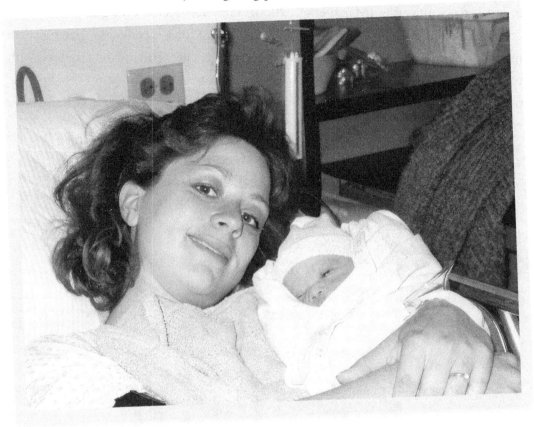

It can be hard to navigate a loss that is ambiguous or intangible, because parents are trying to deal with these feelings of grief and loss, while at the same time caring for and falling in love with their baby who needs them. It can be powerful for new parents to meet other parents who have a positive attitude and who are a little farther along in the journey of raising a child with Down syndrome. Getting advice and help from more experienced parents can be both helpful and encouraging. Parents start to realize they have a choice about how they view their child's diagnosis, and they have a choice in how they view their *child*. Knowing there are choices means they can reclaim their sense of control (De Clercq et al., 2022; King et al., 2006). If you're a parent somewhere along this journey, then you've likely already learned that enduring friendships with other parents become extraordinarily meaningful and valuable. The people in your life who understand you become treasured allies and friends.

In the past, there was a strong focus on supporting parents new to the Down syndrome diagnosis assuming there were only difficult emotions; there was a clear assumption that every parent must be devastated by the news. In the past few years, however, an exciting movement has taken place in our culture that has generated a shift in the previously assumed parental response to having a baby with Down syndrome. It started through social media with parents who developed such slogans as, *I had a kid with Down syndrome before it was cool* and Mica May's extraordinary innovation, the "*The Lucky Few*" tattoo, which features a simple, minimalist design of three arrows that Mica says represent "the three 21st chromosomes and how we rise up and move forward." It began as a simple bonding moment for a few new friends, but quickly went viral when pictures of their matching tattoos were shared on social media. Soon hundreds of mothers were getting The Lucky Few tattoo (Trisomy 21 Update, 2019).

Parents continue to post photos of their tattoos in this viral trend on social media. Many in this newer generation of parents have begun to embrace these slogans as a battle cry over their lives and the life of their child. This pioneering social construct has turned the negative narrative on its ear; parents are increasingly choosing to be part of a community filled with positivity, belonging, and *exclusivity*, thereby spreading goodwill and enthusiastic Down syndrome awareness throughout the entire world.

Additionally, there is a podcast called, "The Lucky Few," about which the National Down Syndrome Congress recently published a post on Facebook:

> *The Lucky Few Podcast has received the Media Podcast [Award] for the 51st Annual Convention. With over 850,000 total plays from 200 episodes over 5 years, The Lucky Few Podcast is a leader in the podcast world for organizations covering Down syndrome. Led by Heather Avis, Micha Boyett, and Mercedes Lara, this podcast shifts the narrative in the media and shouts the value of people with Down syndrome. This award recognizes their commitment to covering a variety of topics and creating an open culture in the media to change the way people perceive people with Down syndrome (National Down Syndrome Congress, 2023).*

No matter where a parent finds themself emotionally at any point, either justifiably struggling or exclaiming the "DS parent" rallying cry—or somewhere in between—we must honor them and support them right where they are.

GETTING THE AUTISM DIAGNOSIS
(WITHOUT DOWN SYNDROME)

You may not be surprised to learn that receiving a diagnosis of autism alone (without Down syndrome) involves a lot of the same emotions that we just described. There are important differences, however, which we will cover in this section. Parents who find out their child has autism go through similar stages of grief and adaptation and have similar questions about their child's future. *"How will other people treat my son? What level of independence will my daughter achieve? What will happen to him after I'm gone?"* Not unlike parents of children with Down syndrome, these parents are often able to adjust their expectations for themselves and their child and settle into their lives with newfound acceptance.

Having said that, getting an autism diagnosis also comes with its own unique set of experiences. For starters, the autism diagnosis is not presented to the parent when their baby is born. While research has shown that autism can reliably be diagnosed at 24 months, the average age that a child is diagnosed falls somewhere between 4 and 5 years old (Leader et al., 2022). Imagine the differences in the parents' experience in terms of getting an autism diagnosis for their child. Most parents who have a child with autism start out with a happy, healthy baby who fits all the standard expectations of a typically developing infant, which means there usually aren't the dashed dreams or unexpected surprises like there can be for parents who immediately learn about Down syndrome. A child who eventually receives a diagnosis of autism can experience developmental regression in later months and years. When certain social, communication, and behavioral challenges start to present themselves, parents usually know something is amiss. This is generally the point at which they seek professional advice and an eventual diagnosis.

For parents of children with autism alone, this process can be complex and emotionally exhausting. Sometimes parents feel they aren't being heard or taken seriously. This can add to the feelings of relief for some parents when an autism diagnosis is finally attained (De Clercq et al., 2022). Because autism is a spectrum disorder, it looks very different in each individual, making diagnosis sometimes difficult; characteristics of autism might be mistaken for other non-neurodevelopmental conditions and can be misdiagnosed. With Down syndrome, the diagnosis is easy for practitioners; it either is Down syndrome or it isn't. With autism, it's much more complex than that, and requires an evaluation conducted by an interdisciplinary team; it's not so black-and-white. When parents finally get the formal autism diagnosis, they may be relieved to obtain guidance and professional support to help them understand their own child better, and to help surround that child with more opportunities to be successful.

Parents of children with autism may struggle a bit more with how their child is perceived by others. Children with Down syndrome, after all, have the general stereotype of being cute, lovable, happy, stubborn, and fun. Autism doesn't necessarily enjoy such a reputation. Parents must wrestle with how to navigate a life where their child, who may appear "typical," self-isolates, where they are often misunderstood because they may have decreased communication skills, or where others may avoid interactions with them—or even be afraid of them—because of unusual or problematic behaviors. Parents of children with autism can also struggle with changing their expectations related to their own personal relationship with their child. Where kids with Down syndrome generally show affection and love for their parents, children with autism may not demonstrate that kind of connection or affection and may never verbalize their love or attachment to their parents, or they may share their affection in unconventional ways.

There are likely more similarities than differences in the experiences parents have when they find out their child has a disability, whether it is Down syndrome or autism. Perhaps those experiences are delayed for a few years for parents whose children have autism. Regardless, parents frequently experience the various stages of grief, adapt their expectations to the reality of who their child is and who they now are as parents, and then they can get to work supporting their child to the best of their ability with the resources they have at their disposal.

GETTING THE DS-ASD DIAGNOSIS

"Why won't anyone believe me…?"

"Isn't the Down syndrome enough? Why are you asking for more problems?"

When a child or adult has both Down syndrome and autism, the result is a completely different, unique, and complex condition. While there is abundant empirical research into the emotional responses of parents who receive a single diagnosis of either Down syndrome or autism for their child, there is little research into the experiences of parents who find themselves facing a diagnosis of autism on top of Down syndrome. Despite this lack of formal research, some important information has evolved from our professional work with hundreds, even thousands, of families over the past few decades. While we cannot describe every possible scenario, we have discovered three recurring themes reported by parents regarding their path to DS-ASD.

Theme #1:

Some parents, extended family members, and professionals may attribute a child's autism-like traits to the simple fact that they have Down syndrome. When characteristics, symptoms, or signs of behavior are reflexively attributed to a person's primary disability rather than considering other medical or diagnostic causes, it is called *diagnostic overshadowing* (The Joint Commission, 2022). In this scenario, there may be more than a few of the red flag behaviors of autism present, but it happens that no one notices or questions them because the child has Down syndrome, and life goes on. One mother said that her son had never communicated verbally and would sit alone and stim on the same toy for hours if she let him. When she asked her husband if he thought maybe their son had autism, he said, "No, I don't think so—I just think we have to accept that he is lower on the cognitive scale than other kids we know with Down syndrome." The behaviors and characteristics are attributed to Down syndrome, and autism is not considered, or may even be disregarded. Additionally, individuals with DS-ASD may exhibit scatter skills which can make diagnosis difficult. For example, an individual may be reading at a first-grade level yet have social skills more in line with an 18-month-old level. Perhaps this child will be identified as having autism later in life, and perhaps not. We believe that there are adults with Down syndrome who are assumed to have a high level of cognitive impairment when, in reality, they are quite intellectually bright, and their challenges could be better interpreted and appreciated when looking through the lens of autism.

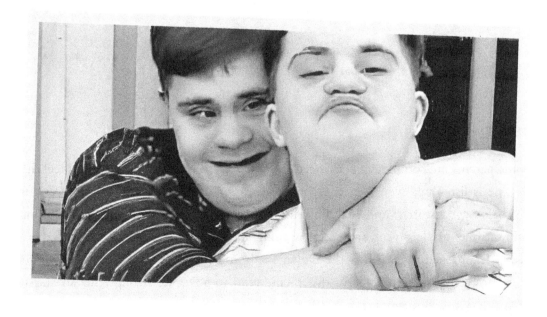

Theme #2:

Some parents may have suspicions that their child has autism, or is somehow *different*, because they have observed other children with Down syndrome and realized their child does not really fit the "DS mold." Other kids with Down syndrome do not exhibit the same characteristic behaviors of autism that their child does, but they aren't convinced or do not see the value in "going down that road." Others may not want to saddle their child with yet another label, and as a result, they may resist or reject any suggestions from others that their child may benefit from undergoing an autism evaluation.

Theme #3:

Some parents are completely convinced that their child has autism, but often feel that no one is listening, even over the course of months and years. They ask questions, do their own research, and may be told "no, they can't have both Down syndrome and autism," or "let's wait and see how things progress." One parent reported that a pediatrician asked them, "Isn't the Down syndrome enough? Why are you asking for more problems?" The parents in this theme tend to advocate strongly for an autism evaluation so they can prove that they are not imagining things. When an autism diagnosis is confirmed for the child, the parent may feel utter vindication that they did not invent the red flags, and they may feel affirmation that they really *are* the expert on their own child. *"Now people will better understand my child!"* Parents can inform others that the behaviors they see are not due to *bad parenting* (quite the opposite, they are likely fabulous parents), and that their child is in no way "less than." They can finally get the ball rolling and access funding, resources, and treatments to help their child live a life filled with more compassion and understanding from the people in their extended family and community.

HOW DO PARENTS GENERALLY FEEL ABOUT THE AUTISM PIECE?

Robin Sattel, MS

In this section, I would like to offer you, the reader, a rare glimpse into the various mindsets that parents have conveyed to me, and that I, myself, have experienced. Some of the information I will share in this section may be difficult for parents who are newer to DS-ASD, but my hope and intent is that you will come away from it with a newfound realization that you are not alone, that there are people out there who understand, and that there is hope for the future. This section may also guide professionals toward increased empathy and understanding when a parent reaches out to them for resources and support throughout their lifelong endeavor to care for their child with DS-ASD.

I am a mother of four remarkable children, including an adult son with Down syndrome (Tom) and a daughter with DS-ASD (Janet Kay) who passed away at the age of 15 over a decade ago. In addition to being a parent, I have worked professionally with parents in the disability world for almost 30 years. I first started working in the Down syndrome community providing support to new and expectant parents at a local Down syndrome association. Later, I supported parents at a statewide chapter of a national autism support group where I became keenly acquainted with the journey of parents of children with autism. Overlapping with those professional experiences, I cofounded the Down Syndrome-Autism Connection nonprofit organization with Margaret Froehlke and supported hundreds—if not thousands—of parents in the DS-ASD community. My extensive experience while being immersed in these three disability communities has given me a bird's eye view into the three separate experiential realities when it comes to the general parent perspective.

In the world of intellectual and developmental disabilities (IDD), there is a well-known "magic pill" question that is often discussed among parents: *If you could, would you give your child a magic pill that would take away their disability?* Generally, some would administer the pill, but it might be surprising to learn that many parents in the Down syndrome community would answer no, they would not administer a magic pill that would take away their child's Down syndrome. Even though there are challenges involved in raising a child with Down syndrome, and parents may rethink their answer at times, their eventual acceptance of their child's Down syndrome diagnosis often evolves to a position of honor and joy.

What I learned from the autism community is that some parents struggle with and resent the autism diagnosis long-term, and many experience very high stress levels depending on their child's challenges. In fact, Kharisma et al. (2021) reiterated that parents of children with autism experience similar levels of stress hormones as do combat soldiers. Therefore, many would answer yes, they would give their child the magic pill to take away the autism.

On the flipside, however, there is also immense pride within the autism community. Since autism is such an expansive spectrum disorder, the magic pill question would likely end up with diametrically opposed responses. In the larger autism community, there is much celebration—and rightly so—for the abilities and accomplishments of individuals with autism. There are talented celebrities and other famous people who self-identify as *autistic*, and many of our world's brightest and most prolific scientists, inventors, and musical prodigies are people with autism who have changed our world for the better. In short, people with autism are amazing regardless of their status; famous or not. Autism Pride Day is organized and celebrated globally to "show the world that we are proud of being autistic and that we are not…in need of a cure" (Autistic Empire, n.d.). There is no doubt that autism can be extremely challenging for some, is a tremendous gift for others, and everything in between.

My experience with parents of children with DS-ASD (as well as my own experience as a mother) is decidedly different from my experiences among the previous two communities. As I have listened to parents, I have learned that many of them downright lament the autism piece of their child's diagnosis. Parents in the DS-ASD community often stated that they would administer the magic pill to eliminate their child's *autism*—in a heartbeat—and admittedly, I was one of them.

I had adopted my daughter Janet Kay *because* she had Down syndrome, so I was not expecting autism to be part of our lives when I brought her home as a tiny newborn.

I loved her with every cell in my body, and I would adopt her all over again, but it would be wrong to omit the fact that autism generated a profound sadness at times, as well as frustration with certain behaviors, that I never experienced while raising my son who has Down syndrome alone. Janet Kay was nonspeaking, and at times this pained me. Oh, how I longed to know what she was thinking! Was she sick? Was she in pain? Why didn't she react when her finger was pinched in the wheel of her stroller? Why did she frantically refuse to go into certain restaurants? Will she ever call me "mom"? Did she have any idea how much I adored her? Did she love me back? Even though I anguished over these types of questions when she was alive, as I've grieved her death I have often found myself missing her characteristic ASD behaviors—with all my broken heart. These behaviors and quirks were a part of the precious, little cherub I fell in love with—the child who will leave me pining for her sweetness, hugs, giggles, and the way she would "flap her wings" …for the rest of my life.

Many parents have shared their feelings over the years, asserting that while Down syndrome makes their child "really cute," the autism piece was what caused so many challenges for the entire family, most notably due to the distinctive autism behaviors that the child exhibited. When word got out that a second edition of this book was being developed, several parents asked us not to sugarcoat the issues; they wanted us to speak the truth about the stresses many families deal with as an everyday reality. Author, blogger, and DS-ASD advocate, Teresa Unnerstall, described her feelings about her son Nick's autism in her book, *A New Course: A Mother's Journey Navigating Down Syndrome and Autism* (Unnerstall, 2020):

> *February 27, 2006*
>
> *(Nick, age 12)*
>
> *I HATE autism. It pisses me off how much it has robbed Nick of his speech and potential. If only Nick just had Down syndrome. He could shower, dress, and make his breakfast like his brother. He'd play Madden football on the Xbox with Hank. He could ride a bike and shoot hoops with the neighbor kids. He could play Super Mario on his Gameboy instead of holding it by his ear and rock side to side.*
>
> *If he just had Down syndrome, I could be like the other moms at the pool. I could lie on a chaise and read a book. I could go to the store for milk and let him stay home by himself. I could leave my car keys on the hook, and he wouldn't set off the remote alarm button.*
>
> *I feel so alone, and nobody understands what this is like to deal with these behaviors. I listen to the tennis gals talk about their kids in honors classes, playing sports, and going out with friends. Meanwhile, I'm in the backseat sitting there tight-lipped on the way to the match. What am I going to say? My son made it two weeks without smearing or eating his poop. I wish there were someone to commiserate with about all of this (p. 97-98).*

Unnerstall's entry from almost two decades ago describes a stark reality that so many of us understand because we have lived it. Parents—don't lose heart; here's where you can be encouraged! In the years since, Nick has grown and matured into adulthood. He has come a very long way, including being 100% toilet trained a few years after this journal entry. Our adult children with DS-ASD do continue to grow and develop, even if the pace of that progression is not on our preferred timeline. We can find joy as we witness their successes throughout their lifetimes. We might see those in the form of a full night's sleep, a new word they have learned, or a skill that they have refined. We can have hope for their future by seeking out meaningful program activities and jobs that build upon their strengths. We can celebrate those triumphs as the true victories that they are.

Unnerstall became an expert on DS-ASD educational and coping strategies by researching evidence-based approaches, which she has been sharing since 2012 in her blog *Down Syndrome with a Slice of Autism* (http://nickspecialneeds.com). Unnerstall and other parents and experts, including The Down Syndrome-Autism Connection support group, have paved the way for parents new to DS-ASD to find support and encouragement as they embark on their journey. These founding parents wanted future families to have a smoother ride than they had when first breaking ground with the fledgling dual diagnosis of DS-ASD.

THE BENEFITS OF PURSUING THE AUTISM DIAGNOSIS FOR YOUR CHILD WHO HAS DOWN SYNDROME

Parents and professionals agree that there are important benefits related to receiving a formal diagnosis of autism for a child who has Down syndrome. The benefits presented in the graphic below are directly from and attributed to the Down Syndrome Medical Interest Group-USA (2022), working in collaboration with Autism Speaks, and is used here with permission.

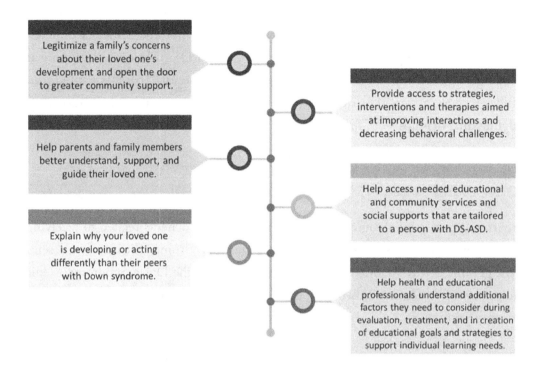

Getting A Diagnosis Can...

Legitimize a family's concerns about their loved one's development and open the door to greater community support.

Provide access to strategies, interventions and therapies aimed at improving interactions and decreasing behavioral challenges.

Help parents and family members better understand, support, and guide their loved one.

Help access needed educational and community services and social supports that are tailored to a person with DS-ASD.

Explain why your loved one is developing or acting differently than their peers with Down syndrome.

Help health and educational professionals understand additional factors they need to consider during evaluation, treatment, and in creation of educational goals and strategies to support individual learning needs.

YOUR CHILD HAS DS-ASD—NOW WHAT?

As we have learned from the research described above about parental reactions to receiving diagnoses for their child, parents can experience a lengthy and complex adjustment period that may or may not always fully actualize into a place of complete acceptance or adaptation. It is possible to land somewhere in between. There is no right or wrong way to respond to such life-changing news. Additionally, while some believe that conflicting emotions, such as happy and sad, are *mutually exclusive*, research has shown that "bittersweet events can elicit pairs of opposite-valence, mixed emotions" (Larsen & McGraw, 2014, p. 263). In the world of parenting a minor or adult child with DS-ASD, parents can experience cognitive dissonance as they encounter conflicting feelings of fear and anger juxtaposed with feelings of intense love and protectiveness. It is also common for parents to feel cheated by the autism, and what it "stole" from them, when they observe the lives of families raising children with Down syndrome alone. Parents in the DS-ASD community can look at parents sporting their Lucky Few tattoos, for example, and long to be part of that alliance.

If you experience conflicting emotions, please know that this is normal. Hold onto hope, as your journey may take you along a path where the joyful emotions take precedence, and the difficult emotions diminish over time. Parents have described the journey from receiving the initial Down syndrome diagnosis to receiving the additional autism diagnosis as a veritable roller coaster ride. If you can relate to this roller coaster experience, you are definitely not alone. If you feel that you continue to struggle long-term, please know that seeking professional support in the form of counseling and/or parent support groups is something to be commended and can play a significant role in your self-care. Taking good care of yourself helps to replenish your energy and focus so you can move forward every day in a healthy way.

SELF-CARE

You matter!

Self-care is a particularly important concept for parents to embrace so they can protect their long-term physical, emotional, and spiritual well-being. Self-care strategies can mitigate the negative ramifications of stressful life situations and provide strength and endurance for what lies ahead. Sometimes it can be a struggle for caregivers to preserve their own sense of self, fearing a loss of their personal identity to the additional diagnosis of autism. Their world tends to shrink around them and become restrictive because they are less able to be spontaneous or spend time with friends (Woodgate et al., 2008). As a caregiver to a child with DS-ASD, these feelings of isolation are the very reason that self-care is so important. Neglecting your own needs will diminish your ability to care for the needs of others. Think of self-care as *filling your gas tank*. When you can ensure that your tank doesn't run dry, you will ideally have enough energy and internal resources to keep going every day.

Research has shown that self-care is a "critical resource" (Kautz et al., 2020, p. 4) for the mental and physical health of parents who have children with developmental disabilities. Parents in the DS-ASD community are known for pouring everything they have into their child. They devote constant, selfless acts of love while forgetting to give themselves the same compassionate and gentle care that they give to their child. Parents, you are important. You are needed. You are precious… and you matter. Please consider doing more for yourself—because you deserve it and because self-care will help you to be your best in your crucial role as a caregiver. Remember, taking care of *yourself* can result in more positive outcomes for your *child*, as well (Kautz et al., 2020; Woodgate et al., 2008).

Parents and caregivers, you can utilize any number of self-care strategies to avoid stress and burnout, including eating healthy foods and getting regular exercise; getting a massage; enjoying movies and books with comedic or light content; practicing deep breathing; engaging in faith-based activities; spending time in nature; doing an art project; meditating or praying; journaling; and making a habit of surrounding yourself with positive people. The point of self-care is to take a break from the demands of caregiving and simply do something that is meaningful to you. Setting aside time to engage in self-care helps you to make a conscious decision to refresh your mind, rejuvenate your body, and renew your spirit.

What Does Self-Care Look Like?

Eat healthy foods; get regular exercise

Watch a movie; read a book with a light theme

Get a massage; do an art project; keep a journal

Surround yourself with positive people

Practice deep breathing; spend time in nature

Engage in faith-based activities; meditate; pray

ASKING FOR HELP

Try saying yes and try not to feel guilty.

Parents have relayed that this journey can be a lonely one as they may feel exhausted, isolated, stigmatized, and left out (Resch et al., 2010; Woodgate et al., 2008). Parents who are engaged in intensive caregiving may also find it difficult to accept others' overtures to provide some relief. We want you to know we see you! We understand the complexities involved in recognizing that we need support in the first place, feeling that we are worthy of that support, finding someone who is able to provide the quality of care we want for our loved one, the guilt we sometimes feel in asking for help, the rejection that we experience, and the pain of isolation when there's no one left we feel we can ask.

These emotions are quite common for caregivers of children with DS-ASD; we tend to decline offers of support due to reasons many of us share. We may have feelings of self-imposed guilt leaving our minor or adult child with someone else. The guilt might come from leaving them, even for a couple of hours, instead of us personally meeting every single one of their needs 24/7. Or we might feel guilty for leaving our child with someone else because we know how challenging it can be to care for them.

Sometimes, we might be fortunate to have someone offer to spend time with our loved one so that we can have a few hours of respite, but we are conflicted because we may not trust that the person who is offering to help can meet the challenge of our child's demanding behaviors. We might become protective of our child with DS-ASD, knowing that there isn't really anyone else who knows how to care for them like we do. Sometimes it's just more work for us to get things in order so that someone else can take over for us than it is to just keep doing it ourselves. Trying to do it all, however, is not sustainable. This kind of thinking eventually begins to take its toll on us.

Maybe you aren't getting offers of support from anyone. Oftentimes, family members or friends might think that unless we ask them for help, that no help is needed or wanted. They might think they would be intruding, or they don't want to bother you. Other times, they want to support you, but they don't know what to say or how to approach the subject. We want to encourage you to *ask* for help when you need it. That may be hard for you to do, but it's so important for your well-being.

One idea that might make it easier to ask for help is writing a practical list of things you need to get done and identifying which items on the list can be delegated to someone else. That list might not include providing direct care for your loved one. It might include running errands, making phone calls, doing laundry, or other practical tasks that anyone can do. Having a list in hand when you approach someone for help will be better received than simply talking ambiguously about your situation and hoping they'll pick up on your silent plea for help. Even if the first person you ask isn't the one who ends up helping you, oftentimes they can point you to someone who can. Keep in mind that some people you approach for help may say "no." Of course, that's never what you want to hear, but an honest "no" is better for everyone in the long run. Knowing who can help and who cannot help is important information for you to have.

We encourage you to accept any form of help that may come your way. If someone wants to provide you with some respite, try not to automatically dismiss it because you think it might be too challenging for them. They wouldn't offer it they didn't want to help. Trust someone else to be able to do what you are doing; *you* are their best teacher and trainer for what your child needs. If someone wants to bring meals, help around the house, go shopping for you, or offer some financial assistance, try saying yes—and try not to feel guilty. Sometimes we can drive the helpers away, or steal their joy, if we constantly say, "no, thanks." We should try to accept that when others are caring for our child so that we can take a needed break, we are still doing our job of facilitating their care. In fact, it's often a mutually beneficial experience for our child to spend time with someone else, and for our friends and family members to spend some time with our exceptional child with DS-ASD. When you can identify any kind of meaningful support, no matter how small or seemingly insignificant, capitalize on it.

HOW GRANDPARENTS, EXTENDED FAMILY, AND FRIENDS CAN HELP

Show up for the family.

When a minor or adult child receives the DS-ASD diagnosis, family and friends of the parents must also process the news. Many grandparents (and others close to the family) experience a form of *triple grief*—they grieve for their own child, for their grandchild, and for themselves and their own lost dreams (Moules et al., 2012). For some, the additional autism diagnosis gives them reason to pause and think about the ways they may have reacted to the child prior to the diagnosis and decide how they will proceed now that there is an explanation for many of their concerns. Having this second diagnosis gives grandparents, extended family members, and friends a renewed opportunity to galvanize and unite in their love and support for the family and the child. It is important for everyone to be given the freedom to manage their responses to the situation in their own way; only then can they move toward being a genuine support to the family.

Grandparents, extended family, and friends can play a remarkably strong role in strengthening the family. Interestingly, researchers discovered that grandfathers in particular had a calming effect on families whose child had autism with significant behavioral challenges (Prendeville & Kinsella, 2019). Grandfathers, grandmothers, aunts, uncles, cousins, and friends, when you are able and ready, please *show up* for the family and offer the kind of support that makes the most sense to you. Support can take many forms: verbal encouragement; active listening; doing away with any previous judgments you may have made; offering to provide respite or do errands; taking the other children on special outings; spending quality time with and pampering the parents; locating resources; and, including their family in larger family gatherings and making appropriate accommodations so the visit can be enjoyed by everyone (even if they consistently say they cannot attend, they still would like to be invited), just to name a few. If you're nervous about being involved, keep learning more about DS-ASD and about the child's unique needs. Walk alongside the family and be a beacon of hope. Draw attention to the *positives* every step of the way and remind them that you can be a lifeline for them through the joys and challenges of raising their child. Please know that they need you, but most importantly they need you to love and accept their child.

How Grandparents Can Offer Support

MOVING FORWARD

Make a connection...

We often hear parents say that after getting the official DS-ASD diagnosis, the world opened up for them and for their child. The second label of autism, which isn't something the parent *wanted* but rather was necessary to shine the light of truth, explains a lot about their child's unique gifts, talents, and struggles. It explains why their child seems more like children with autism than children with Down syndrome. In fact, universally, the parents we have worked with have said that the autism "trumps the Down syndrome"—hands down. Most parents say that adding the autism is a total game changer, not because Down syndrome and autism present themselves in a distinct and separate way in their child, but rather the *combination of the two* creates a completely unique and complex condition.

Happily, with the formal dual diagnosis parents are better able to access funding and educational opportunities that were not an option before getting the autism diagnosis. For families living in rural areas where supports are scarce, we advise reaching out to groups that offer telephone, online, and social media supports. Additionally, after receiving the autism diagnosis, parents can pause, take a breath, and prepare for the future. They can start to advocate for their own needs by seeking out specialized supports from the people who understand them—the amazing DS-ASD community.

CONCLUSION

The journey to autism can be a treacherous and perplexing one and can feel like a wild and unpredictable carnival ride. It involves a unique trajectory that begins with the discovery that your baby has Down syndrome. Once you navigate the diverse emotions related to that diagnosis and settle into your new routine, you soon realize that your reality is very different from what the other parents of kids with Down syndrome are experiencing. The differences in social communication and behavior cause you to suspect autism and you start to seek out professional advice and recommendations. Finally, the journey culminates in receiving the autism diagnosis, and you find yourself in a reality that is different, again, from the one you expected.

A Path Toward the DS-ASD Diagnosis

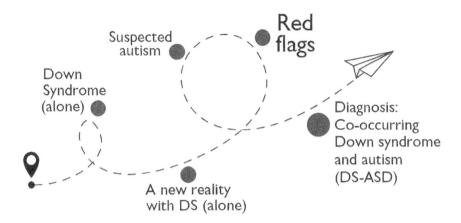

Many have traveled the bumpy road all alone, but this no longer needs to be the case. Other parents, health care providers, and educators are increasingly locking arms with parents on this life-changing, fact-finding expedition. What you are feeling has been felt by so many others, and together we can navigate the unique challenges and opportunities that DS-ASD presents to you and your child. Be comforted: there are others who await the opportunity to support you as you forge ahead, one day at a time (see chapter fifteen).

In our opinion, parents of children and adults with DS-ASD are the real unsung heroes.

Unsung Hero

Someone or something that provides a great benefit, has done very good work, has performed some heroic deed or function, etc., but has not received the credit or recognition they deserve (McGraw-Hill, 2002).

REFERENCES

Autistic Empire. (n.d.). *Autistic Pride*. Autistic Empire. https://www.autisticempire.com/autistic-pride

De Clercq, L. E., Prinzle, P., Swerts, C., Ortibus, E., & De Pauw, S. S. W. (2022). "Tell me about your child, the relationship with your child and your parental experiences": A qualitative study of spontaneous speech samples among parents raising a child with and without autism spectrum disorder, cerebral palsy, and Down syndrome. *Journal of Developmental and Physical Disabilities, 34*(1), 295–329. https://doi.org/10.1007/s10882-021-09800-1

Down Syndrome Medical Interest Group-USA. (2022). *Down Syndrome and Autism Spectrum Disorder (DS-ASD)*. Autism Speaks. https://www.autismspeaks.org/down-syndrome-and-autism-spectrum-disorder-ds-asd

The Joint Commission. (2022). Diagnostic overshadowing among groups experiencing health disparities. *Sentinel Event Alert, 65*, 1–7. https://www.jointcommission.org/-/media/tjc/documents/resources/patient-safety-topics/sentinel-event/sea-65-diagnostic-overshadowing-6-16-22-final.pdf

Kautz, C., Parr, J., & Petrenko, C. L. (2020). Self-care in caregivers of children with FASD: How do caregivers care for themselves, and what are the benefits and obstacles for doing so? *Research in Developmental Disabilities, 99*, 1–24. https://doi.org/10.1016/j.ridd.2020.103578

Kharisma, D. C., Suwandono, A., & Ediati, A. (2021). Characteristics of parents of children with Autism Spectrum Disorder. *Jurnal Medika Hutama, 2*(3), 900–905.

King, G. A., Zwaigenbaum, L., King, S., Baxter, D., Rosenbaum, P., & Bates, A. (2006). A qualitative investigation of the changes in the belief systems of families of children with autism or Down syndrome. *Child: Care, Health & Development, 32*(3), 353–369. https://doi.org/10.1111/j.1365-2214.2006.00571.x

Larsen, J. T., & McGraw, P. (2014). The case for mixed emotions. *Social and Personality Psychology Compass, 8*(6), 263-274. https://doi.org/10.1111/spc3.12108

Leader, G., Hogan, A., Chen, J. L., Maher, L., Naughton, K., O'Rourke, N., Casburn, M., & Mannion, A. (2022). Age of Autism Spectrum Disorder diagnosis and comorbidity in children and adolescents with Autism Spectrum Disorder. *Developmental Neurorehabilitation, 25*(1), 29–37. https://doi.org/10.1080/17518423.2021.1917717

Marsh, L., Brown, M., & McCann, E. (2020). The views and experiences of fathers regarding their young child's intellectual and developmental disability diagnosis: Findings from a qualitative study. *Journal of Clinical Nursing, 29*(1), 3373–3381. https://doi.org/10.1111/jocn.15368

McGraw-Hill. (2002). Unsung hero. In *Dictionary of American Idioms and Phrasal Verbs*. McGraw-Hill.

Moules, N. J., Laing, C. M., McCaffrey, G., Tapp, D. M., & Strother, D. (2012). Grandparents' experiences of childhood cancer, part 1: doubled and silenced. *Journal of Pediatric Oncology Nursing, 29*(3), 119–132. https://doi.org/10.1177/1043454212439626

National Down Syndrome Congress. (2023, June 14). The Lucky Few Podcast has received the Media Podcast for the 51st Annual Convention. [Award image] [Announcement post]. Facebook. https://www.facebook.com/photo?fbid=631287022363906&set=a.318753346950610

Prendeville, P., & Kinsella, W. (2019). The role of grandparents in supporting families of children with Autism Spectrum Disorders: a family systems approach. *Journal of Autism and Developmental Disorders, 49*, 738–749. https://doi.org/10.1007/s10803-018-3753-0

Resch, J. A., Mireles, G., Benz, M. R., Grenwelge, C., Peterson, R., & Zhang, D. (2010). Giving parents a voice: A qualitative study of the challenges experienced by parents of children with disabilities. *Rehabilitation Psychology, 55*(2), 139–150. https://doi.org/10.1037/a0019473

Trisomy 21 Update. (2019). *Trisomy 21 Update: What's behind "The Lucky Few" tattoo?* Children's Hospital of Philadelphia. https://www.chop.edu/news/whats-behind-lucky-few-tattoo

Unnerstall, T. (2020). *A new course, a mother's journey navigating Down syndrome and autism.* Kat Biggie Press.

Woodgate, R. L., Ateah, C. A., & Secco, L. (2008). Living in a world of our own: The experience of parents who have a child with autism. *Qualitative Health Research, 18*(8), 1075–1083. https://doi.org/10.1177/1049732308320112

CHAPTER FOURTEEN

SHARING FAMILIES' LIVED EXPERIENCES

Margaret Froehlke, RN, BSN
Robin Sattel, MS

No one can appreciate the *lived experience* of a parent, sibling, or extended family member as much as another person whose family includes an individual with Down syndrome and autism (DS-ASD). Try as they may, even a highly empathetic person cannot fully appreciate what life with a child, teen, or adult with DS-ASD entails, but it *is* important to try. According to Subramaniam (2021), "lived experience matters for many reasons, not least of which is that only someone who has been through an experience knows the nuances and complexities of dealing with it" (p. 1). With better appreciation for their lived experience, we can approach these parents and other family members with considerably more compassion and respect for the resilience, resolve, and strength that they must cultivate to raise and support their loved one.

Every family has its own lived experience with DS-ASD. Ample research (Estes et al., 2019; Luijkx et al., 2019; Whiting, 2014) has described how families with a child with an intellectual or developmental disability were required to make sweeping changes to their lives. They made numerous adaptations so they could meet the physical, emotional, and educational needs of their child, including in many cases an intensive amount of hands-on support with activities of daily living, such as bathing, toileting, feeding, and challenging behaviors/dysregulation (Oti-Boadi, 2017). Given the fact that individuals with DS-ASD frequently have medically and/or behaviorally complex needs, these findings certainly ring true for the DS-ASD community.

In this chapter, we are sharing anecdotes from parents, siblings, grandparents, and extended family members who have offered to reveal their feelings, beliefs, and intimate details about their life with their child or family member with DS-ASD. We hope that these narratives will touch your heart, bring a smile to your face, and give you comfort and strength. We also hope that these stories will offer valuable information to those who haven't "walked a mile in their shoes." On behalf of families everywhere, we thank you for your tender support of families on their idiosyncratic, complicated, and poignant journey with their family member with DS-ASD.

PARENTS

JOHN DOHERTY, FATHER OF JESSICA, 27 YEARS OLD

Life with Jessica has meant making many sacrifices personally, professionally, and socially. However, it has not been without joy and happiness.

Before and after her official ASD diagnosis, I felt like we were the only ones who had a child with DS that was so different. She didn't seem to fit in with our local DS community or our school community. She was so different, and her behaviors and challenges were difficult to understand. Doctors, teachers, and therapists were not very helpful or hopeful. They had little to no experience with someone like her.

How I have managed to conquer the challenges of DS-ASD is through learning (as a couple with my wife) best practices for DS-ASD. How to approach her education placement and curriculum, therapies, and being a key member of her medical care team because of her challenges with communication. I feel that conquering the challenges is an ongoing journey. We are always learning new things about her. She proves every day that we are all lifelong learners and that brings me hope.

My support system has been my family. My wife and my other children. In the early years, I worked two jobs so my wife could stay home. I feel like I missed out on a lot when the girls were young but that was a sacrifice that I had to make so they could experience typical childhood activities.

Jessica has affected every aspect of our lives. Every decision we make is based on her wellness and ability to adapt. Our goal for her is to always have a meaningful day and life. Every time I look at her beautiful face it brings me joy. She is resilient, funny, quirky, and a phenomenal self-advocate. She gives the biggest and best hugs. Her hugs are the remedy for the times when I am most challenged by her.

CHIARA JAFFE, MOTHER OF JAKE, 14 YEARS OLD

Jake loves to watch music videos on his Kindle and is a wonderful dancer. He has a good throwing arm and likes to throw a ball around. Jake also loves taking swimming lessons.

We became concerned when Jake was a little over one year old because his rate of development began to slow, and he manifested some stereotypic rocking behaviors.

Jake lagged behind his peers with Down syndrome with respect to fine and gross motor development and communication. Over time, the rocking behavior became more frequent, and Jake began to develop other repetitive behaviors, including teeth-grinding and throwing objects. He did not show interest in kids his age, nor did he engage in imaginative play. I remember his occupational therapist commenting that Jake did not know how to play with his toys. Jake began hitting peers, and when he was 7 years old, he was asked to leave his daycare. At that time, we initiated behavioral therapy, and the therapist recommended we have Jake assessed for autism.

I was actually relieved because we now had a diagnosis. The psychologist who made the diagnosis also provided us with resources and referrals, including the Down Syndrome-Autism Connection and the first edition of Robin and Margaret's invaluable resource text, *When Down Syndrome and Autism Intersect: A Guide to DS-ASD for Parents and Professionals.*

Because Jake now had a diagnosis of autism, he was eligible for additional services such as the state Medicaid Autism Waiver, which provides community supports. The diagnosis also helped family members and school and community-based providers to better understand the reason for Jake's behaviors. The co-occurring diagnosis has been a struggle because it adds another layer of challenges. Jake is still working on activities of daily living and his progress has been very slow; he has more functional impairments than kids with Down syndrome or autism alone.

I would encourage [parents new to the diagnosis] to reach out to Down-Syndrome Connection immediately and also to apply for or add their name to the wait list for autism services in their state. I also recommend that they read [this book] to better understand the diagnosis and how to support their child.

Just like anybody else, people with Down syndrome and autism have their own unique strengths and challenges. They can learn new things and should be cherished for who they are.

MARY CARDLE, MOTHER OF AINSLEY, 8 YEARS OLD

Ainsley is an only child, so I didn't have other children to compare her to. I remember a young girl with DS the same age as Ainsley and she was waving hello/goodbye, and I wondered why Ainsley wasn't doing this. Also, Ainsley used to flap her mouth a lot; she would use a small pocket comb or a card, and I remember asking our occupational therapist at the time if she thought that this could be a sign of autism. She felt it was more sensory seeking and not an autism trait. I knew autism was more common in boys than in girls, but I was still a bit concerned.

When Ainsley was about 4½ years old, we were being assessed for the At Home Program. I am in British Columbia, and this is a provincial program for children that looks at their age and what they are and are not doing compared to typical peers. The At Home Program provides funding for therapies, equipment, incontinence supplies, medical supplies, and so forth. As a single parent, I NEEDED her to get in this program. During the assessment, which was held at her daycare, we really played down her abilities. The woman who was doing the assessment asked if I had been to Sunnyhill. I said no and asked her why. (Sunnyhill is a children's hospital that does autism assessments.) She suggested that I get Ainsley evaluated [for autism].

Then a few months later, I was at a Down syndrome presentation, and the presenter afterward asked me if I had had Ainsley assessed. She pointed out that she wasn't being very social. Of course, I was defensive as Ainsley wasn't walking well yet and it wasn't easy access to go where the other children were. But it scared me. Two people who didn't know Ainsley suggested that I get her checked. And so, I put her name on the wait list.

Driving to the appointment to hear the report from the doctors, I had mixed feelings. When I walked into the room, there was a long table, and I could see a box of tissue at the end near where I would be sitting and knew. I knew that they were going to tell me that Ainsley had autism. I was devastated.

Getting the autism diagnosis did not change my love for Ainsley, but allowed me to better prepare her, to get her the appropriate therapies (including music therapy which she loves) and to understand why she does certain things. Nobody wants an autism diagnosis, but actually receiving the diagnosis has opened up so many more doors for Ainsley.

DS-ASD is hard. I am fortunate with Ainsley that she transitions well and adapts very easily to situations, and she rarely has a meltdown or tantrum (and if she does, it's very short-lived). However, it hurts this Momma's heart when I see the gaps between her and other children with Down syndrome who do not have the dual diagnosis. She talks, but not in full sentences, but can certainly makes her needs known. I can't have a conversation with her, yet she understands a lot. She is addicted to her iPad, and I don't know if I'll ever be able to break that habit (thank you COVID). I see that it's harder for her to make friends because she can't communicate and I worry about her being alone, with no friends. The autism makes it hard as I wonder what is going on inside her head and my heart aches. I long for her to call me Momma on her own accord.

Ainsley is quite a funny little girl. She can be silly and fun. I don't hear her laugh a lot, but she is a little jokester. She loves music, Elmo, pasta, cookies, and my boyfriend. Ainsley loves piggybacks and playing in the water-she is a pretty good swimmer! She also enjoys making chocolate chip cookies and stealing the chocolate chips and turning the mixer on full blast! She loves dancing/grooving and going to the park, and she loves Luna the dog from school. Ainsley is easygoing and I can take her anywhere, and for the most part, she is pretty friendly.

It helps to know people who have gone down this path before me. It really helps to know that you are not alone. Like many other families, I often struggle to fit into the Down syndrome world, and I am definitely not a part of the autism community. I see many kids with Down syndrome who I suspect also have the dual diagnosis, but oftentimes the parents don't want to acknowledge it—there is still so much stigma around autism, and I also feel the dual diagnosis. I love sharing our story with others in the DS-ASD community. Down syndrome is hard, but Down syndrome and autism is harder, and you need your village. You need people who can guide you and who understand you.

**KELLY KREI, FATHER OF HUNTER AND KYLE
(IDENTICAL TWINS WITH DS-ASD), 27 YEARS OLD**

Dear Hunter and Kyle,

The last six years have been crazy for us, mom's battle with cancer and the pandemic, and through all of this, you made me so very proud of the young men you've become.

I'm reminded everyday of a quote from a movie, "we're not the ones teaching you, you're the ones teaching us."

I love to hear you laugh and see your joy in your accomplishments. Most of all, thank you for being such gentlemen and for your love. I am extremely proud of you both!

Love, Dad

MICHELLE MORALES, MOTHER OF SAM, 7 YEARS OLD

Sam attended our town's inclusive preschool and had an amazing, loving teacher who connected with him and tried to include him in everything. For example, when he got an AAC (augmentative and alternative communication) device, she did too, and it became part of the class circle time routine. After spending two years in her classroom, we knew that she both understood Sam and really cared about him. As we journeyed with her in those two years, we all came to understand that Sam learns best when he's one-on-one with a teacher in a low-sensory environment. He also needs lots of repetition to really master a new skill. The combination of Sam's IEP meeting, a visit to Boston Children's Hospital Down Syndrome Clinic, and a discussion with a mom in the Down Syndrome-Autism Connection group, confirmed to us that it was time to seek a professional evaluation for autism.

There was a whole range of thoughts when we received Sam's diagnosis of co-occurring Down syndrome and ASD, but I think the biggest one was relief. We finally had a name for why Sam wasn't like other kids with Down syndrome, and we could now move forward with getting him services that would help him learn best.

I think that communication is still the biggest struggle, but we are so proud of how much more Sam communicates now than he used to. Although Sam prefers verbal communication, we lean heavily on total communication because of his small expressive vocabulary. Observing his behavior and using his AAC device helps fill in the gaps. We celebrate the successes, such as a verbal request made from another room or a comment about what is on his plate for lunch.

The biggest advantage that an official diagnosis provided was access to in-home ABA therapists. A benefit that we didn't expect was that it helped us communicate better with our families and close friends about why Sam interacts with people differently than typical kids. We were fortunate that Sam's services at school didn't wait for an official diagnosis—he had already been placed in a classroom that used ABA-based practices for about four months before he was diagnosed.

Sam loves running, swimming in the pool, playing on his tablet, and swinging outside. He can't see a boulder without climbing it, and he laughs and laughs when we are silly together. He loves to have a job around the house; you've never seen someone so excited as Sam to deliver napkins to the dinner table. I think it's fair to say that all of us in the family do anything we can to earn one of his big smiles!

I would like others to know that just because Sam isn't looking at you doesn't mean he's not listening and understanding. Just because he's not engaging with you in a typical way doesn't mean he doesn't want your friendship. Spend the time to get to know him and his interests, and you will be rewarded by knowing someone who is bright, witty, and energetic. And when you really know him, you may get to see his eyes and his smile. It's worth it.

SIBLINGS

Research has confirmed what may seem obvious to the DS-ASD community: having a child with a disability can have a profound impact on the entire family unit. The family's focus is typically on the child with medical, educational, emotional, behavioral, and developmental needs, and understandably so. But what happens when there are other children being raised with the child with DS-ASD? The reality is that siblings in particular feel the effects of the parents' concentration on the other child, often in burdensome ways, but also in potentially positive, illuminating ways. Siblings have reported feeling invisible and fallen to the wayside amidst the flurry of activities that surround their sibling (Naylor & Prescott, 2004), and they are often relied on to provide support with caregiving. While there may be significant challenges for siblings, there are some very encouraging aspects to their experiences, as well.

On a sweet note, siblings often report extraordinarily meaningful and deep-rooted benefits to growing up with a brother or sister with a disability (Rum et al., 2022), and they are known to be mature and wise beyond their years. Many report that their disabled sibling instilled in them a perspective on life that they would not have developed otherwise. Thanks to their sibling, they have acquired valuable attributes, including higher levels of empathy, compassion, devotion, altruism, and the ability to love intensely and with benevolence. Many say that their sibling with IDD changed them to their very core.

Another key quality that siblings often acquire is an increase in helping behaviors (Perenc et al., 2015). Siblings have often chosen a career within disability-related fields, including special education, health care, therapies, and social services, to name a few. Those who follow this path often embrace strong feelings of protection for and devotion to the well-being of people with IDD. Imagine how many lives are being touched because the neurotypical sibling has been so deeply inspired by their brother or sister with disabilities!

In this section, we will be highlighting the stories of several siblings so that you may gain a clearer understanding of their lived experience with a sibling with DS-ASD. Siblings deserve to be recognized, appreciated, and most of all respected, for the special role they play within their families and communities.

EMILY DOHERTY, SISTER OF JESSICA, 27 YEARS OLD

My sister Jessica has taught me many things throughout my life and there are a few I will highlight here:

1. Being nonverbal doesn't mean noncommunicating. Although Jessica uses very few words, she is able to convey a multitude of emotions and thoughts through her body language, change in voice pitch, and even sometimes through a funny facial expression. Not all nonverbal communicators will use an iPad or a communication device to convey their thoughts and emotions, and more people need to realize this. Throughout her life, Jessica has developed quirky and unique ways to communicate with others without these technologies and this is important for all DS-ASD families to understand.

2. The importance of being patient and understanding. There are times where Jessica's stubbornness or negative affect seems unwarranted, yet there is always a reason, whether we understand what it is or not. In a world where she is given such little self-control over her life, there is the need for patience of those interacting with Jessica and we must grant Jessica the self-direction she desires when we can. Growing up with Jessica has taught me to always treat others with respect, dignity, and kindness.

3. In a world that is filled with negative things, Jessica is one that is always positive. She is always down to take a Snapchat selfie or to sing the "Happy Birthday" song any day of the year. Her innocence is something that I will forever cherish.

LIZ VAN WESEP, SISTER OF BRENNAN, 30 YEARS OLD

My brother Brennan has digestive track issues that require a diet that consists of mostly soft foods (bananas, eggs, soft bread) in only small pieces. As a result, we cut up meals into smaller-than-bite-size pieces for him to eat. Recently, we did not cut up a cheeseburger small enough (and Brennan often swallows large bites at once without much chewing) and what we think was a small piece of a burger lodged in his duodenum, causing him to dry heave, vomit, and wretch the whole night and into the next day. Watching him go through this was heartbreaking and reminded me how strong my mom is in helping Brennan every day (she stayed by his side all night), but also how helpless we sometimes are to solve all problems for Brennan.

Brennan is completely pure and innocent of actions that are intended to harm himself or others. He cares deeply about those around him and is extremely empathetic, even coming to tears when he sees that someone else is hurting. As a result, I want to protect Brennan from any and every hardship in the world, but sometimes that is not possible, which is a difficult reality to come to terms with.

Watching Brennan go through this ordeal also reminded me of how he approaches life with a beautiful simplicity and positivity. Any other person who had been up sick all night would have been in a terrible mood the following day, likely (legitimately) complaining and feeling sorry for themselves. But not Brennan. The next day he still would dry heave spontaneously and must have been in pain and discomfort. But other than hearing the heave happen, you would never know it. Brennan was happy to be in the moment and enjoy his day, telling us that "Tummy is all better" even though we knew it was not. He did not feel sorry for himself or seek sympathy or attention. He spent the entire day visiting with the family, watching his favorite shows, and enjoying time on walks in the mountains, even though he was still suffering.

Brennan appreciates life in the moment more than anyone I've ever met. I cannot always protect him from the world and its suffering, but I know that he will always be resilient, positive, and optimistic about life every single day.

GRACE DOHERTY, SISTER OF JESSICA, 27 YEARS OLD

Growing up in a family that is different than most is the biggest blessing in my life. It's not perfect, obviously. But the experiences I've been gifted throughout life and continue to have make everything worthwhile. From a young age, I got to learn what it's like to share my life with someone with DS-ASD.

My sister, Jessica, is my best friend. She has taught me more things than anyone else in my life. She has taught me how to be patient, how to be kind, how to be a self-advocate, and most importantly, how to be a good person. Even though she is nonspeaking, she is still the best communicator I know. Despite all her challenges, she wakes up every day full of love and kindness that radiates to everyone around her. Because of her, I have discovered my passion for helping others. She fills my heart every single day, and I couldn't imagine my life without her. Having a sibling with DS-ASD truly has changed my life for the better. Life is full of ups and downs but the ups always triumph, no matter what.

SARAH FROEHLKE, SISTER OF BRENNAN, 30 YEARS OLD

As the youngest of four, I have always grown up alongside Brennan. First steps, first words, first Communion, you get the idea. Sometimes Brennan would be ahead of me in these steps. Other times, I would be the one leading the way. Though I am his little sister, sometimes it does not feel like that. When I was around 4 years old, I remember when Brennan ran out of the house. No one else noticed and I started yelling for my mom and dad. While Brennan is my older brother, that day I learned I needed to step up as his little sister. It can be a bit confusing trying to find your place and build a relationship with your sibling whose many mood swings and development stages can be tricky to navigate.

One constant for us has been we are always by each other's sides. Today, Brennan and I continue to share many things. Our secret phrases, hand gestures, dance moves, and song lyrics. I am so blessed to grow up not just alongside but hand in hand with

Brennan. We just get each other. We are in sync. And no matter what, he is always my big brother.

JOE ZABOREK, BROTHER OF JANET KAY, (NOTE: JOE'S SISTER WITH DS-ASD PASSED AWAY IN 2012 AT THE AGE OF 15)

Having Janet Kay as a sister was the most beautiful challenge of my life. Now that I am a parent and I know what it takes to raise my two sons, I can reflect on the tremendous amount of energy, both mental and physical, that went into providing the joy-filled life my sister deserved. She was quite medically involved, and she required an astonishing amount of support, from both her mother as her primary caregiver, and from her siblings who often helped out. Even my brother Tom, who has Down syndrome without autism, liked to help take care of her.

Janet Kay's day-to-day life was dominated by medical procedures, therapies, and addressing behavior/sleep issues at all hours of the day and night. She required more active monitoring than perhaps any other human I have encountered, but she was worth it. I never resented her. I didn't then, and I don't today, even though she absorbed the dramatic majority of my parents' attention throughout my adolescence.

I know that there is a great deal of thought that goes into the impact of this type of sibling on a person's development. I cast my lot to say that Janet's presence in my life only served to develop my character for the better. Sure, sometimes it was HARD, but it is also true that there were many positive effects in my life as a response to our family's situation. I can confidently say not one of us would have done it any other way.

Having Janet in my life demonstrated to me so much about the diversity in humanity. I believe that as a part of my general personality I tended to lack compassion. Janet, without ever speaking a word, changed me in this regard. I credit her for softening my heart, and she changed my worldview from one of judgment to one of compassion. Janet Kay taught me so much. Her suffering was significant, but she was always just so joyful. Our family would rush to her bedroom in the morning to see who could wake her up and be the one to get the coveted "first smile of the day". She could make a moment sitting on a porch swing melt away my problems or anxiety. She really helped me just live in the moment . . . I would do just about anything for one more moment like that.

ALEX FROEHLKE, BROTHER OF BRENNAN, 30 YEARS OLD

Growing up, Brennan was (and remains) very routine oriented. Tuesday was taco day. Friday was pizza day. As long as we stuck to the routine and gave Brennan advanced notice, he was as happy as a clam. Brennan's obsession with routines even trickled into his daily snack. He began with a simple snack of Ritz crackers and cheese. As time went on, his plate grew to include the likes of banana slices, goldfish, pretzels, popcorn, etc. We could barely fit everything on the plate. But Brennan is a perfectionist—if we left one item off, he would let us hear about it.

One afternoon Brennan was in a bit of a mood, so I decided to see if he was ready for his snack, in hopes of calming him down. He agreed but had a look of skepticism—almost as if he knew I would screw up his order. I could tell he was ready to pounce if I left one item off the plate. So I carefully put everything together and told him his snack was ready. The plate was so full that you could barely see the pretzels on it. As I put the plate down, Brennan did a quick once-over to check my work and sure enough he didn't see the pretzels at first glance. He looked at me and let out a demanding yell "FRET!. . ." (he pronounced pretzels "fretzels") but stopped in his tracks before finishing the word as he noticed a few stray pretzels hiding at the bottom of the plate. He then happily relaxed and enjoyed his snack. I was cracking up to myself that he thought he "got me" but then caught himself when he realized the snack was indeed to his liking.

It's moments like these that remind me Brennan is not unlike any of us. We all get moody at times, but a simple snack (prepared correctly) can calm us down and make us happy. In many ways, Brennan's obsession with routine was a godsend. It was his way of making it clear what he wanted and needed in a given day, week, or month. I'll always cherish that day where he yelled "FRET!. . ." but stopped himself before being able to finish the ". . . ZEL."

GRANDPARENTS

DONALD A. FROEHLKE, GRANDFATHER OF BRENNAN, 30 YEARS OLD

Dear Brennie,

I can't believe you are going to be 30 years old in June. Where has all the time gone?

Brennie, you are a wonderful person with a lot of love. When we meet, I always get a hug and when I leave, I also get a hug.

You have done a lot through these years. I always enjoyed our time together fishing in Wisconsin. You learned to cast quickly by watching all the uncles and your aim was right on. For many years your Saturday morning volunteer work at the nursing home setting tables or cleaning at your parish, and also being a weekly altar server, are all such great services. Now, you are a Barista at Wellspring Community's coffee house! I would love to get a cup of coffee from you! I cherish the special ceramics ornaments and Christmas cookies you've made for me each year too.

I can tell you love music and are a good dancer. I was so happy to find "Barney" video tapes for your birthday.

Not only as your grandfather, but I am particularly blessed to have you as my godson too.

You are blessed to have such wonderful parents, a brother and two sisters who love you a lot.

I wish you much happiness and all of God's blessings on your birthday and beyond.

All my love,

Grandpa Froehlke

MARY JO LEVY, GRANDMOTHER OF GAVIN, 12 YEARS OLD

For the first eight to nine years of my grandson's life, I was blessed with caring for him in my home most weekends. We developed a very deep bond—he became the "reason I breathe" and being with him brought me so much joy. As a toddler, he was happy and very affectionate. Though his interests and skills were limited (as is normal for children with Down syndrome), he was learning and maintaining knowledge of numbers, the alphabet, colors, shapes, etc. He was an absolute joy to be with. In elementary school, he had many "typical" children who not only watched out for him but competed with each other to sit next to him. Being nonverbal, he learned to use an assistive speech device and became very proficient, even finding words on his own. He had such promise and was so happy.

Then just prior to entering puberty, something in him changed. He began to be unpredictable, aggressive, and eventually destructive. At that time, he was diagnosed with ASD. Eventually he began to have no interest in or seemingly no memory of the skills and knowledge he had learned in school. He became uninterested and uncooperative with speech and occupational therapy. His only interest became his iPad. For a few years, I was still able to care for him. But as he grew physically, it became obvious that it was actually dangerous for me to be with him alone. That is the hardest part for me—not being able to just be with him. I miss the happy boy he once was. But when I begin to "self-pity," I realize my suffering is nothing compared to his. I see the confusion, pain, and unhappiness in his eyes. But once in a while, I see the love and tenderness and I know he is still there.

His parents have been to specialists searching for the cause of these changes in him. The diagnoses of regression and catatonia have been added and treatments are being considered. I pray constantly that he can be happy again, that he can regain all he has lost, that the light will return to his eyes and that beautiful smile and sweet laughter will come back. Then I remember God promised, "I will never leave you nor forsake you," and I have hope.

EXTENDED FAMILY MEMBERS

EMILY WHEELER, COUSIN OF JESSICA, 27 YEARS OLD

Jessica is my cousin and one of my favorite people on this earth. I had the privilege of taking on the role of her PCA (personal care attendant) for about five years. Naturally, this molded a forever special bond and has left an enormously positive imprint on me and my heart. If I could say one thing that she has taught me, it is that actions speak louder than words. Although she is not able to speak for herself, her actions toward me never fell short of appreciation, gratitude, and love. Needless to say, the feelings are beyond mutual. She is kind, silly, and wise. Human value is not measured by abilities and challenges—but by trust, loyalty, and love. I'm a better person because of who she is!

**JOHN SATTEL, UNCLE OF JANET KAY,
15 YEARS OLD AT THE TIME OF HER PASSIING**

Since they both were blessed with the extra 21st chromosome, which gives them the misunderstood label of a "syndrome," I expected my relationship with my niece, Janet Kay, to be very similar to my relationship with my nephew, Tommy. Tommy, once he recovered from his early heart surgery, grew into a real dynamo. He wore his joy on the outside with bold expressiveness. He had, and has, a wonderful sense of humor.

As Janet grew, I realized that she wasn't like Tommy at all. Like Tommy, she had a wonderful smile and a happy response to my loving greetings, but Janet was different in that she was a nonverbal communicator. I did not immediately learn to understand Janet's forms of communication. Sometimes, her expression left me wondering if I was making any connection with her. I was afraid to admit this to Janet's mother (my sister) for fear of hurting my dear sister's feelings. This feeling was not one of trepidation, nor did it prevent me from enjoying being with Janet. I just did not understand her language.

Janet's personality did emerge in its own special way. She found ways to communicate, and she became very skilled at getting her way! Janet's mother and siblings, who lived with her every day, were quite able to understand Janet's modes of communication. They all helped me learn too. The more I learned her nonverbal "language," the more comfortable I became—and the more comfortable I became, the less concerned I was about whether I was succeeding in making a connection with her.

Being around Janet was such a joy. She gave us plenty of laughs with her unique personality, and she gave us such wonderful memories. Simply put, I loved being Janet Kay's Uncle John!

MARY MCCARTHY, AUNT TO BRENNAN, 30 YEARS OLD

It was my great pleasure to live in Colorado near my nephew, Brennan Froehlke, for seven years. It was during that time that I learned many things about Brennan, among them: he loved Notre Dame football, idolized Buzz Lightyear, and was devoted to serving Mass at St. Thomas More Parish in Centennial, Colorado.

Serving Mass required training and dedication. Brennan worked with several youth mentors to learn and perform all the duties required of altar servers. He proudly carried the cross leading the procession to the altar at the commencement of Mass and from the service at its conclusion. He assisted the priest at the altar during the service and sat or stood patiently during the quiet times. Services frequently exceeded an hour in length, yet Brennan understood he must maintain his composure until the conclusion of the Mass.

It was clear that Brennan recognized the solemnity of the duty and the honor of his position. Our family was always proud to see him on the altar knowing it brought him, and all of us, such joy. He was, and is, an inspiration to the entire family.

With Love,

Aunt Mary

KAREN MEDEIROS, GREAT-AUNT OF JACOB, 20 YEARS OLD

In my childhood years, my next-door-neighbor Bobby had Down syndrome. I knew at a young age that he was a special person. He had many challenges growing up. I always tried to support and encourage him, as I do with Jacob. I see the same in Jake; however, his challenges are more due to him having Down syndrome and autism. All of Jake's accomplishments have so much more meaning because he must work harder to reach them. The accolades are in abundance for every goal he reaches to show him love and support. Being a bit familiar with Bobby having Down syndrome, our friendship taught me early on about awareness, inclusion, support, and kindness to others.

As Jacob's great-auntie, I look back to fun times Jake and I have had through the years. Although he cannot verbalize in the traditional way, he communicates through his expressions, feelings, and actions. I clearly remember one night at my home while we were at the dinner table enjoying some sweet treats, he was sitting on the side of me. I gave him a kiss and I made a funny sound which he thought to be hilarious. Immediately after, he communicated with me through his feelings of joy and laughter along with his actions. Jake, with his gentle demeanor, ever so softly put his hands on each of my cheeks bringing my face near his. He communicated by his actions of taking the initiative for me to give him more kisses followed by the funny sounds. As much over the moon I was with his interactions, I think not only was he enjoying our little game, but he was also enjoying all the sweet treats along the way. The ultimate enjoyment that evening was seeing him communicate in his own way and hearing his belly laughs. It was a true joy to everyone seated around the table.

When Jake was born, the love and adoration I had for him would always be there no matter what. He was already so loved before he stepped foot on this earth. Even though Jake is nonverbal, he has shown me his gentle kind heart, his love for others and his endurance through struggles during trying times. He has taught me and given me inspiration that, as difficult as some situations are, you must rise to the occasion as he does. Although he is unable to speak, he communicates volumes in other ways.

JOHN MCCARTHY, UNCLE OF BRENNAN, 30 YEARS OLD

There are lots of adjectives to describe my nephew Brennan: kind, thoughtful, sweet, and polite come to mind right away. His gentleness is his trademark. However, when it comes to sports, you see a different side. Brennan is a fierce follower of the Fighting Irish of Notre Dame and the Denver Broncos. His jerseys tell the story of his devotion to his teams. His cries of "Defense!" and "Come on, guys!" fill the room on game day. He loves the victories and accepts the losses with grace and class. On the odd occasion that Notre Dame is having a bad year, he will even (although reluctantly) root for the University of Michigan. His "Go Blue!" may not have the same energy behind it, but I'll take what I can get. He also loves basketball and has a really good 3-point shot.

My nephew is an amazing young man. Growing up with three siblings and having a huge extended family of aunts, uncles, and cousins made him a team player from his earliest age.

I have spent the last 30 years rooting for Brennan. I am honored to be a part of his team.

ANNE MCCARTHY, AUNT OF BRENNAN, 30 YEARS OLD

I had the good fortune of living with my sister, Margaret, her husband, Bob, and my 29-year-old nephew Brennan after my spine surgery.

Even though Margaret and I were sisters (she's number7; me, number 8 of 12 kids), friends, neighbors and work colleagues, I never spent a lot of after-hours time with the

Froehlke trio. In fact, I rarely, if ever, slept over. I only knew Brennan as one of my 20-plus nephews and nieces from family gatherings, until I "moved in!"

I learned that routines and patterns are amazingly important to persons with DS-ASD. During my multiweek stay at the Froehlke house, I learned that sticking to routines is essential in making the household schedule work.

Brennan knows exactly what he will have for dinner on Mondays (pasta meat), Tuesdays (Tuesday tacos), Thursdays (ravioli), Fridays (pizza), and Saturdays (Chipotle). Wednesdays and Sundays are "wild cards" by design—Bob, a pediatrician, is off on those days and he gets to pick the meal!

But the most astonishing thing I learned was that Brennan made his own lunch—everyday—as soon as he came home from his daily program. Monday–Friday, Brennan made peanut butter and jelly on a soft piece of wheat bread. It was smooth peanut butter and grape jelly. Once the lunch was packed, he put his Broncos lunch bag in the fridge every afternoon until he pulled it out the next morning to take to his day program.

Astonished by this routine, I made up a jingle for Brennan, which he now repeats religiously, "PBJ, every day, that's my way!"

I'm not sure how nutritious Brennan's meal plan is but he sticks to his routine, sings his song, and looks as fit as a fiddle!

**LEAH MARTIN, "AUNT" TO JANET KAY,
15 YEARS OLD AT THE TIME OF HER PASSING**

Janet Kay was like a niece to me, and she'll never know the profound impact she had on my life.

I'm not sure if she was aware that everything revolved around her—but then again, maybe she did know. After all, she was the "Empress" of the household. Things revolved around her for a lot of reasons. Her mom, Robin, took care of her medical needs, her personal care, getting her ready for school, etc. There were moments when I caught Janet Kay staring at her mom with those "love eyes" she had for her, and it melted my heart. I could see the very special kind of "kindred spirit" love they had for one another, and that love helped me see Janet Kay in a different, very special way.

She may not have been like other little girls with Down syndrome. She didn't play with her dolls and pretend to be their mommy. She didn't communicate with words. Her needs required lots and lots of time and attention. Sometimes that meant the other kids didn't get the attention they may have wanted or needed—and sometimes it meant they had to chip in and help to support Janet Kay, as well. But it wasn't just those things that put the focus on her . . . when I was at the house, I could sense the immense love that everyone had for her.

Yes, things revolved around her . . . like she was the sun, and everyone else served as her orbiting planets. There was always a competition for who could feed her something she liked, or who would be able to sit next to her. Who could get her to smile, or who could kiss her neck. I loved how she would grab my hand and lead me to the refrigerator. It was her instruction to me that she was ready for a snack, and I was to get it for her. I just loved that. She was sweet. Yes, she could do the "drop-and-flop" and only move on her own schedule. Yes, she would often be awake all night playing and laughing, and her mom would go to work exhausted the next day. But truly, these were the extent of her "behavioral challenges"—she was sweet and gentle.

Someone with both Down syndrome and autism can require a lot of time and energy. With Janet Kay, all that time and energy was freely given with, through, and because of love. And when she died, it was like the sun had disappeared from her home. For some time, it was void of the light and warmth that the sun used to provide. It seemed there were only clouds, and everyone was lost in the dark. After all, they were all without the central focus of their orbits. They had to find their way again.

When her mom, Robin, decided to start a day program for Tommy (Janet's older brother), I jumped on board with her. I didn't know what I was doing—I had a career in the satellite imagery and remote sensing industry, and I knew nothing about human services. But I had a heart for people like Janet Kay and Tommy. After five years, I left my career and switched full-time to our company. And now after 11 years since starting our program, we are serving more than 70 adults with IDD.

You may ask how Janet Kay had a profound impact on my life personally? If it weren't for her, I wouldn't see people with differences the way I do now. If it weren't for her, Robin and I wouldn't have our day program. I wouldn't have changed careers and earned a PhD; I wouldn't have found the profound joy I feel in my life through knowing the people we serve at our program. Life would be completely different for me if it weren't for her. Yes—Janet Kay changed people's lives for the better, both in her life and through her death. I was happy to be her "Aunt Leah"—and I'm honored to be on the receiving end of her influence.

JANE ROBERTS, AUNT OF BRENNAN, 30 YEARS OLD

Not long ago, the Froehlkes came to North Carolina to sponsor our children as they received the Sacrament of Confirmation. The small private mass included the priest, our family, and the Froehlke family. During the consecration of the bread and wine, the priest offers sacred prayers and elevates first the Host than the Chalice. As soon as the priest elevated each object, Brennan began vigorously shaking his right hand. He stopped only after both items had been lowered and returned to the altar. We didn't know why Brennan had done this. Then after Mass, the priest, Fr. Dan, came up to

Brennan smiling and said, "Brennan, you must be an altar server. Thank you for ringing the bells for us!" (Ringing the bells during this part of the Mass is a sacred practice that is done at many Catholic Masses, and Brennan was making sure this duty was preformed, even with imaginary bells.)

THERESA MCCARTHY, AUNT OF BRENNAN, 30 YEARS OLD

In 1993 my sister Margaret, her husband Bob, their children, and our whole extended family welcomed Brennan into the fold. Our family had little if any understanding of a child on the spectrum or one with Down syndrome. Over the past 29 years we have watched and learned. An amazing young man has emerged softening all our hearts along the way with his accomplishments, humor, and the capacity for empathy Brennan has shown. Brennan comforted our mother, his grandmother, as she declined and passed, at her bedside over many months. He has other special talents too. He never complains. His memory is acute. He is exceptional with directions, never forgetting the route even if only taken once. Margaret and Bob have done a wonderful job exposing Brennan to every opportunity and he has risen to every challenge. He holds a part-time job as a barista, has tasks at home, participates in camping and hiking and assists with the family dog. His admiration for his siblings and excitement to participate in their personal milestones is mirrored by them as they celebrate him, with every race he runs to his fullest. He is an inspiration. XO!

CAROL SHILSON, AUNT OF BRENNAN, 30 YEARS OLD

I will always think of Brennan for the love he brought out in others . . . .

My most special and specific memories of Brennan are how he interacted with my dad, his grandfather. My dad was always a warm and loving man—he and my mom loved children, and together raised 12. I was the baby. After a quintuple bypass and the tragic loss of one son to leukemia, however, a bit of his spark dulled. My whole life to that point, dad's innate charisma and joy for life immediately filled a room. But his sadness put a noticeable damper on his presence and his joy for years. Until Brennan. What a beautiful moment it was to see the bond that developed between my dad and Brennan over the years. He had many grandchildren, but from my perspective it was Brennan who reignited his spark for life, brought back that twinkle in his eye and really let him love again.

I thank God every day for Brennan and all the wonderful things he has contributed to this world and our family—nothing would be the same without him. But I thank him most for being a true angel for my dad.

ISABELLA VALLEFUOCO, COUSIN OF JAKE, 14 YEARS OLD

In April of 2007 my family was blessed with my newborn cousin, Jacob. It was a surprise to the family that he was born with Down syndrome. Shortly after birth, he had to endure open heart surgery, which was incredibly frightening for our family. At 8 years old, I could not understand the extent of the medical risks associated with what he was about to take on, but I could clearly feel the fear running through my family. I remember my sister and I whispering prayers to each other from our bunk beds. These difficult times brought our family closer together, as does Jake. He continues to enrich my life. He reminds me there is always more room for love and play. From his love of music to his contagious laugh, he brings an abundance of joy wherever he goes.

BIANCA VALLEFUOCO, COUSIN OF JAKE, 14 YEARS OLD

I was 3 years old when my cousin Jake was born. I never fully understood what it meant to have Down syndrome or autism, but I knew that it meant Jake had a lot more challenges in his life, and that he had to be a lot stronger than other kids. Watching him grow up has been the highlight of being his cousin. Seeing him walk for the first time or take the first bite of what would become his favorite food (cake, obviously) has brought pure and utter joy to this family's lives with his authenticity. A Jake-smile is both infectious and healing all at the same time.

SUSAN WIGGIN, AUNT OF BRENNAN, 30 YEARS OLD

There was a time in Brennan's younger years, when it was uncertain how much he would be able to understand and interact with family and friends. He always "looked" like he was listening, but, as I recall, we all thought his verbal skills were so limited that he would never progress to a conversational level.

The Froehlke family had a daily routine at dinner where they would go around the table and each person present had to say something about their day. One evening, after each of the kids (Liz, Alex, and Sarah) had shared their event of the day, the meal was proceeding when suddenly Brennan yelled, "ME!" and went on to say "bus, farm, cow!" He wanted to be included in the discussion and shared important highlights of his day at school, which included a bus ride to a farm where he saw, among other things, a cow! What a shock it was! He had been listening and understanding what everybody was saying and didn't want to be left out! I remember crying tears of joy when I heard this story and even find myself tearing up as I recall it now.

Brennan is a wonderful young man who loves to interact with family and friends. The gains he has made over the years, once thought impossible, continue to increase with his innate desire to learn and continue to grow. He is a kind, funny and thoughtful young man who is well loved.

ANNA PUTNAM, LIFELONG FRIEND OF BRENNAN'S, 30 YEARS OLD

Growing up with Brennan had an undeniable, profound effect on my life. He always had a seat at the table, was always included in activities and events that our families did together, which normalized people with disabilities for me. I never saw him as "other" or different, though I did recognize that he had some unique needs. By watching his parents manage those unique needs I learned to have patience, empathy, and respect for people with disabilities. I also learned that every human being has inherent worth and dignity, that every single one of us deserves to have a seat at the table. I have no doubt that growing up with Brennan influenced my choice to become a social worker and was the spark for my passion to support and empower people with developmental disabilities.

CONCLUSION

Parents, siblings, and extended family members have graciously shared their thoughts about how their important person with DS-ASD has influenced their lives. It is impossible to measure the impact of how deeply each life is touched by living with or knowing someone with DS-ASD. Even those in the same family are affected in profoundly different ways, which is why it is important to hear about the lived experiences of each member of the family. A small sampling of anecdotes was provided in this chapter, but there are millions more out there in the world. How fascinating would it be to read them all?

Families in the DS-ASD community are unique and special beyond words. Unlike the fast-paced, busy world we all live in, with its demands of efficiency, perfection, and constant pressures, we mark our relationships with friends and loved ones with DS-ASD with patience, a slower pace, no external pressures, and unconditional love. They, in turn, are filled with acceptance, smiles, and gentleness, and they bring love to us all. We hope that, in your lifetime, you too can experience the special blessing of knowing and loving someone with DS-ASD.

REFERENCES

Estes, A., Swain, D. M., & MacDuffie, K. E. (2019). The effects of early autism intervention on parents and family adaptive functioning. *Pediatric Medicine, 2*, 21–35. https://doi.org/10.21037/pm.2019.05.05

Luijkx, J., van der Putten, A. A., & Vlaskamp, C. (2019). A valuable burden? The impact of children with profound intellectual and multiple disabilities on family life. *Journal of Intellectual & Developmental Disability, 44*(2), 184–189. https://doi.org/10.3109/13668250.2017.1326588

Naylor, A., & Prescott, P. (2004). Invisible children? The need for support groups for siblings of disabled children. *British Journal of Special Education, 31*(4), 199–206. https://doi.org/10.1111/j.0952-3383.2004.00355.x

Oti-Boadi, M. (2017). Exploring the lived experiences of mothers of children with intellectual disability in Ghana. *SAGE Open, 7*(4). https://doi.org/10.1177/2158244017745578

Perenc, L., Radochoński, M., & Radochońska, A. (2015). Prosocial competencies among adolescent siblings of the physically disabled. *Current Issues in Personality Psychology, 3*(4), 195–202. https://doi.org/10.5114/cipp.2015.53897

Rum, Y., Genzer, S., Markovitch, N., Jenkins, J., Perry, A., & Knafo-Noam, A. (2022). Are there positive effects of having a sibling with special needs? Empathy and prosociality of twins of children with non-typical development. *Child Development, 93*, 1121–1128. https://doi.org/10.1111/cdev.13740

Subramaniam, A. (2021, September 29). Why lived experience matters - The limits of empathy. Psychology Today. https://www.psychologytoday.com/us/blog/parenting-neuroscience-perspective/202109/why-lived-experience-matters

Whiting, M. (2014). Children with disabilities and complex health needs: the impact on family life. *Nursing Children and Young People, 26*(3), 26–30. https://pubmed.ncbi.nlm.nih.gov/24708336/

CHAPTER FIFTEEN

WHY PARENTS REQUIRE SPECIALIZED SUPPORT

Robin Sattel, MS

"Not everyone who comes to the table sits. Some lie on the floor underneath, some stim and flap nearby, some run around the table, some twirl and dance at the side. Everyone is valuable. Even if you don't sit, you still deserve space at the table."
— Stalen's Way

When parents begin their journey with their newborn with Down syndrome, they almost always find meaningful support and camaraderie among other parents in the Down syndrome community. For parents whose child with Down syndrome later starts to exhibit characteristics of autism, a gradual realization may overcome them: they don't necessarily fit in with the Down syndrome community anymore (which can cause feelings of loss and grief), and they don't really fit in with the autism community, either. Their child may have both diagnoses but neither "camp" separately fulfills their needs. The tendency for confusion and isolation within the DS-ASD journey is precisely why it is imperative for parents to locate a special kind of support designed just for them. They need a community that understands them and their child. They need people who can embrace and encourage them. They need to find out where they *belong*.

How does this realization about not "fitting in" evolve? Parents may start to feel a sting when they notice that their child does not appear to be like other children with Down syndrome. As a result, they may slowly decrease their participation at support groups, awareness walks, and family-type gatherings at their local Down syndrome association. They may watch the other children who are playing, interacting with each other, or sitting on Santa's lap, while their child is sitting in the corner making vocal stimming noises, covering their ears, or flapping their arms and rocking back and forth. Their child may also have a meltdown because the environment is different and chaotic (i.e., bright lights, loud music, and crying babies). This child, who is *just as adorable and lovable as any other child there*, simply isn't interested in the festivities and appears to be much more comfortable either observing, retreating into their own world, or bolting out the door.

With a few disheartening encounters behind them, parents of children with DS-ASD may begin to feel misunderstood, judged, disrespected, and embarrassed. These feelings cut even deeper when family members, such as grandparents and other extended family members, also judge or avoid the parents and child. Parents often learn to keep their feelings hidden to avoid negative comments about their child's challenges—and about their parenting. Many withdraw and reject invitations to join in gatherings, and many more find themselves no longer being invited over time. Their emotions can create cognitive dissonance; they love their child fiercely but also grieve the life they were promised when their child was born. Why couldn't their child just have Down syndrome without autism?

FINDING THE RIGHT SUPPORTS

Jeanne Doherty, mother of Jessica, and current president of the board of directors for the Down Syndrome-Autism Connection, shares the following about her feelings, and why having specialized support means everything to her:

> *While most days I am positive and optimistic, there is still an underlying sense of grief, sadness, and perhaps fear, that has never quite gone away. I don't perseverate on it, but I have come to realize that grief and fear are emotions that deserve to be acknowledged and shared just as happiness and joy are shared. It is a disservice to parents and caregivers to ignore it, thus creating more feelings of guilt or isolation. My grief and fear are a part of my emotional journey, and they are valid. There is absolutely no shame in feeling this way and sharing with those who understand has been helpful in so many ways.*

> *I think the times I feel the sadness the most is when I am completing assessments about my daughter's abilities. Time and time again, I feel as though I must face the reality of the things my daughter cannot do, and probably will never do, and it is like ripping off a Band-Aid every time. Unfortunately, this is what we often must do to receive the services, support, or supplies we need for our loved one—we must focus on the "cannots." This is where my feeling fearful may creep in, "Who will do for her what I do for her after I'm gone?"*

> *To be clear, there is so much she can do. Like all of us, she is a lifelong learner and continues to surprise and amaze me every day. She is funny, quirky, smart, and loving. She is surrounded by love and understanding. Her life has purpose and meaning, and I am a better person because of her. She truly is my hero.*

Fortunately, thousands of parents and caregivers in this unique situation have discovered a community where they have found help and hope for the future. They were able to connect with others going through the same things in life, and in so doing finally found support among their *own* community. Sometimes parents can find specialized support locally, and if so, they are the lucky ones. Most others must look outside of their immediate community to find information, support, and resources, and to speak to another parent of a child with DS-ASD.

Nationally and internationally, parents have realized that what they are seeking is the *Down Syndrome-Autism Connection* ("the Connection") organization. Many find the Connection by first locating its private support page on Facebook, which provides a safe forum where parents and caregivers of children and adults with DS-ASD gather virtually, offer mutual emotional support, cheer each other on, ask for some advice, share photos, and simply be understood. Indeed, most who have joined the Facebook page have perceived this community as their new "home." They no longer feel alone because there are other people out there walking the same, or similar, path. It is truly an epiphany moment for many, and countless parents have eloquently described their delight at finding the group when they introduced themselves to the rest of the members. They are always met with compassion and kindness, and even the toughest of topics are tackled in a spirit of solidarity.

In addition to providing emotional support to parents, the Connection provides educational opportunities as well. In fact, for many years now, the National Down Syndrome Congress has invited the Connection to host an entire track of workshops related to DS-ASD topics at their annual convention. Parents and professionals alike look forward to meeting together every summer to learn about DS-ASD from seasoned parents and experts in the field.

Charlotte Gray, mother of Jacob, and current executive director of the Down Syndrome-Autism Connection, has shared her testimonial about how the weight of the world fell off her shoulders when she, herself, found the Connection:

> *Having a child with DS-ASD is very complex and can leave families feeling isolated and marginalized. I remember feeling that way myself when my son Jacob got his autism diagnosis when he was 5 years old. I was part of a wonderful playgroup for families who had a child with Down syndrome, and I was so happy to have found my "tribe." However, it was when Jacob was about 3 years old that I started to see the differences in his development compared to his peers with Down syndrome; I just knew in my heart of hearts that something else was going on.*
>
> *When we got that official autism diagnosis, I felt like we were the only family among this group that was different. I felt like Jacob stuck out like a*

sore thumb and that I could no longer relate to these other families because my journey wasn't like theirs. I had become nervous to talk to and support new parents who had a baby with Down syndrome because I didn't want to put this additional worry on them. I also wasn't getting the support I needed; my friend group couldn't relate, and I grieved losing them because I had become so close to them.

I knew I wanted to find other families whose joys and challenges I could better understand. Finding the Down Syndrome-Autism Connection allowed me to do just that and more. Years later, I happily became involved in the Connection, and not only do I now get to support hundreds of families on this journey, but I also get my own needs met, as well. The Connection brings DS-ASD families together for support and encouragement, but it also offers other services, such as providing education about DS-ASD to teachers and health care professionals.

What makes this organization so unique and special is that, currently, each board member has a child with DS-ASD; they live it, and they get it. Sharing our experiences, especially some of us who have been on the journey for a long time, helps new families and interested professionals to learn about this multifaceted condition and shows great insight about living with DS-ASD.

I think the biggest thing that I've learned from being part of this amazing organization and providing specialized support and outreach is that we're all in the same situation. When we run an online sharing session and one-by-one when parents share about their child with DS-ASD, you see the others nodding their heads in agreement. You start to see tears of grief and relief, but there's also laughter about some of the funny things our kids do. We celebrate the victories that our kids achieve, even if they only do it once. We also share some of the hard and scary things that come with a child who may have more severe or even dangerous behavioral challenges; for example, when a parent chooses out-of-home placement. We give guidance, love, and support to all on this journey, but most importantly we show no judgment. We truly are each other's best resource.

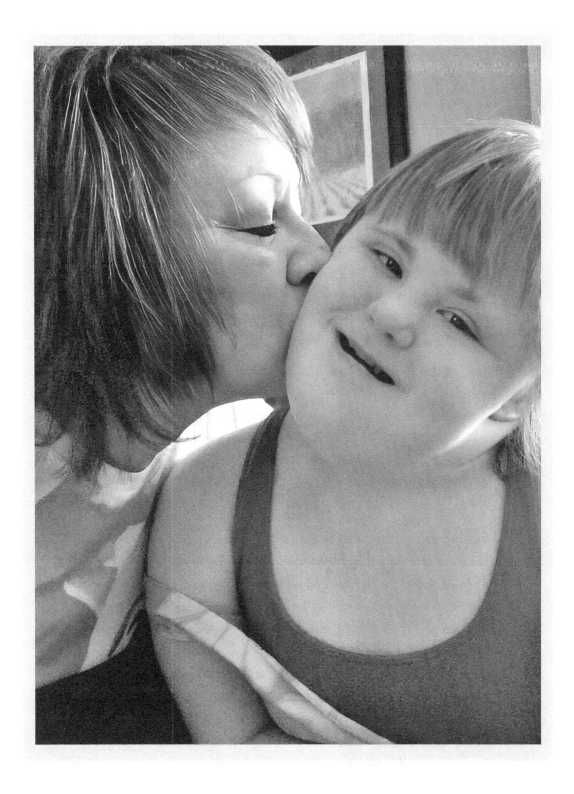

An Example of Meaningful Parent-to-Parent Support

A mother posted on the Connection's Facebook support page (shared anonymously here):

I'm just DONE. [My child] has been impossible. Whining, crying, hitting, screaming. I'm at my wit's end!

Allisa Lembo Rudden, current board member at the Down Syndrome-Autism Connection, answered this mother with compassion and offered hope:

You are not alone!! We had the same experiences at about that same age, and I call it our "dark days." It was overwhelming, exhausting, and debilitating. I feel every emotion in your post.

The good news is that our everyday life is not that way anymore! We do have peace now, and we have calm. When we were in the midst of those dark days, I feared that this was what our life would be every day, all the time, year after year, but it did not turn out that way.

A couple of things I wish I had known or thought of earlier:

1. *As difficult and frustrating as it was for me and our family to deal with [my daughter's] outbursts . . . I needed to keep in mind that the turmoil my daughter was feeling was even greater than ours. People would tell me she was "naughty" or looking for attention . . . somehow making it seem like she could control the outbursts and was enjoying them. That's not at all true. They were torture for her, as well, and believe it or not, she LAUGHED when she was feeling her worst, lending to the thought that she was just being manipulative. But once I realized that the laugh was a false laugh and actually a sign of distress, that was a game changer for me.*
2. *My daughter needed meds to calm her inner turmoil. Putting her on meds at the age of six when physically she looked like a 3-year-old was very difficult, but necessary. I'm not pushing meds, I'm just sharing that we needed help and that it worked for us.*

3. *Even with medication help, it was a long road. Calm, soothing voices worked best for us. Hand massages, quiet space, social stories, and yes, one-to-one support, was necessary but this is not what everyone wants to hear. It was our reality. This isn't a journey paved with rainbows and cotton candy.*

4. *All school districts are different, but ours did offer home training. This allowed us to have therapists hired by the school district come in the afternoons to carry over goals that would be worked on at school, in addition to helping eliminate specific behaviors at home. Schools don't often advertise this, but it's worth asking the special education staff if they offer this service; it's worth an inquiry.*

I wish you the endurance that you will need, and I promise the stress and the pain you feel right now are not going to be the center of your life forever. And lastly, please keep coming back here because we all understand... and we all get it. We've all been there.

Many other parents and caregivers of children and adults with DS-ASD have shared how it felt for them to find the specialized support and sense of community they needed among others who were experiencing the same things they were. Here are just a few of their quotes:

"Interacting with other parents is everything to me. Until now there hasn't been a soul I could relate to. I feel connected and supported for the first time in 11 years. It's the only place where I can vent with people who help me and are understanding. They tell me my daughter is beautiful, and they cheer her on. It makes me so happy that my daughter is appreciated!!"

"I can't believe that I found my people! I didn't feel connected with either the regular Down syndrome group or the autism group. We didn't fit in anywhere until now."

"This community has taught me that I'm not crazy or 'asking for trouble.' My mother's intuition was spot on."

"This group of parents is my lifeline. I don't know what I would do without them. I can ask any question on the private Facebook support page, and no matter how obscure or maybe shocking it may be, someone will have experience and advice to share. No one is fazed, just supportive."

"My DS-ASD community gives me hope for the future."

"I found the Connection group when I was in a state of desperation. Not feeling alone or alienated, judged, or misunderstood is very important. Advice and resource support is important but sometimes we parents just want to be seen and heard."

"The other parents in the DS-ASD group are the only ones who get me. I live in a small town in a mostly rural state on the Canadian border; I have no place close by to go to for answers and suggestions. There isn't even another child with Down syndrome in the nearby environs. The Connection is my 'go to' place if I have a question or a problem. I have made real friends on social media and during virtual support group meetings."

ADDITIONAL SUPPORTS

From Jeanne Doherty, mother of Jessica, and current president of the board of directors of the Down Syndrome-Autism Connection:

In addition to the Connection, Down Syndrome Associations (DSAs) around the nation and world have increased the number of supports and programs available to families with DS-ASD as well as those who have complex medical and behavioral needs. There are currently over 400 DSAs across the country, many of which recognize that a percentage of their membership may be isolated for one reason or another. These members fear that their child will be misunderstood, judged, and not welcomed for a variety of reasons.

A trailblazer on this front is the Massachusetts Down Syndrome Congress (MDSC). They identified families in their membership that needed extra support and have created a support group for those specific demographics, including DS-ASD and complex needs. Communication and information are key components to meaningful support from local DSAs.

How can we expect the world to understand and accept our children if our own DSA does not? As parents, we need to begin community-building, starting with conversations with our local DSAs to ignite change. How can they meet the needs of their most vulnerable members if they do not understand those needs?

What can your local DSA do to provide opportunities for our families to successfully be included in their events? At the heart of each association is a mission to know their members. They want to learn about your loved ones and are making strides to provide extra support and accommodations to enable meaningful participation.

Many DSAs recognize that families may not feel included due to an additional diagnosis or medical or behavioral challenges. Part of their mission is to meet this need by supporting the community on every level. You know best how to support your loved one and should feel empowered to share this knowledge with your local DSA.

What accommodations are necessary to make an event accessible and meaningful? Perhaps it's additional volunteers to provide more support, a more accessible restroom, a quiet area for those with sensory overload, or perhaps a fenced-in park for those who tend to wander or elope. Small but impactful, these accommodations could make a big difference for families as they decide whether to participate.

The Connection will also work with Down syndrome support groups to provide training around how to best support and include our families. Encourage your DSA to get involved.

RELIGIOUS AND SPIRITUAL SUPPORT

Parents, you may wish to consider—if this is something you are interested in—that there can be value in reaching out to religious or spiritual communities for support, as well. A recent study (Karaca & Sener, 2021) found that mothers of children with intellectual and developmental disabilities (IDD) who accessed religious or spiritual support gained effective coping strategies for the stress and anxiety that they were experiencing. The mothers in the study reported that they were better able to make meaning of their child's disability and discovered their own purpose in life through their child's disability. Furthermore, they found that intensified feelings of love and commitment were experienced through participation in religious or spiritual services (Karaca & Sener, 2021). Religious and spiritual support can play a role in assisting parents who are struggling with deep existential questions, if this is something the parent desires.

PROFESSIONAL MENTAL HEALTH SUPPORT

It is normal to ask, "Why me and why my child?" and it is natural to feel a gamut of emotions, including profound grief as well as anger at God or the universe, because your child has DS-ASD. In a recent study, Bravo-Benítez et al. (2019) examined ways that parents of children with autism experienced grief and loss. The researchers noted that there is a specific type of grief that these parents may experience called *ambiguous loss*. Ambiguous loss does not deal with the kind of grief that occurs when someone dies; rather it can happen in the situation where "the child, although physically present, appears to be emotionally absent or distant" (p. 2).

The grief of parents who have children with ASD can develop into *ambiguous loss* or *incomplete/unresolved grief* (Bravo-Benítez et al., 2019). Parents can become "stuck" in their grief, as well, which can prolong the mourning process and hinder their ability to move forward with a measure of resilience, acceptance, and hope. For parents experiencing symptoms of complex types of loss and grief, including anxiety or depression, it can be enormously helpful for them to seek professional mental health counseling. Mental wellness treatments can help parents sort out difficult feelings, cultivate healthy coping strategies, and discover hope for the future. It can take several attempts to find the right fit with a counselor or therapist whom you trust, but it just might be worth the extra effort to find exactly who and what you need. For those who are worried about the costs involved in seeking counseling, there may be free or low-cost options in your area, or, if you have access to the internet, online counseling may be an option if used carefully.

Whether you decide to utilize professional mental health support or not, please take good care of yourselves. Parents, you are beyond valuable in your role, and you are worthy of being well-supported in ways that are meaningful to you. Not only do you deserve to thrive, your child with DS-ASD needs *all* of you to be well—mind, body, and spirit.

Advice for Parents Who Are New to DS-ASD from Mary Cardle, Mother of Ainsley:

The first thing I would tell [parents new to DS-ASD] is to BREATHE! Yes, it's overwhelming. Yes, no one wants this additional diagnosis. But your child is still your child. Knowledge is power. Now you are equipped with information that can help your child live their best life. Start building your team. If you need a consultant, find someone who understands DS-ASD.

I also would tell them that it's going to be ok. It's going to be hard at times, but it's going to be ok. Find your people. Find people who have a child with both diagnoses; these people will be your community, your tribe, they will "get you." And it's ok to grieve this diagnosis, too. Autism is hard on so many levels, but your child can still lead a beautiful, fulfilled life.

Our kids are people, with feelings and emotions just like the rest of us, but they may show it in a different way. [I would tell newer parents] that people with DS-ASD, like Ainsley, can still do things others can, like swimming and for some, reading. They can communicate, maybe not always through talking, but through other means. Just because someone has a dual diagnosis, it does not mean their lives are lesser. Their brains are just wired a little differently, but they can still find joy in life and lead fulfilled, happy lives.

CONCLUSION

Unanimously, parents report that they do not want others to judge them or foist well-meaning but hurtful parenting advice upon them. They simply wish to be understood, supported, included, and respected. Finding specialized support is vital to the well-being of parents who have a child with DS-ASD. They can join a robust community where they feel safe talking about uncomfortable topics knowing that they will not be chastised or rejected. Like-minded, well-matched parents can celebrate a win together or console each other about the challenges, and then offer mutual support and resources. Parents in the DS-ASD community need and deserve no less than this, because, truly, they are valiant caregivers and advocates on the extraordinary undertaking called *parenting a child with DS-ASD.*

REFERENCES

Bravo-Benítez, J., Pérez-Marfil, M. N., Román-Alegre, B., & Cruz-Quintana, F. (2019). Grief experiences in family caregivers of children with autism spectrum disorder (ASD). *International Journal of Environmental Research and Public Health, 16*(23), 1–18. https://doi.org/10.3390/ijerph16234821

Karaca, A., & Sener, D. K. (2021). Spirituality as a coping method for mothers of children with developmental disabilities. *International Journal of Developmental Disabilities, 6*(2), 112–120. https://doi.org/10.1080/20473869.2019.1603730

CHAPTER SIXTEEN

DS-ASD RESOURCES AND NAVIGATING THE HEALTH CARE SYSTEM

Chiara Jaffe, MPH, MSW, LCSW-C

In addition to speech, occupational, and physical therapies, individuals with a dual diagnosis of DS-ASD often require other therapies such as Applied Behavioral Analysis (ABA). Some parents and caregivers also consider nontraditional treatments, including supplements, to treat the ASD symptoms. Navigating insurance coverage for ASD services, understanding Medicaid waivers, identifying other funding sources, and planning for your child's future once you are gone can be challenging, time-consuming, and at times, overwhelming.

This chapter aims to provide guidance for addressing these issues. We will begin by explaining the different kinds of Medicaid waivers, how to apply for them, and how to maximize the waiver services received. We will then review the various types of health insurance and the autism services each is mandated to cover, provide tips for selecting an insurance plan, and offer suggestions for addressing claims processing issues. Next, we will discuss additional funding sources and provide culturally competent and international autism resources. We will then provide tips and resources for financial planning and conclude the chapter with a review of complementary and alternative medicine treatments for ASD.

MEDICAID WAIVERS

History

Prior to passage of the Omnibus Budget Reconciliation Act (OBRA; 1981), children and adults in need of long-term health care, such as those with ASD, were cared for primarily in institutions or similar restrictive, segregated settings. OBRA modified this care model by authorizing state administrators, through Section 1915 of the Social Security Act, to operate Freedom of Choice, Home & Community-Based, and Research and Demonstration Waivers.

In 1999, the US Supreme Court held in *Olmstead vs. L.C.* that unjustified segregation of persons with disabilities constitutes discrimination in violation of Title II of the Americans with Disabilities Act and that persons with disabilities must be provided services in integrated community settings. This decision served to further popularize the use of state waivers (Velott et al., 2016).

"Freedom of Choice" Waivers

Section 1915(b) waivers or "Freedom of Choice" waivers are typically used to mandate implementation of managed care plans for Medicaid recipients. Freedom of Choice waivers allow states the flexibility to modify their Medicaid service delivery systems by allowing the Centers for Medicaid Services (CMS) to waive three statutory provisions in Social Security Act, Section 1902 (which covers implementation of state Medicaid programs):

- Statewideness [Section 1902(a)(1)]: Requires availability of the same Medicaid program to recipients throughout the state. Waiving this requirement allows the state to offer managed care models in specific regions only.

- Comparability of Services [Section 1902(a)(10)(B)]: Requires that the same service amount, duration, and scope be provided to recipients with the same level of need.
  Waiving this provision allows the state to provide additional benefits for specific populations.
- Choice of Provider [Section 1902(a)(23)]: Requires that all recipients be allowed to select from any Medicaid Health Plan. Waiving this condition lets the state mandate that recipients select from a limited number of Medicaid managed care providers, hence the name "freedom of choice" providers (Lewis, 2000).

Home and Community-Based Waivers

The Section 1915(c) waiver is referred to as the "Home and Community-Based Services" (HCBS) waiver because it allows states to serve targeted Medicaid populations in-home or in other community-based settings rather than in state facilities. Similar to the 1915(b) waiver, the state can waive the Medicaid comparability and statewideness requirements, allowing HCBS waivers to offer additional services including home health, case management, personal care, housekeeping, adult day, health, habilitation, and respite care. Other services including in-home support, transportation, and environmental modifications (e.g., room cameras or door locks) also may be covered by HCBS waivers if the state can demonstrate they are needed to prevent institutionalization. HCBS waivers also allow CMS to waive another Social Security Act requirement: Income and Resource Standards [Section1902(a)(10)(C)(i)(III)], which requires states to apply the same financial eligibility requirements to a specific population equally throughout the state. Waiving this requirement allows more recipients to qualify for Medicaid so they can access HCBS (Lewis, 2000).

Services covered under Section 1915(c) waivers vary widely between states, and states may also use different terminology for the same services. Some states use a tiered waiver structure in which multiple waivers serve the same populations but offer different types and frequencies of services or they may cap different waivers at different dollar values or even refraining from placing a cap on some waivers. This allows states to assign participants to the waiver that best meets their needs. Recipients also can receive services from one waiver while being wait-listed for another waiver (Medicaid and CHIP Access and Payment Commission, MACPAC; 2020).

Certain states offer combined section 1915(b) and 1915(c) waivers to provide HCBS by contracting with managed care organizations as defined in Section 1915(b). The managed care organizations then provide HCBS to eligible recipients (MACPAC, 2020).

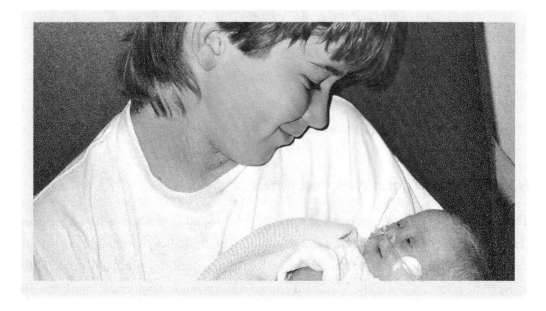

Research and Demonstration Waivers

States can also provide HCBS through experimental, pilot, or demonstration waivers, authorized under Section 1115 of the Social Security Act. Often referred to as "Research and Demonstration Waivers," they are used to evaluate state policy changes in Medicaid to expand eligibility, improve care, and reduce costs without increasing federal Medicaid payments. Research and Demonstration Waivers can be used to waive a much broader set of federal Medicaid provisions than 1915 waivers as long as program changes do not create additional federal costs. As of this writing, 14 states use Section 1115 waivers to provide HCBS, including three states (Arizona, Rhode Island, and Vermont) in which Section 1115 waivers are the only HCBS mechanism. Section 1115 waivers typically cover all or a wide range of Medicaid benefits in addition to HCBS (MACPAC, 2020).

For a dynamic listing of Medicaid Waivers by state, including all current and former 1915(b), 1915(c), and 1115 waiver programs, as well as a complete list of all Medicaid waivers for children (updated annually in September), please see the "Medicaid Waiver Resources" section at the end of this chapter.

State Plan HCBS

Many states provide HCBS through state plan statutory authorities. For example, Social Security Act Section 1915(i) allows states to offer HCBS to people whose needs do not meet requirements for an institutional level of care. Services offered under state plan HCBS are usually more limited in scope and intensity than those provided under waivers. States also are prohibited from creating waiting lists for state plan services because they must be available to all eligible Medicaid recipients if determined to be medically necessary. Therefore, such plans put states at greater financial risk than do HCBS waivers (MACPAC, 2020).

While individuals must be deemed eligible to receive Section 1915(c) (HCBS) waiver services, states are permitted to cap the number of people served under such waivers and to create waiting lists when demand exceeds approved capacity. States typically offer several Section 1915(c) waivers to target one or more identified populations or to offer different groups of services. HCBS waivers are the prime waiver authority states employ to cover HCBS, and as of March 2020, there were 254 Section 1915(c) waivers operating in 47 states and the District of Columbia. At that time, the number of waivers implemented in each state ranged from one (Delaware, Hawaii, and New Jersey) to ten (Colorado, Connecticut, Massachusetts, and Missouri).

According to the Kaiser Family Foundation, in fiscal year (FY) 2018, 41 states reported having an HCBS waiting list for at least one waiver, with a combined total of 819,886 individuals on waiver waiting lists and an average wait of 39 months. Waiting time varied by state ranging from 291 days for one state's waiver to 14 years for another's. Waiting times also differed among waivers in the same state, often by over five years.

Of the 41 states with waiting lists, 33 screen individuals for eligibility prior to placement on the list. The eight states that do not conduct screening beforehand are Iowa, Illinois, North Dakota, Ohio, Oklahoma, Oregon, South Carolina, and Texas.

The method used most often to determine priority for Section 1915(c) waivers is length of time on the wait list. Priority based on need due to functional status, level of care needed, or availability of natural supports was used for a smaller number of waivers. Fewer waivers still used a combination of priority and wait time, such as assigning individuals to priority categories and ordering each by wait time.

Keep in mind that once individuals become eligible and enroll in Medicaid Waiver services, the services will not transfer across states. Therefore, if you are considering moving to another state and it has a waiver wait list, typically you would not be able to be placed in front of other individuals on the list (MACPAC, 2020).

Determination of Functional Eligibility

To determine functional eligibility, some states use "categorical" level-of-care criteria organized by specific "related conditions," such as a diagnosis of intellectual disability, spina bifida, or autism. Other states use "functional" criteria, such as those provided by the federal Developmental Disabilities Assistance and Bill of Rights Act of 2000 (42 U.S.C. Subchapter I Part A §§144-15002). Functional criteria are based on an individual's adaptive abilities or capacity to perform tasks at a specific level. When applying functional criteria, "developmental disability" is defined as a severe, chronic disability resulting from a mental or physical impairment or combination of the two before age 22, which is likely to continue indefinitely and results in significant functional limitations in three or more of the following daily activities: self-care, expressive and receptive language, learning, mobility, self-direction, ability to live independently, and financial independence, resulting in the need for individualized supports or other types of assistance for an extended duration or a lifetime. Most states use a combination of categorical and functional criteria and screening tools may be used to determine waiver eligibility and which waiver is appropriate (42 U.S.C. §15002, 2000).

Once an individual qualifies for waiver services, they are typically reassessed annually to ensure they continue to be eligible for services. States vary a great deal in the stringency of their "minimum level-of-care" criteria and assessment tools vary between states. However, they typically focus on activities of daily living (ADLs), including toileting, bathing, eating, dressing, transferring, walking, as well as behaviors, memory, and cognition.

Points to Keep in Mind Before Applying for Waiver Services

- If you suspect your child may have autism, even if they have not been formally diagnosed, review the list of autism waivers for your state (please see the "Resources" sections) and contact the waiver office for any waiver(s) that your child may be eligible for. If there is a wait list, add your child's name anyway. You can always remove their name from the list if they turn out not to have autism. However, if your child is subsequently diagnosed with autism, they will be one step closer to receiving services.

- If you are considering moving out of state, contact the waiver office in the state to which you are considering moving to determine the wait list length and how priority is determined for each waiver for which the individual may be eligible.

- For autism waivers, some states require that an autism diagnosis be documented within a specific time period prior to enrollment in services (e.g., within three years). If the waiver wait list exceeds the period of time since the initial or most recent autism diagnostic evaluation, rather than pay for another assessment, you may be able to use the autism diagnosis as documented in the Individualized Education Program (IEP) if the person is still in school. Therefore, if autism is not already listed as the primary diagnosis on the individual's IEP, add or promote the diagnosis to primary at the next IEP meeting.

- Once you are eligible to complete the waiver application, you are required to complete an assessment. Unlike IEPs and treatment plans for other services the individual may be receiving, you should NOT focus on their strengths. Instead, think about the individual on their worst day to maximize the chances of their qualifying for the waiver. For an example, please see "Long-Term Services Tools—Colorado Examples" at the end of this chapter.

SIS LEVELS

Once an individual is deemed eligible for and enrolled in a waiver program, a measure is completed to determine the level of support needed. As with the initial eligibility assessment tool, states differ in the measure used. However, given that as of this writing almost a third of states utilize the Supports Intensity Scale (SIS), and measures used by the other two-thirds of states assess similar functional areas, we will focus on the SIS.

The SIS is a nationally recognized, standardized assessment tool developed by the American Association on Intellectual and Developmental Disabilities (AAIDD) to measure the level of support an individual with intellectual and developmental disabilities (IDD) needs to function in community settings. There is a children's version, Supports Intensity Scale-Children's Version (SIS-C), for ages 5–15 years; and an adult version, Supports Intensity Scale-Adult Version (SIS-A), for ages 16 and up. The SIS-C uses the same measurement structure, rating system, and common support need domains as the SIS-A. (AAIDD, 2022).

The SIS-A consists of an eight-page interview and the SIS-C, a 12-page interview between a trained human services professional, the individual with IDD, and at least two people with an in-depth understanding of the individual's functional abilities, including family members, providers, direct support staff, and any others. The SIS-A takes roughly 2 to 2½ hours to complete and the SIS-C 2 to 3 hours; both are intended to be completed in one sitting. In addition to using the SIS results to determine necessary supports and services for the individual, some states use the SIS to determine waiver eligibility and transition needs.

SIS questions are semi-structured so the assessor may ask follow-up questions as needed. Examples include the following:

"What type of support does John need to take a shower?"

"How often does John need this type of support?"

"On a typical day when this type of support is needed, how much time should be dedicated to the task?"

The SIS-A is comprised of three sections and the SIS-C is comprised of two. Section 1, the Supports Needs Scale, assesses the amount of support needed in the following six major life areas:

- Activities performed at home (e.g., toileting, showering, dressing, food preparation and eating, and cleaning).
- Activities performed in the community (e.g., commuting, shopping, and religious and leisure activities).
- Learning activities (e.g., education, training, and social and self-management skills development).

- Employment activities (e.g., job skills development, tasks completion, and interaction with coworkers and supervisors).
- Health and safety activities (e.g., accessing health care, taking medications, exercising, eating nutritious meals, and maintaining emotional well-being), and
- Social activities (e.g., developing and maintaining positive relationships at home and in the community, engaging in volunteer work, and social skills development).

Section 2, the Supplemental Protection and Advocacy Scale, evaluates support levels for activities in the following areas (the SIS-C includes the advocacy component in Section 1):

- Self-advocacy
- Advocating for others
- Financial management, and
- Obtaining legal services

Section 3, Exceptional Medical and Behavioral Support Needs (corresponds with Exceptional Support Needs-Section 2 of the SIS-C), evaluates health needs that significantly impact participant safety, including the following (Human Services Research Institute, 2016):

- Respiratory care (e.g., oxygen therapy, postural draining, chest PT, and suctioning)
- Feeding assistance (e.g., oral stimulation, tube feeding, and intravenous (IV) nutrition)
- Skin care (e.g., turning/positioning and wound care), and
- Other exceptional medical care (protection from infectious disease due to impaired immune function, management of seizures, kidney dialysis, ostomy care, lifting/transferring, and other types of therapy or procedures)

For an expanded description of each SIS topic area, please see "SIS Resources" at the end of the chapter.

The SIS is copyright protected but to print a copy of the SIS-A for your personal use, please see "SIS Resources" at the end of the chapter.

Rating Scales and Scoring

Following administration of the SIS, the instrument is scored, and a report is generated, identifying areas of need. **Note**: It is helpful to have a copy of the SIS-A to reference when reviewing the scoring instructions below.

The SIS-A is scored as follows:

For each activity in Sections 1 and 2, a rating from zero to four is recorded for the type, frequency, and length of support needed. For Section 3, a rating from zero to two is recorded for each type of support need identified.

SECTION 1

Sections 1A to 1E each are scored by adding together the total rating for the type, frequency, and length of support for each activity to get a raw score, adding each activity raw score together to get a total raw score for the section, and then converting each raw score to a standardized score and percentile to determine an overall Support Needs Index. *The higher the Support Needs Index for a specific section, the more intense the individual's support needs for that group of activities as compared to other individuals with IDD on which the scales were normed.*

SECTION 2

Items are scored by adding together the total rating for the type, frequency, and length of support for each activity. The raw scores for each activity are then ranked from highest to lowest score. *The four highest ranked items are considered the areas in which the individual is in most need of support and will be used in the development of an individualized service plan.*

SECTION 3

Items are scored by circling a score of "1" or "2" for each exceptional medical or behavioral support need. The subtotals are then calculated by summing the "1s" and "2s" and then adding both subtotals together to obtain the total score. *If either subtotal is greater than five or a score of "2" is circled for any support need, the individual is likely to have greater support needs than others with the same Needs Support Index; this may impact the level of support needed for activities in sections 1 and 2* (Ascend, 2019).

For information on what to expect during the SIS interview and how to read the SIS report, please see "SIS Resources" to access the links to the SIS-A and SIS-C Respondent Handbooks.

SIS SUPPORT LEVELS

Based on the SIS assessment scores, an algorithm is used to assign the individual to one of seven support levels, from least to most support. Support levels are established when scores meet all criteria of a Support Level Subgroup. Support Level Subgroups reflect variations in the intensity of the individual's basic, medical, and behavioral support needs (Norden & Robertson, 2020).

The Seven Levels of Support Model pertains only to individuals assessed using the SIS-A.

For the Support Level Subgroups Definitions, please see the "Long-Term Services Tools—Colorado Examples" section and for the Seven-Level Support Intensity Framework, please see the "SIS Resources" section.

Tips for the Initial Assessment

Just as when completing the evaluation for receipt of waiver services, you need to focus on your child's most challenging day when completing the initial assessment. Because the SIS is semi-structured, the amount of probing may depend on the evaluator. Therefore, it is extremely important to convey the highest level of support needed even if the need for greater support may wax and wane.

Prior to the meeting, all parties that will participate need to be on the same page with respect to the participant's needs; therefore, be sure to discuss how you will address each assessment item.

The following are questions to ask yourself and tips to keep in mind when providing responses for each section:

SECTION 1—EXCEPTIONAL MEDICAL AND BEHAVIORAL SUPPORT NEEDS

- Does the individual have any congenital conditions?
- Do they require any medical devices/procedures either continuously or on an ongoing basis?
- Have they had in the past or do they currently have any acute or chronic medical conditions that impact the following parts of their body:

  - Ears, nose, or throat
  - Heart
  - Lungs
  - Stomach, intestines, or liver
  - Kidneys
  - Bladder or bowel
  - Muscles, bones, or joints
  - Skin, hair, or nails
  - Brain, spinal cord, or nerves
  - Blood, lymph nodes, or immune system

- Does the individual have any conditions that affect the way their body produces hormones (e.g., diabetes or growth hormone deficiency)?
- Are they allergic to anything and how do the allergies manifest?
- Have they had any surgeries or procedures to treat the conditions?
- Do they take medications to treat any of the conditions?
- How do any medical needs impact behaviors?
- Does the individual engage in any behaviors that are inappropriate and/or could harm themselves or others?
- What triggers these behaviors and what relieves them?

SECTION 2—SUPPORT NEEDS INDEX

- Break down each activity into each of the steps needed to complete it.
- For each activity/topic area, be sure to consider the following in order to report the level of support needed:

o   Is support (e.g., prompting) needed to initiate the activity?
o   What physical, medical, behavioral health, and cognitive challenges impact completion of each step of the activity?
o   What level and type of support is needed to complete each step of the activity and how long does it take to provide the support?
o   How do any exceptional medical and behavioral support needs (as documented in Section 1) impact the activity?
o   What has happened in the past when the individual has not received sufficient support to complete the activity? Are there significant safety issues (e.g., risk of elopement, scalding, electric shock, physical trauma to self or others, etc.)?
o   Is additional support needed depending on the following:
    ←   the setting in which the activity takes place (e.g., toileting at home vs. toileting in the community)?
    ←   different aspects of the activity (e.g., for housekeeping, does cooking require more support than cleaning)?
o   Are there overarching needs that impact every activity? Consider the following:
    ←   Does the individual need a minimum amount of time to transition between activities or to transition between steps of an activity?
    ←   What happens if they are interrupted during completion of an activity?
    ←   What environmental stimuli impede completion of the activity (e.g., loud noises, disorder, crowds)?

SECTION 3 - PROTECTION & ADVOCACY (IN THE SIS-C, THIS IS SECTION 2G—ADVOCACY ACTIVITIES)

·   Consider the areas in which the individual can advocate for themselves. How much support do they need?
·   Consider the areas in which the individual CANNOT advocate for themselves. How does their inability to advocate for themselves compromise their safety (e.g., being unable to protect themselves from exploitation makes the individual vulnerable to physical and sexual abuse).

Reassessment

Some states conduct reassessments at set time points following the initial assessment (e.g., every three years) while others do not routinely conduct reassessments. However, in any state, regardless of whether the SIS or another measure is used, a reassessment can be requested on behalf of the individual at any time if it is determined that the current SIS level (or other value if another measure is used) is not an accurate reflection of the person's support needs (e.g., level of support needed is more significant than that captured in the initial/most recent assessment). Additionally, a support level review can be requested to address support needs not captured in the assessment such as temporary support to ensure the health and safety of the individual (Norden & Robertson, 2020).

As of this writing, 17 states use the SIS statewide, eight states use the SIS at the county or provider level, and four states are considering using the SIS. For a list of states using or considering using the SIS, please see the "SIS Resources" section.

Note: The SIS-A 2nd edition is scheduled to be released later in 2023. To access the URL that provides updates regarding the future edition, please see the "SIS Resources" section.

HEALTH INSURANCE COVERAGE FOR AUTISM SERVICES

Because a formal diagnostic evaluation documenting an autism diagnosis is required for waiver eligibility and receipt of autism services, waiver waitlists can be years long, and even upon receipt of waiver service, there may still be caps on hours and/or payments; health insurance can serve as another significant source of autism service funding.

Keep in mind that many insurers require completion of the Autism Diagnostic Observation Scale-2nd edition (ADOS-2) in order to provide autism-related services, such as ABA. (Please see chapter five, "Diagnostic Evaluations," for additional information regarding the ADOS-2.) In addition, although cognitive functioning level is not one of the criteria that the *Diagnostic and Statistical Manual of Mental Disorders*, Version 5-Text Revision (DSM-5-TR) includes in the definition of autism, some insurance companies also require an evaluation of cognitive functioning level. (The DSM-5-TR is used by mental health providers to diagnose mental disorders.) Therefore, be sure to contact your insurer to find out what documentation they require to verify a diagnosis of autism. The insurance company should have written clinical guidelines that outline the specific requirements (Steps to Progress, 2022).

In addition, even though a diagnosis of autism does not go away, the insurer may require a reevaluation to ensure the diagnosis is up to date and consistent with the latest DSM-5-TR diagnostic criteria. Typically, reevaluations, if required, are requested every three years. Therefore, it is important to ask your insurer whether autism reevaluation is required and if so, how frequently (The Family Guidance and Therapy Center, 2022).

All states require some level of insurance coverage for autism services. However, as with waiver services, some insurance plans may have an upper age limit or cap on the funding level and/or number of hours provided, resulting in disparities in coverage between states. For information on the autism services provided in your state and any coverage limitations, please see the "Health Insurance Resources" section at the end of the chapter.

Insurance Plan Types

Traditional plans (also referred to as "fully insured plans") are established by an insurance company and regulated by either the state Department of Insurance, the state Department of Health, or by special state health insurance boards which issue the plan. Claims are paid directly by the insurance company. However, fully insured plans are bound by the laws of the state in which they are issued, not necessarily the state where the beneficiary resides.

Self-funded plans (also called "self-insured plans" or "non-insured plans") are established by a plan sponsor, including a company, union, association, or state municipal or government agency, and claims are paid out of company/agency assets by the plan sponsor. At first glance, self-funded plans may appear more appealing than traditional plans because they have lower co-payments and deductibles. However, self-funded plans are regulated through the federal ERISA (Employee Retirement Income Security Act), which is implemented by the Pension and Welfare Benefits Administration of the US Department of Labor. Therefore, self-funded plans are generally exempt from state laws and regulations related to the diagnosis and treatment of autism. In addition, state prompt payment rules and standards of network adequacy for providers (i.e., the requirement that there be enough geographically accessible participating providers in a network to meet the needs of members) do not apply to self-funded plans.

State employee health plans (SEHP) provide insurance coverage to state employees in all 50 states. However, the extent of coverage, eligibility, and employee premium contributions differ significantly between states. **SEHPs are also frequently self-funded**. Currently, 48 states self-fund at least one of the health plan options offered to state employees, and 29 states self-fund all state employee health plan options. For a list of states that self-fund some, all, or none of their state employee health care plans, please see "Health Insurance Resources" at the end of the chapter (https://www.ncsl.org/research/health/state-employee-health-benefits-ncsl.aspx).

Medicaid is a joint federal and state program that provides health coverage to qualified children, pregnant women, parents, seniors, individuals with disabilities, and individuals receiving Supplemental Security Income (SSI). As stated above, states may also choose to cover other groups, such as individuals receiving home and community-based services and children in foster care who are not otherwise eligible for waiver services. Medicaid is the biggest single source of health coverage in the nation (Medicaid.gov, n.d.).

The state Medicaid agency and the Medicaid health plan determine if services are medically necessary and which providers can be reimbursed for services. Under the **Early and Periodic Screening, Diagnostic, and Treatment (EPSDT)** benefit of Medicaid, beneficiaries under the age of 21 are entitled to all health care services deemed medically necessary to treat conditions identified in childhood, including autism (Autism Speaks, February 2022).

Under federal law, all other sources of health care coverage must pay claims before Medicaid will pick up any part of the balance (MedicareAdvantage.com, 2021). Keep in mind that Medicaid benefits apply even when Medicaid serves as secondary (rather than primary) insurance. For example, an individual whose primary insurance does not cover ABA but is receiving Medicaid as secondary insurance through a waiver can use Medicaid to cover the ABA (ABA Consulting Services, 2023).

The Children's Health Insurance Program (CHIP) provides coverage to uninsured children up to age 19 who are ineligible for Medicaid but cannot afford private insurance. Like Medicaid, CHIP is funded jointly by federal and state government to provide public health insurance coverage. However, unlike Medicaid, the state method of program administration (either Medicaid expansion or separate CHIP program), determines what benefits are covered. Medicaid Expansion CHIP programs provide the same Medicaid benefit package as is provided for children under each state's Medicaid state plan and/or section 1115 demonstration programs; they must provide EPSDT. However, separate CHIP programs are not required to. Therefore, **coverage for ABA and other autism services under CHIP vary by state.**

To view your state's CHIP benefits profile, please see the "Health Insurance Resources" section to obtain the appropriate URL and then scroll down to "State Medicaid and CHIP Profiles" and select your state from the dropdown menu.

Medicare is the federal health insurance program for individuals aged 65 or older receiving Social Security Retirement benefits, as well as individuals who have been eligible for Social Security Disability Insurance (SSDI) for two years. (Please see the "Government Benefits" section for more information regarding "SSDI.")

Medicare Part A covers hospitalizations and related services, such as home health care, and does not require payment of a premium. Medicare Part B covers outpatient treatment and physician services, durable medical equipment, and preventive services; recipients are charged a monthly premium. Additionally, recipients often need to meet a deductible and then pay a co-pay for a portion of their care. Medicare Part D covers prescription drugs. For individuals who qualify for Medicare and Medicaid, Medicaid will cover the Medicare co-pays and deductibles (Maryland Developmental Disabilities Council, 2018).

To learn how Medicare works in combination with other health care plans, please see the "Health Insurance Resources" section at the end of the chapter.

The Federal Employees Health Benefits (FEHB) Program, the largest employer-sponsored health benefits program in the US, is administered by the US Office of Personnel Management (OPM). As of January 1, 2017, all FEHB plans are required to cover ABA for the treatment of autism, although the extent of coverage and costs of premiums for ABA coverage may differ between plans (US Government Office of Personnel Management, 2017).

TRICARE covers active duty National Guard and Reserve members, and retirees (TRICARE, 2021). ABA is covered under the TRICARE Comprehensive Autism Care

Demonstration (ACD) with an autism diagnosis. Please see the "Health Insurance Resources" section for more information.

The **Health Insurance Marketplace** is an online portal for comparing private health insurance plans and enrolling in a selected plan. ABA is included in the "Essential Health Benefits" package and is required to be covered in Marketplace plans in 33 states. Please see the "Health Insurance Resources" section for a list of covered states.

A child's plan purchased through the marketplace is an option for children not eligible for Medicaid or CHIP and whose parents have a self-funded insurance plan. To learn more about health care plans available through the marketplace, please see the "Health Insurance Resources" section.

Autism Speaks provides an excellent summary of the different types of health insurance as well as a health benefits guide to determine what type of insurance plan you have if you are not sure. Please see the "Health Insurance Resources" section at the end of the chapter for more information.

To access the statutes for states mandating autism coverage, please the "Health Insurance Resources" section.

Choosing a Health Plan

When choosing a health plan, start by making a list of all the providers the individual uses. Be sure to include the following:

- Primary care provider (the doctor or nurse practitioner the individual goes to when they are sick)
- Specialists (e.g., ear, nose, and throat doctors, gastroenterologists, and cardiologists)
- Optometrists and audiologists
- Mental health providers (psychiatrists, psychologists, social workers, and counselors)
- Allied health professionals (physical therapists, occupational therapists, and speech therapists)
- ABA providers
- Health care facilities, hospitals, and urgent care clinics
- Pharmacies

Next, compare plans and prices to determine which plan best suits the individual's needs and whether their providers are in-network. "In-network" means that the insurance plan contracts with the individual provider or facility to deliver medical care to its members. Such providers are referred to as "network providers" or "in-network providers." A provider that is not contracted with the insurance plan is called an "out-of-network provider."

There are four main types of health care plans:

Health Maintenance Organizations (HMOs): These types of plans are the least expensive. However, members are limited to providers who contract with the HMO, so if the individual sees an out-of-network provider (except in an emergency), they will need to pay out of pocket. In addition, they will need a referral from their primary care provider to see a specialist.

Exclusive Provider Organizations (EPOs): Like HMOs, EPOs only cover in-network providers. However, they cover a larger network and are therefore more expensive than HMOs. EPOs may or may not require a referral to see a specialist (Aetna, n.d.).

Point-of-Service (POS) Plans: Like an EPO, a POS plan may or may not require a referral from the primary care provider to meet with a specialist. However, a POS plan covers out-of-network providers, although it will cost more to see them because out-of-network providers are reimbursed at a lower rate and may be subject to higher deductibles. Because of the out-of-network benefit, POS plans have higher premiums than HMOs or EPOs.

Preferred Provider Organizations (PPOs): PPOs generally have a large in-network panel of providers, although the member can see out-of-network providers at a higher cost. PPOs do not require a referral to see specialists. Therefore, this is the most expensive type of health care plan.

Keep in mind that the same insurance company may have different provider networks for different plans so be sure to search the provider network for the specific plan(s) you are considering (Healthcare.gov, n.d.).

A High Deductible Health Plan (HDHP) has low premiums but higher out-of-pocket costs. An HDHP can be an HMO, POS, PPO, or EPO (i.e., any of the four health care plan types). HDHPs can be paired with a Health Savings Account (HSA) funded to cover some or all deductibles (Aetna, n.d.). (Please see the "Other Sources of Funding" section below for more information about Health Savings Accounts.)

When purchasing a health care plan through the Health Insurance Marketplace, compare Marketplace plans and estimated prices before enrolling. Search for the member's doctors and health care facilities to determine if they are in-network for each plan. Please go to the "Health Insurance Resources" section to access the URL for comparing plans.

Addressing a Network Deficiency

If the individual requires ABA or other autism services, but you are unable to locate a provider who accepts your insurance, due to a shortage of providers on the insurer's panel, this is referred to a "network deficiency." In such a situation, you may be able to request that the insurer cover the out-of-network provider at an in-network rate. Such a request is referred to as a "gap exception," "out-of-network exception," "network insufficiency exception," or "gap waiver." However, it requires that the provider accept your health plan's reasonable and customary rate as payment in full through a single case agreement. Depending on the details of the arrangement and your state's insurance laws, the provider may or may not be allowed to bill you for the balance of the charges beyond the agreed-upon amount (Davis, 2022). For additional information, please see the "Health Insurance Resources" section at the end of the chapter.

Prior Approval and Claims Processing

Depending on your plan, ABA may require prior authorization. This involves contacting your insurance company beforehand so they can determine whether the service is medically necessary. It is important to find out if such approval is needed prior to receipt of services because it is rarely possible to obtain pre-authorization retrospectively.

Unfortunately, even if you receive prior authorization, it is not uncommon to run into claims problems.

Below is a list of recommendations for addressing these issues:

- If a claim is denied initially, it should include the reason for the denial and instructions for appealing the decision. When you write the appeal letter, include documentation from the relevant provider(s) explaining why the service should be covered, and if applicable, have the provider document why failure to cover the service will likely result in the need for more expensive procedures in the future. Since insurance companies are most concerned with cost, this may provide an incentive to cover the less expensive service. Note: Since most providers are very busy, they often use a form letter that doesn't meet your needs; in addition, some providers charge for writing letters. Therefore, since you know the individual's needs best, draft the provider letter yourself, and then have the provider edit the letter, print it on letterhead, and sign it.
- If you are unsure of why the claim was denied after review of the denial letter, contact the customer service department for your insurance carrier to obtain clarification. It is possible that the wrong diagnosis or billing code was used, and you may need to call the provider's office to have them resubmit the claim with the correct code.
- If you run into ongoing issues with processing of claims, and the insurance is purchased through an employer, contact the Human Resources (HR) Department. The HR office should have an assigned representative from the

plan who works with them directly. Because it is in the insurance company's best interests to keep the contract with the employer, the plan representative should be helpful in addressing the claims issue.

· If claims issues cannot be resolved using any of the suggestions above, contact your US senator or congressman. They should have contacts at the state insurance administration and the Department of Labor.

To locate your representatives, please see "the "Health Insurance Resources" section.

· If all else fails, contact your local Protection and Advocacy (P&A) Systems and Client Assistance Programs (CAP). Under federal and state laws, P&A/ CAPs are authorized to provide legal representation and other advocacy services to individuals with disabilities. There is a P&A/CAP agency in every state and US territory, as well as an agency serving the Native American population in Four Corners region. Collectively, the P&A/CAP network is the largest provider of legally based advocacy services to people with disabilities in the United States. Please see the "Health Insurance Resources" section for the National Disability Rights Network (NDRN) URL to obtain contact information for P&A/CAPs by state/territory.

Another helpful resource is the **Mental Health and Autism Insurance Project**. The Organization was founded in 2009 to help families of children with autism and other mental health conditions access medically necessary treatments through their health plans. Specifically, the Mental Health and Autism Insurance Project helps families obtain single case agreements, file and follow-up on claims, and write appeals. In addition, they assist providers with writing appeals, billing, collecting unpaid claims, and other services, as needed. For more information, please see the "Health Insurance Resources" section at the end of this chapter.

OTHER FUNDING SOURCES

If your insurance plan does not cover ABA, there are other methods to help pay for these services, either through personal spending accounts or through a grant.

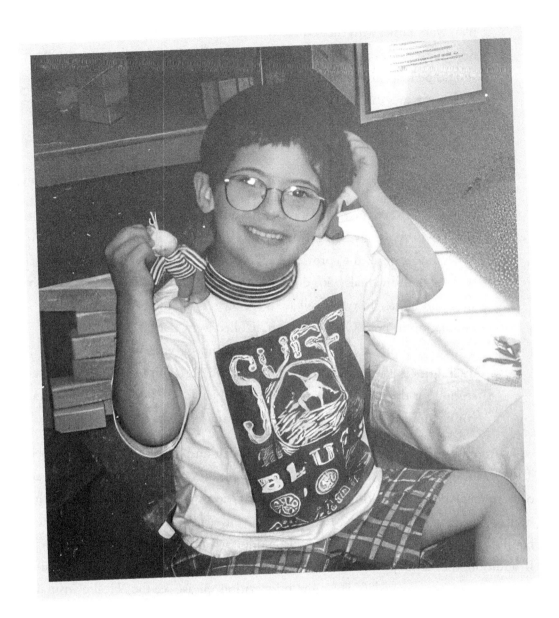

Personal Spending Accounts

Personal spending accounts allow individuals with health insurance to allot money for health care costs referred to by the IRS as "qualified medical expenses." These include health care, prescription drugs, dental and vision care, over-the-counter medications, and other health-related items.

- A **Flexible Spending Account (FSA)** covers medical and dental expenses not covered by insurance, such as annual deductibles and co-payments for office visits, procedures, and medications. For 2023, up to $3,050 in pretax funds can be deducted annually from each wage earner's paycheck toward such expenses. All funds are available at the start of the calendar year but usually must be spent by the end of the plan year. *An FSA can only be set up through your employer.*

· A **Healthcare Spending Account (HSA)** covers medical and dental expenses with high deductible health care (HDHP) plans. For 2023, you can contribute up to $3,850 with self-only HDHP coverage (coverage for the policyholder only), $7,500 with family HDHP coverage (coverage for the policyholder and at least one family member), and an additional $1,000 if the plan holder is age 55 or older. Funds can be rolled over to the next calendar year. *An HSA is also portable; it can be set up through your employer or independently* (Miller, 2022).

GRANT FUNDING

If a personal spending account is not an option, then grant funding should be pursued. However, because most organizations have limited funding, it is important to decide which items/services are the most urgently needed. Two examples of autism-related services for which families commonly seek funding include ABA and speech and augmentative and alternative communication (AAC) devices. (Please see chapter ten for considerations of AAC and ABA Therapy.)

The organizations listed below provide grant funding to cover costs associated with the diagnosis and treatment of autism, regardless of the state in which the individual resides (Autism Speaks, n.d.).

Autism Care Today (ACT) Grants

ACT Grants provide funding between $100 and $5,000. Households with more than one child with ASD, and those with income less than $100,000 per year are considered first. However, income level does not exclude families from receipt of services. The organization also has a separate "SOS" grant program for those with critical imminent needs for service; this program does have an income limit. Families must provide proof of diagnosis and proof of income for all income sources. Providers are paid directly.

Items/services covered include ABA, speech and occupational therapy, medical tests pertaining to autism, supplements, assistive technologies (i.e., iPad, communication apps), safety equipment (e.g., safety fences, GPS tracking devices, and autism service dogs), social skills groups, special needs summer camps, and other items/services to support the diagnosis or treatment of the individual with autism.

Contact Information:
Address: 20750 Ventura Blvd, Suite 160, Woodland Hills, CA 91364
Phone: 877-922-8863 or locally 805-506-5235
General email: grants@act-today.org
SOS Program email: SOSProgram@act-today.org
URL: https://www.act-today.org/our-funds/autism-care-today/

Autism Spectrum Disorder Foundation (ASDF)

ASDF provides funding for iPads, swim lessons, equine therapy, ABA therapy, summer camps, etc., for all ages. Applications for scholarships open on May first and for iPads for Kids on October second. Applications will be available on the website via https://myasdf.org/our-programs/applications/ and will only be accepted through the website. ASDF will need documentation of autism diagnosis from a medical professional. Requests will **not** be accepted through email. There is no income requirement, but preference is given to low-income families. If accepted for the iPad program, the iPads are purchased by ASDF and mailed directly to the recipient.

Contact Information:
Address: 228 W. Lincoln Highway 301, Schererville, IN 46375
Email form: https://myasdf.org/contact-us/
Phone: 877.806.0635
iPad for Kids program URL: https://myasdf.org/our-programs/ipad-program/
Social Skills Summer Camp Program URL: https://myasdf.org/our-programs/social-skills-camp-scholarship-program/

California Autism Resource and Evaluation Foundation (CARE Family Grant Program)

The CARE Family Grant Program provides funding for medication, autism diagnosis/evaluation, therapy sessions (including speech, OT, and ABA) and autism summer camps. Annual family income must be less than $75,000 and families must provide an autism diagnosis from a medical professional as well as IRS documentation of income.

Contact Information:

Address: 1704 Miramonte Avenue, Mountain View, California 94040

Email form: https://careautismfoundation.com/contact-us/

Phone: (833) 222-4226

URL: https://careautismfoundation.com/family-funds/

First Hand

First Hand provides funding for clinical needs, equipment, travel and lodging, and vehicle modification costs related to children's health care needs when insurance and other financial resources have been exhausted. Financial eligibility is based on out-of-pocket gross income and medical expenses, and documentation must be provided. Applicants must be 18 or younger but unusual situations will be considered for individuals aged 19–21. One request can be made annually, with up to three per lifetime. Applications are reviewed monthly.

Contact Information:

Address: 2800 Rock Creek Parkway, North Kansas City, MO 64117

Phone: (816) 201-1569

Email: casegrants@cerner.com

URL: https://www.cernercharitablefoundation.org/request-funding

KNOWAutism

KNOWAutism provides funding through three programs:

- Autism Diagnostic Assistance Program

  o This program provides up to $1,500 for one-time diagnostic testing based on demonstrated financial need for individuals ages 18 months to 18 years. Applications are reviewed on a rolling basis.

- Tuition & Therapy Assistance Program

- o The program provides between $1,000 and $7,500 for behavioral intervention programs, occupational therapy, speech therapy, social skills groups, special needs schools, and/or special education programs based on demonstrated financial need for individuals between the ages of 12 months and 18 years. Preference is given to first-time applications, but families may apply one time per calendar year for up to three awards per eligible child. Applications are reviewed on a quarterly basis and require documentation of autism diagnosis and financial need.

- Special Interest Fund

  - o This program provides between $500 and $2,000 to cover specialized camps, music therapy, art therapy, yoga therapy, therapeutic horseback riding, adaptive swim lessons, and similar programming for individuals between the ages of 12 months and 18 years. Priority is given to families with demonstrated financial need. This fund may also be used to cover up to $1,000 in fees for the services of autism/disability advocates. Applications are reviewed on a quarterly basis and require documentation of autism diagnosis and financial need.

Contact Information:

Address: 6430 Richmond Ave, Suite 410, Houston, TX 77057

Phone: 832-834-6437

Email: info@know-autism.org

URL: https://know-autism.org/apply-for-assistance/

Facebook: https://www.facebook.com/KnowAutismFoundation

MyGOAL, Inc.

MyGOAL, Inc. provides needs-based grants for treatments (including vitamins and other nutritional needs), enrichment, and educational needs that may not otherwise be covered by third-party funding sources such as school districts, county programs, insurance, and/or other grant-making entities for individuals up to age 18 years. A total of 25 grants of $1,000 each are awarded annually. Applicants must submit a health assessment questionnaire completed by a health care provider and proof of household income. Applications can be submitted between February 1 and April 30. Preference is given to first-time applicants.

Contact Information:

Address: P.O. Box 531, Monmouth Junction, NJ 08852

Phone: 877-886-9462

Email: info@mygoalinc.org

URL: https://mygoalinc.org/mygoal-autism-grant-program/

National Autism Association's (NAA's) Give A Voice Program

The intent of NAA's Give A Voice program is to provide assistive communication devices to individuals ages five and above with autism who are nonverbal or minimally verbal. The Program is for families in dire financial need who have exhausted all other resources. An evaluation/recommendation from a speech-language pathologist, physician letter confirming autism diagnosis, and the most recent year's tax return must be submitted with the application.

Contact Information:

Address: One Park Avenue, Suite 1, Portsmouth, RI 02871

Phone: (877) 622-2884

Email: naa@nationalautism.org

URL: https://nationalautismassociation.org/family-support/programs/naas-give-a-voice-program/

UHCCF Grants

UHCCF grants provide financial assistance for families with children up to 16 years of age who have medical needs not covered or not fully covered by their commercial health insurance plan; applicants must be covered by a private health insurance plan. Funding covers costs not covered by health insurance plans, including co-pays, coinsurance, and deductibles. UHCCF funds up to $5,000 annually and $10,000 in a lifetime, depending on the severity and cost/insurance coverage of the child's medical condition compared to similar applicants' conditions. There are maximum household income limits based on family size. Applications must be completed online and require submission of a copy of the insurance card, most recent 1040 form, and a signed physician documentation of medical condition form.

Contact Information:

Address: 9700 Healthcare Lane, Minnetonka, MN 55343

Phone: (855) 698-4223

Email: customerservice@uhccf.org

URL: https://www.uhccf.org/apply-for-a-grant/apply-now/

GOVERNMENT BENEFITS

Federal benefit programs are another source of funding for individuals with autism. They include SSI, SSDI, SNAP, and HUD.

Supplemental Security Income (SSI)

SSI, a federal entitlement program administered by the Social Security Administration (SSA), provides cash benefits to cover food and shelter to people who have limited income and assets, are over age 65, and are blind or disabled. "Entitlement" means that everybody who is eligible receives the benefit, and there is no waiting list. SSA defines a disability as a mental or physical condition that prevents the individual from earning more than a set amount (for adults) or results in severe functional limitations (for children) and is expected to last at least a year. For individuals under 18 years, parents' income and assets are typically considered in eligibility determination (Maryland Developmental Disabilities Council, 2018). Please see the "Government Benefits" section at the end of the chapter for the URL to access information regarding SSI resource and income limits.

Social Security Disability Insurance (SSDI)

SSA also administers SSDI, a cash benefit paid to individuals with disabilities who have worked long enough to accrue payments. Adults with developmental disabilities who have not worked for enough time or have not earned to be eligible for SSDI may still receive dependent benefits through a parent who has retired, has a disability, or has died, the latter through receipt of survivors benefits. The amount of SSDI funding depends on the total the individual earned while working or the percentage of the parent's disability or retirement amount if receiving survivors benefits. The value of assets does not impact SSDI benefits but income may, depending on whether it is earned income (Maryland Developmental Disabilities Council, 2018). To learn more about SSDI benefits and whether your child qualifies, please access the URL in the "Government Benefits" section at the end of the chapter.

Supplemental Nutrition Assistance Program (SNAP)

SNAP provides federally funded nutritional support for low-income families, adults aged 60 years and older, individuals with disabilities living on fixed incomes, and other limited income individuals and households. SNAP operates in the 50 states, the District of Columbia, Guam, and the Virgin Islands, which each splitting the cost of administering the program with the federal government. Eligibility rules and benefit amounts are generally set at the federal level and are consistent nationally, although states have flexibility to tailor some aspects (Center on Budget and Policy Priorities, 2022). For additional information regarding SNAP eligibility and benefits as well as contact information for the SNAP benefits agency in your state, please see the "Government Benefits" section.

US Department of Housing and Urban Development (HUD)

HUD is a federal agency that provides affordable housing options for low-income families, disabled adults, and other vulnerable populations. Applicants must have a household income that falls below a certain threshold, which varies depending on the household size and the housing location. HUD defines "disabled" as having a physical, mental, or emotional impairment that limits one or more major life activities. The applicant must be a US citizen, permanent resident, refugee, or have been granted asylum.

HUD offers several types of housing assistance programs, including public housing, Section 8 housing, and Section 811 housing. Public housing is owned and managed by local public housing agencies (PHAs) overseen by HUD. Public housing units are typically apartment buildings or townhomes owned and operated by the PHA. Residents of public housing pay a portion of their income toward rent, with the remaining cost subsidized by the government.

Section 8 Housing, also known as the Housing Choice Voucher program, provides rental assistance to eligible low-income families and disabled adults. Program participants can select their own housing as long as it meets certain safety and affordability standards. The Section 8 program provides a voucher that covers a portion of the rent, with the tenant responsible for paying the remainder.

Section 811 Housing provides funding to nonprofit organizations for development and management of affordable housing units specifically designed for disabled adults. The units are also equipped with supportive services, such as case management and health care referrals, to help residents maintain their independence and improve their quality of life. Tenants in Section 811 housing pay a portion of their income toward rent, with the remainder subsidized by the government (Affordable Housing Hub, 2023). To learn more about HUD housing options in your state, please see the PHA contact information URL in the "Government Benefits" section. Once accessing the URL, either select your state as listed in the box or from the map to obtain the contact information for local Public Housing agencies.

CULTURALLY COMPETENT AUTISM RESOURCES

The Color of Autism

The Color of Autism supports African-American children with autism and their families by providing parent advocacy training, social skills groups, peer support to individuals with autism and their families, and youth peer support training. The organization also offers a caregiver support group for men of color.

Contact Information:
Phone: (313) 444-9035
Email: info@thecolorofautism.org
URL: https://thecolorofautism.org/
Facebook: https://www.facebook.com/colorofautism/

Grupo SALTO

Grupo SALTO is a support group for Latino families who have children with disabilities, particularly autism. They work to provide culturally competent information. (Please see chapter twelve for more information about this group.)

Contact Information:
Address: 1640 W Roosevelt Rd, Chicago, IL 60608
Phone: (773) 757-9691
Email: gruposalto@gruposalto.org
URL: http://gruposalto.org/
Facebook: https://www.facebook.com/Gruposalto/

AUTISM RESOURCES FOR NON-ENGLISH-SPEAKING FAMILIES AND CAREGIVERS

A total of 53 million Hispanic or Latino people live in the US—17% of the US population. Spanish is the second most-common language spoken in the US after English, with a total of 38.3 million people speaking Spanish as their first language (Temelkova, 2021).

Though by no means exhaustive, the list below was put together by Friendship Circle, a Michigan-based nonprofit organization that supports individuals with special needs and their families by providing recreational, social, educational, and vocational programming (Lewis, 2013).

Autismo Diario

Autismo Diario is a nonprofit publication whose purpose is to share Information about autism, Asperger syndrome, and attention deficit hyperactivity disorder (ADHD). Most of their content is provided by national and international media agencies. Topics include news, general information, education, therapy options, and more.

> **Contact Information:**
> URL: https://autismodiario.com
> Facebook: https://www.facebook.com/autismodiario
> Twitter: https://twitter.com/AutismoDiario

Autism Society

The Autism Society is the United States' oldest grassroots autism advocacy organization and has 34 state affiliates. The Autism Society provides educational materials, trainings, and support. They also partner with other organizations to advocate for individuals with Autism through policy change. The entire website is available in Spanish.

> **Contact Information:**
> Address: 6110 Executive Boulevard, Suite 305, Rockville, MD 20852
> Email: info@autism-society.org
> Phone: (800) 328-8476
> URL: https://www.autism-society.org/en-espanol/

Autismo on Facebook

This Facebook page is 3,800 members strong and provides a support community and place to share information and resources for family members of individuals with autism.

> **Contact Information:**
> Facebook: https://www.facebook.com/groups/141887348126552

Autism Speaks Inc.

Autism Speaks was founded in 2005 by the grandparents of a child with autism. It has 17 affiliates, sponsors autism research, and has developed an online database of autism information and resources for all 50 states. The organization has a landing page that provides information about the identification and diagnosis of DS-ASD and provides helpful resources for family members and professionals (Autism Speaks, 2022).

For non-English speakers who care for or support persons with DS-ASD, Autism Speaks provides educational resources on its website in 13 languages: Arabic, Bangla, Chinese, French, German, Italian, Korean, Portuguese, Romanian, Serbian, Somali, Spanish, and Vietnamese. Resources have been posted for families and caregivers on various topics including new diagnosis, medical and dental considerations, behavioral/life skills, and transition. Resources for medical and dental professionals are also included. **Note:** translation of materials is ongoing so not all resources are available in all languages.

> **Contact Information:**
> Phone: (888) 772-9050
> URL for translated resources: https://www.autismspeaks.org/non-english-resources
> URL to locate your local Autism Speaks affiliate: https://www.autismspeaks.org/autism-speaks-locations
> URL to locate a list of international autism organizations: https://www.autismspeaks.org/international-autism-organizations
> Facebook: https://www.facebook.com/groups/2688492634501289/

The Global Down Syndrome Foundation (Global)

Global was founded in 2009 by the mother and grandparents of a child with Down syndrome. It is a public nonprofit 501(c)(3) dedicated to significantly improving the lives of people with Down syndrome through research, health care, education, and advocacy.

> **Contact Information:**
> Global provides a list of other organizations helping people with Down syndrome:
> URL:https://www.globaldownsyndrome.org/about-down-syndrome/resources/other-organizations-helping-people-with-down-syndrome/.
> The organization also provides educational series and workshops on various topics, including medical care, behavioral interventions and therapies, several of which are available in Spanish:

URL: https://www.globaldownsyndrome.org/
programs-conferences-grants/conferences/
down-syndrome-educational-symposium-series/

Finally, two Down syndrome specialists, one in Australia and another in Brazil, very kindly provided us with resources in Australia, New Zealand, and Brazil. Please see the respective lists below:

AUTISM RESOURCES IN AUSTRALIA

Autism Awareness Australia

Autism Awareness Australia was founded in 2007 to improve the lives of all Australians on the autism spectrum and their families. The organization provides targeted educational programs to families, as well as professionals and the broader community.

> **Contact Information:**
> Phone: 1300 900 681
> Email: office@autismawareness.com.au
> URL: https://www.autismawareness.com.au/diagnosis

Autism CRC Ltd.

Autism CRC was established in 2013 under the Commonwealth Government's Cooperative Research Centre (CRC) Program, as the world's first national cooperative research effort focused on autism across the lifespan. The organization now serves as the independent national resource for delivering evidence-based practices for autism across the lifespan through collaborations with autistic people, families, professionals, service providers, researchers, and the government. It also provides online autism resources for health care professionals.

> **Contact Information:**
> Address: The University of Queensland, Long Pocket Precinct, Level 3, Foxtail Building
> 80 Meiers Road, Indooroopilly Qld 4068
> Phone: +61 (0)7 3377 0600
> Email: info@autismcrc.com.au

URL: https://www.autismcrc.com.au/knowledge-centre/resource/
tools-health-professionals
Facebook: https://www.facebook.com/autismcrc

NATIONAL AUTISM HELPLINE

The National Autism Helpline is a free service that provides national and local information on autism assessment and diagnosis, education, employment, behavior and communication, strategies, peer support, autism friendly places and events, and creating accessible environments.

Contact Information
Phone:1300 308 699
Email:https://www.amaze.org.au/autismconnect/ (scroll down to and click on "Email us")
Live webchat:https://www.amaze.org.au/autismconnect/#webchat
URL:https://www.amaze.org.au/autismconnect/

INFORMATION ON ACCESSING HEALTH CARE THROUGH AUSTRALIA'S UNIVERSAL HEALTH CARE SCHEME

Medicare Benefits for People Under Age 13 Information Sheet:

URL:Information Sheet 24 -Medicare benefits for people under 13 years.pub (developmentalpaediatrics.com.au)

Centrelink: Turning 16 and Disability Allowance Information Sheet:

URL:https://www.amaze.org.au/wp-content/uploads/2019/08/Amaze-Information-Sheet-Centrelink-and-turning-16.pdf

National Disability Insurance Scheme (NDIS) Resources

Supporting Communication in and Contribution to NDIS Planning Conversations for Autistic Adults with Complex Support Needs and Their Parents and Caregivers: URL:https://www.amaze.org.au/wp-content/uploads/2020/02/Supporting-communication-in-and-contribution-to-NDIS-planning-conversations-final.pdf

Evidence-Based Resources for Families, Health Professionals, and Educators:

URL:https://www.amaze.org.au/support/resources/downloadable-resources/

AUTISM RESOURCES IN NEW ZEALAND

Autism New Zealand

Autism New Zealand provides services and support, education, and information on autism for autistic people and family/whānau, caregivers, and professionals.

Autism New Zealand also manages the Autism Outreach Service, which provides support services via coordinators outreach coordinators across 16 branches nationwide and links callers to the appropriate support services in their local region. The Outreach Service is free and available for autistic people, parents/family/whānau, and their support networks, including educators and professionals.

Autism New Zealand also provides a simple step-by-step guide to obtaining an assessment for an autism diagnosis.

Contact Information:

Address: 20 Sydney Street, Petone Lower Hutt 5012

Freephone: 0800 AUTISM (288 476)

Phone: +64 4 803 3501

Email: info@autismnz.org.nz

Main URL: https://autismnz.org.nz/

URL for outreach services: https://autismnz.org.nz/support-from-us/

URL for diagnosis guide: https://autismnz.org.nz/diagnosis-guide/

HEALTH PASSPORT INFORMATION

A Health Passport is a booklet an individual with autism can carry with them when they go to hospital or when they use other health and disability services. It contains the information the individual wants people to know about how to communicate with and support them. A Health Passport can be downloaded here:

URL: https://www.hdc.org.nz/disability/my-health-passport/my-health-passport/

AUTISM RESOURCES IN BRAZIL

National Autism Treatment Guidelines for Health Care Providers and Families

URL: https://bvsms.saude.gov.br/bvs/publicacoes/diretrizes_atencao_reabilitacao_pessoa_autismo.pdf

PUBLIC SERVICE LOCATIONS IN SÃO PAULO

URL: https://www.prefeitura.sp.gov.br/cidade/secretarias/saude/atencao_basica/index.php?p=204204

GENERAL AUTISM INFORMATION

URLs:

https://autismoerealidade.org.br/

https://autismoerealidade.org.br/2020/06/16/
centros-de-referencia-para-atendimento-de-pessoas-com-autismo/
https://www.autistologos.com/

AUTISM BLOGS

URLs:
http://mundodami.com/
https://www.lagartavirapupa.com.br/blog

NONGOVERNMENTAL ORGANIZATIONS (NGOS)

URLs:
https://www.fada.org.br/
https://www.ama.org.br/site/
http://www.autismoevida.org.br/

INSTAGRAM

@alice_neurodiversa
@carolsouza_autistando
@autistas_com_lacos_e_fitas
@omarcospetry
@revistaautismo
@autismolegal
@tea.cerena

PLANNING FOR THE FUTURE

It is never too early to plan for the future. Securing necessary supports will ensure your child is taken care of when you are gone. Four major methods for doing so include shared decision-making/guardianship; wills and trusts; ABLE accounts, and letters of intent.

Shared Decision-Making/Guardianship

Parents have authority to make decisions for their child with a disability until he or she turns 18, at which time a parent will need to utilize a legal process. To support self-determination of the individual, parents should use the least restrictive option whenever possible.

Health Care Agent

One less restrictive option is using a "health care agent" named by the individual with a disability to make medical decisions on his or her behalf through an "advance directive." Such health care advance directives can be used to communicate the individual's wishes regarding medical and mental health treatment and other health care issues. An advance directive also may be referred to as "health care power of attorney," "medical power of attorney," or "living will." Advance directives are usually written but may be made orally; they must be signed in the presence of a witness. The person signing the advance directive must be competent to initiate an advance directive and able to communicate his or her health care wishes, or at a minimum who should make those health care decisions for them (Maryland Developmental Disabilities Council, 2018).

Power of Attorney

Another option that can be used in conjunction with an advance directive is a power of attorney, whereby a competent adult can select a person he or she trusts to make legal and financial decisions on his or her behalf. The power of attorney must be in writing and must be witnessed and notarized. It can be general or restrictive so the agent can only make specific types of decisions or take certain actions (Maryland Developmental Disabilities Council, 2018).

Guardianship

Families, along with their attorneys, should consider all less restrictive options before pursuing guardianship. Guardianship entails going to court to demonstrate to a judge that the person with a disability cannot make responsible decisions regarding food, shelter, health care, finances, or property because of their disability and then transferring some or most of the person's decision-making rights to another person, who is then accountable to the court. However, even if guardianship needs to be pursued, one can limit the guardianship authority to the decisions needed. For example, a limited guardianship could give a guardian authority to make medical, financial, and property decisions while the individual with disabilities continues to make decisions regarding food and shelter (Maryland Developmental Disabilities Council, 2018).

For laws regarding guardianship and supported decision-making in your state, please go to "Future Planning Resources" at the end of the chapter.

WILLS AND TRUSTS

Wills

A Last Will and Testament is a legal document that specifies your wishes and instructions for who will receive your money, property, and other assets when you die. In addition, it stipulates who will implement the will's instructions and any limits or restrictions. Your will also names a guardian for children under the age of 18 or adult children with disabilities (Maryland Developmental Disabilities Council, 2018).

The Mass Mutual Special Care Program, which provides resources to families of individuals with special needs, recommends asking the following 10 questions as listed below when selecting a guardian (Cision PR Newswire, 2010):

1. Have you directly and openly discussed the issue with the adult whom you intend to name as guardian?
2. Have you considered all your children—not just the eldest—as potential guardians to ensure you choose the one that is best-suited for the role?
3. Does the guardian you are naming live in the same state or near your child with special needs?
4. Is the guardian whom you are naming aware of the specifics of the day-to-day care and routine of your child with special needs? Do you have an outline describing this care in detail, and have you given time for the potential guardian to review it?
5. Is the guardian whom you are naming at a time and place in his or her own life to successfully assume the role? Is he or she aware of changes in care that may be required over time for your child with special needs?
6. Have you and/or the potential guardian considered the impact or strain the responsibilities of being a guardian may have on his or her marriage and family life?
7. Have you considered the impact or strain the responsibility of being a guardian may have on the finances of the potential guardian?
8. Have you considered naming two guardians—one for the personal care of your child with special needs and one with responsibility for personal property?
9. Have you considered naming a guardian who is not a member of your family (e.g., a friend or institution) who/which might be better equipped to provide care for your child with special needs?
10. Have you considered naming a successor guardian if the guardian whom you name is unable to assume responsibility?

Trusts

A trust is a legal agreement that serves as a mechanism to manage assets, including money and property, for the individual. Keep in mind that trusts are not just an option for wealthy families. There are multiple options to choose from so even small regularly scheduled contributions can grow into a fund that will greatly enhance a person's quality of life, with proper planning (Maryland Developmental Disabilities Council, 2018).

A **Special Needs Trust (SNT)** preserves the beneficiary's eligibility for needs-based government benefits such as Medicaid and SSI. Because the beneficiary does not own the assets in the trust, he or she can remain eligible for benefit programs that have an asset limit. The trust will supplement the beneficiary's government benefits by covering costs for expenses not covered by benefits such as companions and medical and dental expenses not covered by Medicare or Medicaid (ABLE National Resource Center, 2023a).

A Special Needs Trust may be a first-party trust or a third-party trust. A **first-party SNT** is funded with assets or income, typically a personal injury settlement or inheritance, belonging to the beneficiary (the individual with the disability). For the assets not to disqualify the individual from receiving Medicaid or SSI, the trust must be created before the beneficiary turns 65, must be irrevocable (i.e., cannot be changed without a court order or the approval of the beneficiary), must provide that Medicaid be reimbursed upon the beneficiary's death or upon termination of the trust (whichever occurs first), and must be administered for the sole benefit of the beneficiary (Special Needs Alliance, 2013).

A **third-party SNT**, often referred to as a "supplemental needs trust," is funded with assets belonging to somebody other than the beneficiary. In fact, no funds belonging to the beneficiary may be used to fund the trust. Typical funding sources include gifts, an inheritance from parents or grandparents, and life insurance policy proceeds. This type of trust need not include any provisions to pay back Medicaid upon the trust's termination; instead, the person creating the trust decides how the trust estate is distributed when the beneficiary dies (Special Needs Alliance, 2013).

A **pooled SNT** is operated by a nonprofit organization that selects the trustee and serves multiple beneficiaries. Total assets are pooled for investment and management purposes, but each beneficiary retains his or her own account. Fees are generally lower than for an individual account and may not require as much money to open. Additionally, beneficiaries can access the services of a professional trustee and different investment options are available because there is more money to invest.

A pooled trust may be a first-party trust (i.e., established by the beneficiary) or a third-party trust (i.e., established by a parent, grandparent, guardian, or by the court). Unlike a single-person SNT, when the beneficiary dies, the pooled trust may keep the funds remaining in the beneficiary's account. If the trust does not do so, the assets in the account must be used to reimburse all states that have provided Medicaid benefits to the beneficiary, up to the amount of benefits paid during the beneficiary's lifetime (Maryland Developmental Disabilities Council, 2018).

Choosing a Trustee

The trustee is responsible for administering the trust, so you must select your trustee very carefully. You should also name a successor trustee to take over should the first trustee be unable or unwilling to serve. At the very least, you should pick someone who can select a new trustee if necessary (Maryland Developmental Disabilities Council, 2018).

Finding an Attorney

A will or a trust should be created by an attorney who either specialize in or has a solid foundation in special needs law. If you are unable to obtain the name of a special needs attorney through a friend or family member, try posting on your local Down syndrome, autism, or other special needs listserv. If you are not subscribed to such a listserv or do not receive any viable responses after posting, review the "Future Planning Resources" section below for assistance with locating an attorney.

ABLE ACCOUNTS

History and Contribution Rules

The ABLE Act was passed in December 2014 to amend Section 529 of the Internal Revenue Service Code of 1986 to establish tax-free savings accounts for individuals with disabilities with an onset prior to age 26 (ABLE National Resource Center, 2023b). An ABLE account must be funded using post-taxed money so the funder will not be eligible for federal tax deductions, but some states do provide state income tax deductions. Funds in an ABLE account can be used for qualified disability-related expenses (or, QDEs, which are items or services to optimize health, independence, or quality of life). QDEs include expenses related to food, housing, transportation, employment training and support, assistive technology, personal supports, health care, financial services, legal fees, funeral and burial expenses, and other disability-related expenses.

The recipient can have only a single ABLE account, but anybody can contribute to the account, including the beneficiary, friends, or family. As of this writing, the total annual contributions made to an ABLE account cannot exceed $17,000. The total balance allowed in an ABLE account at any time varies by state, ranging from $235,000 to $529,000. There are currently active ABLE plans in 46 states, and 30 states permit enrollment of residents from other states (ABLE National Resource Center, 2023c).

In addition to the annual contribution limit of $17,000, an ABLE account owner who works may contribute his or her compensation up to the federal poverty level (FPL) amount for a one-person household, as defined during the previous calendar year for the owner's state of residence. The FPL amount for 2023 is $13,590 for the continental US, $16,990 for Alaska, and $15,630 for Hawaii if the beneficiary is working, and they or their employer are not making certain retirement plan contributions (ABLE National Resource Center, n.d.).

Impact on Government Benefits

For SSI recipients, the first $100,000 in an ABLE account is exempt from the $2,000 individual resource limit. If the combination of ABLE savings over $100,000 plus non-ABLE savings exceeds $100,000, the beneficiary's SSI benefit will be suspended until the account falls back below $100,000. The suspension does not impact continued eligibility for Medicaid. However, if non-ABLE resources over $100,000 cause an individual to exceed the resource limit, Medicaid will be suspended (ABLE National Resource Center, 2023d). The ABLE account value does not impact SNAP benefit eligibility (Federal Registrar, 2017) or eligibility and continued occupancy for HUD (ABLE National Resource Center, 2023e).

Medicaid Payback

Upon the death of the beneficiary, the state in which the beneficiary lived may file a claim to all or a portion of the funds in the account equal to the amount the state spent on the beneficiary through their state Medicaid program. This is commonly known as the "Medicaid Payback" provision. However, the state can only recoup Medicaid-related expenses from the time the account was opened after outstanding qualified disability expenses, including funeral and burial expenses, are paid. Some states have taken steps to limit payback (ABLE National Resource Center, 2023f).

For a list of the key benefits and disadvantages of an ABLE account, first-party SNT, third-party SNT, and pooled SNT, please see the three related entries under the "ABLE Account Resources" section at the end of the chapter.

Selecting an Account

The ABLE National Resource Center provides several methods to assist in selecting the appropriate account. Please refer to the appropriate entry under the "ABLE Account Resources" section for a series of questions to consider when determining which account is best for your child.

Once you determine what is most important to you with respect to selecting an account, you can either compare ABLE accounts in three different states, search for an ABLE account with specific program characteristics, or use the map tool to select a specific state program to view its features and sign up for an account using the information provided in the "ABLE Account Resources" section.

Managing Your Account

Useful tools for managing a budget, including a budget worksheet and monthly spending plan can be accessed by going to the ABLE Financial Education URL as listed in the "ABLE Account Resources" section and selecting "Financial Tools."

Letter of Intent

A final important planning tool is a Letter of Intent (LOI). An LOI is not legally binding, but clearly communicates information to family and friends, a personal representative, trustee, guardian, or service provider to help them make important decisions with or on behalf of your child. As with all planning about your child's life, it is important to involve him or her to the maximum extent possible.

The following considerations should be included in a letter of intent (Maryland Developmental Disabilities Council, 2018):

- Living arrangements
- Education
- Employment or other meaningful daytime activity
- Supports and services needed in all aspects of life
- Important relationships to maintain
- Medical history, health care needs, medication, and therapies
- Contact information for friends, medical providers, therapists, and benefit providers

- Abilities and needs with respect to communication, activities of daily living, financial management, and decision-making
- Likes/dislikes and preferences (e.g., social/recreational activities and foods)
- Spiritual and religious affiliations, observances, and practices
- Effective ways to work with and support your child
- Financial information: government benefits, bank accounts, trusts, life insurance
- What a typical weekday and weekend looks like for your child
- Clothing and shoes sizes and where to purchase specific items
- Other "important things to know" about your child (e.g., habits, behavior, wishes)

When developing the LOI, think about what needs to be done for/with your child daily, weekly, monthly, and annually. The LOI should be updated each year to ensure that it remains current. If you store information on your computer that you would like specific individuals to be able to access, be sure to include access instructions.

FUTURE PLANNING RESOURCES

Websites

The Arc

Founded in 1950, the Arc is the nation's largest community-based organization advocating for and with people with IDDs and serving them and their families, with over 600 local and state chapters. In addition to providing residential, educational, and vocational services, the Arc provides several financial planning resources, including a Build Your Plan Tool. This free tool can be used as an LOI to document your wishes with respect to living arrangements, level of support, coverage of basic needs, employment, daily activities, life decisions, and personal relationships.

Within this "Future Planning Resources" section, please refer to the appropriate URLs to create an account and get started or just complete a fillable form, to locate a financial resource directory that you can search by state, or to view videos on future planning topics including housing, financing, employment, decision-making, and creating social connections.

Autism Speaks

Autism Speaks has a resource directory that includes a category for locating a special needs attorney. To search for a lawyer in your area, please access the appropriate URL within this "Future Planning Resources," section, select "Attorneys" > "Attorney Guardianship, Estates, and Trusts" from the "Category" field, and enter your zip code.

The Special Needs Alliance (SNA)

Founded in 2002, SNA is a national organization comprised of attorneys committed to the practice of disability and public benefits law. They provide a 15-step process for developing an estate plan for parents of children with disabilities. Please see the appropriate URL within this "Future Planning Resources" section.

BOOKS

Friedman, Steve. *The Essential Guide for Families with Down Syndrome: Plans and Actions for Independence at Every Stage of Life*. Austin, TX: Peavine Press, LLC, 2023.

This text, penned by the father of a child with Down syndrome, focuses on methods for fostering independence from an early age, recognizing health concerns and financial resources, education and work opportunities, and identifying and evaluating family- and community-based housing.

Hadad, C. R., and J. W. Nadworny. *The Special Needs Planning Guide: How to Prepare for Every Stage of Your Child's Life*, Second Edition. Baltimore, MD: Paul H. Brooks Publishing Co., 2022.

Written by two Certified Financial Planners (CFPs), one a parent and the other a sibling of an individual with disabilities, this text serves as a financial planning guide from the child's birth through adulthood. The authors address family support, emotional, financial, and legal needs, as well as government benefits. The book also offers a suite of online resources, including a Special Needs Planning Timeline, financial planning worksheets, and a Letter of Intent template.

Wright, H. *The Complete Guide to Creating a Special Needs Life Plan.* London, UK: Jessica Kingsley Publishers, 2013.

This guide is written by a CFP who is also the father of a child with Down syndrome. The book focuses on planning for the future with respect to resources, finances, and legal needs. It also includes a section on special situations, including divorce.

COMPLEMENTARY AND ALTERNATIVE MEDICINE (CAM) TREATMENT FOR ASD

Complementary and alternative medicine (CAM) treatment are therapies (medications, supplements, and practices) that are not part of standard medical care (National Cancer Institute, 2022).

In recent years, there has been an increase in the use of CAM for treatment of autism, largely driven by the rapid expansion of social media which has increased access to a diversity of CAM information. While it is helpful to share and receive information with others in the autism community, it is still important to conduct your own research first, and to decide for yourself whether a CAM therapy is appropriate for the individual with autism. Each person is different and what may work for one individual with autism may not work for another (Bennie, 2009).

In this section, we will cover methods for evaluating CAM research, what to look for in a CAM provider, and considerations when starting CAM supplements. We will then review treatments to avoid and how to identify false claims. Finally, we will present a list of organizations that provide information on evidence-based autism treatments.

Reviewing CAM Research

CAM therapies vary from safe and effective to ineffective to dangerous, resulting in worsening of symptoms, serious side effects, or even death. In addition, an increasing number of studies of CAM have yielded inconsistent results (Li et al., 2017). Therefore, it is essential to conduct a review of the research before starting any treatment.

A good place to start is **PubMed Central (PMC)**. PMC is the National Library of Medicine's digital archive of full-text biomedical and life sciences journal articles, which are provided free of charge. You can search for articles using multiple filters, including key word and publication date.

Another place to look is **PubMed**, a database of more than 34 million articles from thousands of journals. It provides links to full-text articles at many journal web sites and to most of the articles in PubMed Central. There is a charge to purchase many of the articles, but the search can be restricted to free articles.

You also can search **Google Scholar**, a web search engine that links to articles, theses, books, and abstracts from academic publishers, professional societies, online repositories, universities, and other web sites. Please see the "Complementary and

Alternative Medicine (CAM) Resources" section at the end of the chapter for the PMC, PubMed, and Google Scholar URLs.

When reviewing research studies on the CAM in which you are interested, you can then use the following checklist of questions developed by the Children's Hospital of Philadelphia Research Institute (2020):

- Are any research studies for the CAM therapy published in peer-reviewed journals? ("Peer-reviewed" means that researchers other than those who conducted the study evaluated the research design, methods, and results, and found them to be of sufficient quality for publication.)
- If you read about the therapy in a book, does it cite a scientific research study?
- Does the therapy target the autism symptoms you wish to treat?

- What types of studies evaluating the treatment have been published? (Large, double blind, randomized control trials are considered the "gold standard." In this type of study, there are at least two groups, one of which receives the CAM intervention. The other group(s) receive either another intervention, no intervention, or a different dosage of the CAM intervention. However, each participant has an equal chance of being assigned to each of the groups.)
- How many studies have evaluated the intervention?
- How many people were enrolled in the study and what was the age range of people who participated? (If you are considering a CAM treatment for a child, make sure the study included children, not adults. Dosage and potential side effects may be different for children.)
- What did the results of the study show? Did the treatment make a difference and if so, how much difference did it make?

If you decide after reviewing the research studies to start the CAM treatment, speak to the individual's pediatrician or family physician before starting to ensure the treatment will not interact with any medications or other treatments they are receiving.

The health care provider can also answer any questions you may have after reviewing the research or be able to direct you to additional research studies.

Selecting a CAM Provider

Before you select a CAM provider, be sure to ask about the following (US Food and Drug Administration, 2019):

- Education and training (the CAM provider should have received coursework and training in prescribing CAM).
- Experience in delivering CAM therapies to children and those with Down syndrome and/or autism (some CAM providers may have limited experience prescribing CAM for children and/or adults with a dual diagnosis of Down syndrome and autism).
- Experience working with non-CAM ("traditional") medical providers to ensure coordinated care. (CAM providers should be comfortable working with traditional medical providers. Beware of CAM providers who recommend discontinuing care with current providers.)
- Licensure, if your state requires it.

Beginning CAM Treatment

Once you start CAM treatment, keep the following things in mind (Children's Hospital of Philadelphia Research Institute, 2020):

- If you are planning to start multiple treatments, make sure to only start one at a time so you can accurately determine which treatment is working.
- Do not increase the dose or length of treatment beyond what is recommended; more is not necessarily better and can be dangerous.
- Monitor symptoms to see if they are changing, as well as other behaviors, overall mood, and potential side effects. If the person with DS-ASD experiences any side effect(s) from a CAM therapy, contact their health provider immediately.
- Keep track of what happens when you stop giving the CAM therapy.
- Store herbal and other dietary supplements out of the sight and reach of children.

CAM Supplements

The Food and Drug Administration (FDA) is the federal agency responsible for regulating human drugs and biological products, animal drugs, medical devices, tobacco products, food, cosmetics, and electronic products that emit radiation. However, under the Dietary Supplement Health and Education Act (DSHEA) of 1994, the FDA is not authorized to approve dietary supplements for safety and effectiveness before they are marketed. Therefore, supplement manufacturers can legally begin marketing dietary supplements without even notifying the FDA (US Food and Drug Administration, 2022).

For these reasons, it is important to consider the following before initiating CAM treatment (US Food and Drug Administration, 2019):

- Some dietary supplements may interact with medications or other supplements, may have side effects of their own, or may contain potentially harmful ingredients not listed on the label.
- The side effects of CAM therapy may be different in children than in adults. Most supplements have not been tested on children.
- You may not get the same ingredient in the same amount every time, and the medium the ingredients are dissolved in can also change.
- "Natural" does not necessarily mean "safe."

- CAM can be expensive and is typically not covered by insurance or grant funding.

CAM Treatments That Are Contraindicated

The FDA has warned and/or taken action against a number of companies that have made false claims about their products' use as a treatment or cure for autism or autism-related symptoms.

Some **CAM therapies** carry significant health risks. Several of those promoted most widely are listed below (US Food and Drug Administration, 2019):

- **"Chelation Therapies."** These products claim to cleanse the body of toxic chemicals and heavy metals by binding to them and "removing" them from circulation. They come in several forms, including sprays, suppositories, capsules, liquid drops, and clay baths. **FDA-approved chelating agents are approved for specific uses that do <u>not</u> include treating or curing autism.** Chelation therapies are intended for the treatment of lead poisoning and iron overload and are available by prescription only. FDA-approved prescription chelation therapy products should only be used under professional supervision for the purposes intended. Chelating important minerals needed by the body can lead to serious and life-threatening outcomes.
- **Hyperbaric Oxygen Therapy.** This treatment involves breathing oxygen in a pressurized chamber and has been cleared by the FDA only for certain medical uses, such as treating decompression sickness suffered by divers.
- **Detoxifying Clay Baths.** Added to bath water, these products claim to draw out chemical toxins, pollutants, and heavy metals from the body. They are falsely advertised as providing "dramatic improvement" for autism symptoms.
- **Various products, including raw camel milk, MMS (chlorine dioxide), and essential oils.** These products have been marketed as a treatment for autism or autism-related symptoms but have not been proven safe and effective for such use.
- **The FDA also has provided some tips to help identify false or misleading claims** (US Food and Drug Administration, 2019):
- Be suspicious of products that claim to treat a wide range of conditions.

- Personal testimonials do not replace scientific evidence.
- Be suspicious of any therapy claimed as a "quick fix"; few diseases or conditions can be treated quickly.
- Products that claim to be "miracle cures" result from scientific breakthroughs or that contain "secret ingredients" are likely a hoax.
- Beware of treatments claiming to "cure" autism. While symptoms of autism can change and/or improve across the lifespan, autism is a lifelong condition and cannot be "cured."

If you have a question about CAM treatment, talk to a health care provider who specializes in caring for people with ASD.

RESOURCES FOR OBTAINING INFORMATION ON EVIDENCE-BASED AUTISM TREATMENTS

Below is a list of reputable organizations that provide information regarding evidence-based autism treatments. *Contact information for each organization can be found in the "Complementary and Alternative Medicine (CAM) Resources" section at the end of the chapter.*

The National Center for Complementary and Integrative Medicine (NCCIM)

The NCCIM sponsors research designed to determine which CAM therapies are safe, whether they work for their intended purpose, and, if so, how they work.

The National Institute for Child Health and Development (NICHD) and Centers for Disease Control and Prevention (CDC)

NICHD and CDC provide information about evidence-based treatments for autism.

The Organization for Autism Research (OAR)

OAR funds pilot studies on autism diagnosis, early intervention, education, transition to adulthood, housing, employment, and life care. They also provide resources for families, including a parent's guide to research, which is available for download in English and Spanish.

The National Autism Center

The National Autism Center is a nonprofit organization dedicated to providing evidence-based information about the treatment of autism, promoting best practices, and offering comprehensive and reliable resources for families, practitioners, and communities. Their National Standards Project was implemented to provide parents and professionals with guidance to make informed choices about autism intervention. Report Phase 1 (released in 2009) evaluated autism interventions in individuals through age 21. Phase 2 (released in 2015) provides an update on interventions through age 21, as well as an evaluation of treatment studies for individuals aged 22 and older.

The Association for Science in Autism Treatment

The Association for Science in Autism Treatment website provides research summaries of the full array of autism treatments for families and professionals to make informed choices before selecting a therapy. They also publish a monthly newsletter, cosponsor several autism conferences and have a media watch initiative to respond to accurate and inaccurate portrayals of autism treatment in the media.

CONCLUSION

We sincerely hope this chapter has been helpful to you and that you come away feeling better able to navigate autism waivers, insurance coverage for autism services, sources of additional funding, future planning, and hopefully have identified one or more resources that are helpful to you. In addition, we hope that if you are considering CAM, you feel better able to evaluate the safety and effectiveness of any treatments you are considering.

ADDITIONAL RESOURCES

ABLE Account Resources

ABLE account, special needs, and pooled trust comparison chart
https://www.ablenrc.org/wp-content/uploads/2022/11/2022_SNT_ABLE_comparison.pdf

Becoming ABLE ready
http://www.ablenrc.org/becoming-able-ready/

Choose the program that's right for you!
https://www.ablenrc.org/select-a-state-program/

Compare state programs
https://www.ablenrc.org/compare-states/

Financial education
http://ablenrc.wpengine.com/resources/tools/financial-education/

Search to find your best fit
https://www.ablenrc.org/state-plan-search/

Understanding ABLE accounts, special needs trusts and pooled trusts. What are key advantages and disadvantages of each type of account?

https://www.ablenrc.org/understanding-able-
accounts-special-needs-trusts-and-pooled-trusts/
what-are-key-advantages-and-disadvantages-of-each-type-of-account/

Complementary and Alternative Medicine (CAM) Resources

Association for Science in Autism Treatment
https://asatonline.org/

Google Scholar
https://scholar.google.com/

Health Information – Autism
https://www.nccih.nih.gov/health/autism

National Standards Project
https://nationalautismcenter.org/national-standards/

OAR's free resources_
https://researchautism.org/resources/

PubMed Central (PMC).
https://www.ncbi.nlm.nih.gov/pmc/

PubMed.gov
https://pubmed.ncbi.nlm.nih.gov/

Treatment and intervention services for autism spectrum disorder.
https://www.cdc.gov/ncbddd/autism/treatment.html

What are the treatments for autism?
https://www.nichd.nih.gov/health/topics/autism/conditioninfo/treatments

Future Planning Resources

Achieve with us
https://futureplanning.thearc.org/assets/CFP-LOI-225742be9adf0a44017a713dd7ec
0d7c2e79514bb29f592a45e4b446e02a52c4.pdf

Developing an estate plan for parents of children with disabilities: A 15-step approach

https://www.specialneedsalliance.org/the-voice/developing-an-estate-plan-for-parents-of-children-with-disabilities-a-15step-approach-2/

Find a listing

https://pathfindersforautism.org/business-directory/?wpbdp_view=search

Let's get started on your plan!

https://futureplanning.thearc.org/users/sign_up

Locate sources near you

https://futureplanning.thearc.org/professionals/landing

Making social connections

https://futureplanning.thearc.org/pages/learn/where-to-start/making-social-connections

Supported decision making.in your state

https://supporteddecisionmaking.org/in-your-state/

Government Benefits Resources

Disability Benefits | How You Qualify

https://www.ssa.gov/benefits/disability/qualify.html

PHA contact information

https://www.hud.gov/program_offices/public_indian_housing/pha/contacts

SNAP eligibility

https://www.fns.usda.gov/snap/recipient/eligibility

SNAP state directory of resources

https://www.fns.usda.gov/snap/state-directory

Supplemental Security Income (SSI)

https://www.ssa.gov/ssi/

Health Insurance Resources

Autism and insurance coverage state laws
https://www.ncsl.org/health/autism-and-insurance-coverage-state-laws.aspx

Autism Care Demonstration
https://www.tricare.mil/Plans/SpecialPrograms/ACD

Children's Health Insurance Program (CHIP)
https://www.medicaid.gov/chip/index.html

Disability Rights Network
https://www.ndrn.org/about/ndrn-member-agencies/

Down Syndrome and Autism Spectrum Disorder (DS-ASD)
https://www.autismspeaks.org/down-syndrome-and-autism-spectrum-disorder-ds-asd

Find your members
https://www.congress.gov/members/find-your-member

Health insurance coverage for autism
https://www.autismspeaks.org/health-insurance-coverage-autism

How Medicare works with other insurance
https://www.medicare.gov/supplements-other-insurance/
how-medicare-works-with-other-insurance

Marketplace health insurance
https://www.autismspeaks.org/marketplace-health-insurance

Mental health and autism insurance project
https://www.mhautism.org

Resource guide
https://www.autismspeaks.org/resource-guide?state%5B166%5D=166

See plans and prices
HealthCare.gov/see-plans

State directory of resources
https://www.fns.usda.gov/snap/state-directory

State employee health benefits, insurance and costs

https://www.ncsl.org/health/state-employee-health-benefits-insurance-and-costs

State regulated health benefit plans

https://www.autismspeaks.org/state-regulated-health-benefit-plans

Still need health insurance?

https://www.healthcare.gov/

When out-of-network care can be covered in-network.

https://www.fairhealthconsumer.org/insurance-basics/your-costs/
when-out-of-network-care-can-be-covered-in-network

Long-Term Services Tools—Colorado Examples

Eligibility assessment

https://hcpf.colorado.gov/sites/hcpf/files/ULTC%20100.2-Eligibility%20
Assessment.pdf

Support level subgroup definitions

https://hcpf.colorado.gov/sites/hcpf/files/Support%20Level%20Subgroup%20
Definitions-June-2017.pdf

ULTC 100.2: Determining level of care [PowerPoint slides]

https://hcpf.colorado.gov/sites/hcpf/files/ULTC%20100.2%20Training%20-%20
FINAL.pdf

Medicaid Waiver Resources

State Medicaid waivers list

https://www.medicaid.gov/medicaid/section-1115-demo/demonstration-and-waiver-
list/index.html

Full list

https://www.kidswaivers.org/full-list

SIS Resources

How support needs can be used to inform the allocation of resources and funding decisions

https://www.aaidd.org/docs/default-source/sis-docs/supportneeds.
pdf?sfvrsn=a88b3021_0

SIS-A 2nd edition
https://www.aaidd.org/sis/sis-a/sis-a-2nd-edition

SIS-A respondent resources
https://www.aaidd.org/sis/sis-a/sis-a-resources

SIS-C respondent resources
https://www.aaidd.org/sis/sis-c/sis-c-resources

States and provinces in North America using the SIS
https://www.aaidd.org/sis/states-using-sis

Supports Intensity Scale Expanded Item Descriptions
https://www.aaidd.org/docs/defaultsource/sis-docs/sisexpandeditemdefinitions.pdf

Supports Intensity Scale Interview and Profile Form
(Adult Version Ages 16 and up) [Measurement instrument]
https://www.aaidd.org/docs/default-source/sis-docs/sis-interview-and-profile-form-
(do-not-copy).pdf?sfvrsn=2

REFERENCES

ABA Consulting Services. (2023). In-network insurance and financial resources. https://stlaba.com/resources/financial-resources-insurance/

ABLE National Resource Center. (n.d.). Calling all employers! You are ABLE to support a diverse workforce. https://www.ablenrc.org/wp-content/uploads/2023/03/Employer-Toolkit-Flyer-v3.27.23v2.pdf

ABLE National Resource Center. (2023a). ABLE Account, Special Needs and Pooled Trust comparison chart. ABLE Account, Special Needs and Pooled Trust Comparison Chart (ablenrc.org)

ABLE National Resource Center. (2023b). History of the ABLE Act. https://www.ablenrc.org/what-is-able/history-of-the-able-act/

ABLE National Resource Center. (2023c). Step 3: How can funds be used? https://www.ablenrc.org/get-started/what-can-funds-be-used-for/#

ABLE National Resource Center. (2023d). Are there limits to how much money can be put into an ABLE account? https://www.ablenrc.org/frequently-asked-questions/#contributions

ABLE National Resource Center. (2023e). Housing and Urban Development (HUD) releases guidance on ABLE accounts. https://www.ablenrc.org/housing-and-urban-development-hud-releases-guidance-on-able-accounts/

ABLE National Resource Center. (2023f). Are you concerned about Medicaid Payback? https://www.ablenrc.org/understanding-able-accounts-special-needs-trusts-and-pooled-trusts/are-you-concerned-with-medicaid-payback/

Aetna. (n.d.). HMO, POS, PPO, EPO and HDHP with HSA: What's the difference? https://www.aetna.com/health-guide/hmo-pos-ppo-hdhp-whats-the-difference.html

Affordable Housing Hub. (2023, March 2). Affordable housing for disabled adults: HUD programs and resources. https://affordablehousinghub.org/affordable-housing/hud-housing-for-disabled-adults

American Association on Intellectual and Developmental Disabilities. (2022). Supports Intensity Scale - Children's Version (SIS-C). https://www.aaidd.org/sis/sis-c

Ascend. (2019, June 19). DIDD Provider Training: The SIS Assessment. [PowerPoint slides]. https://maximus.com/sites/default/files/svcs/documents/DIDD_provider_training%20DE.pdf_

Autism Speaks. (n.d.). Autism grants for families. https://www.autismspeaks.org/autism-grants-families

Autism Speaks. (2022, February 1). Medicaid EPSDT. https://www.autismspeaks.org/medicaid-epsdt

Bennie, M. (2009, September 14). Choosing a treatment/therapy for individuals with ASD. Autism Awareness Centre, Inc. https://autismawarenesscentre.com/choosing-a-treatmenttherapy-for-individuals-with-asd/

Center on Budget and Policy Priorities. (2022, June 9). Policy basics: The Supplemental Nutrition Assistance Program (SNAP). https://www.cbpp.org/research/food-assistance/the-supplemental-nutrition-assistance-program-snap

Children's Hospital of Philadelphia Research Institute. (2020, June 8). Evaluating complementary and alternative medicine (CAM) for treating symptoms of ASD. https://www.research.chop.edu/car-autism-roadmap/evaluating-complementary-and-alternative-medicine-cam-for-treating-symptoms-of-asd

Cision PR Newswire. (2010, April 5). MassMutual's Autism Awareness Month advice for parents: 10 questions to ask when choosing a guardian for your child with autism, special needs. https://www.prnewswire.com/news-releases/massmutuals-autism-awareness-month-advice-for-parents-10-questions-to-ask-when-choosing-a-guardian-for-your-child-with-autism-special-needs-89927932.html

Davis, E. (2022, June 6). Network gap exceptions. Verywell Health. https://www.verywellhealth.com/network-gap-exception-what-it-is-how-it-works-1738418#citation-6

The Family Guidance and Therapy Center. (2022). Re-evaluation assessments._https://familyguidanceandtherapy.com/re-evaluation-for-autism-california_

Federal Developmental Disabilities Assistance and Bill of Rights Act of 2000, 42 U.S.C. §§144-15002. (2000). https://www.law.cornell.edu/uscode/text/42/15002

Federal Registrar. (2017, January 6). Supplemental Nutrition Assistance Program (SNAP): Eligibility, certification, and employment and training provisions of the Food, Conservation and Energy Act of 2008. https://www.federalregister.gov/documents/2017/01/06/2016 30663/ supplemental-nutrition-assistance-program-snap-eligibility-certification-and-employment-and-training#p-96

Healthcare.gov. (n.d.). Health insurance plan & network types: HMOs, PPOs, and more. https://www.healthcare.gov/choose-a-plan/plan-types/

Human Services Research Institute. (2016, January). Building personal supports budgets for adults with intellectual/developmental disabilities information brief: Supports Intensity Scale and assessment levels. https://ddsd.vermont.gov/sites/ddsd/files/documents/HSRI-Building_Personal_Supports_Budgets-SIS_and_Assessment_Levels.pdf

Lewis, L. (2013, October 23). 12 autism resources for those who speak Spanish. Friendship Circle. https://www.friendshipcircle.org/blog/2013/10/23/13-autism-resources-resources-in-spanish-you-should-know-about/

Lewis, V. (2000, March 1). Medicaid waivers: California's use of a federal option. Medi-Cal Policy Institute. https://www.chcf.org/wp-content/uploads/2017/12/PDF-medicaidwaivers.pdf

Li, Y. J., Ou, J. J., Li, Y. M., & Xiang, D. X. (2017). Dietary supplement for core symptoms of autism spectrum disorder: Where are we now and where should we go? *Frontiers in Psychiatry*, 8, 155. https://doi.org/10.3389/fpsyt.2017.00155

Maryland Developmental Disabilities Council. (2018). Planning now: A future and estate planning guide for families of children with intellectual and developmental disabilities. https://www.md-council.org/wp-content/uploads/2018/12/Planning-Now-Guide-2018-4.pdf

Medicaid and CHIP Access and Payment Commission (MACPAC). (2020, August 1). State management of home- and community-based services waiver waiting lists. https://www.macpac.gov/wp-content/uploads/2020/08/State-Management-of-Home-and-Community-Based-Services-Waiver-Waiting-Lists.pdf

Medicaid.gov. (n.d.). Medicaid eligibility. https://www.medicaid.gov/medicaid/eligibility/index.html

MedicareAdvantage.com. (2021, December 8). How Medicaid works as secondary insurance. https://www.medicareadvantage.com/medicaid/medicaid-as-secondary-insurance

Miller, S. (2022, April 29). 2023 health FSA contribution cap rises to $3,050. SHRM. https://www.shrm.org/resourcesandtools/hr-topics/benefits/pages/2023-fsa-contribution-cap-and-other-colas.aspx

National Cancer Institute. (2022, March 21). Complementary and alternative medicine. https://www.cancer.gov/about-cancer/treatment/cam

Norden, L., & Robertson, V. (2020, January 1). Supports Intensity Scale: Overview of requirements and processes. [PowerPoint slides]. Colorado Department of Health Care Policy and Financing. https://www.tre.org/wp-content/uploads/2021/03/Supports-Intensity-Scale-Presentation-NordenRobertson-January-2020.pdf

Special Needs Alliance. (2013, January). Your Special Needs Trust ("SNT") defined. https://www.specialneedsalliance.org/the-voice/your-special-needs-trust-snt-defined-2/

Steps to Progress. (2022, March 14). Autism evaluation requirements: What to expect. https://www.stepstoprogress.com/blog/aba-therapy/autism-evaluation-requirements-what-to-expect

Temelkova, K. (2021, January 18). The prevalence of the Spanish language within the US. Milestone Localization. https://www.milestoneloc.com/the-prevalence-of-the-spanish-language-within-the-us/

TRICARE. (2021, October 4). TRICARE 101. https://www.tricare.mil/Plans/New_

U.S. Food and Drug Administration. (2019, April 17). Be aware of potentially dangerous products and therapies that claim to treat autism. https://www.fda.gov/consumers/consumer-updates/be-aware-potentially-dangerous-products-and-therapies-claim-treat-autism

U.S. Food and Drug Administration. (2022, July 28). Information for consumers on using dietary supplements. https://www.fda.gov/food/dietary-supplements/information-consumers-using-dietary-supplements

U.S. Government Office of Personnel Management. (2017). ABA coverage in FEHB for 2017. https://www.opm.gov/policy-data-oversight/worklife/news-attachments/aba-coverage-in-fehb-for-2017-questions-answers.pdf

Velott, D. L., Agbese, E., Mandell, D., Stein, B. D., Dick, A. W., Yu, H., & Leslie, D. L. (2016). Medicaid 1915(c) Home- and Community-Based Services waivers for children with autism spectrum disorder. *Autism: the International Journal of Research and Practice*, *20*(4), 473–482. https://doi.org/10.1177/1362361315590806

CONTRIBUTOR BIOGRAPHIES

Rudaina Banihani, MD, MHPE

Neonatologist and Developmental Paediatrician
Newborn & Developmental Paediatrics, Sunnybrook Health Science Centre
Assistant Professor of Paediatrics, University of Toronto

Dr. Banihani stands as an accomplished neonatologist and developmental pediatrician, with a special focus on Down syndrome. Based at Toronto's esteemed Sunnybrook Health Science Centre, her career reflects her dedication to Neonatal-Perinatal Medicine and Developmental Pediatrics. As a director of the Neonatal Follow-Up Clinic, she pioneers an initiative ensuring the growth of Neonatal Intensive Care Unit (NICU) graduates up to age ten.

Her academic journey began with dual fellowships in Neonatal-Perinatal Medicine and Developmental Pediatrics at the University of Toronto. Complementing this, she holds a master's degree in health professions education from Maastricht University and received clinical research training from Harvard Medical School. As an Assistant Professor in the Department of Pediatrics at the University of Toronto, she shares her knowledge passionately.

Notably, Dr. Banihani served as the medical codirector of the Down syndrome clinic at Toronto's Hospital for Sick Children from 2014 to 2018. Guiding the DSMIG-ASD assessment subgroup within the Down Syndrome Medical Interest Group showcases her commitment to enhancing care and understanding for this community.

Dr. Banihani's research delves into developmental aspects of Down syndrome and its link with autism spectrum disorder. She explores early identification, risk assessment, and intervention strategies for those with Trisomy 21. She also navigates the intricate neurodevelopmental challenges faced by NICU graduates and infants with genetic syndromes.

Adding a deeply personal touch, Dr. Banihani is also a mother to a 19-year-old young man with Down syndrome. Her narrative resonates as a holistic endeavor to improve lives. Through her clinical expertise, dedicated research pursuits, and influential roles, she orchestrates remarkable contributions, elevating care, and knowledge in this pivotal field.

Nicole T. Baumer, MD, MEd

Neurodevelopmental Disabilities
Director, Boston Children's Hospital Down Syndrome Program
Assistant Professor, Harvard Medical School

Nicole T. Baumer, MD, MEd, is a child neurologist/neurodevelopmental disabilities specialist at Boston Children's Hospital and an Assistant Professor of Neurology at Harvard Medical School. Dr. Baumer is Director of the Boston Children's Hospital Down Syndrome Program. She completed medical training at Harvard Medical School, pediatrics training at Massachusetts General Hospital, and Neurodevelopmental Disabilities Training at Boston Children's Hospital. Dr. Baumer also studied special education and has a master's degree in education from Harvard Graduate School of Education. She specializes in clinical care of children with Down syndrome, autism spectrum disorder, attention deficit hyperactivity disorder, and other neurodevelopmental and behavioral disorders. Her research is focused on neurodevelopment in Down syndrome, and on interventions to optimize health, learning, and development. Dr. Baumer also serves on the board of the Down Syndrome Medical Interest Group-USA (DSMIG-USA), and the National Down Syndrome Congress (NDSC). Dr. Baumer's sister has Down syndrome and has been a huge inspiration in her life and career.

Kimberly Bonello

Kimberly Bonello is the mother of three adult children; including her youngest daughter, Emily, who, in addition to being born with a cleft lip and palate, was born with Down syndrome and autism spectrum disorder (DS-ASD). She is the founder and facilitator for Parent Advocates Lending Support (P.A.L.S.) support group. Kim was involved in the Down Syndrome-Autism Connection in Colorado, providing support to other parents who were newer to the DS-ASD diagnosis. Additionally, Kim was a contributing writer on the book *When Down Syndrome and Autism Intersect: A Guide to DS-ASD for Parents and Professionals,* first and second editions. After many years of navigating the medical field while dealing with Emily's physical and developmental conditions, Kim decided to go to school to become a Certified Medical Assistant (CMA). In 2004, she graduated magna cum laude from Remington College in Lakewood, Colorado. Kim is currently a Certified Nursing Assistant (CNA) with a local home health agency. She utilizes her CNA training daily while caring for Emily.

George T. Capone, MD

Director, Down Syndrome Clinic & Research Center, Kennedy Krieger Institute

Since 1990, Dr. Capone has been on the medical staff at the Kennedy Krieger Institute where he serves as Director of the Down Syndrome Clinic & Research Center. He has a wide range of interests in topics relevant to people with Down syndrome, including health care, development-neurobehavior, mental health, Alzheimer's disease, sleep, and medication trials in children and adults. Past service includes serving on the advisory boards of the National Down Syndrome Conference (NDSC), National Down Syndrome Society (NDSS), National Institutes of Health Down Syndrome (NIH DS) Consortium, DS International, and DSMIG-USA, where he is a cofounding member. Dr. Capone lives in Towson, Maryland, with his wife Mary, son, Daniel, and dog, Katara.

Brian Chicoine, MD

Medical Director, Advocate Medical Group Adult Down Syndrome Center

Brian Chicoine, MD, is the cofounder and Medical Director of the Advocate Medical Group Adult Down Syndrome Center in Park Ridge, Illinois. The Center has served over 6,000 adolescents and adults with Down syndrome since its inception in 1992. Dr. Chicoine graduated from Loyola University of Chicago Stritch School of Medicine. He completed his Family Medicine residency at Lutheran General Hospital where he is now a faculty member. He has published many articles regarding the health of people with Down syndrome. He has coauthored two books *Mental Wellness of Adults with Down Syndrome*, and *The Guide to Good Health for Teens and Adults with Down Syndrome*.

Paige Terrien Church, MD

Neonatologist & Developmental-Behavioral Pediatrician
Associate Professor, Paediatrics, University of Toronto

Dr. Church was first a graduate of the Neonatal Intensive Care Unit (NICU) at the University of Vermont, and then a few years later became a graduate of the University of Vermont College of Medicine. Her pediatrics training was completed at the University of Chicago, focusing on inner city medicine and complex care. She then completed a combined fellowship in Neonatal-Perinatal Medicine and Developmental-Behavioral Pediatrics at Tufts University School of Medicine in Boston. She is board certified through the American Board of Pediatrics in both Neonatal-Perinatal Medicine and Developmental-Behavioral Pediatrics.

Dr. Church is on staff at Beth Israel Deaconess Medical Center and Boston Children's Hospital, where she works as a neonatologist and developmental-behavioral pediatrician in the Neonatal Intensive Care Unit and in the Growth and Development Support Program (GraDS clinic). Her academic interests include developmental care, long-term outcomes of babies who were cared for in the NICU, systems of care, spina bifida, and disability.

Angelica Davila, PhD Student

Angelica Davila, a doctoral student at University of Chicago (UIC), is an autistic individual who was diagnosed as an adult. She also has a younger autistic sister who was diagnosed as a child and who Angelica provided support for. Her background includes having worked as a Senior Disabilities Specialist at University of Illinois at Chicago's Resource Center for Autism and Developmental Delays for seven years, as well as having conducted autism-specific workshops for The Autism Program of Illinois (TAP), The Arc of Illinois, and the National Center for Families Learning Conference.

Deborah Fidler, PhD

Professor, Human Development & Family Studies, Colorado State University

Deborah Fidler, PhD, is a Professor in the Department of Human Development and Family Studies at Colorado State University (CSU) and Director of the Intellectual and Developmental Disabilities (IDD) Division of the CSU Prevention Research Center. Her research focuses on development in individuals with neurogenetic conditions associated with IDD. Dr. Fidler has served as editor of the American Journal on Intellectual and Developmental Disabilities and coeditor of the International Review of Research in Developmental Disabilities. She is the author of over 100 manuscripts and book chapters focusing on development in individuals with IDD and their families and the codirector of the Ram Scholars Inclusive Postsecondary Education program at CSU.

Katie Frank, PhD, OTR/L

Occupational Therapist III, Adult Down Syndrome Center Advocate Medical Group

Katie Frank, PhD, OTR/L, has worked as an occupational therapist at the Adult Down Syndrome Center in Park Ridge, Illinois, since 2016, and in the field of occupational therapy since 2001. She also serves as the president of the Down Syndrome Medical Interest Group-USA. Dr. Frank earned her degree in occupational therapy from Saint Louis University and her doctorate in disability studies from the University of Illinois at Chicago. Most of her work has been with individuals with Down syndrome of all ages. Dr. Frank's experience includes treatment and evaluation as well as facilitating groups for people with Down syndrome, conducting trainings for staff, families, and caregivers, and offering a variety of other educational opportunities across the globe. Her research has been published in peer-reviewed journals.

Margaret Froehlke, RN, BSN

Margaret Froehlke is a registered nurse and the mother of four adult children. Her 30-year-old son, Brennan, has DS-ASD. In addition to working as a pediatric nurse early in her career, Margaret also worked in the IDD community as executive director of the Denver Adult Down Syndrome Clinic, a program team member with Adam's Camp, and helped prepare an oral health care grant for the Autism Society of Michigan. Margaret also worked in the private sector in the Baxter Travenol Quality Assurance Department, and most recently for a boutique marketing agency in Denver. Margaret's life passion is advocating for individuals with IDD and DS-ASD. She helped launch the nonprofit, the Down Syndrome-Autism Connection, the leading support organization for families of individuals with DS-ASD, coauthored the first and second editions of, *When Down Syndrome and Autism Intersect: A Guide to DS-ASD for Families and Professionals,* and authored the Catholic resource book, *A Guide to the Mass for Visual Learners, 2008 and 2013*—a resource book designed to assist individuals with ASD in attending the Catholic Mass. Margaret received her Bachelor of Science in Nursing (BSN) from Wayne State University and lives in Denver with her husband Bob and their son Brennan.

Robert Froehlke, MD

Robert Froehlke, MD, is a pediatrician and the father of four adult children. His 30-year-old son, Brennan, has DS-ASD. Bob recently retired as a physician and partner with the Littleton Pediatric Medical Center, LLC, in Littleton, Colorado. He worked as a general pediatrician for 40 years with a large portion of his practice caring for children with IDD, including many patients with Down syndrome and autism. Dr. Froehlke received his medical doctorate from St. Louis University and completed his residency in pediatrics at Northwestern University/Children's Memorial Hospital. He spent three years working in Fort Defiance, Arizona, as a pediatrician for the Indian Health Service then joined the Center for Disease Control as an Epidemic Intelligence Service Officer in Atlanta. In addition to general pediatrics, Bob has served in several roles including assistant to the US Surgeon General, assistant professor of pediatrics at Michigan State University School of Human Medicine, commander in the United States Naval Reserve Medical Corps, and director of Sparrow Hospital inpatient pediatric service in Lansing, Michigan. Bob and his wife Margaret live in Centennial, Colorado, with their son Brennan.

Julie Hearrell, MA Ed

Julie Hearrell, MA Ed, is currently the Goal Development Specialist at A Brighter Community in Wheat Ridge, Colorado. Prior to her retirement, she was a special educator and instructional coach with Jefferson County Public Schools in Colorado for 20 years. Preceding her instructional career in Colorado, Julie taught elementary and secondary special education in Texas and for the Department of Defense Dependent Schools. Julie earned her bachelor of science in special education from Texas Tech University in 1985, and her master of arts in education, curriculum, and instruction from the University of Phoenix in 2007. Julie credits her brother, Gary, who had developmental disabilities, as her inspiration for a lifelong dedication to advocacy for persons with IDD.

Susan Hepburn, PhD

Professor, Human Development and Family Studies, Colorado State University

Susan Hepburn, PhD, is a professor in the Department of Human Development and Family Studies at Colorado State University. Trained as a clinical psychologist with a specialization in assessment of autism, Dr. Hepburn studies ways to identify autism symptoms in people with other known conditions. For over 25 years, she's focused her clinical work on public school settings, where she provides consultation and training in educational identification of complex students.

Chiara Jaffe, MPH, MSW, LCSW-C

Resource Specialist

Chiara Jaffe, MPH, MSW, LCSW-C, is the mother of two boys, the older of whom has DS-ASD. She serves on the Maryland State Department of Education, Division of Early Intervention and Special Education Services State Advisory Committee, which is tasked with improving the delivery of special education services to children between the ages of 5 and 21. Previously, she served as the resource coordinator for the Down Syndrome Network of Montgomery County (DSNMC) for 10 years during which she provided clinical and social service referrals and linkage in response to requests from professionals and community members. She also served as a parent mentor, providing emotional and informational support to parents of children with Down syndrome, through the Parent-to-Parent Program. Chiara has served as a Parent-Educator for the Uniformed Services University of the Health Services (USUHS) Medical Student Ethics Course, educating first-year medical students on working with families of children with Down syndrome. She is a licensed clinical social worker and has 20 years of medical and behavioral health research experience. Chiara works as senior study director for a survey research company. She received her bachelor of arts in psychology from Georgetown University, her master of social work from the Catholic University of America, and her master of public health from Johns Hopkins University.

Terry Katz, PhD

Psychologist, Developmental Pediatrics, Children's Hospital Colorado,
University of Colorado School of Medicine

Terry Katz, PhD, is a licensed psychologist and Senior Instructor with Distinction at the University of Colorado School of Medicine. She has worked with children with developmental disabilities and their families for over 30 years. In 2009, she cofounded a sleep behavior clinic for children with special needs at Children's Hospital Colorado and continues to work in this clinic. Dr. Katz has helped develop educational materials for caregivers and providers to help address difficulties with sleep, toileting, and completing medical procedures. Her research interests include assessment of sleep problems, the association between sleep and daytime functioning, and behavioral sleep education.

Katarzyna Kowerska, MA, CCC-SLP

Speech-Language Pathologist, Audiology, Speech, and Learning Services,
AAC Team, Sie Center for Down Syndrome

Katarzyna "Kat" Kowerska, MA, CCC-SLP, earned her master's degree in speech and language pathology at Queens College, City University of New York, and has been focusing on supporting children with complex communication needs for over 16 years. Her clinical experience includes working in private practice and public schools in San

Francisco, Las Vegas, and rural Minnesota, before joining Children's Hospital Colorado Augmentative and Alternative Communication (AAC) Team and the Sie Center for Down Syndrome in 2016. In the Down syndrome clinic, she provides multidisciplinary in-person and telehealth evaluations for hundreds of children, teens, and young adults with Down syndrome and dual diagnoses, including autism. She also provides AAC therapy and evaluations for complex communicators who benefit from multimodal/ AAC tools and strategies for consistent and effective communication. Kat consults and collaborates with schools and private therapists, provides in-person and virtual training and hands on experience for parents regarding implementation of AAC tools and optimization of communication skills in children of all ages and abilities. Her passion lies in empowering communication partners to feel competent and confident when supporting children in communicating to their highest potential. Additionally, she has presented in various settings to school districts, parents, and therapists, and has mentored graduate students.

Kathleen Lehman, PhD

Clinical Professor, Department of Psychiatry & Behavioral Sciences,
University of Washington School of Medicine

Kathleen Lehman, PhD, is a licensed psychologist, clinical professor in the Department of Psychiatry & Behavioral Sciences, and the associate director of the University of Washington Leadership Education in Neurodevelopmental and related Disabilities (LEND) at the Institute on Human Development and Disability (IHDD). Dr. Lehman conducts psychology and developmental evaluations and supervises psychology trainees, including residents and postdoctoral fellows in a variety of clinics at the IHDD including the Child Development Clinic, Cardiac Neurodevelopmental Clinic, Infant Development Follow-up Clinic, and Down Syndrome Specialty Clinic. The IHDD specialty clinics are interdisciplinary and serve infants through adults with and/ or suspected of having neurodevelopmental disabilities, including autism.

Lauren A. Lewis, DDS

Board Certified Pediatric Dentist

Lauren A. Lewis, DDS, is a Board Certified Pediatric Dentist and owner of Drs. Ensor, Johnson & Lewis in Rockville, Maryland. She received her DDS from the Baltimore College of Dental Surgery, University of Maryland and completed her pediatric dental residency at the University of Pittsburgh, School of Dental Medicine. Dr. Lewis has worked extensively with patients with special needs during her residency at Kernan Hospital in Baltimore and in private practice. She is originally from Pittsburgh, Pennsylvania, but has called Maryland home for over a decade. Her mother is a retired dental hygienist who introduced her to the care of special needs children, and her brother just graduated from dental school. Dr. Lewis is also married to a dentist and has two children who are too young to know if they want to follow in their family's footsteps.

Leah Martin, PhD

In addition to being an owner and founder of A Brighter Community (ABC), Dr. Leah Martin serves as its operations executive. She received her bachelor of science in cartography and her master of science in geography from Brigham Young University, and she received her doctorate in industrial and organizational psychology from Grand Canyon University. Leah left a career in the satellite imagery/remote sensing industry to devote her life to individuals with IDD. Her dissertation explored the topic of Direct Support Professional (DSP) role modeling for job seekers with Down syndrome. Dr. Martin is also an author, having published the novel, *Joshua's Tree*, which is a fictional memoire. She has found fulfillment and joy in providing a meaningful life to her exceptional friends who attend ABC, including several amazing individuals with DS-ASD.

Elina R. Manghi, PsyD, LMFT

Elina R. Manghi, PsyD, LMFT (1952-2012), was a family therapist and child psychologist who helped create a support group in Chicago for Spanish-speaking families with autistic children in 2003 called Grupo SALTO. She was formerly a clinical professor in the Department of Disability and Human Development at the University of Illinois at Chicago, and codirector of The Autism Program. The author of many publications based on her research and clinical work in the United States and internationally, particularly on the topic of autism, Elina was a strong supporter and dear friend of the Down Syndrome-Autism Connection.

Dennis McGuire, PhD

Private Practice

Dennis McGuire, PhD, is the former director of psychosocial services for the Adult Down Syndrome Center of Lutheran General Hospital in suburban Chicago. Dr. McGuire helped to establish the Adult Down Syndrome Center which has served the health and psychosocial needs of over 6,000 adults with Down syndrome since its inception in 1992. Dr. McGuire received his master's degree from the University of Chicago and his doctorate from the University of Illinois at Chicago. His work experience includes over 30 years in the mental health and developmental disabilities fields. He presents regularly at national and international conferences, and coauthored two books with Dr. Brian Chicoine on Mental Wellness of Adults with Down Syndrome: A Guide to Emotional and Behavioral Strengths and Challenges, Second Edition (2021), available on the website of the Adult Down Syndrome Center and, The Guide to Good Health for Teen and Adults with Down Syndrome (2010), published by Woodbine House press.

Darren Olsen, PhD

Licensed Clinical Psychologist
Division of Developmental and Behavioral Health, Section of Psychology
Children's Mercy Kansas City
Assistant Professor of Pediatrics, UMKC School of Medicine

Dr. Olsen received his doctorate in clinical psychology from the University of Hawaii at Manoa in 2018. He completed his predoctoral internship and postdoctoral fellowship in child psychology with a focus on autism spectrum disorder at Indiana University (IU) School of Medicine. Currently, Dr. Olsen is a clinical child psychologist at Children's Mercy Hospital Kansas City and assistant professor of pediatrics at the University of

Missouri Kansas City (UMKC) School of Medicine. He conducts evaluations of children and teenagers suspected of having autism spectrum disorder and other developmental differences. He also conducts individual and group therapy for parents of children with autism spectrum disorder and other developmental differences including the Research Units in Behavioral Interventions (RUBI) parent training program. Dr. Olsen also partners with colleagues in further developing and maintaining the Down Syndrome-Autism dual diagnosis clinic at Children's Mercy Hospital. Dr. Olsen's clinical and research interests involve the assessment and treatment of behavioral difficulties associated with various developmental disorders and dissemination of evidence-based information related to Down syndrome and autism spectrum disorder.

Matiana Ovalle

Cofounder, CEO, and Coordinator, Grupo SALTO

Matiana M. Ovalle, also known as Matie, is cofounder, current CEO, and coordinator of Grupo SALTO, and the mother of two adults with autism. Her interest is to keep the group functional and up-to-date to meet the needs of the Spanish-speaking community with developmental disabilities, with a focus on autism. She recently retired from University of Illinois at Chicago (UIC), worked for the Developmental Disabilities Family Clinics, DHD at UIC, and was the Illinois LEND's family discipline coordinator. She has a bachelor of science in communication disorders, an associate degree in early childhood education and is the children's artistic director and vice president of the Mexican Folkloric Dance Company of Chicago, Inc.

Lina Patel, PsyD

Associate Professor, Department of Psychiatry,
University of Colorado School of Medicine

Lina Patel, PsyD, is an associate professor of Child and Adolescent Psychiatry at the University of Colorado School of Medicine, practicing at Children's Hospital Colorado. Dr. Patel is the director of the Down Syndrome Behavioral Health Collaborative, a virtual clinic providing tele-behavioral health services to children, teens, and young adults with Down syndrome. She provides consultation with schools, parent training regarding the management of challenging or unsafe behaviors, toilet training, and desensitization to medical devices (such as hearing aids and CPAP), and evaluation for dual diagnoses, including autism. She has worked with hundreds of individuals with Down syndrome. Outside of her clinical work, she conducts research as the Director of Neurodevelopmental, Behavioral and Cognitive Assessment at the Linda Crnic Institute for Down Syndrome. Additionally, she has presented to numerous organizations across the country and internationally and is the coauthor of Potty Time for Kids with Down Syndrome: Lose the Diapers, Not Your Patience.

Laura Pickler, MD, MPH

Chief of Family Medicine, Associate Professor University of Colorado School of Medicine, Director Pediatric Feeding and Swallowing Program

Laura Pickler, MD, MPH, is a family physician who has completed two fellowships in Developmental-Behavioral Pediatrics and Clinical Genetics and Metabolism. As a resident in family medicine, she became aware that young adults with complex medical and intellectual disabilities often experienced suboptimal health care and lacked fundamental access to basic primary care services. Over nearly 20 years, she has worked in diverse ways to impact the health of this patient population through direct health care delivery, clinical research, public health systems building, clinical leadership positions, student mentorship, teaching, and administrative leadership roles. Currently she is a faculty member at the University of Colorado School of Medicine and chief of Family Medicine at Children's Hospital Colorado, and uses these roles as a platform to improve transition from pediatric to adult health care for young adults with Down syndrome.

Ann Reynolds, MD

Section Head, Developmental Pediatrics
Professor of Pediatrics, University of Colorado School of Medicine

Ann Reynolds, MD, is a professor of pediatrics and section head of Developmental Pediatrics at the University of Colorado School of Medicine and Children's Hospital Colorado. Dr. Reynolds received her undergraduate degree from Emory University and her medical degree from the Medical College of Georgia. She did her residency training in pediatrics at Children's National Medical Center in Washington, DC, and her fellowship in neurodevelopmental disabilities at Baylor College of Medicine. Dr. Reynolds has a clinical and research interest in co-occurring medical conditions in neurodiverse children, including sleep and gastrointestinal issues. In 2009, she cofounded a sleep behavior clinic with Dr. Katz for children with developmental delays at Children's Hospital Colorado and continues to work in that clinic.

Robin Sattel, MS

In addition to being an owner and founder of A Brighter Community (ABC), a private company that serves adults with IDD in Colorado, Robin serves as its programs executive. She received her BA in French and secondary education from Beloit College, and she received her MS in mental health and wellness with an emphasis in grief and bereavement from Grand Canyon University. Robin is a longtime disability advocate, and she has won several community awards for her work with disability-related nonprofits. Robin also cofounded the Down Syndrome-Autism Connection nonprofit, and she coauthored the first and second editions of, *When Down Syndrome and Autism Intersect: A Guide to DS-ASD for Families and Professionals.* Most importantly, Robin is a mother of four, including an adult son with Down syndrome (Tom), and a daughter with DS-ASD (Janet Kay) who passed away at the age of 15 in 2012. Robin founded ABC to create a gold standard program that keeps Tom and all his friends safe, healthy, and engaged, and as a special way to honor Janet Kay's life.

Noemi Alice Spinazzi, MD, FAAP

Medical Director, Charlie's Clinic
UCSF Benioff Children's Hospitals' Down Syndrome Clinic

Noemi Spinazzi, MD, FAAP, is a primary care physician at UCSF Benioff Children's Hospital Oakland and an assistant professor at the UCSF School of Medicine. She provides primary care services to hundreds of children with complex care needs and developmental disabilities. She is the founder and medical director of Charlie's Clinic, a specialized clinic serving patients with Down syndrome in Oakland, California. She is also the director of the developmental and behavioral pediatrics resident rotation at Children's Oakland. She serves on the board of the National Down Syndrome Congress and of Through the Looking Glass. Dr. Spinazzi, who identifies as an immigrant, was born and raised in Milan, Italy, and moved to the United States when she was 15 years old. Her work with children and families from all over the world motivates her to be an advocate for immigrant rights and immigrant health. She received her medical degree from the University of Pennsylvania in Philadelphia, Pennsylvania, and completed her residency at UCSF Benioff Children's Hospital Oakland, where she was the chief resident.

Maria A. Stanley, MD, FAAP

Clinical Professor of Pediatrics
Chief, Division of Developmental Pediatrics and Rehabilitation Medicine
University of Wisconsin School of Medicine and Public Health
Medical Director, Waisman Center

Maria A. Stanley, MD, FAAP, is a developmental-behavioral pediatrician and clinical professor of pediatrics and chief for the Division of Developmental Pediatrics and Rehabilitation Medicine at the University of Wisconsin School of Medicine and Public Health. Her career has focused on clinical care for individuals with Down syndrome, autism spectrum disorders, and other developmental disabilities. She also participates in research efforts and education for families, caregivers, and medical providers. She is based at the Waisman Center, a facility dedicated to advancing knowledge about human development, developmental disabilities, and neurodegenerative diseases. She serves as Waisman Medical Director and as director of the Down Syndrome Clinic.

Mary M. Stephens, MD, MPH, FAAFP, FAADM

Co-Director, Jefferson FAB Center for Complex Care
Medical Director, Continuing Care Program; Associate Professor, Family & Community Medicine

Mary Stephens, MD, MPH, FAAFP, FAADM, is an associate professor in Family and Community Medicine at Jefferson. She is a family physician with more than 25 years of experience in patient care and teaching. In 2015, she cofounded the Teen and Adult

Down syndrome program at Christiana Care in Wilmington, Delaware, and continues to serve as the clinical leader. In 2018, she returned to Jefferson to help launch the Jefferson Continuing Care Program (JCCP), a new primary care practice for teens and adults with complex childhood-onset conditions and currently serves as codirector with Karin Roseman. Dr. Stephens is actively involved in medical student and residency education at Jefferson and is also on the board of directors of the Down Syndrome Medical Interest Group-USA (DSMIG-USA), and as a member of the volunteer committee for the Global Down Syndrome Foundation's adult health care guidelines. The mother of an 11-year-old with Down syndrome, she is a parent-member of the Down Syndrome Association of Delaware (DSA of DE) and has been actively involved with the Special Olympics since 2014, as a parent to an athlete and a unified partner and both a medical and Class A volunteer in Pennsylvania and Delaware.

Teresa Unnerstall, BS Ed

DS-ASD Consultant and Author of A New Course:
A Mother's Journey Navigating Down Syndrome and Autism
www.teresaunnerstall.com
Blog: www.nickspecialneeds.com

Teresa Unnerstall, BS Ed, is a DS-ASD consultant and the author of *A New Course: A Mother's Journey Navigating Down Syndrome and Autism*. Teresa has presented to the National Down Syndrome Conference (NDSC), National Down Syndrome Society (NDSS), and other national organizations, universities, and medical groups, and has been featured on webinars and podcasts about her work in the field of co-occurring DS-ASD. Since 2012, she has written a blog, *Down Syndrome with a Slice of Autism*, about her son Nick and navigating DS-ASD. Teresa currently serves on the board of directors for the Down Syndrome-Autism Connection.

ACKNOWLEDGMENTS

MARGARET AND ROBIN:

Our sincere gratitude to the experts who donated their knowledge and experience to this resource guide. Thank you for your devotion to serving individuals with DS-ASD, their families, and fellow professionals. You are changing lives.

We send special thanks to all the parents who shared their stories and photos of their beautiful children for this book. You helped us to accurately portray the humanity and loveliness of individuals with DS-ASD.

We wish to acknowledge Dr. Leah Martin for being this book's "Citations and References Editor." We couldn't have done it without your magnanimous support.

We also wish to recognize Janica Smith (https://www.publishsmith.com/), our publishing consultant and project manager, who ensured a beautiful and worthy final product.

MARGARET:

To my husband, Bob, for his constant support and valuable professional counsel in the editing process.

To the Down Syndrome Medical Interest Group, especially the DS-ASD Workgroup members, for passionately investing your time and life's work to improving the health and lives of individuals with DS-ASD and their loved ones.

ROBIN:

My thanks to my friend and business partner, Dr. Leah Martin, for her unwavering moral support and assistance with troubleshooting the technical issues we encountered during the process of writing and assembling this book. Everything she touches turns to gold.

My thanks to Jeanne Doherty and Charlotte Gray for their guidance in covering the most pressing issues currently facing families who love and care for a child or adult with DS-ASD.

INDEX

ABOUT THE AUTHORS

 **Margaret Froehlke, RN, BSN** is the mother of four adult children, including her 30-year-old son Brennan, who has DS-ASD. Brennan's birth was the catalyst of Margaret's life passion, advocating for and supporting individuals with IDD and DS-ASD and their families. Margaret lives in Colorado with her husband Bob and Brennan.

Robin Sattel, MS is a mother, grandmother, author, entrepreneur, and passionate advocate who has devoted her 30+ year career to individuals with IDD and their families. Her son, Tom, entered the world with an extra 21st chromosome 36 years ago. Later, Robin adopted her daughter, Janet Kay, who also had Down syndrome - plus a little something extra - which Robin suspected early on was autism spectrum disorder. Janet Kay's official DS-ASD diagnosis (at age 10) immediately inspired Robin's uncompromising devotion to,  and love for, the DS-ASD community. Robin lives in Denver, Colorado, where she co-owns A Brighter Community, an enchanting day services program where she has the privilege of hanging out with scores of friends with IDD every single day. Not surprisingly, she reports that her ABC friends are the coolest people on planet earth.